A
C. H. Sisson
Reader

Edited with an introduction by
Charlie Louth and Patrick McGuinness

FyfieldBooks

CARCANET

First published in Great Britain in 2014 by
Carcanet Press Limited
Alliance House
Cross Street
Manchester M2 7AQ

www.carcanet.co.uk

A CIP catalogue record for this book is available from the British Library

ISBN 978 1 84777 265 7

The publisher acknowledges financial assistance from Arts Council England

Supported by
ARTS COUNCIL
ENGLAND

Typeset by XL Publishing Services, Exmouth
Printed and bound in England by SRP Ltd, Exeter

Contents

From *Metamorphoses* (1968)

From the new poems in *In the Trojan Ditch* (1974)

From *Anchises* (1976)

From *Exactions* (1980)

From the new poems in *Collected Poems* (1984)

Translations

Essays

Introduction

'For about a year (*circa* 1932) I must have been contemporary', wrote C.H. Sisson in his autobiographical essay, 'Natural History': 'How I got over this is mysterious, but it was not all done by literature'. The essay, which falls into the 'making of a writer' genre, has a characteristic Sissonian emphasis on the writer's unmaking, which is usually also his real making. If we wanted a brief insight into Sisson the poet, thinker and cultural critic, we could do worse than start here. In an essay on Pound's *Pisan Cantos*, Sisson recalls being drawn to *Hugh Selwyn Mauberley*, a poem he encounters first in piecemeal, quoted form while still living with his parents. 'For three years, out of key with his time...', it begins. The power of that line, and something one suspects Sisson responded to, lies in the enticing perfection of its rhythm even as it speaks of something, of someone, out of 'rhythm' with his time. There is also the possibility, the probability even, that there is no better sign of being of one's time than advertising one's estrangement from it. Certainly that modernist passion for locating oneself on either side of the present, and, if possible (Pound, Eliot...), on both sides at once, is something Sisson understands and stays attuned to throughout his long career. *In Two Minds* is the title of one of his books of literary criticism, and in a review of a book on the Leavises he jokes that two minds is 'surely the minimum number for any reflection of any interest'. It is a witty, penetrating comment, and one that goes to the heart of Sisson's own work, which is authoritative but never comfortable, articulate but always suspicious of articulacy.

Sisson began as a mostly urban poet:

I was born in Bristol, and it is possible
To live harshly in that city

Quiet voices possess it, but the boy
Torn from the womb, cowers

Under a ceiling of cloud. Tramcars
Crash by or enter the mind

A barred room bore him, the backyard
Smooth as a snake-skin, yielded nothing

In the fringes of the town parsley and honey-suckle
Drenched the hedges.

('Family Fortunes I')

There are quiet voices there, but they are drowned out by the
crash of tramcars, and the smooth surface of the yard stifles the life
of the land beneath that only emerges elsewhere, an erotic
drenching that does not touch the centre. Sisson's direct experience of modern bureaucracy, as a civil servant in the Ministry of
Labour, prepared also by an early reading of Kafka while in Berlin
in 1934–35, sharpened his sense of humans as trapped animals
estranged from their instinctual life by a system of regulatory
structures. But at the same time, he had a clear idea of how the
history of those structures had for better or worse shaped us into
what we are. 'A person becomes, not what he thinks he is, but
what he is, or at any rate what is', he writes in 'Le roi soleil'.
Becoming what you are consists for Sisson not in inhabiting the
interstices, which might be thought to be one way of enjoying
some freedom from the control of the state (or the state's failure
to limit the profit motive), but, as he spells it out in the 1939 essay
'Order and Anarchy' – and also thirty years later in an editorial for
PN Review – to 'understand' government and 'our inherited institutions' (*Avoidance*, p. 555). This leads him to align himself with
cultural and political order, and yet, because his version of that
order, rooted in the seventeenth century, was so against the times,
and the reality he saw such a counter-reality, his work is always
radical and oppositional, critical and sceptical, an irritant. 'Good
writing alone may be described as independent of government',
he says in 'Order and Anarchy' – 'alone', that is, in contradistinction to bad writing – and part of what makes his writing good is
its independence not just from government but from literary
fashion and consensus, its unwillingness to swallow the ortho-
doxies of the day.

Being in or of one's time matters little to Sisson, if by that is
meant being fashionable, or courting an existing readership, or
being part of a group or generation with an identifiable collective
ethos. Yet ideas of continuity and community are central to his

work. An English poet first and foremost, he is also one of English poetry's most European-minded, and his sense of a specifically English (as distinct from British) cultural inheritance is matched by his understanding of the European traditions it partakes of and diverges from. The translator of Virgil, Catullus, Lucretius, Dante, Du Bellay, Racine, La Fontaine in bulk, he also assayed a range of writers including, among others, Ovid, Horace, Petrarch, Labé, Gryphius, Boileau, Heine, Corbière and Valéry. 'Fishing in other men's waters', he called translation, though as a poet, and despite his self-avowed short spell as 'contemporary', he fishes almost entirely in his own.

There must have been a time when Sisson was young, and perhaps that was when he was contemporary too. But 'late style' came early to him. We are struck, as we read him, by how weathered and disabused Sisson's writing can be, how ambiguously freighted it is by the past, by history, and by a sense of community that often constrains as much as it enhances us. His preoccupations with the relations between Church and State, literature and national life, his special understanding of conservatism, which is civic and pragmatic as well as something more numinous, are hardly fashionable. His writings on administration and governance are so far from the sort of cultural interventions we are used to seeing from poets that it would be tempting to set them apart from the body of his properly literary work (the term 'properly literary' is one Sisson would have rejected). But they are not; they are part of it, part of its informing vision.

Even when Sisson's conservatism might have been fashionable, it was rendered inaudible by noisier simplifications – notably the amnesiac, historically illiterate conservatism of the 1970s and 1980s, and the softly sentimental attachments to tradition and history that accompanied it, often as ways of distracting from its ravages. Where the easier forms of conservatism look to history and tradition for comfort, Sisson tends to look to them for something harder and more testing. In this he resembles another poet-critic, Donald Davie, and both writers, despite differences, were conscious of their common ground: an attraction to modernism (notably Pound) that often seemed at odds with a specifically British literary and cultural inheritance. And the word 'inheritance' seems more apposite than mere 'tradition', because one cannot choose one's inheritance, though traditions can always be managed in ways that suit us. In this respect, Sisson is perhaps the true heir of T.E. Hulme, a poet and thinker about whom he writes perceptively and with sympathy. Those Hulmean ideas he responds to – a belief in order and continuity, support for democracy that understands its imperfections, a sense of what Hulme called 'the religious attitude' that is independent of a belief in God and by no means implies it – are the least glamorous attachments a writer can admit to. After all, they are forms of self-denial, retreats from the grandiloquent statement or the vertiginous insight. But they are what Sisson values and what he stands by. Sisson, who was a witness to German developments before the war, who admired the French nationalist Charles Maurras, and who saw through Pound's attraction to fascism and Yeats's Celtic essentialism, resists, in his own work, exactly that tendency certain writers have – poets especially – to become drawn into politics of the extreme. The gesture of his entire work is against this, and against, too, the temptations of the very poets he most values. 'Maurras founded his politics on his esthetics, and that is a lunacy', he writes. That ability to divorce politics from aesthetics while registering the temptation to conflate them, is what makes his lifelong engagement with Maurras so revealing of Sisson's own mind.

A good place to approach Sisson is the three pamphlets, all privately printed, of 1967–68: 'Essays', the long poem 'The Discarnation', and 'Roman Poems', five poems derived out of Virgil and Horace. The 'Essays' are a kind of fundamental Sisson text, though more enigmatic and even gnomic than his usual prose: they are perhaps best read as long aphorisms, like Nietzsche's. They are fundamental in the sense that they try to get down to what really matters, to 'what is', what he elsewhere calls the 'sensible realities' that are continually in danger of being covered up and forgotten. The 'Essays', eight short texts with an introduction, begin by asking what politicians are here for, but since 'the conduct of government rests upon the same foundations and encounters the same difficulties as the conduct of private persons' also what *we* are here for. And they then ask *how* we are here, and answer that it's by virtue of the past: 'Words are not ours but the words of a myriad, having point only because of their history, ultimately of their prehistory' ('A Possible Anglicanism'). 'If we are selves,' Sisson goes on, 'it is by virtue of other selves that we are so. And our speaking is that of a race, of a tribe, of a time. There is no speech which is not of a here and now and it is nothing except in terms of other times and elsewhere'. We are born into particular circumstances and cannot remove ourselves from them by adopting an outside perspective 'like Kant's, trying to elevate our thinking above the world of sense'. In Sisson's view there simply is no such place, it is a nothing. When it comes to religion, the situation is the same: 'I am of a religion,' he writes in a later essay on Coleridge's *Church and State*, 'in which – to adapt Coleridge's phrase – Christianity is an accident; the religion of our fathers, or the *mère patrie*, of the spirits buried in the ground, of the religion of England, I cannot help it' ('Coleridge Revisited': *Avoidance*, p. 553). This is a pagan Christianity, and a helpless one. The uncertain syntax reflects a kind of willing self-abandon, a settling into what is felt to be there. The Anglican Church is the native church, the inherited one: 'The starting-point cannot be justified; it can only be loved' ('A Word of Apology': *Anglican Essays*, p. 138). But the historical church 'is a congregation of meaning and there is no meaning without congregation' ('A Possible Anglicanism').

This congregation is focused on the incarnation, which was a 're-affirmation of the kind', but the present is characterised by 'discarnation', the flight of meaning, the loss of the realities. We are becoming, as the poem telling 'how the Flesh became Word and dwelt among us' puts it, 'the heirs of an emptiness', detached from tradition, 'The crowd / Soothed as it never was'. 'The Discarnation' is a deeply unfashionable poem, but one fixed unhesitantly on the present, using its strict and awkward stanzas to peel back the layers of illusion and trying, like the 'Essays', to 'restore our minds to a perception of the sensible realities' ('Helps to a New World': *Avoidance*, p. 29). Of these, an important one is place:

> Places have names because a thought
> Lives in them, changing like our own
>   And grown
> Wily with years, not to be caught,
>   So meant
> Only by words we don't invent.

Place-names are part of our inheritance, they remind us of a past and of the dead we have grown from. They are the opposite of 'emptiness': rather, they are a kind of embodiment, where the place is contained in the name and the name gives texture to the place. Named places – some from Dorset and Somerset follow in the poem – offer the possibility of correspondence between humans and nature in which no diminishing occurs. They are traces of such ancient correspondence that reach through the present into the future, loci of meaning to set against abstraction and distraction.

'Roman Poems', the final part of the triptych, are all in different ways poems of decline. The much-admired imitation of Horace's 'Carmen Saeculare' surveys the unreal city of London; in 'Palinurus', the first of two ventures into the *Aeneid*, Aeneas loses his friend and helmsman, and in 'The Descent' he goes down into the underworld to discover 'the whole kingdom was empty'. 'Age falls', the other poems say, and 'this is over': they all contemplate a world in which a process of attenuation is at work everywhere. Virgil, Sisson says in his introduction to his translation of the *Aeneid*, 'had, to an exceptional degree, the gift of seeing the present as streaming out of the past and moving into the future'. The formulation is equivocal perhaps, the streaming out is a kind of emptying as well as a sustaining flow. The 'Roman Poems' remember the past in the form of Horace and Virgil in order to get an angle on the present, and the way they part company with their originals (especially in 'The Descent' and 'Hactenus arvorum cultus') is an acknowledgement of the loss they discern. It is because we are estranged from these texts that we go back to them, that we *can* go back to them.

As Sisson writes in 'A Possible Anglicanism': 'There is no speech which is not of a here and now and it is nothing except in terms of other times and elsewhere'. These Roman poems are of course English poems, but their Englishness involves a retracing of the historical and linguistic threads that make up the here-and-now, threads which extend far beyond England and so extend England far beyond itself. Englishness, for Sisson, is a consequence of where and when he was born and brought up, part of the necessary inheritance, but it doesn't preclude a deep engagement with other times and places and modes: this is visible above all in his enormous and various work of translation, which few poets in the twentieth century, even poet-translators like Pound or

Hughes, have as much to set beside. It enriched and pointed his poetry, affecting its movements and its preoccupations.

Sisson's idea of what it was to be English was anything but unexamined, just as his conservatism, if that's the best word for it, was never unexamined. Both were influenced by his stays in Berlin, Freiburg and Paris in 1934–36, the time he spent in India during the war, and by much reading in foreign literatures, especially French, throughout his life. Although his sense of the 'English inheritance' (*Avoidance*, p. 558) and its roots in the constitutional quarrels of the seventeenth century was strong, he didn't believe that 'the national character should be encouraged. It is the fund of vitality from which the conscious life of a nation springs, and if one exploits it one debauches the source of life' ('English Liberalism'). This slightly mystical notion recalls the parsley and honeysuckle drenching the hedges 'in the fringes of the town' in 'Family Fortunes' and is probably also related to his belief that poems 'just happen' and should not be too consciously pursued (see 'Natural History'). Despite all the analysis, the historical knowledge, the insistence on the value of knowing where you come from, and the immense amount of learning which he absorbed from diverse sources, there is never just a resigned acceptance of things as they are, but a holding to the fact that what really matters eludes definition and happens somewhere round the edges of consciousness.

The preface to the second edition of *The Spirit of British Administration* points out that 'the real inventiveness of the human race is usually to be found not at the centre but at the periphery, and in a democracy it can hardly be otherwise'. Sisson's main argument with contemporary culture, put most forcefully in *The Case of Walter Bagehot* and even more apposite now than it was then, is that 'number has replaced intent' ('The Discarnation'): the obsession with counting and accounting for everything leads to a neglect or, worse, a perversion, of anything that cannot be quantified. The diagnosis in the Bagehot book is unerring: 'The central object of Bagehot's writing – and it is a destructive one – was to give exclusive respectability to the pursuit of lucre, and to remove whatever social and intellectual impediments stood in the way of it. Intellectual pursuits, and whatever strives in the direction of permanence and *stillness*, have to give way to the provisional and divisive excitements of gain. In the end one is left contemplating numbers over a great void' (*Avoidance*, pp. 423–24). While one might not regret 'the ancient feeling of rank and ancestry' (Coleridge) or even the 'hold and intellectuality of religion' which Sisson includes among the 'checks' operative in the past, it is hard not to accept the justness of this as a view of the present.

It is because he believed in the necessity of these checks that he remained attached to the Church, the monarchy, and the civil service at a time when their hold on society was becoming visibly weaker. For him they were all forms of order imposed on chaos, but *regulating* democracy and not, as Maurras or Pound would have wanted, *replacing* it. This is a specifically English suspicion of the grand scheme, the total plan, a willingness to work with what is fallen and imperfect (namely: us, as we are, in the world we have made and has made us). It is a version of what Hulme called 'Original Sin', and writers such as Chesterton less dramatically saw as the unexciting conservatism of liberal democracy. These imperfect and imperfectly regulating systems are also greater than the sum of their imperfections – the banality of the monarchy in person is made up for by the binding nature of its pageantry, the dullness of the civil service is its strength, because if it were not dull it might not be either *civil* or a *service*, the Church of England, a pragmatic melding of religion and state, and the only church designed for agnostics, is an expression of spirituality rather than its home. It is the tired, already-disappointed way in which Sisson treats these, yet still holds out for them, that makes him so English. These allegiances, moreover, are not chosen but inherited, and our links to the past, to our own collective history, cannot simply be ignored. We are more than what we are, though there is often little comfort to be drawn from this.

The scrupulously downbeat way in which Sisson defends the institutions he values often contrasts with the tension and struggle in his poems as they wrestle with desire, old age, loss and cultural oblivion. Those barely enthusiastic, pre-emptively jaded essays about politics and governance are more conservative than they are reactionary, though they are frequently written against a prevailing leftism Sisson feels has become the *bien pensant* orthodoxy of the literary class. It is hard to think of a poet or critic less suited than Sisson either to the materialist right of post-Thatcher Britain or to the slippery pseudo-inclusive left of Blairism and since. And hard to imagine a less appropriate poet laureate than

C.H. Sisson, despite the probability that he alone among his contemporaries really *believed* (spiritually, institutionally, culturally) in the post.

Sisson represents what Hulme would have called 'a certain kind of Tory', something that means pretty much nothing these days, but which played its role in the development of a conservative cultural politics that tends to be forgotten in the crude binarism of the left/right narrative, as well as the corporatist post-ideological culture we have today. What is interesting and valuable about this brand of conservative cultural politics is that it is essentially modernist, not just in its poetics but in its ideological and cultural bearings. It does not tarry with the radical right. It is not the conservatism of, say, Larkin or Betjeman, and it is barely part of the 'native tradition' of British poetry (whatever we mean by that). It represents a sort of lost or marooned tradition, and Sisson's essays exemplify it in its purest, as well as its most isolated, form. The political essays are among the most deep-reaching engagements any British poet has shown with the world of politics in the twentieth century – not just political theory or political ideology, but politics in all its mess and slop and chaos. They have a remarkable degree of political literacy too, and attain this early on. Those essays and reviews Sisson wrote for *New English Weekly* in the 1930s seem like the work of a much older man, and have an extraordinary range for a writer then in his early twenties, with reviews and articles on Maurras, Weber, Curtius, Federalism, English Liberalism, Péguy and a great deal more besides.

In one of the 1967 'Essays' already referred to (later called 'Sevenoaks Essays' and then 'Native Ruminations'), Sisson writes (in the brief but capaciously titled 'An Essay on Identity'): 'It is, indeed, very hard to understand what makes up "I". And the mere existence of the pronoun should not at once persuade us of the existence of the thing'. There is something metaphysical about Sisson's treatment of the self, however drily and undramatically he writes about it:

> consciousness [...] flows, but its contents are historical rather than individual. It is a matter of 'culture' what we are conscious of. The 'thought' is a common thought; only so could it be understood. A stream loaded with old bottles, the vegetation of several countries, rags of clothing perhaps, flows

around the world. It makes no sense to talk of the individual mind. The individual body, perhaps.

It is clear that notions like this go somewhat against the prevailing current: in a time of confessional poetry, a political emphasis on the individual as locus of truth, and a cultural premium on self-fulfilment, Sisson's writing was never going to be consensus-building stuff. 'Out of key with his time' as he was, he was also expressing a Hulmean world-view, the sort of conservatism that emphasised limits and limitation, that resisted the lure of idealism, and never believed in perfectibility, on either the individual or the collective level.

His poetry, likewise, situates itself on the margins of the fashionable, emphasises the boundedness of our experience and the uncertainty of our projections:

> The future has not lasted yet
> Even the second that it can
> And so is good for any bet:
> It is the guessing makes the man.
>
> ('Uncertainty')

The 'guessing' is his characteristic mode, something we can sometimes overlook in the face of the weary confidence of so much of his writing. In his engagement with Maurras, Sisson shows how a mid-century English writer with interests that go beyond writing can be drawn to the great totalising projects of someone like Maurras, and yet still see through them. It is partly the failure of Maurras that attracts, and we can sense that Maurras was to Sisson what Péguy was to Geoffrey Hill in 'The Mystery of the Charity of Charles Péguy': an exemplary failure but perhaps a necessary one. And when, in a review of Hill's 'Péguy' in *PN Review* 33, Sisson writes

> All this raises the question how far the 'mystic' who – with whatever disclaimers – dabbles in the matter of politics, has a right to dissociate himself from the practical consequences of his actions. Péguy had an invincible conviction of his own rightness. [...] Such a man was hardly made for success.

he could as easily be talking about Maurras, to whom he quickly
compares Péguy, himself the subject of an essay first published in
1946. A few lines on, Sisson quotes Daniel Halévy imagining a
polemic between the two, born a few years apart, on opposing
sides of the Dreyfus affair (Péguy, the socialist, a Dreyfusard,
Maurras a lifelong anti-Dreyfusard) and each becoming a symbol
for a particular kind of French nationalism in the midst of historical turmoil.

There is a place for the mystical in Sisson, though we sense
him resisting it too, fending off its allure, something he captures
in his poetry with its refusal of grand style or high lyric, and by
the mattness of his language and diction. This mattness extends to
his translations too. Perhaps surprisingly, Sisson's work is often
extremely personal, even in its way confessional, though always
undercut by a sense of the self's dispersal, its unbelonging in relation to the 'I' that speaks it. His view of the self, and of the poet's
point of voice – many of his poems are spoken by an 'I' – is one
that calls the self into question as a stable, sufficient thing:

> What is the person? Is it hope?
> If so, there is no I in me.
>   Is it a trope
> Or paraphrase of deity?
>   If so,
> I may be what I do not know.
>
>   ('The Person')

There is nothing of the mystic in Sisson when it comes to culture
and politics, however, and yet in his way he believes that writers
should engage with political reality. 'Scarcely any writer since
Hulme has formulated a precise political idea. Inevitably, both
poetry and political analyses are the worse for the lack of political
doctrine.' His interest in Bolingbroke, Bagehot, Keynes,
Montesquieu and others, in T.S. Eliot as critic of culture and
Marvell as poet-politician, and his writings on administration,
government and economics ('Economics used to be called Political Economy, and has lost the adjective in the search for scientific
status. But political it remains...') mark Sisson out as the most
politically literate poet of his time. He is certainly more politically
literate, if by 'literate' we mean coming to the subject with a grasp

of detail as well as overlooking sweep, and pronounces on culture from a less high place, than Eliot. This is in part because of his own dual career as poet and civil servant; or perhaps it is the other way around: that he came to practise both because he was always intellectually invested in both.

In the flyleaf to the first and only edition of *Art and Action* (1965), his first collection of essays, we may read what we assume to be Sisson's own words: 'At present he is an Under Secretary at the Ministry of Labour [...] Although he is very hard-worked, not to say over-worked, he still finds writing difficult to avoid.' *The Avoidance of Literature* (1978) reiterates this theme: a sort of reluctant weakness for what the French, in exactly these decades, were calling *engagement*, which we could roughly translate as commitment to a cause, usually an eye-catching one, and always involving plenty of publicity. Sisson's cause, however, could not be further from the radical postures of his contemporaries. As John Peck writes in an essay on Sisson, 'what makes for a lively mind in truly urgent political situations is not a *posse comitatus* of like views, but of unlike views converging upon limited, principled grounds'.[1] It is in that spirit that Sisson, as a cultural critic, engages: offering a critique, or a set of critiques, of commodity capitalism, not from the left but drawing on the older forms of conservatism.

Walter Bagehot, his most polemical and urgent intervention, was published in 1972, an important time for Sisson, who took early retirement in 1973, moved to Somerset, and saw the publication of *In the Trojan Ditch* in 1974, the Collected Poems that established his presence in English poetry. The new poems in that book, those written since *Metamorphoses* (1968), and the following two collections, *Anchises* (1976) and *Exactions* (1980), probably concentrate his best work. As several readers have pointed out, 'The Discarnation' is in some ways subject to its own strictures in that it is ruled by number and by a severely reductive take on human nature. Although it is of course an over-simplification, there is at around this time an observable shift – a movement, nothing more – away from a poetry of analysis, very often with a satirical edge and always an edge of some sort, towards a poetry

---

1   John Peck, 'Charles Sisson and the Distantly Raised Voice', in *Agenda*, Vol. 45, No. 2 (Spring 2010), C.H. Sisson Special Issue, pp. 28–36 (p. 32).

of association. In the Foreword to the poems in *In the Trojan Ditch* there are some interesting remarks which perhaps relate to this shift. 'The writing of poetry', he says, 'is, in a sense, the opposite of writing what one wants to write', and translation is seen as one of several 'enabling distractions' which can let the 'unwanted impulses free themselves'. When they do, it is as a rhythm that they make themselves felt, and it is rhythm – 'that unarguable perception' – that holds the otherwise unreckonable impulses together. If the earlier poetry is too much bound up in the world it criticises, the later tries to escape it by finding ways of suggesting or even entering the life that subsists beneath the grid of meaning we order it by. In doing so, it is also seeking to escape the vigilance of the conscious mind, which in Sisson's case, as poem after poem shows, is tormented by its own interfering intelligence. What Rilke called 'the interpreted world' ('die gedeutete Welt') is necessary for our living in it but also impedes or forces our apprehension of what it might be. The glimpses through it follow the injunction of 'The Red Admiral':

Its fingers lighter than spiders, the red admiral
Considers, as I do, with little movement;
With little of anything that is meant:
Let the meaning go, movement is all.

Some of the best poems are those that let the meaning go, that give the over-inquisitive mind the slip and embrace a movement, a rhythm, that of course belongs to consciousness too but at a deeper, more instinctive level. Sisson's own description is best, talking of Hardy in words that apply as truly to himself: 'less awkwardnesses than aspects of his speaking mind, like a particular lurch or other movement which is habitual to some bodies. The rhythm of the verse, with its hesitations, sudden speeds, and pauses which are almost silences, is the very rhythm of thought'. Thought, that is, that resembles the way we think, with its false starts, interruptions, leaps, slidings and empty patches, rather than the philosophical moves and reasonings which plague the mind elsewhere. Compared to the earlier poems the later are less governed by argument, they are more of the body, and thus have that incontrovertible quality that Sisson identifies in 'Natural History': 'the poem exists as a natural object exists, so that you can look at it, hear it, smell it, as you can wind, waves or trees, without asking why you are doing so':

> And so with the natural surfaces,
> Like comfrey gone to waste, there is no loss,
> Only the passage of time. And the singing mind,
> Like a telegraph wire in the waste, recording time:
> Intervals, sounds, rustling, there is no peace
> Where the wind is, and no identity
> Clapping with herb or tree…

This is from a poem called 'The Surfaces' and many of the later poems seem able to abandon the distinction between surface and depth, or to assume that surface is the only depth, and take readings of the Somerset landscape as earlier they scrutinised the life of the commuter-belt. It is always a landscape inhabited by the past, a version of England both imaginary and real:

> Do you know it? It is Arthur's territory
> – Agravaine, Mordred, Guinevere and Igraine –
> Do you hear them? Or see them in the distant sparkle?
> Likely not, but they are there all the same.
>
>   ('In Flood')

In poems like this, and the major and most challenging example is probably 'In insula Avalonia', an extended meditation on the known landscape which is inevitable and elusive in equal measure, Sisson is speaking as one who has fully absorbed the modernist moment but is at the same time instinct with the English tradition. He is not the only modernist to have read Malory, but perhaps he is the only one for whom Malory had such real presence, so that we witness a fusing of the language and the landscape in which the movement of the mind, as it is embodied in words both inconsequential and unanswerable, finds its exact correspondence in details of the observable world, the river, the willows, the geese 'in a careless skein / Sliding between the mort plain and the sky' ('In insula Avalonia'). The modernism is not attenuated by its Englishness but fuelled by it, and it is an English-ness in which Dante and Virgil play as much a part as Hardy or Vaughan. The result is 'durable speech' – to quote Sisson's own words for literature that matters – which has a savour and accent quite its own.

In a very late poem, 'Tristia', contemplating a version of the same landscape, the often-flooded Levels spread out south of the house in Langport, he stands 'at this far tip of the world', a metaphor above all for old age as a last 'promontory' of life. But in a sense it was where he had always been, late and 'lost', an 'exile' from the world he loved and so from his own life. The poems are nearly all written from that place, avoiding literature, giving little consolation, and leading us into territory quite different from that of most modern poetry.

★

The span and variety of Sisson's work is so great that any selection is bound to leave out not just particular texts but whole aspects. The poetry from all periods is well represented, but a few essential poems apart – some of them would be 'A Letter to John Donne', 'On my Fifty-first Birthday', 'The Usk', 'In insula Avalonia', 'Troia', 'The Herb-garden', 'The Red Admiral', 'In Flood' and 'Burrington Combe' – an almost equally good choice could have been made of other poems, which says something interesting about the kind of poems Sisson wrote and the nature of his achievement. Nothing has been included from the two novels, *An Asiatic Romance* (1953) and *Christopher Homm* (1965, but written in the mid-50s), though the last is a masterpiece in its way, like the poems radically different from other novels being written at the time. In the end they represent a mode he abandoned. Also left out is *On the Look-Out: A Partial Autobiography* (1989), though this is made up for by the inclusion of the essays 'Autobiographical Reflections on Politics' and 'Natural History'. A greater omission given its importance for the poetry is the great body of translation, but we felt that in a book of this kind it made little sense to draw from large works such as the versions of the *Divine Comedy* and the *Aeneid* which are in any case easily available, and that this might be the place to draw attention to (a very few) smaller things otherwise liable to be overlooked. It is a distortion nevertheless. *The Spirit of British Administration* (1959), Sisson's book on the civil service, is also absent, but a couple of essays which formed earlier versions of chapters there are included instead. The short study

David Hume (1976) is entirely absent, and only one chapter is taken from *The Case of Walter Bagehot* (1972), despite its importance and readability; and only two and half from *English Poetry 1900–1950: An Assessment* (1971). From among the essays proper we have included all that we really wanted in, but there is a great deal more that could also have been included. Sisson wrote essays and reviews all his life, and together they are a fascinating education in the sources of his thinking, as well as being lucid, thought-provoking, and often very witty. There is in the end little from the ecclesiastical essays (only one from *Anglican Essays* (1983)) – the writing there is often more polemical and context-bound. What we wanted to bring out is Sisson's close engagement with the times and with politics throughout his writing life, and the independence, intelligence and civility of his opinions. No poet has written with anything like his intimate knowledge of the workings of government, and few have had a clearer sense of the role of literature in participating in civic life.

The poems themselves are uncompromising, contradictory, afflicted, savage, sometimes abrasive, and pursue disquieting truths. Much of the time, they seem to invite dissent, and their positions, though growing out of a clearly recognisable English tradition, have never been those of the mainstream, not even the mainstream which likes to see itself as marginal. Yet his work has a certain centrality too. Civically, in that it is concerned with the public sphere and with keeping channels open to the past; with maintaining clear-sightedness and countering a world where 'the denial of the sources of our thinking' has become 'an indispensable preliminary to any intervention on the public stage' (*The Case of Walter Bagehot*). And then poetically, in its crossing of a tradition that flows out of Edward Thomas, Hardy and Barnes with the nervous energies and disruptions of Eliot and Pound:

> There is one God we do not know
> Stretched on Orion for a cross
>   And we below
> In several sorts of lesser loss
>   Are we
> In number not identity.

('The Person')

POEMS

From *The London Zoo* (1961) and other early poems

On a Troopship

They are already made
Why should they go
Into boring society
Among the soldiery?
But I, whose imperfection
Is evident and admitted
Needing further assurance
Must year–long be pitted
Against fool and trooper
Practising my integrity
In awkward places,
Walking till I walk easily
Among uncomprehended faces
Extracting the root
Of the matter from the diverse engines
That in an oath, a gesture or a song
Inadequately approximate to the human norm.

In Time of Famine: Bengal

I do not say this child
This child with grey mud
Plastering her rounded body
I do not say this child
For she walks poised and happy
But I say this
Who looks in at the carriage window
Her eyes are big
Too big
Her hair is touzled and her mouth is doubtful

And I say this
Who lies with open eyes upon the pavement
Can you hurt her?
Tread on those frightened eyes
Why should it frighten her to die?
This is a fault
This is a fault in which I have a part.

The Body in Asia

Despite the mountains at my doorstep
This is a hollow, hollow life.
The mist blows clear and shows the snow
Among the dark green firs, but here
Upon the cold, scorched, dusty grass
The camels looped together raise
Their supercilious noses.
Upon the road the donkeys trot
And mule-teams with their muleteers pace.
The country lies before me like
A map I carry in my mind –
A wall built by the Hindu Kush
A plain that falls away to sea
I on the foothills here between
Sniffing the cold and dusty air.
Too long of longing makes me cold
The heart a tight and burning fistful
Hangs like a cold sun in my chest
A hollow kind of firmament.

I can imagine my exterior
The body, and the limbs that run off from it
But there is nothing in it I am sure
Except the ball of heart that weighs one side
Like the lead ballast in a celluloid duck.
And in my head a quarter-incher's brain
Looks out as best it can from my two eyes:
It can imagine how the country lies
To left and right, extensions of the limbs

But has no thoughts that I can understand.
Not only in this land I have felt it so
But on the Brahmaputra where
Bits of the jungle floated down
Black heaps upon the coloured river
When night fell and the sun
A red and geometric disk
Above its square reflection stood
For half a moment and then dipped:
I heard it sizzle in the water.
The flat and muddy banks, remote
Beyond the miles of plashing water
Diminished me
Till, smaller than the skin I stood in
I leaned against the rails and watched
The searchlights on the licking water.
The secret of diminishment
Is in this sad peninsula
Where the inflated body struts
Shouting its wants, but lacks conviction.
Conviction joins the muscles up
But here the body flaps and flutters
A flapping sail in a fitful wind.

In a Dark Wood

Now I am forty I must lick my bruises
What has been suffered cannot be repaired
I have chosen what whoever grows up chooses
A sickening garbage that could not be shared.

My errors have been written in my senses
The body is a record of the mind
My touch is crusted with my past defences
Because my wit was dull my eye grows blind.

There is no credit in a long defection
And defect and defection are the same
I have no person fit for resurrection
Destroy then rather my half-eaten frame.

But that you will not do, for that were pardon
The bodies that you pardon you replace
And that you keep for those whom you will harden
To suffer in the hard rule of your Grace.

Christians on earth may have their bodies mended
By premonition of a heavenly state
But I, by grosser flesh from Grace defended,
Can never see, never communicate.

In London

I float between the banks of Maida Vale
Where half is dark and half is yellow light
In creeks and catches flecks of flesh look pale
And over all our grief depends the night.

I turn beside the shining black canal
And tree-tops close like lids upon my eyes
A milk-maid laughs beside a coffee-stall
I pray to heaven, favour my enterprise.

But whether there is answer to my prayer
When with my host at last I redescend
After delicious talk the squalid stair
I do not know the answer in the end.

Sparrows seen from an Office Window

You should not bicker while the sparrows fall
In chasing pairs from underneath the eaves
And yet you should not let this enraged fool
Win what he will because you fear his grief.

About your table three or four who beg
Bully or trade because those are the passions
Strong enough in them to hide all other lack
Sent to corrupt your heart or try your patience.

If you are gentle, it is because you are weak
If bold, it is the courage of a clown
And your smart enemies and you both seek
Ratiocination without love or reason.

O fell like lust, birds of morality
O sparrows, sparrows, sparrows whom none regards
Where men inhabit, look in here and see
The fury and cupidity of the heart.

In Kent

Although there may be treacherous men
Who in the churchyard swing their mattocks
Within they sing the *Nunc Dimittis*

And villagers who find that building
A place to go to of a Sunday
May accidentally be absolved

For on a hill, upon a gibbet ...
And this is Saint Augustine's county.

Maurras Young and Old

1

Est allé à Londres
Monsieur Maurras jeune
From a land of olives, grapes and almonds
His mind full of Greek.
Under the shadow of the British Museum
He reflected on the many and foolish
Discourses of the Athenians
And on the Elgin marbles.

The fog settled
Chokingly around the Latin head

Of the eloquent scholar.
Quick like a ferret
He tore his way through
Scurrying past the red brick of Bloomsbury
To the mock antique portals.

The Latin light
Showed on the Mediterranean hills
A frugal culture of wine and oil.
Unobserved in their fog the British
toto divisos orbe
Propounded a mystery of steam
In France they corrected the menus
Writing for *biftec*: beefsteak.
Monsieur Maurras noted the linguistic symptoms
He noted, beyond the Drachenfels
The armies gathering.

2

The light fell
Across the sand-dunes and the wide *étang*.
In their autochthonous boats
The fishermen put out
And came back to the linear village
Among the vineyards and the olive groves
Place de la République
Rue Zola
In which names the enemy celebrated his triumphs.

Twenty-five years:
Beyond the Drachenfels
The armies gathered again
irruptio barbarorum
The boats are moored on the *étang*
For Monsieur Maurras
The last harvest is gathered.

A Latin scorn
For all that is not indelibly Latin

A fortiori for the Teutonic captain
Passing him on the terrace of the Chemin de Paradis
Enemy and barbarian.
Inutile, Monsieur, de me saluer
His eyes looked out towards the middle sea
He heard not even that murmur
But an interior music.

On the Way Home

Like questing hounds
The lechers run through London
From all the alley-ways
Into all the thoroughfares

Until, shoulder to shoulder, they vanish
Into the main line stations
Or the Underground traps them.

A moment of promiscuity at nightfall
Their feet go homewards but their attentions
Are on the nape of a neck or the cut of a thigh
Almost any woman

As Schopenhauer noted
Being more interesting to them than those
Who made their beds that morning.

Silence

Let not my words have meaning
And let not my bitter heart
Be expressed, like a rotten
Pomegranate. Guts full of pus
And a brain uncertain as a thunderstorm
Do not, I think, amuse the muses.

Ightham Woods

The few syllables of a horse's scuffle at the edge of the road
Reach me in the green light of the beeches
Les seuls vrais plaisirs
Selon moy
Are those of one patch between the feet and the throat.
Maybe, but the beeches
And that half clop on the gravel
Indicate a world into which I can dissolve.

Family Fortunes

I

I was born in Bristol, and it is possible
To live harshly in that city

Quiet voices possess it, but the boy
Torn from the womb, cowers

Under a ceiling of cloud. Tramcars
Crash by or enter the mind

A barred room bore him, the backyard
Smooth as a snake-skin, yielded nothing

In the fringes of the town parsley and honey-suckle
Drenched the hedges.

II

My mother was born in West Kington
Where ford and bridge cross the river together

John Worlock farmed there, my grandfather
Within sight of the square church-tower

The rounded cart-horses shone like metal
My mother remembered their fine ribbons

She lies in the north now where the hills
Are pale green, and I

Whose hand never steadied a plough
Wish I had finished my long journey.

III

South of the march parts my father
Lies also, and the fell town

That cradles him now sheltered also
His first unconsciousness

He walked from farm to farm with a kit of tools
From clock to clock, and at the end

Only they spoke to him, he
Having tuned his youth to their hammers.

IV

I had two sisters, one I cannot speak of
For she died a child, and the sky was blue that day

The other lived to meet blindness
Groping upon the stairs, not admitting she could not see

Felled at last under a surgeon's hammer
Then left to rot, surgically

And I have a brother who, being alive
Does not need to be put in a poem.

In Honour of J.H. Fabre

My first trick was to clutch
At my mother and suck
Soon there was nothing to catch
But darkness and a lack.

My next trick was to know
Dividing the visible
Into shapes which now
Are no longer definable.

My third trick was to love
With the pretence of identity
Accepting without proof
The objects 'her' and 'me'.

My last trick was to believe
When I have the air
Of praying I at least
Join the mantis at its prayers.

Nude Studies

They are separate as to arms and legs
Though occasionally joined in one place
As to what identity that gives
You may question the opacity of the face.

Either man is made in the image of God
Or there is no such creature, only a cluster of cells
Which of these improbabilities is the less
You cannot, by the study of nudity, tell.

Tintagel

The clear water ripples between crags
And the Atlantic reaches our island
A clout on the outer headland.

A small band gathered God into this fastness
Singing and praying men; while others
Climbed up the perilous stairway shod in iron.

In every clearing a mad hermit
Draws his stinking rags about him and smoke rises
From thatches lately hurt by rape or pillage.

Cynadoc, Gennys, names as clear as water
Each hill unfolds, and the sheep
Pass numerous through the narrow gate.

To Walter Savage Landor

No poet uses a chisel in quite the same way
You do, or lays the marble chips together
In the sunlight, chip by chip.

If you had this girl before you, you
Would make her excel in some way by mere words
But I have only my pity and little to show
For forty-five years. Memoranda
Are strictly not to be memorised. It is the fleeting moments
Sunlit leaf upon leaf, your speech
That remains.

Cranmer

Cranmer was parson of this parish
And said Our Father beside barns
Where my grandfather worked without praying.

From the valley came the ring of metal
And the horses clopped down the track by the stream
As my mother saw them.

The Wiltshire voices floated up to him
How should they not overcome his proud Latin
With We depart answering his *Nunc Dimittis*?

One evening he came over the hillock
To the edge of the church-yard already filled with bones
And saw in the smithy his own fire burning.

Knole

The white hill-side is prickled with antlers
And the deer wade to me through the snow.
From John Donne's church the muffled and galoshed
Patiently to their holy dinners go.

And never do those antlered heads reflect
On the gentle flanks where in autumn they put their seed
Nor Christians on the word which, that very hour,
Their upturned faces or their hearts received.

But spring will bring the heavy doe to bed;
The fawn will wobble and soon after leap.
Those others will die at this or the next year's turn
And find the resurrection encased in sleep.

On a Civil Servant

Here lies a civil servant. He was civil
To everyone, and servant to the devil.

Money

I was led into captivity by the bitch business
Not in love but in what seemed a physical necessity
And now I cannot even watch the spring
The itch for subsistence having become responsibility.

Money the she-devil comes to us under many veils
Tactful at first, calling herself beauty
Tear away this disguise, she proposes paternal solicitude
Assuming the dishonest face of duty.

Suddenly you are in bed with a screeching tear-sheet
This is money at last without her night-dress
Clutching you against her fallen udders and sharp bones
In an unscrupulous and deserved embrace.

Ellick Farm

The larks flew up like jack-in-the-boxes
From my moors, and the fields were edged with foxgloves.

The farm lay neatly within the hollow
The gables climbing, the barn beside the doorway.

If I had climbed into the loft I should have found a boy
Forty years back, among the bales of hay.

He would have known certainly all that I know
Seeing it in the muck-strewn cobbles below.

(Under the dark rim of the near wood
The tears gathered as under an eyelid.)

It would have surprised him to see a tall man
Who had travelled far, pretending to be him.

But that he should have been turning verses, half dumb
After half a lifetime, would least have surprised him.

The Un-Red Deer

The un-red deer
In the un-green forest

The antlers which do not appear
And are not like branches

The hounds which do not bay
With tails which do not swish

The heather beyond and the insignificant stumble
Of the horse not pulled up

By the rider who does not see all this
Nor hear nor smell it

Or does so but it does not matter
The horn sounds Gone away

Or, if it does not, is there hunter,
Hunted, or the broken tree

Swept by the wind from the channel?

The London Zoo

From one of the cages on the periphery
He is brought to London, but only for duty.
As if radio-controlled he comes without a keeper,
Without any resistance, five times in the week.
See him as he rises in his ordered household,
Docile each morning before he is expelled,
Take his bath when he is told, use the right towel,
Reliable as an ant, meticulous as an owl.
His wife, until he is gone, is anxiously protective
In case after all one morning he should resist,
But all is well each day, he hasn't the spirit
− He is edged out of the door without even a murmur.
The road to the station is reassuring
For other black hats are doing the same thing
Some striding blithely who were never athletic,
Others, who were, now encased in Cadillacs,
Snug and still belching from their breakfast bacon,
All, halt and well, keen to be on the train.

Each sits by other whom a long acquaintance
Has made familiar as a chronic complaint,
Although the carapaces they wear are so thick
That the tender souls inside are far to seek.
First there is *The Times* newspaper, held before the eyes
As an outer defence and a guarantee of propriety,
Then the clothes which are not entirely uniform
So as to give the appearance of a personal epidermis,
But most resistant of all is the layer of language
Swathed around their senses like a mile of bandage;
Almost nothing gets in through that, but when something does,
The answering thought squelches out like pus.

These are agreeable companions. At this hour
The people travelling are certainly superior
To those you would have the misfortune to see
If you came up one morning by the eight fifteen
− Typists and secretaries talkative and amorous
With breasts like pears plopping out of their bodices.

Mr Axeter's companions do not distract him:
Carefully he spreads out his copy of *The Times*,
Not unwilling to be stimulated by disasters
Less likely to happen to him than sex,
Disappointed when he finds so boring a centre page
That this morning his mind is not going to be raped.
As an alternative he begins to eavesdrop
On the holidays and cars which a lot
Of people have larger and more expensive than he does.
He computes their incomes and their intelligences,
The one larger, the other smaller than his own,
Though his intelligence has shrunk and his income grown
– A not unsatisfactory bit of co-ordination
Which comforts him as his train enters the terminal station.

Out on the platform like money from a cashier's shovel
The responsible people fall at the end of their travel.
Some are indignant that their well-known faces
Are not accepted instead of railway passes;
Others faithfully produce the card by which the authorities
Regulate the movement of animals in great cities.
With growing consciousness of important function
Each man sets out for where he is admired most,
The one room in London where everything is arranged
To enlarge his importance and deaden his senses.
The secretary who awaits him has corrected her bosom;
His papers are in the disorder he has chosen.
Anxieties enough to blot out consciousness
Are waiting satisfactorily upon his desk.

Mr Axeter's office is designed theologically;
Upstairs there is one greater than he;
Downstairs there are several he must keep in submission
Who smoothly profess they are doing what should be done.
Yet the conflict here is no simplified battle,
As you might think, between God and the Devil.
Swords go ping on helmets in every direction
– It is not the fault of God if there is not confusion.
Every man may speak according to his conscience
If he has had it regulated in advance.

A man who goes out to meet a bullet
Is after all some sort of a serious character,
For it is him the bullet goes through all right, though he wishes
For an MC or a *Croix de Guerre* or loves spit and polish,
But the man who makes money or who gives wise counsel
Is prostitute or pimp to more live originals
– Still, this is what he takes his money for;
He wouldn't be more honest if he were less of a whore.

Meanwhile from the same train Professor Tortilus
Has gone where they allow him to profess.
Already his zealous students are reading their comics
In the library of the School of Economics
– Judicious journals where those who think thoughts
For a living lay out their unappetising corpses.
The long-haired, the beautiful and the black
And those whose only distinction is to be ignorant
Learn that to be intelligent is to be dull
And that to be perfect you should be statistical as well.
To these hopefuls Professor Tortilus
Will explain the maxims of his own mysterious
Speciality which is nothing less than the complete science
Of correctly conducting human government.
The morning papers, which to many brought only diversion,
To him brought irrefutable demonstration
That all who exercise power will certainly fail
Simply through not following his principles.
All round the School is utter confusion
– The city, Whitehall, industry in ruins –
Only Professor Tortilus, as in a calm season
Still swimming happily in a pool of reason.

There are many others, of course, in the same trainload
As Mr Axeter and Professor Tortilus.
Each has his pretensions and his importance,
Worth good money at the price of utter dependence.
The happiest are convinced by their own rackets,
And there is no racket that does not provide a pretext
For those who are willing to be convinced: one
Incidentally produces something useful as well as money;

Another can be shown, although itself despicable,
To prevent what can be thought of as a worse evil.
Each actor thinks of the particular part he acts
As producing only beneficial effects;
He does harm and picks up his money as unobtrusively
As a physician taking a tip or a waiter a fee.
This lawyer, a vehement defender of the rich against the poor,
Pays no attention to that part of his behaviour,
But advertises himself as a kind of John Hampden
As, without risk to himself, he becomes eloquent
On the unalterable right of the poorest he
That is in England to have an advocate, for a fee
To be paid for by the public out of those taxes
The evasion of which is the object of his main practice.
Many who, in a more rational system,
Would be thought mad if they behaved as they do in this one
Are obsessed by the more insidious forms of property:
They buy and sell merchandise they will never see,
Hawking among Wren's churches, and, if they say their prayers,
Say them, without a doubt, to stocks and shares.
– One can barely imagine what scandal would be caused
If they were to be found on their knees in Saint Paul's.
For everything is turned from its right use, so that
Even the lobster that climbs on the business man's plate
Is there less for its colour or its marine taste
Than to impress a customer, or conclude a bargain
– A species of harlotry in edible materials
As the tax-free limousine is a harlot on wheels.

And who am I, you may ask, thus to belly-ache
At my betters? I tell you, I am one of the same lot
– Without lobster and limousine, but, like the rest,
Expending my best energies on the second-best.
There are those who do not, who accept no pay
For work they know would better be done otherwise
– Not the scabs of culture for whom any talk of the arts
Brings money to their purses and a throb to their silly hearts,
But the few still remaining who have decided to live
Without taking account of what is remunerative.
You will hardly believe it, but it is those few

Who are the only spectators in this zoo
– And yet to call it a zoo is certainly an injustice
To the family of hyenas, apes and bustards
Who have no difficulty in speaking with their own voice
And do not look to be respected for their price.
It is rather as a somewhat extravagant machine
That the managerial classes should be seen,
Whose only animal activity is when
Mr Cog returns at the end of the day to his hen.

From *Numbers* (1965)

My Life and Times

I would not waste this paper for
(I hope) a merely personal bore
But write about the singular
Because 'I am' may read 'We are.'
So damn the individual touch
Of which the critics make so much;
Remember that the human race
Grins more or less in every face.

My mind unfocussed like my eyes,
When young I showed, not felt, surprise.
Perhaps. But what comes from the womb
Is all that goes into the tomb
Or more than all. And what we mean
Or may imagine in between
Is trivial by comparison.
It is the gloss that we put on.

My elders recognised my shape.
Thereafter there was no escape
For parents do the best they can
To capture us and make us Man.
So I became subjective too
And what was hopeful now is true.

As my especial mode of thought
Was finding where I had not sought,
When Love at last possessed my mind
It was exactly of that kind.
There was no exercise of will;
It came, I saw it and stood still.
It was a blaze and I was dark.
The grief that scorched me left the mark.

No money and much time to spend.
I walked the streets for hours on end
Then lay upon my iron bed.
Some have their youth. This was instead.

What mattered when I left this shore
And found the classic world of war?
I understood the natural hate
Of man and cruelty of state
And the Schutz Staffel was to me
The natural heart of Germany.

War happened like a second birth
Upon an even blinder earth:
Some happy to increase the rate
At which they drink and fornicate
But exile and anxiety
For others. This included me.
From this excitement then I come
To settle soberly at home
And, blindly occupied with work,
I live completely in the dark.
For I have reached that slippery place
Where Nisus fell upon his face
While his young friend ran on. The truth
Took over from the hopes of youth.
Rather, I saw the limits of
Even the promises of love.
This moment comes, early or late.
Rather, you slide into a state
In which the heart is running on
Perhaps, but expectation's gone.
For the first part of life we move
To get to where we came from – love.
Then time is moving and we stand.
Something descends and is at hand.
There are innumerable ways
Of marking the *nel mezzo* phase
But all men understand that breath
Grows shorter long before our death.

So I, improvident, looked round
And saw that I was losing ground
And that it did not matter for
To win would also be a bore.
I could say, like some wily man
I had thought out a clever plan.
In fact, it worked the other way;
I did what offered day by day.
Small children climbed upon my face
Or ran in front to set the pace.
The only secret of 'I go'
Is following what you do not know.
I burrow in an office where
There is no purpose in despair.
This is, indeed, the last descent.
But how await the sure event?
For time will wave his arms about
Until he gives his final shout.

The Nature of Man

It is the nature of man that puzzles me
As I walk from Saint James's Square to Charing Cross;
The polite mechanicals are going home,
I understand their condition and their loss.

Ape-like in that their box of wires
Is shut behind a face of human resemblance,
They favour a comic hat between their ears
And their monkey's tube is tucked inside their pants.

Language which is all our lies has us on a skewer,
Inept, weak, the grinning devil of comprehension; but sleep
Knows us for plants or undiscovered worlds;
If we have reasons, they lie deep.

A and B

A

I was in the lane and saw the car pass.
The white face of the girl showed through the windscreen,
Beside her a youth with a tight grip on the wheel.

B

There was a blue Anglia; I remember.

A

I caught the girl's eyes as she passed;
They were in deepest contentment.
She communicated in perfect freedom to me
The candour with which she would undress when they reached
the wood.
It was a point that had been troubling the boy.

B

And what has their pleasure to do with us?

A

You think a philosopher should stick to his port.
That is not my opinion.
What is enacted in these hills
Is a sacrifice as certainly as any propounded
Under the shadow of the Giant of Cerne
And sacrifice is not for the actors.

B

What nonsense is this about a sacrifice?
This is what two people did, and that is all.

A

What they did in a flurry of consciousness,
Their hands upon one another's sides,
Was trivial enough. But what were their intentions?
Some hope perhaps of giving or taking pleasure.

B

I should think they might have been partially successful.

A
I met an old man on a tall horse
He had ridden for thirty years. It was his intention
When he had seen the last of it, to bury it
Out in that field beside his dead mare.
Do you think he had planned that harmony?
Did not a spirit seize him by the throat
And tell him what to do: there, under the old church
Rising there on that mound above the groin?

B
I am afraid, A, you are not a philosopher.
You are merely an inconsiderate fool who loves his country
At the very moment when love has become vain.

A
See there where a party of picnickers
Trace their way over the springy turf
And the world proceeds without understanding.
Perhaps all will be well.

A Letter to John Donne

On 27 July 1617, Donne preached at the parish church at Sevenoaks, of which he was rector, and was entertained at Knole, then the country residence of Richard Sackville, third Earl of Dorset.

I understand you well enough, John Donne
First, that you were a man of ability
Eaten by lust and by the love of God
Then, that you crossed the Sevenoaks High Street
As rector of Saint Nicholas:
I am of that parish.

To be a man of ability is not much
You may see them on the Sevenoaks platform any day
Eager men with despatch cases
Whom ambition drives as they drive the machine
Whom the certainty of meticulous operation
Pleasures as a morbid sex a heart of stone.

That you should have spent your time in the corruption of courts
As these in that of cities, gives you no place among us:
Ability is not even the game of a fool
But the click of a computer operating in a waste
Your cleverness is dismissed from the suit
Bring out your genitals and your theology.

What makes you familiar is this dual obsession;
Lust is not what the rutting stag knows
It is to take Eve's apple and to lose
The stag's paradisal look:
The love of God comes readily
To those who have most need.

You brought body and soul to this church
Walking there through the park alive with deer
But now what animal has climbed into your pulpit?
One whose pretension is that the fear
Of God has heated him into a spirit
An evaporated man no physical ill can hurt.

Well might you hesitate at the Latin gate
Seeing such apes denying the church of God:
I am grateful particularly that you were not a saint
But extravagant whether in bed or in your shroud.
You would understand that in the presence of folly
I am not sanctified but angry.

Come down and speak to the men of ability
On the Sevenoaks platform and tell them
That at your Saint Nicholas the faith
Is not exclusive in the fools it chooses
That the vain, the ambitious and the highly sexed
Are the natural prey of the incarnate Christ.

Words

I have noticed that words are not understood.
Where the dappled fawns walk in the sunlight
In contrast with their sisters dark against the sky-line
The beeches crack.

The Thrush

You do not see your speckled breast and bright eye;
What you eat is what interests you. I do not eat
You but I am interested and have the name beauty
For your feathered and energetic stand and sharp beak.

This is what it is to be the image of God:
I am it because I reflect your image,
Loving without eating. But eating
Is the end of loving. No wonder if I am confused.

And this young beauty is aware of herself
From shoulder to shank she is for discovery
By herself as well as by the hungry who would eat her.
Her mind is out of the order of nature.

It is puzzling that the form of natural good
Is a little different from the specifically human.
Those who out of congress invented lechery
Were the first inventors of man and woman.

Adam and Eve

They must be shown as about to taste of the tree.
If they had already done so they would be like us;
If they were not about to do so they would be
Not our first parents but monsters.

You must show that they were the first who contrived
An act which has since become common,
With head held high when it is conceived
And, when it is repented of, dangling.

There must be not one Adam but two,
The second nailed upon the tree:
He came down in order to go up
Although he hangs so limply.

The first Adam, you will recall, gave birth
To a woman out of his side;
For the second the process was reversed
And that one was without pride.

Easter

One good crucifixion and he rose from the dead
He knew better than to wait for age
To nibble his intellect
And depress his love.

Out in the desert the sun beats and the cactus
Prickles more fiercely than any in his wilderness
And his forty days
Were merely monastic.

What he did on the cross was no more
Than others have done for less reason
And the resurrection you could take for granted.

What is astonishing is that he came here at all
Where no one ever came voluntarily before.

In Memoriam Cecil De Vall

late garrison chaplain, Barrackpore

You can count me as one who has hated
Out of spoiled love rather than malice.
Let me lie now between tufts of heather,
My head in the grass.

The sky is too high, I prefer to be far under it
The road is happily distant.
No angel shall catch me here, nor tourist
Abase me with his talk.

Out from this patch of dust the flat plain
Extends like Asia under a blue sky.
It is no misanthropy that binds me here
But recognition of my own failure.

I ask no better than that
The long convolvulus shall grow over me
And prickling gorse
Keep the children away.

Soon the fallen flesh will begin to crawl
Making off in the worm's belly
Into the undergrowth, and the polished flies
Will riddle me like hat-pins.

I bid their rising lives welcome because
It is better to be many than one;
The mirrors of blue-bottle and worm
May reflect to more purpose than I.

Curl my fin where the shark
Lurches in the blue Mediterranean;
Open my wizened eye
Like a lizard under a tropical leaf.

As I bite the dust of this flat land
For the last time, with dissolving chaps,
Keep me free from all such reflection
Lest the mind dazzle as it goes out.

I do not wish to recognise Christ
As I enter the shades.
What other company could I have
In darkness of my own choosing?

Perhaps it is no more than a recollection
– The banks of a river,
The heavy vegetation wet with the monsoon,
My friend on the verandah?

He brought out the long whiskies and proved
That God hated nothing that He had made:
At no time did I take at his hands
Any but his own hospitality.

Fill my mouth with sand, let the passer's boot
Unwittingly fold my skull.
I have resigned the pretensions
Of the individual will.

From the darkened shores of the river
The dogs howled;
I was alone with the famished and the dead.
Whatever stirred in those shadows was not God.

The Death of a City Man

Quantum meruit was what he got
When he hung by his braces on the door.
He had often – had he not? –
Looked on the lift-shaft with desire.

Well, he could have loved another way
But all falling is one.
See him with his burning eyes
Up and down in the lift, John.

How much for his sagging flesh
Laid out in the bath-room?
With black tights and a gold chain
Quantum meruit has gone home.

No Title

I will tell you the story of my success:
I had lived in great obscurity before,
The room was literally dark, I came and went
As a person without mystery, gifted with reason.
It was a hell and an obscure one,
But the more specious hell I live in now
Full of light and colours, and predestination
Moving my arms like windmills and my legs like a treadmill.
My nature is not what I am
But what these manipulations appear to be.
It is not the world that is reflected in my eye
But the dark interior of my face.
There are two kinds of being, recognition
Making the larger out of the dust
Which composed the meaner and more exact person.
It is as if I had become somebody else
Not by becoming another person but by becoming
Some of the things one person may seem to another.
As if, by pretending, I had become a stone,
Not as something inert but a seen thing

Instead of a seeing thing, and the corruption
Which should wait to seize the body till death
Already begins to eat at my living carcase.

Being is not necessarily at one with person;
It is rare indeed for the conception
To fit in the body or even the manner of walking.
This person who conceives ideas
Carries a tangle drawn from all quarters
His own mind is unexpressed
It is the last of those that find voice.
This hair, these toes, and these excreta
Walk in the form of fashion, not their own.
The body is not more clad than the mind:
The bowler hat and the supporting stick
Give courage to the unadmitted nude.
It is this lie and this silence
Which comprise the excellence of the world.
I have that excellence now;
It is certainly a splendid thing to be successful.

Thomas de Quincey

Thomas de Quincey lying on the hearth-rug
With a finished manuscript at his side,
His bare feet in slippers and, tied up with ribbon,
There was his mind.

Of course it was stupor that he wanted
But his mind would work.
He followed the eloquence whose end is silence
Into the dark.

The Theology of Fitness

This is what I call mind:
Your behind,
That patch of hair in front,
Your navel, your cunt,
Your nipples, your lips;
The hair in your arm-pits
(If a depilatory
Have rased that memory
The hair on your head
Will do instead).
Starting at the nape
I examine your shape;
It is intellectual
And accordingly small.
There is the line
As I descend your spine
To your two legs
Split like a clothes peg.
Quelle heureuse pensée!
You will probably say
If I want a ewe to tup
I should start higher up
And, for example, surprise
Your intellect in your eyes.
Wishing merely to understand,
Lady, I kiss your hand.

Consider, since that is you
Who I am, who
Address these courtesies
And seek to please.
Shall I admit my mind
Starts in my behind
Or that my balls and hair
Gives my verse its air?
(Less pleasant to dwell upon
I find, it is all one.)
This is my fund of wit

And cavity for shit.
Oh, there is much else
Still, when I see myself
I do not over-emphasise
The intelligence of my eyes.

So, when we resurrect
That which was once erect
(Although, in paradise
The suits are without flies)
Your spirit and your bum
Will certainly be one;
Every orifice
Will receive a kiss;
The lowly heart
Will trumpet out a fart;
There will be hosannas
From long bananas.

That being so
What shall we do now?

What a Piece of Work is Man

The man of quality is not quite what he was
In the days when that was a technical term
But there are, happily, a number of qualities
You can be a man of, and it is hard if there is not one
In which you can claim distinction.
Like speaks only to like, and without quality
Which you cannot communicate because you have it by blood
Or some subtler misfortune known as intelligence
There can be no speech.
It is by quality that you are not alone.
Those gathered around the bar, as they lift their beer-mugs
Tremble to break the enchantment of what is common:
It is so by the well or the dhobi-ghat
Or the club where charm may not exceed a pattern.
Pray do not address me in Japanese

In which language my hopes express themselves ill.
Yet what I have in common with the cat
Suffices for a very short conversation
Each time we meet.

Love is of opposites, they say: but the opposite
Is by way of being a philosophical refinement
And what wedges itself in the female slot
Though apposite enough, is hardly that.
If what goes on there is understanding
Then understanding is something different.
Do not imagine the body cannot lie;
What else have we for lying or for truth?
We talk by species and genus.
God who created us made himself understood
First in the thunder, then in the cloud and then in us.
I wish I did not hear him in the thunder.

How does it happen that the table leg
Has this curve in one age, that in another?
Or that the carved figures of men
Differ more than the men themselves?
Conception rules the art.
How then can one man speak to another?

Is it not the conception
Past any man's thinking, that is expressed
Even in the voice that seems to speak clearly?
And in the million voices that chatter together
Over this peninsula or that continent
A peculiar god looms
And what seems to be said between two people
Is only part of a complex conversation
Which they cannot hear and could not understand.
Yet it is only by taking part in that conversation
That they can give names to their own movements.
I lift my hand: there is a hand, certainly.
I touch your cheek: a hand touches a cheek.
In the name of what god? I have no name of my own.
Can I see my own movement except in conception?

What art has the heart, how does it understand
Its own beat?
The heart opened and the body chilled
Or the mind unneeded because the body is perfect.
The leaves of the jungle are parted. There comes out
One who moves like a deer.
And in the city the tapes record the prices,
Which is also a mode of understanding.

Words are not necessary between bodies.
O admirable attempt to forget to be human.
But you are clothed in words
Less of your own devising than your own body
And of which nothing can strip you but death.
Age and forgetfulness may leave you mumbling,
The words eating your toes or soft belly:
How are you speaking now?

The Reckoning

My life dates from the day of my father's death
When I lay weeping and it was not for him.
Now I am to continue the degenerescence
Until I enter his dream.

There is nothing a drink cannot settle at forty
Or money at fifty, the cure of all is death.
But all lovers can remember a moment
When they were not alone.

From a Train

Two on a railway bank
They do not need their own thoughts
Their organs hanging on the verge.

The hanging gardens of Babylon
Flower in vast space between their legs
They crouch with great knees side by side.

Hands laced across the shoulders O
The light electrical touch of reason
O need they give each other names?

Go home at last to parents' eyes
The spirit unscaling as you go
Unlace those arms and be alone.

What you will not believe as you lie down
And call on God for the fornication you did not dare
Is that by chastity you have begun your age.

This loneliness will become your natural condition
When everything has been added and taken away
You will be left with a small grit which is yourself.

Numbers

1

Now you have left that face I am perplexed
To find no-one where I have loved best.
That is why, in the High Street, I stare
Wondering whether there is anyone anywhere.

2

Nothing that is remembered is true
– And what precisely does that make of you?

3

Please now leave indignation alone.
It is enough if you are a stone.
There are the mountains, the waving trees, and you
Flat on the open ground from which they grew.

4

If there were time it would be time to go
— It is the lack of it makes me rage so.
Yet you may say, laughter would do as well
Since for the eternal all things are possible.

5

I said this man would fall and he fell.
With power dreams become terrible.
The power is nothing and the dream is all.

6

Let me escape the burning wheel of time.
There is no other purpose in rhyme
— As if a man could be identified
At least for his folly after he had died.

7

You come from sleep like a body from the womb
A moist wisp, and straggle into bloom.
There is an instant of delicacy, then
You strumpet unnoticed through a world of men.

8

Lechery in age is not kind.
It is the last exercise of the mind.

9

Do not burn, my heart
— That would be to exaggerate your part.
It would not do for you to reduce to tears
One who has carried you for fifty years.

10

If there were not air what would there be?
The voice passed my ear musically
Yet somehow I managed to be aware
Of what she was talking about – the air.
There were spirits in it, not least her own.
They are a substance immediately known
So there was no trouble about using the body
And that, for the moment, satisfied me completely.

11

Clifford says the mind is destroyed by work
And I agree my mind is destroyed by work.

12

Age, you have reached others before me.
They do not again expect to see me.
As they say good-bye they do not even have tears
Lest they seem to acknowledge their fears.

13

They do not know whether they are going to rest
Or a long recession from what they have loved best.
The truth in those old eyes and in my own
Is all that was said in that conversation.

14

He says good-bye from his wooden chair.
We go out and he is left there.
But which of us sees most vividly in the street
The boys and girls passing on featherweight feet?

15

I saw five hares playing in the snow.
That was only a winter ago
Yet they dance in my eyes and are as wild
As if I were old and had seen them as a child.

From *Metamorphoses* (1968)

Virgini Senescens

I

Do you consider that I lied
Because I offered silent hands?

And are my lips no use at all
Unless they have a lie to tell?

Because my eyes look doubtfully
Must they not look on you at all?

And if my hands drop to my sides
Are they then empty of desire?

And are my legs unusable
Because the linked bones of my feet

Rest where they are upon the floor?
I could have used them otherwise

And brought my legs across the room,
Lifted my arms and caught you up

And housed my eyes under your brows
And fixed my lips upon your own.

Or would you then have said that I
Performed but did not speak the truth?

II

Although the body is your truth
The mind may have some part in it

As, mine that holds your body fast
And yours, said to keep house inside

Perhaps the yawning mind of God
Which folds us in his universe.

The mind that holds you is my eye
The quicksilver inside your own

Which, seeing me, collects and runs;
It is the mucus in my skull

And your intestines tight with fear
Our several secret, hirsute parts

Our finger-nails which dig the flesh;
It is our flushed or dented skin

The toes we clench inside our shoes.
Or do you think it less than that?

The spidery numbers you can read?
The tricks they play among themselves?

The art by which you hope to draw
A self from chaos, and be pleased?

A reputation? Who admires?
Oh, I am old and sly, I twist

A way through ribs and weeds and trees
And mark my body as I go:

While you are young, and hardly dare
Moisten your lips upon a stone,

Your fluttering look is hardly out
And does not reach your nearest parts.

Do not imagine I am bold.
It is this terror I admire:

It is the shaking universe
I too inhabit, but in me

Age has reformed the hope of love.
The *quia impossibile*

Drifts with me as, I make no doubt,
It travels with the astronaut.

III

I turn myself from you, to think
Upon the gravity of age

Which bears upon me now until
My weightless body floats in space.

I want it anchored where I live
Why should I bother with the mind?

It is an old excuse for death
Or else a young man's sleight-of-hand:

Attend to that and he will grow
And, silent as a savage, steal

Upon the world of sex and war.
He will grow up while I grow down

And hold you firmly in his arms
Still talking of the intellect

And, turning to me, will pretend
That we are equals in our minds

Although my body will shrink until
He well could throw me out of doors

Or push my huddled frame against
The fender, while he pokes the fire.

It has not come to that, but I
Must plan now my civilities

While I can give him knock for knock.
I will accept his gambit and

Use all my thin and polished words
To make him feel my harmless ease

Whereas my burning heart prepares
To snatch you from him if I can.

It can do you no good, this war
In which you gain by my defeat.

Do not suppose I shall give up
Till I have hurt you if I can.

Iago was an honest man;
I have that reputation too.

IV

The honest thing for you to do
Is take your clothes off while you can

And let me look upon your mind.
I had intended this request

The day I asked you for a kiss
And now the truth is out I give

The comprehensive reason why.
But you will not be taken in:

The complication is in me.
The history riddled in my brain

Protects me now against the world
But does not hide the man I am

And you see clear the face of lust,
The last dance of an ageing man.

I would not have you think I lied.

Catullus

Catullus walked in the Campus Martius.
He had seen all he needed to see,
Lain on his bed at noon, and got up to his whore.
His heart had been driven out of his side
By a young bitch – well, she was beautiful,
Even, while the illusion was with him, tender.
She had resolved herself into splayed legs
And lubricity in the most popular places.
He had seen Caesar who – had he not been, once,
The drunken pathic of the King of Bithynia? –
Returning in triumph from the western isles:
Nothing was too good for this unique emperor.
Against these fortunes he had nothing to offer
– Possibly the remains of his indignation,
A few verses that would outlive the century.
His mind was a clear lake in which he had swum:
There was nothing but to await a new cloud.
We have seen it. But Catullus did not;
He had already hovered his thirty years
On the edge of the Mediterranean basin.
The other, rising like a whirlwind in a remote province,
Was of a character he would have ignored.
And yet the body burnt out by lechery,
Turning to its tomb, was awaiting this,
Forerunning as surely as John the Baptist
An impossible love pincered from a human form.

VALEDICTION
Catullus my friend across twenty centuries,
Anxious to complete your lechery before Christ came.

In Allusion to Propertius, I, iii

When I opened the door she was asleep.
It is thus I imagine the scene, after Propertius.

The torches flickered all over the world
My legs staggered but I went to her bed

And let myself down gently beside her.
Her head was propped lightly upon her hands.

I passed one arm under her body
And with my free hand I arranged her hair

Not disturbing her sleep. She was Ariadne
Desolate upon the coast where Theseus had left her;

Andromeda, no longer chained to the rock,
In her first sleep. Or she was Io,

A milk-white heifer browsing upon her dreams,
I Argus, watching her with my hundred eyes.

I took kisses from her and drew my sword.
Then, through the open window the moon looked in:

It was the white rays opened her eyes.
I expected her to reproach me, and she did:

Why had I not come to her bed before?
I explained that I lived in the underworld

Among shadows. She had been in that forest.
Had we not met, she said, in that place?

Hand in hand we wandered among the tree-trunks
And came into the light at the edge of the forest.

The Person

What is the person? Is it hope?
If so, there is no I in me.
    Is it a trope
Or paraphrase of deity?
    If so,
I may be what I do not know.

Do not be proud of consciousness
For happiness is in the skin.
    What you possess
Is what another travels in.
    Your light
Is phosphorus in another's night.

It does not matter what you say
For any what or who you are
    Is of a day
Which quite extinguishes your star –
    Not speech
But what your feelers cannot reach.

There is one God we do not know
Stretched on Orion for a cross
    And we below
In several sorts of lesser loss
    Are we
In number not identity.

Every Reality is a Kind of Sign

The self is the bit that has not yet emerged;
It is therefore completely unknowable.
It is perfect before the discovery of sex.
When sex is known and the children have grown up
What blindness remains to me? And I cannot live without it.
There is only the dark arcanum of religion;
I prowl round the outside and am not let in.
Every reality is a kind of sign.

On my Fifty-first Birthday

I

Hare in the head-lights dance on your hind legs
Like a poor cat straggling at a rope's end.
Everything is cruelty for innocence.
If you could mark this escape from death
In your thin mind you would have eaten what I have
And, running from form to form, you would consider
The immeasurable benignity of the destructive God.

II

A great sunlit field full of lambs.
The distant perspectives are of the patched earth
With hedges creeping about. If I were to die now
No need of angels to carry me to paradise.
O Lord my God, simplify my existence.

III

The whole hill-side is roofed with lark-song.
What dangerous declivities may I not descend?
It is dark green where the horses feed.
Blackthorn and gorse open before my eyes.

IV

The gulls come inland, alight on the brown land
And bring their sea-cries to this stillness.
It was waves and the surf running they heard before
And now the lark-song and the respiration of leaves.

From the new poems in
In the Trojan Ditch (1974)

The Discarnation
or, How the Flesh became Word and dwelt among us

I

The individual is the thing
Or it is either me or you.
    I do
Not care which way I sing
    This part
So long as I can somehow start.

There are two ways of looking at
The subject, either from within,
    As in
A scallop, diving bell or hat,
    Or slope
The eyes up through a telescope.

They are two different animals,
It sometimes seems, the man
    Who can
Reflect, and does, the swaying walls
    And he
Who sways himself for all to see.

For to be seen and stir within
The porridge of the consciousness
    Is less
One action than to flash a fin
    And sink
Down to the bottom of the ink.

The seen continuum of act
Of something else, makes that a thing.
        A wing
Or speaking head is doubtless fact
        And far
More so that you can show you are.

But the observer is observed,
You think. He is not. What you see
        Is me
As something linear, straight or curved,
        Which I,
As I, should certainly deny.

Though all the time, to understand,
Men make a certain sort of face
        Or pace
Impatiently, or lift a hand
        To greet
Another pair of travelling feet,

Yet this proves nothing. Every look
Is attribution. What I see
        Can be
So little more than what I took
        Before
As imprints on my mind's clean floor.

From what? What passes there? All ghosts?
Or able spirits like my own?
        The moan
The tree makes touches me, the hosts
        Of eyes
Around me also sympathise.

– And I with them. A comity
Is what we make for comfort's sake
        To break
Our prison, not to be let free
        But bind
Some obligation on our mind.

For our supremest wish, ourself,
Must find its equal, or we die.
   The sky
Is peopled; Ghibelline and Guelf
   Stick out
Of history books like a pig's snout.

And we admit companionship
In people passing in the street.
   The beat
Suggests the heart, likewise the quip
   The mind
Which, multiplied, makes out mankind.

While these unsure companions dance
Before our eyes, we can forget
   The set
They move in is our glance,
   The tears
They shed a humming in our ears.

Also forget that, worst of all,
There is no bottom to our well.
   To tell
What is reflected there, what wall
   Is there
We peer into a breathless air.

But whether in or out, or who
It is that peers, one does not know.
   A flow
Of sorts is there; there are some few
   Dark bits
That float on what are called our wits.

But I is not found there. It is
Not found at all. Descartes
   Was smart
Enough to catch a glimpse of his
   But since
A cogitat has only been a wince.

Conscience perhaps? Or consciousness?
A pool of that is not a man.
          What can
The lizard say? And yet the guess
          Is that
He sees, although perhaps non cogitat.

And the computer reads my cheques
And thinks as well as you or me.
          May be
Our calculus is more complex;
          Its trick
A variant of arithmetic.

But number is concealed in verse
And every preference we show.
          We know
The good from better, bad from worse
          Without
Counting what brought the choice about.

Or do we count but, like machines
Simply not notice what we do?
          Have you,
Choosing a summum bonum, seen
          The hands
Clock up the number of the sands?

The things we notice are a spot
Of light in a dark countryside.
          The wide
Part is unknown but not
          Unten-
anted by animals and men,

Alive and dead. The small part is
What passes for the mind of man
          Or can
Be seen upon its surfaces,
          A glade
In which he dances unafraid.

How came the mind to be that shape?
Or there at all? How first the axe
      Made cracks
In that wide forest, how the nape
      First said
The word that grew into the head:

All that is Logos, and obscure.
The shape is history. A mind
      Will find
The way it has been taught. Past cure,
      It sees
No hope except in its disease.

And when you think you are yourself
It is a kind of learned joke.
      You croak
A dead man's words, take from the shelf
      A book
In which all generations look

And read a line which two or three
Imagine they made their own,
      Though known,
With variants, throughout history.
      A form
Of language is a human norm

And it is made in several styles,
As, 'Dozōō' in the Japanese
      For 'Please'
(Used sometimes in the British Isles)
      Which may
Mean 'Bitte' or else 'S'il vous plaît.'

That is the simplest proof there is
That similar is not the same.
      The name,
Likewise, of Gert or Bert or Liz
      Conceals
Less difference than the subject feels.

And everything we do is form
Of manner, language or physique.
        The meek
And violent equally are norms
        And we
Are less than our mythology.

Yet what we think is less, for sure,
Than what we are, and that is flesh.
        Its fresh
Bloom is the best we know. Its dure
        Descent
The hardest way that we are sent.

It starts in comfort, or at least
It does not know it is a start.
        A part
Unwittingly and, when released,
        It finds
One body has become two minds.

Whether its first thought comes with breath
Depends on what you mean by thought;
        But caught
In air, it feeds on it till death
        And takes
As sauce the ripples the air makes.

Its softness becomes strength, its coos
Turn into words and bite. Its sex
        Will vex
Itself and everything it woos.
        Its eyes
Will see the world and show surprise.

But youth once lost, a lizard skin
Envelops organs with a twist.
        All's missed
That called the appetite within.
        Pretence
At last replaces every sense.

To die is best at last, and yet
The last kick struggles after life.
        The knife
That enters like a prince is met
        By will
Which is the last thing to be still.

                    II

As I approach my second theme
Decorum stares me in the face.
        No place
For ribaldry or pretty dream
        Which lure
The senile and the immature.

Man is conventional, he lives
According to imagined laws.
        The cause
Is partly in himself who gives
        The rule;
In part they are discovered by the fool.

Confused between discovery
And natural error of the heart,
        By art
He finds he may be free;
        By right
Searches the arrow of his flight.

Two bodies in one mind – the mark
If any, of the lover's knot –
        And not
As something hollowed in the dark,
        But found
As paradise to build around.

And if this cannot be, the flesh,
Which is not dildo or mere meat,
            Will bleat
Outside another mind's thin mesh
            Till cross-
Petition makes a general loss.

Or, falling back upon themselves,
Each mind admits the other's fears.
            Then tears
Pour out over eroded shelves
            As of
The dried-up torrent-bed of love.

When they are spent the stones are seen.
There is an end of all soft charm.
            The harm
That lovers do has always been
            The mind,
More calculating then than kind.

And if one mind two bodies touch,
– But not the two of unity –
            The he
Both him and her, and she as much
            Both her
And him, they are not as they were.

No innocence, deliberate love,
Pleasure, but not the blinded hope,
            The slope
But not the precipice above
            The prec-
ipice, high above emptiness.

The body turned to instrument?
As if it could be! But that lie
            Will try
To turn the drift of each intent
            And wear
A face that's slightly more than fair.

And so the flesh betrays the mind
And must be guarded like a jewel,
        So cruel
It is when it is unconfined
        And yet
Imprisoned, it is overset,

Bedevilled, peeved. But bond or free
Are parables of servitude,
        While prude
And lecher both are equally
        Without
The key that lets the body out.

Because the body is the mind
To speak of gaolers is absurd.
        The word
Is friend, the blind leading the blind.
        And so
In tears the man and woman go.

They were not always in one yoke.
They issued out of separate wombs,
        The tombs
Of separate affections, broke
        In fear
Into a separate atmosphere

And lived for years without their sex
Or with so little that the heart
        Was part
Of everything and could annex
        A tree
As well as an identity.

Then doubt and reason grew a twig
On branches formed of love and hate.
        A late
Comer was lust, who is so ig-
        norant
Because it does not hear, and can't.

If lust had raised its roaring voice
Before the mind had formed its ring
       Nothing
Could have withstood it, and no choice
       Been made,
Or else it would have been afraid.

But as it grew, provoked by mind,
By whom it was contained, it caught
       The thought
(Which, nascent, is so near combined
       With flesh)
And so drove on to lust afresh.

The intellectual pursuit
Of all, desire then became.
       The name
Was often changed, although the root
       Remained
And sap in everything complained.

So adolescence turned into
A trap for ingenuity.
       The key
Of everything it tried to do
       Was lust
It would not own unless it must.

So hearts and heads and other parts
Became confused. Analysis
       Which is
So bright, picked out the darts
       Which hurt
And then the youth became alert.

His object then, through thick and thin,
Was much and falsely simplified.
       He cried
For certain patches of bare skin –
       But, kind,
Paid his addresses to the mind.

More wise than he, his elders then
Obstructed all that he essayed
          And made
A ritual with a long amen,
          The which
Denatured quite his primal itch.

But gave him a society,
Anxious and troubled all his life,
          A wife
In whose routine embraces he
          Might find
A body had become a mind.

This practice for paternal love
Employed his economic strength.
          At length
He'd house and crockery to prove
          The plan
Is more important than the man.

Then children came to make complete
His service to the commonwealth.
          By stealth
We have good done to us. We eat
          The food
Others prepared for their own good.

Since every thought must have its act
And not all thought begins inside,
          The wide
Extension of a private fact
          Will give
The failed man an excuse to live.

He fails because there is no man
Except in number and exchange.
          The range
Of one man's mind in no way can
          Invent
A world in which a life is spent.

And there are engines make us go
Without our knowledge. So the mind
      Confined
To what we tell ourselves we know
      Is ill
Accomplished to direct the will

And does not do so. And the heart,
So-called, is only a vague belt
      Of felt
Impressions, so a dimmer part
      Of the
Same instrument of cecity.

But facts and bodies operate
Upon our whims and so we are.
      The jar
Of honey and the sting don't wait
      Till you
Imagine hives, and flowers in dew

Or the digestion or the cure.
The world is ready-made and we
      Who see
And taste and smell are too unsure
      To make
Any resolve but a mistake.

No reason therefore to despise
A little magic in your drink
      Or think
That antiseptic thoughts comprise
      The best
And highest that can be expressed.

Reflect: the first, near-simian men
Put in their rods without a thought.
      They sought
And found, but knew it no more when
      They'd done
Than omne animal post coitum.

The second men observed there was
An act worth taking notice of,
      Though love
Is not imputed to this phase,
      Indeed,
Nor the analogy of seed.

The third men noticed, very sly,
That nine moon cycles brought a birth
      Though earth
And air might have to join the cry.
      But still
They knew the act was not the will.

The fourth man is the Onan-Stopes
(The latter the more technical
      But all
The same in terms of fears and hopes
      – Technique,
However, makes the hope more weak).

Children are born through platitude,
Error or love or anything,
      The spring,
Long winter evenings, or mood
      Or al-
cohol, the same moons bring them all.

And, having come, like stars themselves,
They govern others' destinies
      But ease
No favour in their own behalves
      For love
Comes from around if not above.

So, drawn out by these facts, the man
Who acts the part of father finds
      That minds
Grow in and out of things, and can
      Be grown
Like lichen on from stone to stone.

III

And so with place. A habitat
Is habit in a certain space,
    A face
With thought behind it. It seems like that
    And who
Shall say it has less thought than you?

Places have names because a thought
Lives in them, changing like our own
    And grown
Wily with years, not to be caught,
    So meant
Only by words we don't invent.

Cerne Abbas is a name I like;
Toller Porcorum even more.
    Ebbor
Valley by Priddy has a psych
    -e which
Can be counted to make you twitch.

It is painful that men should die
And be forgotten. Places prove
    That love
Or even hatred will long try
    Not to
Be, and names are to remind you.

If you sit on a barrow and
Play your transistor, still the dead
    Will head
Their way out of the ground, the hand
    Which slew
Your ancestor will be on you.

It does not matter if you don't
Feel it, it is certainly there.
          You dare
Admire yourself because you don't
          And close
Your eyes upon the dead man's toes.

Your ignorance does not seal up
The innumerable petitions.
          The guns
Emplaced upon the coast still plop
          The shell
Into the sea although you are well.

Thomas Tusser still ploughs these hills
Though you may not have heard of him.
          You trim
Your smile to contemporary wills.
          Who said
That you too would not join the dead?

They are living, as well as you;
And their thoughts creep into your bones.
          Rough stones
May have more to say that is true
          Than men
Who do not know how to say Amen.

Labour instead of thought will do
To form the man, for what he makes
          Soon takes
Its part in shaping me and you.
          We are
The subtlest artifacts by far.

The house that grows upon a hill
Remembers like the hill itself.
          The self
Which likes to think it is a will
          Is but
The image of an acre and a hut

And certain kind words are spoken too
Before it knew what they could mean.
            The seen
Enters beside the heard, the true
            Image
Burrows inside the living rage.

That is the man. The furrows eat
His aching brain out as he ploughs.
            To rouse
Him there is the sun. To greet
            His bit-
-ter end there is the mud pit.

Happy if between rise and fall
Some creature greets him for a day
            And clay
Cakes on his boots and a few tall
            Trees rise
Before him to excite surprise.

He is happy indeed if such
As Salisbury spire teach him to expect
            Direct
Fruition outside his own hutch.
            This is
The best of man's artifices.

But number has replaced intent
For most; they are not cattle they
            Betray
The heritage of cattle, bent
            On what
They think they cannot say is not

But no more attentive to what is
Than a sewing machine to cloth,
            And loth
To reject an analysis
            Which tells
At least how to avoid bad smells

And ensures that they die in peace
In well-furnished euthanasia.
                    These are
The objectives of our police
                    Although
It does not always work out so.

Quiconque meurt, meurt à douleur
– Or so it used once to be said.
                    The dead
Do not report on it. There were
                    No doubt
Once more who screamed as they went out.

Do not under-rate benefits
Everybody seeks to enjoy
                    The boy
Shut away because out of his wits;
                    Foetus
Smothered lest it should bother us.

We are the heirs of an emptiness
Of which we are extremely proud;
                    The crowd
Soothed as it never was, a less
                    Extreme
Nightmare, and a less hopeful dream.

And artifacts less regarded
Than ever before, because made
                    For trade
And not for use, and by the dead
                    Hand of
Number instead of by our love.

Not even made to be consumed
As is sometimes said. Made so that
                    The rat
In the sewer is well groomed;
                    The count
Of nothing will continually mount.

Over the hills now there advance
The artifacts, both man and thing,
    A string
Choking the leaders of the dance;
    Their blood
Cannot do their brains any good.

So, departing into Thing
As if the Pied Piper had called them,
    The hem
Of the garment is untouched, to sing
    Is not
Necessary, and that's my lot.

No Address

In my leprosy I have lost speech
Which before I had with several.
Now no voices, not even my own.

Pliny, Horace, Cicero, talk to me;
I am a dead language also.
The poetry owners cannot make me out

Nor I them. And the big mouths of learning
Open and close over my thoughts without biting.
Under the shadow of politics I have no teeth.

I am no man, Caesar, to stand by you,
Nor have the whimsical humour of pre-war Oxford
But my unrecognised style was made by sorrow.

Inching towards death, let me go there quickly.
Silently, in the night or in the day-time,
Equally, I would take it like a Roman.

Evening

Sleep has my muscles and a cord my throat.
Faint heart! The rooks at evening repair,
Climbing upon so many steps on air,
To the elm tops; caw, on the balustrade,
Caw from the church-tower, where the dead are laid
Under a passing shadow. I to tea,
Beside the fire in the old house, quietly.

Aller Church

The art, the artifex, and I.
    Let the wind blow softly.
Currents of air over the plain.
    When shall I see England again?
The mouse creeps in the sedge. The fire runs
    Over the stubble against the sun.
This world is not yours. Walk here
    Under the half edge of Sedgemoor.

The Usk

Christ is the language which we speak to God
And also God, so that we speak in truth;
He in us, we in him, speaking
To one another, to him, the City of God.

I

Such a fool as I am you had better ignore
Tongue twist, malevolent, fat mouthed
I have no language but that other one
His the Devil's, no mouse I, creeping out of the cheese
With a peaked cap scanning the distance
Looking for truth.
Words when I have them, come out, the Devil
Encouraging, grinning from the other side of the street

And my tears
Streaming, a blubbered face, when I am not laughing
Where in all this
Is calm, measure,
Exactness
The Lord's peace?

II

Nothing is in my own voice because I have not
Any. Nothing in my own name
Here inscribed on water, nothing but flow
A ripple, outwards. Standing beside the Usk
You flow like truth, river, I will get in
Over me, through me perhaps, river let me be crystalline
As I shall not be, shivering upon the bank.
A swan passed. So is it, the surface, sometimes
Benign like a mirror, but not I passing, the bird.

III

Under the bridge, meet reward, the water
Falling in cascades or worse, you devil, for truthfulness
Is no part of the illusion, the clear sky
Is not yours, the water
Falling not yours
Only the sheep
Munching at the river brim
Perhaps

IV

What I had hoped for, the clear line
Tremulous like water but
Clear also to the stones underneath
Has not come that way, for my truth
Was not public enough, nor perhaps true.
Holy Father, Almighty God
Stop me before I speak

— per Christum.

V

Lies on my tongue. Get up and bolt the door
For I am coming not to be believed
The messenger of anything I say.
So I am come, stand in the cold tonight
The servant of the grain upon my tongue,
Beware, I am the man, and let me in.

VI

So speech is treasured, for the things it gives
Which I can not have, for I speak too plain
Yet not so plain as to be understood
It is confusion and a madman's tongue.
Where drops the reason, there is no one by.
Torture my mind: and so swim through the night
As envy cannot touch you, or myself
Sleep comes, and let her, warm at my side, like death.
The Holy Spirit and the Holy One
Of Israel be my guide. So among tombs
Truth may be sought, and found, if we rejoice
With Ham and Shem and Japhet in the dark
The ark rolls onward over a wide sea.
Come sleep, come lightning, comes the dove at last.

Morpheus

Naked people
Stepping, under mackintoshes
Through the dim city

The elect, the dead
The indifferent, head on
Into the underground. Morpheus.

What underneath? Proserpine dances
Exactly with legs, arms curled
About her head like a duster

There are green fields, below
Memory cannot reach, trees discover
Or old tales render probable.

It was a snake, some say
Bit at her ankle. So
I would myself.

It was a thorn
Entangled her. I
Could wind about her.

It was the wind
Caught and advanced her flying
Hair. It was tears distresses

Of my hope and finding
Destroyed, unkindly, what hope there was.
That was my failure.

So against the crowd, perfect
I stand like a lamp-post, they flow past me
Stoney eyes, mine or theirs.

Somerton Moor

I

You are unusual, but the touch
Of innocence may sear a mind.
I know who say so, for I am
The prisoner of a loving ghost

O death, come quickly, for the fiend
Crosses the marshes with my tears.

II

Under the peat, dark mystery of earth,
Fire of the hearth, enchanter of my heart
The smoke that rises is a sacrifice
The peat moves over in its sodden sleep

And I, who should have touched her with my wand
Let her evade beneath the burning turf
And now through smoke and bitterness I speak
Words she would recognise and no one else
And she can no more hear than oyster-ears.

III

Last speech. Accustomed as I am to speech
And she to silence, excellence is hard
For nothing that is facile can be heard
And nothing hard can be endured for long.
So sleep. Pass out between the willow-boughs
Out of my dream into the cool of death.
There, where the resurrection that you hope,
Though tardy, comes at last
The instrument I carry is untuned.

In insula Avalonia

I

Huge bodies driven on the shore by sleep
The mountain-woman rocks might fall upon
And in the cavity the heaped-up man.

Sleep on the island like a witty zone
Seas break about it, frolicking like youth
But in the mists are eyes, not dancers, found.

Hurt is the shepherd on the inland hill
He has a cot, a staff and certain sheep
Stones are his bed, his tables and his bread.

This is not where the sirens were, I think
But somewhere, over there, the next approach
Behind that other island in the mist.

That was the song, beyond the linnet-call
At the cliff's edge, below the plunging gull
The fish it found, the enemy or Christ.

II

Counting up all the ways I have been a fool,
In the long night, although the convent clock
Winds several hours around Medusa's locks,

Geryon and Chrysaor are with me now
– Sure there was bad blood in that family –
And yet the worst of all was done by love.

The fool: but not the bow and naked babe
But top-coat murderers with sullen looks
And yet Medusa was a temple harlot.

Under the river-bank a seeping wind
Ripples the bubbles from a passing fish
No colder memory than gloomy Dis.

Look, for you must, upon the fine appearance,
The creature had it and is formless dead.
Now come no nearer than to straws in glass.

III

Dark wind, dark wind that makes the river black
– Two swans upon it are the serpent's eyes –
Wind through the meadows as you twist your heart.

Twisted are trees, especially this oak
Which stands with all its leaves throughout the year;
There is no Autumn for its golden boughs

But Winter always and the lowering sky
That hangs its blanket lower than the earth
Which we are under in this Advent-tide.

Not even ghosts. The banks are desolate
With shallow snow between the matted grass
Home of the dead but there is no one here.

What is a church-bell in this empty time?
The geese come honking in a careless skein
Sliding between the mort plain and the sky.

What augury? Or is there any such?
They pass over the oak and leave me there
Not even choosing, by the serpent's head.

                              IV

O there are summer riders
On the plain
                    in file or two by two

It is a dream

For Winter, one by one, is wringing us
The withers, one, and scrotum-tight the other

Yet I am here
Looking down on the plain, my elbow on
The sill

From which I night by night and day by day
Watch
          for the moon pours swimmingly

Upon this field, this stream
That feeds my sleep.

Be night
Be young
The morning half begun
Palls on the waiting mind and makes it scream

O Minnich, Minnich

Who is the lady there by Arthur's lake?
None is. A willow and a tuft of grass
But over bones it broods, as over mine

Somewhere
Except
      nowhere

Bind up your temples and begone from here
No need to answer. What is there to fear?

Only the wind that soughs, and soughs, and soughs.
Some say it does, and others contradict
Some say sleep strengthens, others that it kills
This music comes
              from Wendover I think
Where meaning is at least, there, sure, am I.

V

Out in the sunlight there I am afraid
For dark depends upon the nascent mind
The light, the envy and the world at large

A field for flood, and fish and such-like deer
The willows standing in between the pools
Great siege this morning, in the morning-time

The water rustles like a turning page
Write then who will, but write upon the stream
Which passes nonchalantly through the hedge

No word of mine will ever reach the sea
For mine and words are clean contrary things
Stop here for envy, go there for your love

For love of persons are the passing geese
Swans on the flood, the dopping water-fowl
The cloud that cumbers while the sky is blue.

Awful at nights, the mind is blue today
Enlarged without a purpose like a lake
For purpose pricks the bubble of our thoughts.

Climb back to sleep, the savage in that mine
Picks with his teeth and leaves his skull to dry
O skull and cross-bones on the earthen floor

My earth, my water, my redundant trees
Breaking the surface like a stitch in skin.
No word but weather, let me be like that.

VI

A ruminant in darkness. So am I
Between the skin and half a hope of hell
Tell me till morning where the savage stops.

His eyes beside the fire. The burning peat
Is quiet, quiet, quiet till it shrieks
Not what the hammer was but what it says

The eyes on Thursday and the mind that waits
For sabbaths of intent but does no thing
Not seeking, waiting for a peaceful end

What wind is in the trees? What water laps
Extravagantly round the seeping hedge?
A house on sticks, where several yearned before

The skin, the furze, the movement into sleep
The watery lids beside the river bank
Mirrors of emptiness, O what way in?

VII

A mine of mind, descend who can that way
As down a staircase to the inner ring
Where figures are at liberty, and play

A plain of ghosts, among the rest a girl
(And none had touched her, though the serpent's teeth
Met in her heel below the flying skirt)

She gathered flowers, exacting from their grace
An outward parallel for grace of skin,
Petals for fingers, petals for arms and legs.

This transient surface is the thing I seek
No more, perhaps, than scale upon the eyes
Do not walk with her, winds are blown that way

A storm of leaves and all may disappear
And yet below the circle of my mind
Playing in spring-time there is Proserpine.

But I am rather Cerberus than Dis
Neither receive nor yet pursue this child
Nor am I Orpheus who could bring her back.

I stand and roar and only shake my chain
The river passes and gives others sleep
I am the jaws nothing will pass between.

VIII

The mind beyond the reach of human time
Mine or another's, let me now perceive
Time has turned sour upon the earth for me

A little earth, walking upon the earth
A molehill, Mother, on your credent slopes
But moving, time against me, everywhere

This is the lump out of which I was made
The hands, the feet, the brain no less is mud
What does not crumble must remain in shape

The shape of man, but moles are better off
Boring the hill-side like a nit in cheese
They asked for blindness, that is what they have

But I for light, for sleep, for anything
Moving my hands across the surfaced world
Exacerbate in darkness, though alive

I never came from any natural thing
To take this shape which is not mine at all
Yet I am I am I and nothing more

If any took this shape I took this shape
Yet taking what I did not ask to have
And being nothing till I took this shape

The shape of shafts of light and falling suns
Meteors incarcerate in balls of mud
A cracked example of a better kind

Admit you came because you could not know
Walk in the garden as you did one day
And if you cannot flatter, answer back.

IX

Some seek examples in the world of sense
They slide across the retina like dreams
Yet are objective in the world of deeps

Which swimmers may attempt, that move all ways
Across the current, from the pebbly floor
Up to the surface where the morning breaks

If any capture what the water-weed
Holds brightly like a bubble on its stem
Or what may disappear in lengthening dark

Volumes of sleep will turn the swimmer's arm
His leg will gently bump the feathered rock
Gulls cry above, sleep has no place for them

A call, a cry, a murder in the street
Is sign of others lonely as yourself
The Lord have mercy, others may as well.

X

I do not know and cannot know indeed
And do not want a word to tell me so
A sentence is construction more than I.

I feel, I vomit. I am left to earth
To trample and be trampled, in my turn
But always rotting from the day I came

Thy kingdom come. And could I pray indeed
I would be höhnisch and destroy the world
This is not what is meant and nor am I.

So let my silence fasten on a rock
Be lichen, that is plenty, for my mind
And not be where I was. Where is he? Gone

The empty space is better than himself
But best of all when, certain winters past,
No one says: There he was, I knew him well.

Martigues

I

Myrtle, roses and thyme
And the rose laurel:
I too have something that I wish to forget
There, where the woodland path
Passes into the concrete
And my tears are for a master.
At the gate I picked a leaf of laurel and said:
Dante
Wore these pointed leaves.
Here, in the bitter south,
A madman, between gaolers.
Whisper it to the myrtles we may, crushing the past
In our tingling fingers,
Or picking the thyme.
But the rose laurel

It is all I have, the bitten past,
Not all I came to.
Speeches were made and names taken, the heart
Burst out of his side.
No love like the unspoken
Ferocity, the bitter tears, a battle
Standing instead with brimming eyes
Looking out over the *étang*
The poverty of a few fish
And a garden of roses.

I too have something that I wish to forget.
Myrtle and roses, the same.
Controversy among apes is no custom
And my limbs fell hard
Against the rail of the scuttled ship. You may cup your eyeballs
For ordinary uses now.
My faith
Sprang into the air with indignation.

II

At the corner of the streets
The fishermen stand in groups
With brown faces: they have them from the Moors
And the wind blowing across the *étang*.

In the garden
Pierre, or perhaps Adam.
I shake him by the hand, brown also,
A fisherman's face, gardener's rather.
Help us with the language of saints.
Adam spoke
Softly, and in the old *patois*,
Knowing no other.
Myrtle, roses and thyme
And the rose laurel
Never to be let go.
I took him by the hand
Old friend

Whom I have never seen
Your ghost is my beginning, I have tears
For what is here forgotten
And in the winter of my age my hand
Cut the air with scimitars.

III

Roses and thyme
But leave the myrtle, leave the myrtle here
Roses and thyme
Fed on a garden where I made my home
And southward facing over the *étang*.
In Somerset I crumble up the soil
And linger on a terrace looking south
So minds have ears no voices
They have eyes
Which look upon the land and do no harm
But avarice is cupid in this game.
Yet love came after all, olive and rush,
The tart wine held under the cupping hand.
One taste of death. Good-night to all this lake.
The olives in the garden after all
Eat up the man and put him under ground
How should he turn his hand?

IV

Pallas Athene, wisdom in all this,
Mistress of olives and the curling prow
Let not your lids drop on this falling earth.
Set enmities at rest or let there be
Sufficient enmity to stir up love
And bring the sword before you bring smooth tongues,
Harsh enmities are best
And Judas put his silver in the ground.

V

Night falls, perhaps, upon my wide *étang*,
Joseph of Arimathea riding home.
The Saintes Maries
Await another pilgrim at this time
But now must sleep. And did he sleep or wake
Who walked upon this terrace in his dream?
The Saintes Maries put out their lights at last
And Joseph's ship touches a barren stone.

VI

He took a flower
And gave it in a morning without hope.
Hand down the rose
Hand down the myrtle, stuff the air with thyme.
There in the garden where it all began
Seek nothing for yourself. Seek nothing more
Than time will offer to dishonesty
And patience and the like. Silence at last
And Abraham's voice seeps through the air.
David is King. And then the dragons come
The thud of horses over the Camargue,
But silence first. The rose,
Myrtle crushed in the hand
And the rose laurel.

A Ghost

Nothing is more mysterious than a ghost. There are such
To be seen, between sleep and waking. Thomas Stearns Eliot,
For example, flashed between my eyelids and the waking room
And he was still there when I went downstairs,
Pottering among the books or admiring the view,
Quizzical, old, realising that there was little point
In his being there, but admitting that he had once met me
And so, a ghost had to do as he was told:
Tiresome, perhaps, but he put up with it.
He did not bother to go off down the garden
He would go, he knew, the moment my interest faded
And an old man could not be that interesting,
Above all to one already approaching those bournes
From which he had come. So he took his leave politely
As if raising his hat, at the very moment when I
Thought, after all, I would make myself some tea.

(1974, uncollected)

From *Anchises* (1976)

Cotignac

River, deep as death, deeper, Avernus,
Red water of ox-hide, ox-blood, clouded,
Drawn across these caverns like a taut sheet,
What is down there, under the cliff edge,
Deeper than hell? Village
Lost to all time, under the sick archway,
The lost steps lead there, the life
Stirs like a movement of moss.

If I were to awake in that underworld, whom should I see?
Not Nestor, not Paris,
Not any heroic shadow, long putrescent,
Blown into dust: no woman
Caught my wandering eye last summer
Or any summer gone. The friends of shadows,
The commonplace merchants of ambition,
These are the ones, bragging in the market-place
So vain is all philosophy
My teeth were set on edge by such merchants
Half a caravan back: and when they came
To the high street where the palms set the form
It was eating and drinking who must,
Who laughed loudest, who spat,
While I stood by discreetly.
Worn hours! bitter heart! petty mind below all
No kiss of sun can cure, autumn eyes
Seeking rather between shadows the hurt.

There are gigantic shadows upon the cliff-face
I have seen them scowl and lour over the village.
All villages have them: they are the governors
Living among themselves without passions

Touching our parts. I had lived among them as evil
No man knew better their vain twists,
Admired what he hated most
Or so fell to dreaming of impossibles
Which are only eaten ambition
Knives in the heart, or pure reason.

A handful of almonds, a few grapes
All that the fine fingers could pick
Out of the residue of the world
Was not enough for this termagant.
The fine surface of bodies touched
By the sun and rendered potable
Was not enough for the eye-palimpsest;
The half-eaten moaner must moan.
What cages for tigers, whips for scorpions or other
Replicas of effete damnation
Had been prepared, must find a place
Within the cataclysm of each mind.
Mine was none of the stablest, I felt,
Looking over the impeccable scene,
The cicada chipping the hillside.

The Quantocks

Sheep under the beeches: the old dykes
Reflective over centuries, the sheep
Stationary over escaped time.
My nails are ground by biting,
There is no remembrance
Does not taste like aloes.

Gardening

What night, corrupt, as this must be, with dreams
Gathers around this age and finds me now
Here in this garden, not in Eden, no
Another garden and another time

But there is neither slope nor sun can make
Amends for what I missed under your hands.
Old fool. Reproaches I could buy for nothing
In any market-place. How can I turn
This ageing sorrow to a biting wind
To catch me like the tangles of your hair

Gone and imagined? How can I turn
This burrow in the crumbling earth to peace?
Like a worm under stone. Or like a beetle
Making away and does not understand
Its movements, passions, parts.

The Evidence

If you had hopes once they have turned to reason
If you had reason it has turned to evidence:
The evidence is against you.

Eastville Park

I sat on a bench in Eastville Park
It was Monday the 28th of October
I am your old intentions she said
And all your old intentions are over.

She stood beside me, I did not see her
Her shadow fell on Eastville Park
Not precise or shapely but spreading outwards
On the tatty grass of Eastville Park.

A swan might buckle its yellow beak
With the black of its eye and the black of its mouth
In a shepherd's crook, or the elms impend
Nothing of this could be said aloud.

I did not then sit on a bench
I was a shadow under a tree
I was a leaf the wind carried
Around the edge of the football game.

No need for any return for I find
Myself where I left myself – in the lurch
There are no trams but I remember them
Wherever I went I came here first.

Marcus Aurelius

I do not want to pour out my heart any more
Like a nightingale bursting or a tap dripping:
Father no more verses on me, Marcus Aurelius
I will be an emperor and think like you.

Quiet, dignified, stretched out under a clothes line
The garden of my soul is open for inspection
As the gardener left it, chaque cheveu à sa place
And if you do not believe me you can comb through my papers
                                                      yourself.

Of course you may not agree with: No hurt because the lips are
                                                      tight.
The psychologists have been too much for you, but that rascal
                                                      Freud
Did nothing but devise his own superficial entanglements
For his readers to trip over, while he smiled.

Old devil of Vienna, moving among the porcelain,
You were the beetle under the ruins of an empire
And where the Habsburgs had protruded their lips
You pinched your nostrils.

If I were a plain man I would do the same,
Dexterous, money-making, conforming to another pattern
Than the one I seek which will cover me entirely:
I hope to be an emperor under my own mausoleum.

The Garden

Am I not fortunate in my garden?
When I awake in it the trees bow
Sensibly. There is a church tower in the distance,
There are two, underneath the maze of leaves

And at my back bells, over the stone wall
Fall tumbling on my head. Fortunate men
Love home, are not often abroad, sleep
Rather than wake and when they wake, rejoice.

Anchises

This is my proper sightlessness,
The invisible pack hunting the visible air.
There are those who exist, but it is not I.
Existent are: bodies, although their existence is
Not proven; tremors
Through the vast air expecting some other thing
Not known, or hopeless; or else hoped for and lost.
One could devise invisibility,
Walking by it as if it were not obligatory
As it is with me, *moi qui n'existe pas*
NON SUM, therefore NON COGITO, although there are shapes
Upon a mind I sometimes take to be mine.
This is not much to show for sixty years
Here by the Latin gate, or where the Baltic
Spreads its white arms over the barren sand.
Do not number me on this seashore
Where the effete light from the north
Floods over the ice-cap. I came from Troy
It was not after she had ended, but before.

Troia

So in the morning light she came to him
Light-footed

But Troy the common grave of Europe and Asia
Troia (nefas)

The Sibyl's cave
Aeneas standing there
and it was only a descent

ad inferos
Speaking any words
wildly
Hair streaming: Aeneas founding a city
among the dead
Troy speaking again
only through the mouths of the dead
the city pardoned
the libation poured out and the ox-hides spread

I noticed this peculiarity in Troy
That the soldiers, looking out over the walls
Were sightless, they had long been dead
and a Roman capital
Stood in the desert, half broken.

Est in conspectu Tenedos

I

The day goes slowly, it is the first day
After the fall of Troy. I walk upon the beaches,
A ghost among ghosts, but the most shadowy I
O Tenedos O the thin island
Hiding the ships. They need not hide from me
I am the least figure upon the shore,
Which the wind does not notice, the water refract, or the sands
                                                                      count

As one of their number. I was a warrior,
Yes, in Troy
Before all reason was lost.
Where did Helen come from? Where is she now?
All reason is lost and so is she.
I was only a parcel of her reason
Now of her loss
Ghosts
Cannot be companionable; parts, shreds,
All that I am, ghost of a part of a part

II

Desolate shore, dark night
I have lost so much that I am not now myself
That lost it, I am the broken wind
The lost eagle flying, the dawn
Rising over Tenedos

III

Not any more I, that is the last thing
Rise or fall, sunrise or sunset
It is all one. The moon is not friendly
No, nor the sun
Nor darkness, nor
Even the bands of maidens bringing offerings
Pouring libations, buried
Among the ineluctable dead.

IV

Dead, ineluctable, certain
The fate of all men.

From *Exactions* (1980)

The Desert

1

This is the only place that I inhabit:
The desert.
No drop of water: no palm trees: nothing.
No gourd, no cactus: sand
Heaped on all sides like mountainous seas
To drown in.
Luckily I cannot see myself, I am alone
No mirror, glass, plastic left by an Arab
Nothing
I cannot say it too often
Nothing.
The sand itself would diminish if I said yes.
No rascally Bedouin,
Praying mantis, or nice people
– A mirage of them, occasionally.
But they are not there, any more than I,
For all my vocables, eyes, 'I's,
Other impedimenta of the desert
– Khaki shirt, shorts, chapli,
Mess-tin, for nothing to eat;
Water-bottle, nothing in it.
It is an amusing end, because desired.

2

Alone
But to say 'alone' would be to give validity
To a set of perceptions which are nothing at all
– A set as these words are
Set down
Meaninglessly on paper, by nobody.

There were friends, they have faded into the distance;
With my disintegration the vision becomes blurred,
Rather, disintegrated, each bit
For all I know
Tied to a separate nothing, not I.
Enough of laughter, which echoes like a tin eccentric
Round the edge of the desert:
Tears would be ridiculous
If I could shed them,
Eyes shed them, one
Then another again, weeping
For different things, not joined.

Shatter the retina so that the eyes are many
– Hailstones, now, it can be sand for all I care.
The damned unrepairable, I sit
Like a vehicle sanded up, the desert
Is frequent with images.
Could night come, that would effect a change,
But the sun blazes:
'I am all you have to fear, extreme, hot, searing
But the end is dust, and soon.'

Place

We have only to live and see what happens
– Nothing perhaps; for it may be that history,
As Mairet remarked, is coming to an end
And we shall wander around without meaning.
That is what most of us would like, and it is death
However it puts on the masks and opinions of life.
If we live here, it is indeed here that we live.
We cannot afford to scoff at the *pays natal*,
Unless our minds are to be born without content;
Nor at the acres in which we spend our childhood,
Unless the things we see are of no account,
Do not fill our minds, are nothing but generalities.
What do we see? Faces on a television screen
Which are more vivid than those we pass in the street.

So we live no-where, but somewhere there is a *place*
Where life is lived, a kingdom of the blest,
Perhaps, in which the programmes are prepared.

The Zodiac

And so we need divide the year;
Also, the human character.
Aries at first, Aries the Ram
Whose neighbour in the sphere I am:
Taurus who, lowing for Europa,
Must be content with grass for supper;
The other neighbour being Gemini,
Though two might be thought two too many.
Cancer crabs everyone in sight
And therefore has the shortest night,
While Leo tries to be benign
In spite of his ferocious sign.
Virgo, we all know, cannot last
Even until the summer's past;
Her Libra seeks to equalize
With equal balances of lies,
Though Scorpio would bite the tail
Of any too ambitious male
And Sagittarius shoots arrows
At aeroplanes, and brings down sparrows.
Capricorn is a goat, and cannot
Conduct himself as if he were not;
Aquarius with watery eye
Does nothing else but cry, cry, cry;
Pisces, however, swims in tears
Till harmless Aries re-appears.

Why quarter and divide in three?
Too much brilliant astronomy:
The heavens would not stay still, and grew
Quickly to circle out of true,
Till all the scholars, from their book,
Knew that the sky must be mistook.

Then came a learned supposition
That the erroneous position
Taken by the wandering stars
Must reflect on the characters,
Not of astronomers and pedants
But all the new-born innocents
Who had not yet twisted their minds
Into the pattern of mankind.
In case the constellations faltered,
Science would see that they were altered:
So anything you care to hope
Is enlarged in your horoscope;
Whatever makes you shake with terror
Is grimmer in the written error.

If Aries only were a ram
And Gemini, twins in a pram,
Taurus among the cows, and Cancer
Not so much favoured as the lobster;
If Leo kept his woolly head
Inside his cage, and Virgo's bed
Were no more visited than most;
If Libra weighed up pounds of tea
And Scorpio died of DDT,
Who'd be afraid of Sagittarius
Or find no life-belt in Aquarius?
If Capricorn were only goat,
The fear of butts would be remote,
And indeed, but for scholarship,
Pisces might end as fish and chips.

The Pool

1

All options close: a devious life
Flows no more beyond this point.
Devious and plentiful stream, you come to a stop
Here, in this meadow, I am incredulous
– Instead of a river, a pool, no bigger than nothing,
As if the source must end as it begins.
Does it go underground, does it go at all?
Liquid and deep and still, that seems to be all.
So deep, that it has transparency
Like a cube of glass. I could get through easily:
Yet not, for a million reflections this way and that
Warn against any movement, better stand pat.
If I moved, I should go topsy-turvy,
More like a hall of mirrors. While I waited
On the bank, looking at the interior,
It sometimes seemed farther and sometimes nearer.
Seen through a telescope: if so, through which end?
Stutter foot, slur speech, you slide, my friend.

2

I held the meaning of life in my hands
For a while: then I abandoned it.
Why? There were several reasons: first,
The life it was the meaning of was not mine.
Then it was a mistake I made about God.
I simply imagined that there was somebody there
And, having imagined it, strove to be polite to him.
But egotism is all I have to say,
God, the lot! He and I are much of a muchness;
More than that, he is the principle of identity
Which I should certainly find hard enough without him.
The imagination ends: the self disintegrates.
Good-bye to a bad self, and the good god with him,
Who was rather better, because imaginary.
Flies and whiskers growing out of a dead cunt.

3

Somebody else's egotism, the prime motive
In most rational action, if it is rational
To curl and twist and do as others command:
The egotism of self, which is also God's,
Noticeably has a more urbane look,
Twisting others, perhaps, which should be pleasant;
Or finding excuses for non-intervention
In quarrels which are too silly for speech.
So I pray to myself: O God,
Allow me to be extraneous to myself,
Using the word YOU to MY SELF
– Playing with one's own genitals, it might be said.

4

All that has now gone, because
For many years I imagined another YOU;
Not so ingenuous as to push for the Magna Mater,
Or Diana come down from the sky to admire Endymion:
No! but a principle of heterogeneity,
Masked by desire which, being my own,
I put myself behind. Snap!
God and myself are one.

5

Hope was my primary theological virtue,
But this I never succeeded in placing anywhere
Except on the surface of a female body:
Tactile corpus, visible also, the image
Ever before the mind, in Christian torture.
The torture was mine, the body itself was blind
– Reversing the evidence of the crucifix,
Where the body was tortured and the onlooker, benign.

6

I will act my senile part as the Furies desire,
Having discovered too late what I knew already:
Nothing is new, nothing miraculous;
The tree grows and flowers in order to fall.

7

In order to fall, in order to fall:
Only my life is without deflection,
The *declinatio* which created the world
And might create me now, were any permitted.

I have been the fool of myself long enough,
Mocking, impeding, now in permanent discourse,
And now it appears there is not one fool, but two.

8

The only fact that matters is the fact
Of the matter which happens to be the matter today.
How the blow falls, why nothing is anything,
Everything nothing, remain secrets from me.

9

Pass down, pass down the explanation;
Credit it if you can, if not, pretend to:
Guide yourself on a banister of air
As if your fingers were touching something solid.

10

Damn all extravagant moralities,
The Muses say, the Muses say:
Let horror have a holiday,
And be content to please.

11

I should say nothing but the mouth will open.
Although the last man on the last shore
– I say, but the whole thing is a pack of lies –
Etc., etc. But why finish the sentence?

12

I end the year in discouragement.
There can be no more years: a rubble of time
Only, to be pushed before one in the stead
Of winter, spring, summer and autumn, which mark
The evading hours for those who are in life.
It is a cold tunnel I go through, the other end,
Which was dreams, not even an hallucination.

The door on the outside world has shut for ever.
It is not night, for night implies day;
It is not prison, for prison implies escape.
There is none.
The world, which was made in six days,
Has contracted. A week, a minute, an hour,
Are short enough to comprise it.
The pinhead light
Has gone out:
Nothing more here, for hope or for consolation.

And yet not despair,
Which also implies hope, and I have none:
Equally held, because blackness
Knows no points, up or down;
Because nothing
Has no weight, has no self to be conscious of,
Neither exists in itself nor by any reference.

Reference would be too much, the long and short of it,
Which has neither long nor short, nor any enigma,
Nothing to solve, no question to ask.

Differently

If I had done differently I should have done well;
Differently is better, it could not have been worse.
I cannot stand, looking, as into a fire,
Into the past. There is only the charred wood.

Style

Although a person is a style
– Whether a woman or a man –
I am past style.

I am not speaking of writing now,
Fads or labours, or anything
To do with how

Anything is done, if that means
Deliberately, but even helplessness,
Which is in between

How and what and more like what.
A quiddity is amusing, but
It does not take me in.

Ham Hill

Nothing means much now,
I am stone;
Cool, golden, not cold,
The temperature of the air-flow.

You might have spoken to me
Or across, it would not matter;
Sat on me, or not regarded
My location or entity;

Not seen me entirely
Or expressly said, A stone;
There is no occasion
For such familiarity.

It is enough to be here,
Not too much, enough;
The equal of love;
That is why I am here.

Moon-rise

It is the evening brought me here,
Or I the evening.
So I, which is the writing finger,
The hand placed on the sill, the night
Coming up from beyond Kingsbury:

Another foot, or hand, perhaps,
Perhaps a train, passing along
Down the line by the signal-box;
Or that rising star which may be
The next one to come out of the west.
Which way? has no meaning because
Here and there relate to what:
The moon rises, as we say.

Nightingale, you sing no more;
The tree you sat on is not there;
The night you sang has also gone:
And I alone remember you,
Or am the nightingale tonight.

Night of the day, because succeeding;
Or of the night, because pleading;
Or of the Lamb of God because
Bleeding.
Useless to ask any question of
This night or any:
Answer as lightly as you ask.

from *The Garden of the Hesperides*

★ ★ ★ ★

However, something has happened. The thin air
Is certainly thinner and finer than before:
I can see things. It is not that there is light
Anywhere in particular, unless it is every night
Has its moon, every day its sun,
Equal everywhere. Trees tower and streams run
Everywhere lighted. Animals come out
In broad daylight fearless, minnow and trout
Agitate in a water clear as air.
What is the meaning of this? The meaning is where
The objects are, it does not bother me.
All of us are disproven, but gently.

The Herb-garden

When a stream ran across my path,
I stopped, dazzled, though the sparkle was at my feet;
The blind head moving forward, Gulliver
Walking toweringly over the little people.

Not that smaller in size meant, in any way, lesser;
It was merely that I could not see them, my eyes
Crunched on them as if they had been pebbles,
And I blundering without understanding.

Large is inept: how my loping arms fall,
The hands not prehensile, perpendicular
Before an inclined trunk. The legs do the damage,
Like the will of God without rhyme or reason.

Epithalamia are dreamed in this atmosphere
Which towers like a blue fastness over my head.
My head is full of rumours, but the perceptions
Dry like lavender within my skull.

Herb-garden, dream, scent of rosemary,
Scent of thyme, the deep error of sage,
Fennel that falls like a fountain, rue that says nothing,
Blue leaves, in a garden of green.

The Surfaces

And so with the natural surfaces,
Like comfrey gone to waste, there is no loss,
Only the passage of time. And the singing mind,
Like a telegraph wire in the waste, recording time:
Intervals, sounds, rustling, there is no peace
Where the wind is, and no identity
Clapping with herb or tree, or the wild waste
Of skin and shrub-land, which are only perspectives
On time

No heart to be eaten out, a womb to be caught
Sometimes as it were casually, for a new flower.

The Red Admiral

The wings tremble, it is the red admiral
Ecstatically against the garden wall;
September is his enjoyment, but he does not know it,
Name it, or refer to it at all.

The old light fades upon the old stones;
The day is old: how is there such light
From grey clouds? It is the autumnal equinox,
And we shall all have shrunk before daylight.

A woman, a horse and a walnut-tree: old voices
Out of recessed time, in the cracks,
It may be, where the plaster has crumbled:
But the butterfly hugs the blue lias.

The mystery is only the close of day,
Remembered love, which is also present:
Layer upon layer, old times, the fish turning
Once more in the pond, and the absent.

All could not be at once without memory
Crowding out what cannot be remembered;
Better to have none, best of all when
The evening sunlight has ended.

Its fingers lighter than spiders, the red admiral
Considers, as I do, with little movement;
With little of anything that is meant:
But let the meaning go, movement is all.

The Morning

I do not know what the mist signifies
When it comes, not swirling,
Gathering itself like briony under my window

The trees stand out of it,
Wading, you might say,
Have their dark tresses trailing in the water
Which began the world.

For Passing the Time

For passing the time it is a very good thing
To say, Oh, how are the vegetables growing?
How are the artichokes? Are the leeks coming on?
Will there be decent parsnips when the time comes?

I expect so: nature does not deny her abundance
To those who are patient and don't expect too much;
The leaves wither, and the leaves sprout again;
It is unchangeable as change can be.

Down by the river there are events
In every season; and the river flows
In all seasons, sometimes more, sometimes less:
It is hallowed time which passes along its banks.

But for me how can the time be hallowed?
I seek no remedy in it; there can be none.
The scent of rosemary is pungent in the nostrils:
Break the lavender stem, and recorded time.

Leaves

Leaves are plentiful on the ground, under the feet,
There cannot be too many, they lie below;
They rot, they blow about before they are rotted.
Were they ever affixed to trees? I do not know.

The great connection is from the leaf to the root,
From branch, from tendril, to the low place
Below the burial ground, below the hope of the foot,
The hand stretched out, or the hidden face.

On all occasions, or most, remember this:
Then turn on yourself like a small whirlwind of leaves.

Autumn Poems

En rond, nous sommes en rond
Ainsi, nous danserons.

I

The plunging year, the bright year. Through the clouds
Comes sunlight, sunlight, making iron-grey
The under-belly of the cloud it comes from.
Golden the dull leaves September wants to turn,
But dust is everywhere, not free, but plastered
Thinly over road, pavements, even bark
Branches and leaves, and the old iron buildings,
Ochre walls, fall. Not so, and yet it seems so.
Dust is the country way and dust the rhyme
Which equals everything in this sad time.

II

Broken-backed willow, elder and the sharp tree
Which is loaded with berries presently,
Heap upon heap, hawthorn, while the rose-hip
Beside her offers me her paler lip.

III

The world which was not mine, should I have wanted it?
By eating deceived, as Adam was,
I tell myself, but I do not believe it:
Belief is difficult after sixty years.

IV

Once there was bitterness which had regret in it
Or even hope, now there is none of these
The bitterness itself is muted,
Not by satisfaction, which is not
But by etiolation, defoliation, the leaves
Growing whiter and thinner, and no wind through them.

Once I found sleep, it was
In the hollow of anybody else's hand
As the world sleeps in God's; now there is waking:
Not to receive the world, as some do,
But to watch, as the old, suspiciously.

I am looking for contentment out of nothing
For new things are made out of what is new
And I have none except this: the birds' song,
The rain, the evening sky, the grass on the lawn.

V

I am a tree: mark how the leaves grow
Sparsely now; here a bunch, there,
At the end of this thin twig, another
And the bark hardening, thickening. I am allowed
No respite from the wind, the long
Thorn trunk and branches stretching like a swan's neck
In torment. And the hiss
My own malice makes of this wind
Gentle enough, in itself: I can imagine myself
As this tree but what consciousness
Should go with it – that,
Screeching neck, I am blind to.

Across the Winter

1

Quiet. It is winter and the frost
Stretches away into the mist;
A circle of dark closes in
Under the predicated stars.
How, under them, can you be content
With the light, the fire and the Christmas tree?
Or the gesticulating screen
There by the bottles in the corner?
What spirits move? What memory
Stirs in the human race today?

What in me, for I cannot find
In my drunk and incapable mind
Any entrance. There must be one.
Exit you mean? No, a way in
From this disorderly side of a hill
Which does not matter to me at all.
To what? To what? We must first get in
In order to know. But whether we go
Into the hill or into the blue,
Opening it like a money-box,
Is not a matter I can determine.
A dream is an entrance. It would be better,
Perhaps, to spell out every letter
Of the rational alphabet,
Tekel, Upharsin, on the wall.
Or not. But with enough reason
We may go in and turn about
The chambers of the past. It is this
Monstrous alternative to living
I now attempt. On the underside,
There also, where the inverted life
Has its beginning and its end.
Useless to talk of freedom in
The corridors of an old castle;
Gaolers lurk at every corner,
Clanking their keys. Grill after grill
Goes down, a chiaroscuro of
What may, possibly, be love.
But first, it is a memory.
Stapleton Church, which is not fine,
Or only so because it is mine
To skirt and go down to Black Rocks
– Better to go there over Snowdon,
Dangerous because well-known,
With roar of waters from a barrel
Of drains, a gap from one to the other;
A stony track, a shallow river,
A cave for crawling and for terror.
Eastville Park! Down through you
I came to this Elysium

– Which I call it in irony,
In old man's language, because no freedom
Was without terror or was mine.
I walked, yes, and climbed the daring
Slippery places under the alders.
A dog would frighten me, a fall
Threaten me, an eye – my own –
Fear to look. Where the brown
Eddies smoothed themselves was calmer,
Yet there was no safety, nor I either
For if I was alone
Trees might descend on me, the whole bank fall;
If there were enemies they would know all.

There was also, below Stapleton Church,
That entrance to a superior world
– I mean, just, higher up, but hills are green,
Distant and open. To get there between
High walls of pennant grit, with bridges over,
A lane for a dog to shit in, or a lover
To press a squealing girl against a wall.
This kindness also was terror, like the demented
Ill-spoken louts, with faces screwed or gaping,
Roaring, if they said anything, rather than speaking,
Who looked down from the walls and seemed to jeer
As I passed by, also a pilgrim there.

What of the further path, the falling tower,
The lake, Stoke Park and all defences down?
When will you ever be where you want to be,
My treason-top? There is a long track,
Passing the dangerous gates, of white chalk
– It seems in this moment's memory,
But is not – winding away – it does not –
Under a sky extravagantly hot,
For here the journey is long.

2

In this holy season there is remembrance
Here also for me; my enemies rise up
– But not here, for all is in the past –
Only the dark season of Christ brings them
Here to my door, with the snow.
But it is a summer's morning when I go
Along by the fishing stream, through the meadow
Which brings me to the edge of the plunging pool
In the quarry, from whose appalling ledges
The green water looks like a kingdom.
Is that a newt there, dragon-like?
Or, further, where the reliable stepping-stones
Cross the river, shallow but
Alive with brown bubbles, and the froth
Of unknown causes, interlaced with twigs,
A leaf fallen, or a stray blossom,
Minnows, perhaps, may wink.
I, far in mid-stream, the bank
Holding, like watchers over me, great trees.
No enemies there: but on the way back,
The boy with the stone, the big girl
Looking curiously at me: 'What is it?'

But this deep season, in which remembrance
Is not mine, takes me rather,
All that is gone. The mind that hovers
Over me like a hawk, is mine:
Its prey, and yet itself distinct,
Finite in looking, infinite being looked at.

Against the pavement where my feet had chattered
Thousands of miles, here I am, here is she,
Two distances, distance beyond distance.
Yet Shoe Lane is sharper where I stooped
On the hill-side, surely my purgatory,
To buckle my mistress's shoe, eight years old,
And that dark look of love so pitiful,
Or so it seemed. All love is infinite,
And now there is only memory,

Axbridge and Bleadon Hill and bleak Shute Shelve
Where I encountered her beside a well,
Ate my burnt porridge, slept under the wind
And flapping canvas, hold that love for me.
I am, she sang, the inescapable siren
Who sings to mariners on the high seas
Until they fail, and the green sea goes over them.

3

But Uncle George and Auntie Ju
Find place in my memory too
– The Lodge, The Conifers and all
There is beyond the garden wall.
How dusty the road was, I came,
How silent the precincts of Ham Lane:
And how extraordinary, when I was there,
The apple-tree in the always vernal air.
How strange the summer-house, with rotten sticks
Holding it uncertainly, with the planks
Sloping to make a dangerous floor,
And the grass tousled round about and deep,
An occasion for looking, rather than sleep.
How far the Lodge, where Uncle George
Leaned on his spade, looking over the garden
Which edged upon mysterious territory,
The Big House, with its lawns and walks and swing:
That is where the nightingales sing
In retrospect, that did not do at the time
– Uncle George, watchful, saying little, a smile
Was his language, gleaming more than his shirt-sleeves
Always rolled up. He limped when he moved.
It was he that my Aunt Julia loved,
Her face hollowed a little, but always sweet,
Full lips, eyes in hesitation
There in the stone kitchen, neat and small,
Aunt Julia dominant over all,
Sweet in each corner, with her lumpish daughters.

There should be a ballad for Auntie Kate
Who lived at Hambrook, the address, Myrtle Cottage,
Stumpier friend and confidante of Miss Good.
The two kept a shop, there it is,
With small panel windows, it was called the store;
The grain in the bins ran in the hands like money.
Beside it, under the archway, was the yard
And, opening out of that, the coffin-maker's:
Carpenter, joiner, priest of the great saw-pit,
With wooden ladder that ran out of it,
Up to the loft, where there was work to do
But what exactly it was, nobody knew.

There should be a choral for Aunt Anne
Who had been a beauty and whose face glowed still
With the pleasure she had given and could give.
Neat as a Prayer Book, no aunt could be smarter,
And she was trenchant even in her chatter.

Aunt Bessie queened it in an old farmhouse
She was not queen of; none of them was queen
And yet not one of them but might have been
And all of them had had untidy loves,
Perhaps.

4

The dark season runs into sunshine
In which nothing more is illuminated,
The paradise of snow that the cold holds.
Do not turn that into imagination.
It is better to see the peace the New Year brings,
The sky blue as it need be, sunlit branches
Motionless on the beech, waiting for green.
Spring will come, and after it the summer
Extending across the moors like a bow drawn,
Waiting to shoot its arrows into autumn,
The line of hills which always promise winter
And beyond that.

In Flood

A word for everybody, myself nobody,
Hardly a ripple over the wide mere:
There is winter sunshine over the water,
The spirits everywhere, myself here.

Do you know it? It is Arthur's territory
– Agravaine, Mordred, Guinevere and Igraine –
Do you hear them? Or see them in the distant sparkle?
Likely not, but they are there all the same.

And I who am here, actually and statistically,
Have a wide absence as I look at the sea,
– Waters which 'wap and wan', Malory said –
And the battle-pile of those he accounted dead.

Yet his word breathes still upon the ripple
Which is innumerable but, more like a leaf
Curled in autumn and blown through the winter,
I on this hillside take my last of life:

Only glad that when I go to join them
I shall be speechless, no one will ask my name,
Yet among the named dead I shall be gathered,
Speaking to no man, not spoken to, but in place.

Burrington Combe

Not what I think but any land beside
Hidden from human speech, is where I go
As that dark leaf of thyme pushes its way
Into the empty world, and so speak I

Blackdown and Burrington and the deep combe
Which was my land, is also what shall be
Arraigned by time. I make my way only
Backwards, where I may look indulgently

And yet the indulgent land, where silence is
Is not my friend nor ever was before
The great ferns held terror as well as love
Who was lost on the heather-covered moor?

If I could climb out of this bitter combe
Into a lucid world, nothing there said
Could equal now the silence of your grief
Or the exchanges of the recorded dead

The word stands still upon the frozen lip
The eye is glazed that should have danced with love
For such days as are uneaten by the years
A nod, a commonplace will be enough.

★ ★

O Light, I do not want you
The years have taken away
Whatever there was lovely
In the day

The land stretches to doomsday
The rivers to the sea
And nothing done and nothing said
Matters to me

The age laughed in its hollow skull
And strove to be polite
But how can the dazzling fingers equal
The shepherd with his pipe?

Travel across the lips you bones
And do not stop for me
If there is nothing but death in the whistle
It will do for me.

★ ★ ★

So I address the musing mind
Which has no mind to speak
Which can hear nothing, see nothing
And has no heart to break.

The key of the kitchen is frenzy
And the cook stands by the door
Pobble-de-hope fair stranger
What is the ladle for?

A fortune for your porridge
The hope of a transitive verb
Is only to find its object
But the best word here is, Starve.

★ ★ ★ ★

But this is where I came
And where I wish to be
Burrington Combe, half in the dark
Half in the light of the moon

Ellick Farm you are buried
Deep in your greenery
And there is nothing miraculous left
Under the sky.

★ ★ ★ ★ ★

Cry up the pastures of the moon
They stretch from here to nowhere else;
A weed grows on a mossy bank
Its roots go down and down and down.

Down to the dark the dark the dark
Forget the light it is ending soon;
A cloud scuds over the face of the grass-land
Down-a-down and a hurrying moon.

I stood exactly over the valley
Looking down on the changing light.
What vixen cries in the hollow?
What owl passes the barn tonight?

I am not caught in the falling thunder
I am not pierced by the spits of rain;
Six foot long and six foot under
Never to speak on earth again.

Yet the mind hovers like a falcon
A bird of daylight and of dreams
Over the meadows and over the willows
But only hears the barn-owl scream.

★ ★ ★ ★ ★ ★

I came to speak to her
It was no good
No sign in the bushes
Or in the wood.

No sign on her lips
When I found her
There was nothing nothing nothing
But the chill around her.

The willows, she did not see
Or the ditch
Her eyes stared as if the day
Were black as pitch.

Me it may be she saw
As I were any thing
Stoned and stoned and stony
Not living.

And scarcely I am
Or I would not stay here
Walking, talking, proferring
And cannot break her fear.

* * * * * * *

If night falls, there is nothing more
If night falls, there is nothing more
If night falls, there is nothing more

And it does fall, it is falling now
The light is less already, see how it goes
Smaller, smaller, smaller, the circle of light;
But the scent of the rose

The scent of the wallflower, the night-scented stock
The scent of thyme, never off my hands
Except when rue chases it, or fennel, or sage
– Whose hands? –

Except when the bonfire that I have tended
Leaves me with nothing but its acrid air
In my clothes, in my finger-nails
In my hair.

Wherever I sit, as night falls
A last blackbird, perhaps, such things are
The moving night, and I awaiting it
And the first star.

It should be enough, but it is not
When night falls, it will take away
All I wanted and all that I did not
With the last day.

Patience, it is all that is required
Night is patience itself, when it falls
Not even memory disturbs its dream
Loser takes all.

* * * * * * * *

When I walk out there will be nothing missing
That I can see;
The pond will be there with its fish,
The rosemary

Spreading itself over the garden
As if still aided by my hand;
The mulberry-tree I planted, and the cherry,
The old apple-trees and

The plums stretching up against the wall
Over which the church-tower still looks;
Starlings and swallows, the swans flying over,
And always the rooks.

And that distance into which I shall have vanished
Will still be there;
It was always dear to me, is now
In the thickening air.

No distance was ever like this one
The flat land with its willows, and the great sky
With the river reflecting its uncertainty
But no more I.

From the new poems in *Collected Poems* (1984)

The Time of Year

She asks me how I do
It does not matter how
Well and ill are all the same
Now.

I live beyond touching
Beyond friendship now
Do not ask oh do not ask
It does not matter how.

The night has gone from me
And the day is going
Oh the world oh the world turns
And I on it.

Who, I? Or the world itself
Turning, turning
Between the moon and the clouds
Its head spinning.

What price the cul–de–sac
Where you must certainly go?
Patience is getting in
– And the rest you know.

Know it as unknowing
No-way-to-go, unknown.
The fields whisper to harvest
– You go home.

Death, though I cannot go there
Is a neighbouring land
Stretched before my window
But not touched by my hand.

The willows are brown now
It is the time of year
– Look again, look again, orange!
So have no fear.

Two Capitals

'Sieg Heil! Sieg Heil!' It came then like a roar
Across Berlin in nineteen thirty-four.
Herr Bargel, Dr Mohrhoff and young Schmid
Answered its echo like a natural need.
By the old Reichstag torches lit the sky
As the brown-shirted Fackelzug went by.
The heart of Germany! But not my heart;
I stood with thousands but I stood apart.
What peace for England? That is all I knew,
The awful menace of a dream come true.
And France? Months later, there was I, as one
At table, rue du cardinal Lemoine,
At breakfast, lunch and dinner: René Chave,
Febrile as autumn, nineteen and a half;
Old Monsieur Duchemin, discoursing reason;
Madame, who bought the vegetables in season
And clacked over the price of artichokes;
Jacques who irrupted with his silly jokes;
Hélène who once let slip an awful word;
The Madame Picart who was so refined,
Contrasting English Sport with the French Mind;
Henri her studious son, who chose the latter;
Kreitmann, who had his own thoughts on the matter
As on most others. What do I make of it,
Forty-five years later, in Somerset?

Winter has come and I welcome it
Despite grey cloud which hammers down its lid
Upon the flat world, flat as it, and still.
Oh, it is cold, but not with that cold will
Which laid itself over the multitude
That hurried, clouded, gathered or just stood
Below me in the Schäferkampsallee.
There it was cold, there there was steel to glint
If in no more than in a massive hint
As the leaves fell, had fallen. Yet again
Can I not feel it in the icy rain
Threatening to fall over gabbling Europe?
I am too well instructed to have hope
Yet softly, do not speak. Only prepare
To walk out naked in the bitter air
Trusting what is not to be trusted, love.

Athelney

The apple trees are dulled in the red sun,
The fruit unpolished and the day is done.
This is where Alfred crept by on his marsh,
Wet straggling country still, but now the harsh
Road runs on blue and dark beside his ghost.
Headlamps begin to count the sodden posts
And catch a nosing heifer here and there.
The squawking ducks are home, and the wet air
Settles more heavily as the night comes.
'A bit of fire-stuff, like': a voice close by
And a dead branch is dragged to Athelney.

The Broken Willow

It was an old willow with a dark
Hawthorn bush underneath its leaning stem.
(The bush was dark not because of shadow
But from the rustling silver of the willow

Poring over it like an attentive head.)
Over the stile and to the river-side
I went to examine this conjunction.
It was no girl poring over a lover

Or comforting a child dark but her own.
It was an old broken sexless thing
Which time had ripped open and its tubes
Rings and soft places open in their rot,

Yet more like a circuit than a man,
A control panel with the cover off,
Saving a natural grace, a contentment
Of ruin sinking into renewed life.

Blackdown

Here was a distant and remote youth
– I saw them on waking under the old apple-tree –
And a girl smudged by time but not remote,
Withdrawn that is from him but not from me:

Wind perhaps but not much against her dress,
Enough to show the outline of a girl.
I see them both against the blackened earth
– Burnt heather, it would be, from the smell.

Walking or standing, with the sky huge
About them on all sides except one
– It might be everywhere and they hung
Among the improbabilities of youth.

What was he saying? For it is his words
Which spring as from my lips from that image.
They are obscure now but they pierced the sky,
The future, but they have not reached me.

And yet I half suspect: 'There must be something
I could do' – or 'do well' – 'I don't know what.'
But 'well' was what I meant yet this was not
Ambition, you might rather say definition.

Yet it is she has become definite;
I never did. We twist and grow together
Like old trees with their attendant ivy
And it is I who am the parasite.

From *God Bless Karl Marx!* (1987)

Read me or not: I am nobody
For myself as for others, and so true:
If only it were also so with you
Every accommodation would be easy.
But so it is not, for what we see
Assumes as we look the mask of who,
Doing convincingly what others do:
So you become yourself without falsity.
Or so it seems. But when delusion stirs
It dreams of a mask, of his or hers,
And so must you. Where is the truth in that?
And you who read me read nothing or, worse,
What you make out for yourself, some borrowed features.
Who is what you say but I answer, what?

Vigil and Ode for St George's Day

Déjà il ne cherchait plus le bonheur
RENÉ BÉHAINE

What is the cure for the disease
Of consciousness? The cures are three,
Sex, sleep and death – two temporary
And only one that's sure to please.

In sex the circles of the mind
Close to a point and disappear
And that is something, till we hear
The world again and are not blind.

Sleep closes round us from without
Until it has us in its grip
And then the pincers start to nip:
It tells us what to dream about.

And death? Then all is gone, or so
There is best reason to believe.
In manus tuas: what we leave
Is certain, and enough to know.

For we are stone, or so they say
And how should we have ears to hear
Any objection, we who are
The treaders of the obvious way?

Either the truth is what we see
Or else it is not to be seen.
No more is it, perhaps; that green
Is grass, that tall thing is a tree.

But what else is it cunning men
Invite the suckers to believe?
All manner of follies weave
Their ways past us with if and when.

Yet there is truth which we assert
And I myself would die for one
If there were need, as there is none:
Better the world should be inert.

There is a time, it is enough
To know, there have been, will be times
And places when and where the crimes
Habitual to mankind, grow rough.

But we can rest in comfort, no
Mind need assert what all betray.
We in the light of common day
Without concern watch the light go.

So must it be, that only death
Relieves us at the sentry-box;
The guard comes marching up, the flocks
Of augurs' birds catch at our breath.

I watched them once, when harmlessly
They flew as martins near the house,
Dipping and soaring, and could rouse
No trouble but in memory.

A line of sceptical recruits,
Myself among them, waited for
What fortunes there might be in war
But no-one found the one that suits

Because no fate is suitable
To any man who hopes for more
Than comes his way, or comes before
He has decided it is well.

For fortune like the birds that fly
Takes its direction from the wind
Which no man changes or holds pinned
And which blows on us till we die.

The first, the bitter lot of all,
Is to be born, for so it is
As time and place and parents please
Or rather, as their fortunes fall.

Then come the choices: none is right
For none is as the birds allow;
By Aldebaran and the Plough
They pass, we into darker night.

That much is tolerable, but that
The same should swallow up our land
May not be borne, and yet the hand
Points to the hour that we are at.

The time that bore us runs away,
The place must follow, the extreme
Edge of the world is here, the dream
Breaks on another homely day.

The strong will always be unjust,
The weak will cringe and run away
Or find their comfort in a day
When they will do as all men must:

And who would dare to boast of that?
We who survive, though not for long,
May envy those who do most wrong
Yet soon enough they too fall flat.

And who is he who in the end
Loves life more than he longs for death?
Does not the most exulting breath
Turn at last to the only friend?

The spirit which was proud to be
Collected in a little earth
Finds what the privilege is worth
And in that knowledge he is free.

Fortune which holds us in its grip
Does not change, though it seems to do,
The same for me, the same for you
Whatever words are on your lips.

For what we say and what we are
Are different things, and we console
Our patience when we take a role:
Only one voice will carry far.

Christ comes to all, because belief
Is necessary for our peace,
The world cannot give it, release
Can only come by way of grief.

The Man of Sorrows is the one
Who represents the way we go:
He is the only one we know
However furious our fun.

For he knows better than the most
Experienced practitioner
Whatever comes to him and her
And that their pleasure is a Ghost.

And of death too he understands
The comfort and the mystery;
The secrets of mythology
Lie always open in his hands.

The bark of Charon and the bite
Of Cerberus, are jokes to him
Yet in his mind no single whim
The pagans have, is lost from sight

For all is laid upon the cross,
The auguries, the sacrifice,
The marching armies, every vice
And virtue, every gain and loss.

There, all was nothing to the God
Who was inside the man, who was
The man and all was all because
He died where Adam first had trod.

The intervening years were gone:
All this he did for Adam's sake
And so the future reeled to take
Another face from that time on.

The face is sorrow, like the Man,
The underworld no longer waits
To have our shadows and our fates
And where our God hung, others can.

He has gone climbing out of space
And time, yet taken with him all
That we have here, the world is small
Beside his new appointed place

Which also leaves him where he was
Before he came, but with a new
Body which he already knew
From his intent to visit us.

Our bodies too, so lifted up,
Will shine as his does, so they say,
But that is for another day
When we have also drunk the cup

Which will not pass, and when we leave
The world we credit now for one
Invisible under our sun
And in which none of us can believe.

So glory, laud and honour, all
To the impossible, and most
To Father, Son and Holy Ghost
And let our own pretensions fall.

They may, but only if we love
No other as we love our end.
The night comes down upon our friends
As on ourselves, yet still above

Their graves, the grass grows and the sun
Shines upon others as on us:
The fieldmouse and the weasel pass
And do not ask whose will is done.

But we, who saw our friends depart
Into the shadows of the moon
Leave others, as it may be soon,
Glad we are gone or, in their hearts

Holding our tiny memory
A moment till that too goes out.
Why not? For we can never doubt
The comfort of mortality.

Yet may Time's treasure still remain
Until it quietly ebbs away
Beyond our knowledge, England's day
– I cannot help it, for the pain

Of her demise is more than all
The mind can suffer for the death
Of any creature that draws breath,
And should her time come round again

Our dust will stir, not to a drum
Or any folly men devise
But to the peace which once our eyes
Met in her fields, or else in some

Of her best children, from the first.
All this is folly too and yet
Rather than any should forget
Let this sad island be immersed

In raging storm and boiling seas.
Let no man speak for her unless
He speaks too for her gentleness
And it is her he seeks to please.

Waking

May has her beauties like another month,
Even June has her pleasures. I lie here,
The insistent thrush does not trouble me
Nor the slight breeze: a tree stump looks like a cat.
Yet all is not altogether well
Because of memory; crowd round me here
Rather, you ghosts who are to drink of Lethe.
Who else would go back to the upper world
Or take again the nerve-strings of the body
Or will to suffer grief and fear again?
Once I did: and the echo still comes back,
Not from the past only – which I could bear –

But from the young who set out hopefully
To find a bitter end where they began
And evil with the face of charity.
I have seen some such and do not want
Ever to pass along that road again
Where blind beggars hold out their hands for coin
And saints spit in their palms. This I have seen
And shall see if I wake from sleeping now.

The Absence

How can it be that you are gone from me,
Everyone in the world? Yet it is so,
The distance grows and yet I do not move.
Is it I streaming away and, if so, where?
And how do I travel from all equally
Yet not recede from where I stand pat
In the daily house or in the daily garden
Or where I travel on the motor-way?
Good-bye, good-bye all, I call out.
The answer that comes back is always fainter;
In the end those to whom one cannot speak
Cannot be heard, and that is my condition.
Soon there will be only wind and waves,
Trees talking among themselves, a chuchotement,
I there as dust, and if I do not reach
The outer shell of the world, still I may
Enter into the substance of a leaf.

The Hare

I saw a hare jump across a ditch:
It came to the edge, thought, and then went over
Five feet at least over the new-cut rhine
And then away, sideways, as if thrown
– Across the field where Gordon and I walked
Talking of apples, prices and bog-oak,
Denizens of the country, were it not

That denizens do not belong, as they do
And the hare tossing herself here and there.
And I? If I could, I would go back
To where Combe Farm stood, as Gordon's stands
Trenched in antiquity and looking out
Over immense acres not its own
And none the worse for that. You may say
It is the sick dream of an ageing man
Looking out over a past not his own.
But I say this: it is there I belong,
Or here, where the pasture squelches underfoot
And England stirs, forever to hold my bones.
You may boast of the city, I do not say
That it is not all you say it is
But at the Last Judgment it will stand
Abject before the power of this land.

God Bless Karl Marx!

A centre in a kingdom is absurd
You say? And where else would you find a word?
A theory, like a skein of mist that covers
The sacred members of a pair of lovers,
Mythological giants strewn by the way
Of history? The proletariat, say,
Reluctantly embraced by the middle class
Or some such dream? I at least
Prefer the ground under the two-backed beast:
Wet or fine it is less phantasmagorial,
You may even get a damp touch of the real
Or so it seems to me. Not only giants
But field-mice, rabbits, creatures more compliant
With grass and molehills – even human beings –
Shaped and sized more conveniently for doing
Whatever moles and men and women do,
Live in that terrain, having private limits
Less subject to the theoretical gimmicks
Of Marx and others living in a library.
Their words and noises are the things we see

Or hear or touch or smell, the mist that swirls
Around them is not everything in the world,
Just one delusion butting against others;
They say their piece and then their life is over.
If history rolls on they are not with it,
They understand for only half a minute
And then go blank. But the great sage Abstraction
Flies like a pterodactyl, with an action
Appropriate for imaginary millennia
Before or after there were any men here.
Here? Yes and now. Enough past for a man,
Some sunlight, moonlight, changing clouds that can
Be caught for a moment in an eye
Which must wear spectacles and then must die.

Looking at Old Note-Books

It would seem that I thought,
At that time, more than I ought;
I noted the reflections
Of those for whom perfection
Came in a sudden phrase:
How one should behave,
How others did, the wise
Remarks of men in difficulties
Or who observed others
Making a great pother
While they were easy themselves.
All this should have been useful
To a young man rising twenty,
Yet one finds that at thirty
He was still floundering.
If he understood anything
It was by way of suffering
For his first incompetence
Or third or fourth inability
To do anything sensibly.
How much had the wise helped?
They could do nothing themselves,

Being dead, buried in books
In octavo or folio, works
In several languages
And always, phrases that pleased.
What price then Schopenhauer,
Throwing a woman downstairs,
Fénelon, Proudhon,
Goethe in Eckermann
Or Plutarch in North?
I might add, 'and so forth'
– Out and around
The world but all bound
In antique leather,
Mercure de France yellow
Or the elegant brown or black
Of the *Insel-Verlag*.
There was the London Library
Doing its best to confuse me
– Then back to Valéry,
Antoine de St-Exupéry,
Barrès, Cocteau, Jouhandeau
And what d'you know?
On oriental customs,
To confirm my observations
There was the Abbé Dubois
Or the Japanese school reader
For children of five.
It can cause no surprise
That with such learning
For half an hour each morning
And a supplement at night,
I knew my way all right.
The world opened before me
Like a speck in memory,
I grew in wisdom
Like a mastodon
Or other inept animal.
Behold me now, in old age,
Seated in my cage,
Pulling through the bars

What leaves can be reached from there.
Naturally I advise
The young who would be wise
To follow my example.
They should all read examples
Of the philosophers, I recommend
The moralists of course and
The epistemologists,
There is a long list.
They are not to reject
The theologians, I expect
They will find them illuminating.
Imaginative writing
Isn't all it's cracked up to be:
Take it cautiously.
Avoid writing poems, a frequent
Cause of discontent;
You may read one occasionally
And that is all
– And all I can tell
You about how to live well.

Taxila

There is a rail-head at Havelian
– Or was, for I was there long ago –
Around it a sweet plain circled by hills:
This was my Greece, the only one I know.

It was a ghost of olives that I saw:
I had not seen the Mediterranean light
Where it falls, but I had dreamed of it.
I who had not been born woke to the sight.

Rus in urbe, urbs in the dazzling grey
– Or was it green? – green, but so grey and brown,
A spot of light in the surrounding darkness:
Taxila was the name of the town,

The heart of all I loved and could not have;
And in that limy track, as I approached,
A child with bright eyes offered a coin.
It was a bargain that was proposed.

Would I, the soldier of an alien army,
Neither the first nor last to come that way,
Purchase for rupees certain disused drachmas
Left by the army of an earlier day?

Alexander himself came down from those hills,
Over the mountains beyond them to the north
– Far lands, the boy said, but mine was farther
And longer ago still my setting forth

For my exile burned me like the sun.
I should have bought that coin, I often thought of it
After that time, and in far different places:
It would have carried me over the Styx.

I would have returned, but there is no returning.
Yet you may rise, ghosts, or I sink to you.
The world is in my hand, breathing at last
For now I know, only the past is true.

From *Antidotes* (1991)

Fifteen Sonnets

1

The minutes have gone by, the hours, the days,
The years have counted themselves up, and now
That little piece of time, a life, is proud
To show itself complete: 'fini' it says.
Yet I who speak for it in so many ways
Cannot say this: the when, the where, the how
Must be determined first, and who knows
Less well than I what may be the delays?
To be on the outside and yet to speak
Is not a thing the mind of man can compass,
Yet inside I am inside something else
Than the completed life and cannot break
The circle of it to see it as it is
Even now, at the end even less.

2

No other language but that of the Creed
Will serve to say the things which must be said.
And what things are they? All things, I said:
Or did not all things come from the same seed
– The seed which is unsowable indeed?
When we name that, we say what we cannot know,
Much less express, the inexpressible, so
Beyond our every thought or word or deed.
So no word counts which is not beyond speech,
No action but what is beyond our reach,
And if we rest, it is in mystery.
No explanation touches us, no word,
Once spoken, is not more or less absurd:
Why then, not *quia impossibile*?

3

Why should one write poems when one is old?
Not, to be sure, in hope of reputation
Which has either come, or else will escape one.
In hope of love perhaps? But what is told
Now, will not strengthen anybody's hold
On me or mine on them: the time of truth has come,
And yet I lie as I have always done
And leave myself and others unappalled.
Poets are liars, yet no more than others,
Those who are not their sisters are their brothers,
All of the same lying family,
Children of Adam, fond of all evasions,
Blaming, beguiling on the least occasions
And to the last, and so it is with me.

4

Of all that can be said silence is best
In which God can be heard and none but He,
But that silence has not come to me,
Rather I lie and babble with the rest.
Quiet may come, but in it can be guessed
Voices like shadows which I hear or see
Hunched in a courtyard under a great tree,
Dark and faint, with nothing clearly expressed.
Then words come, or else shapes, and what they say
Is nothing to the torture of this day
Which is all cloud, above me and without.
Or maybe like lunatics they rush
Out of the gates of reason and so flush
The mind not knowing what they are about.

5

To look back is to look back on a thing
Which never was, because it then was *is*
And I was going forward in a mist
Which cleared without revealing anything
– For what showed then at once disappearing,
Another scene flashed, another, this
With no sign that what is seen exists
Beyond the blind instant of its coming.
Even the hour does not contain the minute,
Much less the day the hour, the year the day.
How, in the end, can anybody say
That his life had this or that thing in it,
Or that it failed or succeeded, caught,
As all time is, in multiples of nought?

6

More is what they say, what I say is less,
And so, naturally, will each of us be served.
Do we get our wishes then? No, our deserts.
Asking there must be, for happiness,
Yet one may ask for it and find distress;
Door after door closes, the right words
Are never spoken, the wrong silence observed.
Who is responsible for all this mess?
It is not a mess: the end is always found,
The young go roaring over new ground,
The old come to a stop. So it should be.
The world must either grow or shrink, or seems
So to do, for life is only dreams
For time to wind up in eternity.

7

The only dream I had did not come true
And we are to believe it never does:
Dreams are like that, they represent the fuzz
Of what might be beyond the things we do:
Integer vitae is the way you grew,
Sceleris purus is ridiculous,
And every other character no less.
What makes you think that you are really you?
No names, no pack-drill, and the simple act
Amounts to no more than a pile of fact
No-one can know unless you lay a claim to it.
Truth is in action, but your words will lie
Until, escaping into truth, you die
And then what might be and what must be fit.

8

All such excitements are illusory.
How prove they are more illusory than most?
They are not illusory, more than a ghost
Or any ordinary thing daylight can see.
What makes the difference, it seems to me,
Is that they are so entirely lost
– Some careless Rubicon having been crossed –
They are a past which is a past completely.
Such an excitement I had on the way
And often think of it: and what is thought
Except a finding of something we have sought,
Which, being found, has nothing more to say,
Or, being said, must then be changed for new,
Thoughts being many and the truths but few?

9

'What?' said the World, 'You come to beg from me?
Where are your papers then, who are your friends?
Will they serve me? I love a man who bends
To every whim I have, and I have many.
Here come the cohorts of the wise who slily
Swerve when the word goes round, whose common ends
Waver to suit my smile, tend where mine tends, ·
Constant only to instability.'
They are in the right of it, for well I know,
Nothing endures that any man can say,
The lips that spoke the words will fall away,
The words precede them or else quickly follow.
But what in this can ever hold a man
As the impossible Eternal can?

10

When time stands still, it is you who have stopped,
For time goes on and leaves you standing there
And crumbling, for as long as you breathe air
You are mined, and your little growth is cropped,
Like a field tunnelled and yet grazed on top,
And soon the empty surface will lie bare.
You stand? You lie. Lie still, time will repair
Your pride and see your last pretensions drop.
And if time moves again, what do you see?
A hurrying world in which you have no part:
Either way you have lost the fruit of time,
Which was to live as if you had been free
To choose some other error which your heart,
Always deluded, would have turned to rhyme.

11

The world in which I wander on my own
— For who is there? To whom can I speak now? —
Spreads like a terror round me, and I go
As one to whom no mercy can be shown
Across the acres of a shadowy down
Over which clouds determine all I know,
While barrenness flavours the earth below
— So impervious to hope has my age grown.
If through the darkness there appeared a rift,
A streak of moon-light, a square inch of blue,
If there were any breath to start a drift,
Real or imagined, or if one blade grew,
I would rejoice, and stretch a living hand
To touch the surface of this once loved land.

12

To cast off, as a boat that puts to sea,
Is difficult, the eyes are fascinated
By all that lies ashore. It is too late
Now to enquire the meaning of what I see,
The little houses, the great rock, the trees
Standing against the hill, the tempting gate
Leading into the fields. And those who wait
Idly beside the lane, what are they to me?
If I had taken that turning, found them there,
Exchanged a word or else a look, what air
That I did not draw in, should I have spent?
Was this land my land? Or I made of it,
As part and parcel of its growth and grit,
Incapable of being different?

13

As the mind shrinks, the body withers too.
And whither does it wither? To the ground,
Where at once nothing or else all is found.
But the poor mind? It flies into the blue,
And who knows what is there? A plant that grew
Cannot grow rootless, and in heaven abound
The principalities and powers, while here around
The earth the lingering air holds nothing true.
So the faint voice of fame is only lies,
Misprisions, misapprehensions, and the heart
Moves silently, or not at all, is lost
As memory vanishes and no-one tries,
Though generations flow past and depart,
To reckon up the little that it cost.

14

What I imagine is the least of things,
The less than nothing that I call my own
In place of what might actually be known,
The world beyond me and the gifts it brings,
Colour and size and shape — no, trees and limbs,
What else God knows, all that his art has grown:
Knowledge can count only what stands alone
Beyond the harm of my imaginings.
If there is truth I need to look at it,
Well knowing that my mind will never fit
Even the objectivity of sense:
So back to images and back to me,
Who cannot trust the slightest thing I see,
Much less come to the edge of penitence.

15

If love and death are one and the same thing,
As Ronsard said – others have felt it too –
Yet neither he nor they can make it true,
Nor anything, by mere imagining.
Whatever evidence the world may bring,
The mind fills like a pond and what looks through
The waters is the sky's cloud and blue,
But what have images to do with naming?
The names of love and death we have from far
But who can say what their originals are
Or whether the names they have are their own?
When we sail into that unexpected harbour
The moment of trespass beyond words is there,
All freshness and newness begin, or nothing is known.

The Christmas Rose

A spray of myrtle and the Christmas roses
Come from the garden like a grail of light.
They climb out of the mist into a hand
Which holds them till they flower in her sight:

Myrtle for Myrtilus, who died for treachery
And yet found a place among the stars:
The Christmas rose for peace and chastity
– Old stories both, if any of them are.

Yet love remains, although I cannot see it,
The myrtle berries hovering among leaves,
Dark for sorrow, white petals of the rose
Straggling from the gold centre to grieve.

Rapacity and lust will not forbear
And there is no retreat from injury
Except one: *amor vincit omnia*,
And rose and myrtle float in the same sea.

Myrto a woman, Myrtos an island, the Mare
Myrtoum where the rival of Pelops fell.
What light now plays across the sea?
Is there any? O Christmas rose, Noël!

Uncertainty

The future is the only thing
That makes for thought, the past is past:
It brought its presents, had its fling,
But what it flung could never last.

The future has not lasted yet
Even the second that it can
And so is good for any bet:
It is the guessing makes the man.

Human uncertainty is all
That makes the human reason strong:
We never know until we fall
That every word we speak is wrong.

Muchelney Abbey (from On the Departure)

The quiet flood
Lies between hedges and turns back the light,
Black and blue like the bruises of the time
– Sheet after sheet of record where the crime
Is lost beneath the water. Rushes write
Illegibly in mud

And willows point
Downward without weeping, or else raise
Flourishing heads topping gigantic trunks.
Uneasily the shadows of dead monks
Move past an abbey in which no-one prays.
Who will anoint

The wounds they did not,
More than we do ourselves, attempt to cure?
Grey evening behind which the sun, unseen,
Sets to the sound of church-bells, which still mean
No more than echoes: and, for sure,
Nature will rot.

O come away
To death O human race! Accept no more
This watery world in which the fox and hare
Have lost their scent, in which the livid air
Promises nothing on this wasted shore
But closing day.

Yet spring may come,
Who knows? with drought and terror, or else flowers,
For time may circle back, once more pretend
A grammar of renewal without end,
A summer with its vacuum of bright hours.

From *What and Who* (1994)

The Mendips

The stream that runs
Under the earth and is the stream of death
Is also that of life: without
Its sombre, unheard flow
What pulse would beat here or what ghost
Re-visit? Where
The sparkling shapes come tumbling from the mouth
Of that dark cave into the light of day,
The living are, and see
The splash and laughter of their ecstasy:
No sound. Imagination only made
That single figure dancing in the shade,
Naked as air, and it is she who slides
Into the mind and eats the heart away.
Turn back the spring
Which feeds the torrent: let the stream flow back.
The falling water mounts and disappears
Into the cave-mouth. All is quiet now.
The eaten heart goes with it, and the man,
Empty of grief as hope,
Watches the sunlight on the glinting rocks,
The tufts of bracken and the scattered flocks
Upon the hill-side. Age has come again,
And found its victim patient and at ease
Upon a world that has no power to please.

Et in Arcadia ego

And in Arcadia never have I, Charles Sisson,
Passed a day, my days have been otherwise:
I am the old Adam, in another garden,
Driven by tormenting angels from my prize.

The living days are over, and I remember
Only where I have failed, as any might,
On this or that occasion, with him or her,
When almost could perhaps have turned to quite.

So ends a journey which was hardly necessary,
Or so it seems, but what is done is done:
Fact has replaced illusion and I see
With what ineptitude the course was run.

Steps to the Temple

What is belief? A recognition?
Who knows of what? If any say
He knows, he lies.
Who knows what never was begun
And will not end? God is a way,
And a surprise.

And in that way we cannot choose,
For choice deceives us, as it must.
We live in sense,
Certain at least that we shall lose
That urgency, for we are dust.
Our recompense,

If any, cannot be to find
That beauty and that bitterness
Again. A new
Perception must await the vanished mind
– Or none, and which of these we cannot guess.
That much is true.

So here, we who are fallible
As shifting sands, may feel the tide
Flow over us, or in, or out.
If in, then all will then be well;
If not, then we should feel no pride
Even in doubt.

April

Exactly: where the winter was
The spring has come: I see her now
In the fields, and as she goes
The flowers spring, nobody knows how.

The Lack

All is past that is not now:
How long ago it seems!
What was, when life was, is remote
Beyond the reach of dreams.

The life was in the wants we had,
And now what do we need?
Less every day. True riches are
In hope, intent and greed.

How we fared in that starving time
Is less than the starvation
Which gave the future all its worth
And negatived negation.

But now, we only lack the past,
And now is less than then,
Less even than the direst lack
Which will not come again.

Peat

If I could only return to where I am
From where I have been or from the vague reaches
Passing imagination saw, but not I,
The darkness would softly occlude the sky
And all sound faint before the barn-owl's screeches
Or the cry of a solitary lamb.

The sum of everything would be the peat
Which runs cool and dark between my fingers.
It is night itself, a peaceful shower
Which not one minute falls, not for one hour,
But endures while consciousness lingers
And follows it into its final retreat.

Trees in a Mist

The mist is so thin, the world stands still
Before my eyes: there is no vanishing.
Dead figures ape the live ones which before
Breathed and were blown about by wind or will.
The winter cold embraces everything:
Death is the country I must now explore,

Yet cannot, and my corpse is not among
The number that I count before my eyes
– Trees which another time will bud and fruit,
And do not wait for any season long,
Though time seems long under these hazy skies
And there are trees which perish at the root.

So plays the outer world with that within,
And maybe that within with that without
– Consciousness no more than an interface
Between the two, with roots under the skin
And in the natural objects round about,
Housed where it occupies no shred of space.

And as the body perishes and finds
Itself confounded by the world of sense
– Taste, scent and hearing joining touch and sight –
The mist comes and goes; the river winds
Into the darkness: can there be pretence
Where there is neither confidence nor light?

The Levels

Summer has come, with no comfort
Except the cattle munching as they think,
And green being green where they bow their heads.
The river runs low, emptying itself
As if the sky itself were going out,
Streaming to westwards as the evening falls.
When light comes again, what shall we see?
Only the ruin of this ancient land,
And hear no more the old authentic words.
Yet somehow out of silence truth is born,
Which nothing now can harbour but herself,
And so succession will make all things new.
Let autumn come, and winter fill the dykes.
Spring will succeed, and the incredible
Prove itself by the plenty that it yields.

Broadmead Brook

O you haunting ghosts, I move towards you.
Could I go over these flooded plains
It would not be to any Paradise:
I came from none and I expect to find none;
It was a long journey, or so it seemed.
The scene changed, and thoughts went through my head,
But even the possibility of knowledge
– Never coveted – seemed no more than a slide
From one thing to another. First the child
Tasting the world, and finding that it hurt;
Then the youth, felled by the bolt of love,

Then labouring where the knowledge was acquired
In self-defence or else in mere ambition.
But late in time and after all deceits,
I came to stand beside Broadmead Brook
As in the very hollow of my hand.
A woman stood there who had been a child
Where in another century my mother
Had played and laboured. Now all was changed,
Yet Broadmead Brook flowed, exquisite woods
Marked her course, for in my fantasy
It was she guarded the bounding deer,
The rabbits and the partridges, and all
Who dare to dream, and be, of England still.

Absence

Go back, or forward, to a time
When I am not here. What remains?
What is here is what I see,
For I trust visibility,
Find that I get wet when it rains
And think that sense and reason chime.

No sense, no reason. For the past,
The living stand in for the dead
And try to see what others saw,
Though disappearance is the law
For what is seen, and what is said,
Though cast in bronze, can never last.

And so one can imagine sand
Carried back by receding tides,
And yet not understand a word
The ocean said when it was heard.
The present never co-incides
With any past that comes to hand.

Go forward. I am here no more:
No word of mine can extricate
The listener from the cord that binds
Him in the twist of other minds.
Unheard before, and now too late,
My words have lost the flesh they wore.

I am not even silence, as
The rows on rows of marshalled dead
Who left no word they did not speak.
An echo that is faint and weak
Remembers me for what I said,
Happy to lose the man I was.

Casualty

It is not the spoken word but the word spoken
In silence, not directed at anyone,
But holding meaning till it spills over,
Which finds its way into the casual mind.
Poetry, ha? The bed-rock of that art
On which those few can build who lose themselves.

Poems from *Collected Poems* (1998)

Five Lines

The splashed light on the rain-wet stones
Is in the eye, not in the sun:
Eyes dimmed, the light is gone,
And all the wonder of the world
Cannot withstand the touch of age.

Triptych

1

Now I am come to that strange place
Where those must come who wait for death:
We expect no familiar face,
But one who takes away our breath.

So welcome to the visitor
Who comes but once, and as a friend,
Seen only as an open door
Through which we go to find our end.

He brings release, after so long
In business and captivity,
And when we go where we belong
– *In manus tuas* – we are free

2

We live within, although we hope,
Ambitiously, to live without,
In the world where we only grope,
And see no more than we can doubt.

To be, to be as others are
– Visible, moving as a mind –
Seems an ambition not too far
Out of the way of human kind.

Yet to be other is to be
The true impossible for us:
Within, it is outsides we see,
Our own not less extraneous.

We move without but live within,
Like it or not, that is the way,
And when we move no more, the in-
And out-side vanish quite away.

The only hope is in belief
In all the gross absurdities
The Creed contains, of which the chief
Are of a kind the least to please

Abstracted and ingenious minds
Which trust in thoughts but not in things,
While he who swallows it will find
Reality is King of Kings.

3

All the estates of life are done:
We wait with alms to please the world,
Which will refuse our gifts and run
From us whose empty shells are hurled

Into the dustbin of intent,
Where meaning was, but is no more.
And how should anything be meant
When life is that which went before?

For what is now is emptiness,
Engendering nothing that can be
The object of desire or guess,
Or any future memory.

The empty plain extends beyond
All human being, into what
Lies quiet as a darkened pond,
And is is overpowered by not.

Tristia

1

It is because of exile I am here,
The utmost tip of the world, for old age
Brings one to the edge of what one lived among.
Before departure I was of that race
Which passed the time but thought of something else,
But now time fills the whole horizon:
Not what yesterday was or what tomorrow
Will bring, for what it brought is dead,
And what it will, will never come to life.
When will it pass? is all I have to ask.
No-one is implicated in that question
But I who now no longer live among
Even those who see me now as I do them.
But 'as' is not the word I should have used,
For age has given sight its own blindness,
And no impression is conveyed to me
Which tells me it is here that I belong.
I am the utmost tip of what once was,
Beyond which there is nothing but the sea;
The stationary Pontic cold holds all.
I look towards it, not to those I know,
Though casual bodies hurrying in the street
May hold the eye enough to make a glance,
But where they go is not where I will go:
I turn back to the water and am lost.

2

No-one will speak to you, nor you to any:
This is the end of all communication
Which was the hope which brought you to this end

And served delusively to coax you on.
The road that leads to death goes single file,
And so it always was. Though each in turn
Surrounds himself with dreams of other minds,
The bodies which should hold them have no voice.
The voice of every lonely traveller
Is loud with silence as the company
He sees around him as he passes on.
Why then these verses? Nothing can be heard.
But speak on as you will, you who are young.
Collude with one another on the way:
Proximity may do what words will not.

                    3

The hollow name of Love sounds through the streets,
The newsboy crying while the city burns.
The lack of any purpose of my own
Cries louder, and the city is consumed.
The state denies the Church, the Church the state;
The promises of neither have come true,
Or so it seems, here at the door of death.

                    4

The past is only past which never present was:
Nor is there present now but that vain show of past.
Reality has faded into dream
– A dream without cohesion or event.
Oddities now show nothing but oddities,
For meaning has escaped. Where purpose was
Is nothing but consecutive array
Of matters past which do not matter now.

                    5

The day is over and the night begins,
But what is day which so resembles night?
Forgetfulness and sleep are of a piece.
The tail-end of the world: and here am I
Pledged to a narrowing prospect. I stand here
While the world fails or falters in my eye.

6

Here on this promontory by the sea,
Speech has no meaning, yet we use it still:
The flagged signal, the gesticulation,
Serve better to elicit a reply.
Yet we talk on, dazed and with hollow voice.
The empty shell you see is what you hear:
The tolling bell will tell the truth at last.

7

The crystal world that was, when I was there:
The broken morning and the silver eve,
The flashing woodland and the dew on grass,
The moon lighting up what the sun has left.
Such a world must be somewhere, but not here.
Even the sea breaking upon the rocks
Crashes no more, but laps this final shore,
Soon to be frozen. There is wind,
But only hissing as it sidles by.
O send the blustering past in new array,
And let me find the quartz within the stone.

8

The naked person is the only one
Who speaks within the chatter of our speech:
There is no truth in reason or abstraction.
They are the garments that the body wears,
The chatter of the magpie, not the bird
Which walks before the eye in black and white.
The body gives direction to our speech,
As to our thoughts: your shape is what you are,
And what you are is what I seek to know.
The brilliant knowledge which escapes me here,
At this far tip of the world, is what the mind
Can take immediately from what it sees,
Plain without any need for explanation.
So strip before my eyes and speak in tune
With what you are, and that will be the truth
– A momentary revelation

To clear the clouds which else envelop me.
But if you think cloud is where I belong,
Pile on your clothes and chatter in the words
The magpie uses and the world applauds.

9

Speech cannot be betrayed, for speech betrays,
And what we say reveals the men we are.
But, once come to a land where no-one is,
We long for conversation, and a voice
Which answers what we say when we succeed
In saying for a moment that which is.
O careless world, which covers what is there
With what it hopes, or what best cheats and pays,
But speech with others needs another tongue.
For a to speak to b, and b to a,
A stream of commonalty must be found,
Rippling at times, at times in even flow,
And yet it turns to Lethe in the end.

10

I am the place where I belong,
For other self or place is not:
The horror of the world extends
Beyond that bourn and never ends.
No friend, no other haunts that space
Which, empty as infinity,
Means no more to me than myself.
Send me particulars and limits,
The tactile and the visible.
Here only nullity is left:
What was lost has lost its place
– No, place has gone as time has gone,
And I have never been, nor am.

The Verb To Be

Nothing comes out of the forest of my mind,
So what can be? There is the outer world.
Or how should I know if there were to be
A fight of dragons or a shower of rain?
For I stand at the entrance of the world
– Of my world, of the only world I know,
Or can know – I who am limited.
There is one God who made the world complete
And all the little worlds, beetle or man,
Who see as much as their small natures allow.

Indefinition

As death approaches, I look back –
Même pas, for I see nothing.
Nothing is what it was, for what is now
Is nothing – or so tenuous
As not to lead a purpose by the nose.
Indefinition reigns, and who am I
Who, after long ranging among things
Which summoned words to say that they were definite,
Am lost in nothingness which now I am?

Finale

Nothing means anything now:
I am alone
– My mind a vacant space,
My heart of stone.

A tuneless thing I am,
A broken lyre.
I cannot even boast
A flameless fire.

There is the work I did
– Paper and ink –
I have no part in it:
There is no link

Between the man who wrote
– And more, was once alive,
And this relic for whom
The end does not arrive.

Although the life has gone
There is no corpse to show:
When others find it, I
Alone shall never know.

TRANSLATIONS

Roman Poems

Carmen Saeculare (Horace)

O sun, and moonlight shining in the woods,
The best things in heaven, always to be worshipped
As long as they give us exactly what we want

Now, at this season when selected girls
And the boys who are about to venture upon them,
Though still in bud, sing what will please London,

As you bring out one day and conceal another
Shine on the arms and legs and make them brown.
May all you see be greater than we are.

The time will come to open thighs in child-birth.
Gently, supervising god, look after the mothers.
Bringing to light is the true meaning of genitals.

Could you bring up these children without laws?
The statute-book is crowded, what wonder therefore
If all that interests them is an obscure kindness?

A hundred and ten years it may easily be
Before songs and games which come as speedily
As these three days, ah, and delicious nights.

You have sung truthfully enough, O fates.
Once it was ordained that everything should be stable
And will be again, but not now, or for ever.

Rich in apples, yes, and seething with cattle,
The succulent earth is dressed in barley whiskers.
And grow plump, embryo, from the natural gifts.

The sun will shine, as long as the boys are suppliant,
That will keep sickness away; and you girls,
Listen, for the moon will hear you if you do.

If you made London, as before it Engelland,
The Jutes coming over in ships, but only to be Romans,
Part of that remnant to join this one

The ways that have led here are multifarious,
Even Brutus from Troy, our ancestors believed,
But whatever they left they found better here.

You cannot credit the wish, that the young should be teachable
And old age quiet. Yet it is these wishes
Spring from the earth at last, when the country flowers.

Might you not even remember the old worship?
I could name ancestors, it is not done any more.
It remains true that, before you are king, you must win.

We have been through it all, victory on land and sea,
These things were necessary for your assurance.
The King of France. Once there was even India.

Can you remember the expression 'Honour'?
There was, at one time, even Modesty.
Nothing is so dead it does not come back.

There is God. There are no Muses without him.
He it is who raises the drug-laden limbs
Which were too heavy until he stood at Saint Martin's.

It is he who holds London from Wapping to Richmond,
May he hold it a little longer, Saint George's flag
Flap strenuously in the wind from the west country.

Have you heard the phrase: 'the only ruler of princes'?
Along the Thames, in the Tower, there is the crown.
I only wish God may hear my children's prayers.

He bends now over Trafalgar Square.
If there should be a whisper he would hear it.
Are not these drifting figures the chorus?

Palinurus (Virgil, *Aeneid* V, 835ff.)

Ho! Palinurus. Night came
Softly upon your dream.
The sailors lie, wherefore?
Slumped at the oars.
Your dream wakes still.
Not for long, while
Sleep hangs over the sea.
It is you she seeks.
Palinurus, innocent,
In quiet spent.
'Shall I entrust Aeneas to
This monster? Not so.
I have watched the fallacious air.'
Behold, god, the Lethean
Dew-laden branch is shaken
Over the sinking head.
You may call your comrades.
Palinure,
When Aeneas stirs.
'Naked and unknown,
Palinurus, your bones.'

The Descent (Virgil, *Aeneid* VI)

It follows my footsteps over these hills.

Some seek the seeds of flame
Hidden in the veins of flint.
Some crash through the undergrowth, point
To new rivers. But the same
Passions do not seize Aeneas.

He climbs where Apollo is.
And the secret parts
Of Sybil, in a dread cave,
Open, having the future.

Cut in the rock, lying huge,
A hundred mouths, you might say,
A hundred voices, Sybil responds.
To ask the Fates,
Time, it is time.
God.
Not one face or colour,
Her hair would not stay, nor colour. Panting,
Her breast like an earthquake,
Her heart swelling.
Not an ordinary voice. There is breathing
That is not her own, nearer to the god's.
'Do not stop praying, Trojan
Aeneas, must you stop? If you do
No gates can open.'

'Do not trust
Verses to the winds, but speak.
Leaves will not hold them.'
There was no prophecy. In such words,
Truth wrapped in darkness, that the utterance
Escaped my patience.
In such words, thus speaking:
'God's blood, Anchises'
Son, and a Trojan.
To descend, yes, through my entrance is easy.
Will you see the light again?
But if your mind is love, go down, cupid
Of the Stygian lakes, twice black Tartarus.
On a dark tree,
Golden, in leaf, the stem bending, a bough
This for Proserpina, a gift,
When it is torn, another and another
In its place, the same bough,
The same metal.

There lies your friend,
A corpse.'

Two doves flew.
They were my mother's birds, and therefore
Indicate.
Discoloured, in dark foliage,
As it were mistletoe,
Luminous on the oak.
Aeneas breaks it off
And carries it away under the roof of the Sybil
While on the shore the Teucrians
Paid to the last dust,
Misenus, your wishes.
The ground rumbled and the ridged
Woodlands dipped.
Through the unstable shadows
The dogs howled.
The goddess was approaching.
Then the vatic: 'Far
From everything, from this grove
Those who do not know love.'
The sword now out of the scabbard.
She entered herself, and Aeneas after.

Gods of the world of spirits, silent shades,
Chaos and Phlegethon lying in night,
Allow me to speak.
They went darkly, through night and shadows.
The whole kingdom was empty.
If there were moon's light, a wood,
A path in the undergrowth.
Night has taken the colours.
On the threshold, but inside,
Where Orcus begins,
Straw laid for Care,
With Sorrow upon her.
There are sick-beds enough. Age,
Fear, Evil Persuaders, Shortage.
They have terrible faces. Death,

Passing us ruthlessly. Sleep,
Also a brother, and the evil
Pleasures which exist only in the mind.
There were others. War
And one coifed with vipers.

A dark elm, huge, with dreams under every leaf.
Aeneas offers his sword to all comers.
I cannot however see the dead
Wailing by the water-side.
Why should they go over? A sordid
Old man, watching the girls.
Let them come to him. Charon,
Do not tip the boat in your excitement.
The dead are not lovers when
They pass your way.

I can hardly move now,
Aeneas, without your wishes.
There are several ghosts
I would wish to see.
And one especially, her hair
Plentiful where they have it,
Weeps from her head,
Too fragrant to be among the dead.
And beyond her,
One whose matted hair
Resembles Charon's.
Of him
Nothing is to be said, except
I came to seek him and
He does not exist.
The mist
Swirls up over Tal-y-maes.
He is gone with it.
An empty hill-side.
Fortune, if you are old.

Tu ne quaesieris, scire nefas, quem mihi, quem tibi
(Horace, *Odes* I, xi)

You do not ask – useless to ask, Leuconoë –
What end the gods will give, to me, to you.
Consult no augurers. Suffer what comes,
Whether some winters still, or this one only
Which now wears out the sea under the cliffs.
Think, take your wine. You are better off with sleep
And no long hopes. For, while we speak, age falls.
Collect your day, and have it. The next, you may not.

Hactenus arvorum cultus (Virgil, *Georgics* II)

Up to now the fields
Have been ploughed and the stars
Sent us home to our cottages
At the end of the day.
There has been the vine,
Even on these hills, and the slow
Growing olive.
Not only the Cotswold shepherd
But I too, with even pace,
Treading where the wind can be heard
Or some horn perhaps. But this is over.
Not even metal ringing
At the smithy, or a voice.
Water sucking the rotting
Piers,
The algae lifted
Tide by tide.
A single gull
Banking, back to the dead sea,
Cries.

★

Eheu fugaces, Postume, Postume
(Horace, *Odes* II, xiv)

The years go by, the years go by you, nameless,
I cannot help it nor does virtue help.
    Wrinkles are there, old age is at your elbow,
    Death on the way, it is indomitable.

Not if you choose, as you will choose, to doctor
Yourself with hope, will you weep out your pain.
    The underworld is waiting. There are monsters
    Such as distended you before you died.

The subterranean flood is there for everyone who has taken food and drink on earth.
    A light skiff will put out, you will be on it –
    And, win the pools, you still will go aboard.

The blood dried on you and you came home safely
– Useless. You blew out an Atlantic storm.
    – No need to fear the wind, it can do no harm.
    It brings you where you will be brought at last.

The dark, the black and, in the blackness, water,
A winding stream, it will not matter to you.
    The fifty murderesses are there, the toiler,
    Exhaustion beyond hope, condemned to dreams.

Your house, your wife, and the familiar earth,
All will recede, and of the trees you prune
    Only the cypress follow you, ill-omened.
    You were here briefly, you are here no more.

The heir you leave is better than yourself,
What you kept closest he will throw away.
    Your books are on the pavement, and his laughter
    Sounding like broken glass through all the rooms.

ESSAYS

From the *New English Weekly* (1937–1949)

Charles Maurras and the Idea of a Patriot King

We have several political poets and too many publicists, yet scarcely any writer since Hulme has formulated a precise political idea. Inevitably, both poetry and political analyses are the worse for the lack of political doctrine. I believe that Charles Maurras is almost the only writer capable of re-directing our political enquiries. He is not, by Englishmen, to be swallowed whole, but to be used. What is needed is a transposition of his ideas to fit our own place and prejudices. That difficult transposition is not attempted in this essay, which is a simple experiment. I have taken a single idea of Maurras (an idea not peculiar to him no doubt) and placed it beside an idea of Bolingbroke; the two are allowed to react in such a way as to expose a common contemporary English error.

Maurras finds in the identification of a king's interest with the public interest a chief guarantee of the efficacy of monarchy. While not without a good word for personal qualities which his taste disposes him to admire, he aims at showing the value of the monarchy independently of the value of the monarch.

Bolingbroke is concerned with a 'rare phenomenon', a patriot king, but there are fortunately passages in his essay which are susceptible of commoner application. He claims at the start that his method is sceptical, yet he is soon engaged in discussing 'duties' in a manner which is not sceptical. His intention, however, is coherent. '"Salus reip. suprema lex esto", is a fundamental law: and sure I am, the safety of a commonwealth is ill provided for, if the liberty be given up.' Liberty is justified because it contributes to the safety of the state. Similarly, we read:

> I speak not here of people, if any such there are, who have been savage or stupid enough to submit to tyranny by original contract; nor of those nations on whom tyranny has stolen as it were imperceptibly, or had been imposed by violence, and settled by prescription. But I speak of people who have been

wise and happy enough to establish, and to preserve, free constitutions of government, as the people of this island have done. To these, therefore, I say, that their kings are under the most sacred obligations.

The king must be moral because the people has a mind to be free. The constitution is such, Bolingbroke says elsewhere, that 'no king who is not a patriot can govern with sufficient strength'. The need for morals arises from the nature of the constitution. The famous English talent for humbug is not all stupidity; it corresponds to the facts of our situation.

Maurras, despite his comparative unconcern for rights and wrongs, does not represent a contrary point of view. The government he wishes to realize is decentralized; the monarchy is therefore not unlimited. In national affairs, however, the king exercises a power which he may delegate but which he shares with no one. The English constitution provides for a division of power in national as well as in local affairs; the business of the king is merely to prevent the disintegration of the central authority. The difference between the theories of Bolingbroke and Maurras, therefore, arises out of the difference of function of the English and French monarchies; it is accidental. In essence, Bolingbroke and Maurras aim at the same thing – the utilization of the king to secure the unity and coherence of the nation.

The morals of Bolingbroke are forced into their place in an empirical system. They are in no sense the starting point of his political theory. In this, Bolingbroke is at one with Maurras, who, at every point more consistent, declares himself an atheist.

If we are content to identify, as for this purpose we may, the 'justice' and 'injustice' of the Pinks with the 'absolute standards' of the Oxford Group and the 'development of consciousness' of the Artists' International Congress, it will be clear that this relegation of morals, or sentiments, to a position of dependence in politics, is in conflict with the assumptions of a wide section of political writers in this country. While Bolingbroke, attempting to justify the position of the king deductively, was taking notice of the habits of his countrymen to such an extent that his method was in fact empirical groping, most contemporary writers, while claiming to adhere more or less to scientific schools of political thought, deduce their politics from their ethical and sentimental prejudices.

An English interpretation of the ideas of Maurras would make their fault evident, and might rid us of those humane philosophies which provoke violence by demanding excessive change.

Prejudice as an Aid to Government

permitting the innocent to be possessed with laziness and sleep in the most visible article of danger.

In the fourth and fifth books of *De l'Esprit des Lois*, Montesquieu defines three springs of government and describes the education which favours each. Honour is the spring of monarchical government, fear of despotism and virtue of democracy. The 'principle' of a government is what makes it work. The government does not, however, entirely stand on its own legs; an appropriate education is required for the production of suitable citizens and subjects.

No European state now belongs wholly to one or other of Montesquieu's three types of government. England, for example, is a democracy pervaded by snobbery which is in part a decadent left-over from a monarchical caste system and by a little tyranny more lately introduced. Democracy is, of Montesquieu's three, apparently the chief ingredient of England as it is of all modern European states. (All are at least governments in which the people appears to have some voice.) We should therefore examine more closely the virtue which makes democracy work.

This virtue is, Montesquieu insists, a 'vertu politique' and has nothing to do with morals. In a later book, he illustrates this by telling us that the avarice of the Chinese is a 'vertu', whereas the honesty of the Spaniard is bad for the prosperity of the state. These examples, however, prove nothing about the nature of 'vertu politique'; they merely show that a moral virtue may cause the state to disintegrate, and a vice may hold it together. 'Vertu politique' is more closely defined in the fourth book, and there it is not successfully distinguished from moral virtue. As one might expect, if many are to govern they must be possessed of honest manners, uprightness and forbearance. Otherwise the government will disintegrate or be transformed either into a monarchy or a despotism by the vice of one man or of a group.

The 'sentiment de l'éducation' which, according to Montesquieu, is appropriate to democracy, is the honesty learned from
the manners of one's parents. Englishmen, with their long democratic tradition, should obviously be instinct with this honesty. As
everyone knows, however, the young do not imitate their
parents; rather, perhaps, the old prefer to be like their children
rather than to be models for them; the family, except as a
breeding-ground, is disappearing. There are few opportunities of
exercising virtue in public life. The citizen drops his paper in the
ballot-box with a cross against the name of one of two or three
distasteful candidates. This action may help the state to cohere;
the mere repetition of it produces a sense of easiness; it is not,
however, 'virtuous', or in itself even 'politically virtuous' and it
has little to do with democracy. There is virtue in the air,
however, in England, of the sort that the League of Nations was
built on. We may examine it more closely.

The first thing to notice is that the citizen does not do anything
with it politically. He carries it about with him and he can
produce it like a driving licence. It does, however, enable him to
react in a certain way, or rather, it is a label which tells one how
he will react. If it is useless to him, therefore, it may still be of use
to someone else and it is in fact useful to the man who makes him
react – the advertiser with something to sell, or the politician. The
passive sense of what is right does therefore help to hold the state
together. It is, however, a mechanical sentiment and by no means
an active quality.

The political thoughts which drift in most minds in England
are 'Is it right?' and 'It's not fair.' That these should be the most
popular thoughts is due partly to our tradition of democracy and
partly to our liking for religion of a certain brand. It is clear,
however, that the function in the state of passive virtue is precisely
the same as that of the passive sense of national honour which is
exploited by the leaders of Germany. Hitler has said that the
German soul has two or three strings, and one can count on
getting a certain response by plucking them. An English statesman
might say the same of the English soul. The notes would be
different, that is all.

The modern governor uses in an unprecedented fashion the
sentiments of his subjects as an instrument of government. The
typical modern state is in fact run by propaganda. Wherever the

nominal government is, the power will lie with whoever controls opinion and a government which offends public opinion will go under. Most governments, of course, once established, take care that they shall more than anyone else control opinion.

The sentiments appealed to usually are of some nobility. In England they are moral and sporting canons; everywhere they are meant to dispose people to be disinterested. Hitler has written in *Mein Kampf* an interesting chapter on propaganda. He says: 'All propaganda must appeal to the people and must be put at the intellectual level of the most limited of the minds it is directed to…. The capacity of the mass of men is very limited, their understanding small, but their forgetfulness great.' The second sentence at once recalls Machiavelli – 'It is to be asserted in general of men, that they are ungrateful, fickle, false, cowards, covetous…' Hitler is speaking of peaceful persuasion; the fact that he is an unpleasant Nazi should not blind us to that. His words might be used by any politician or man with muffins to sell. Machiavelli recommended the utmost violence. If he were our contemporary he would change nothing in his view of man; he would, however, no doubt see that a subject who can be clubbed into obedience by propaganda is not in need of rougher treatment. One may, by friendly words, give a despotically-governed people the illusion that it is free. The nobility of the sentiments the new despot governs by, makes it hard for people to understand his tyranny. Blows have this advantage, that even the stupidest do not think them signs of good intentions.

English Liberalism

Anthony Ludovici, *English Liberalism* (New Pioneer Pamphlet)

Mr Ludovici's thesis in his new pamphlet, is that the Anglo-Saxons, a race of particularists, were civilized against their will by wise rulers from Henry I to Charles I and forced to admit the authority of the state to order certain matters for the common good. Then the Puritans got the upper hand, defeated the king and made property absolutely private, at the same time re-admitting to the country the Jews, an 'uncivilized' race (in the proper sense) little better than the Anglo-Saxons. Despite the

Tories of the king's party England declined from that day. Englishmen grew both sentimental and scraggy and the stock declined so far that some are now born liberals.

I am not competent to discuss Mr Ludovici's account of the history of our decline, but on his methods I will offer a few observations. It is undeniable that races, or at any rate nations, have peculiar characters, but these characters are difficult to define. Wherever it is possible, therefore, to explain a change in a society without reference to them, one should, I think, in the interests of clarity do so. There is a further reason. Whoever talks of the national character comes near to encouraging it, and I do not think that the national character should be encouraged. It is the fund of vitality from which the conscious life of a nation springs, and if one exploits it one debauches the source of life. To develop a personal life it is perhaps best to fix one's eyes on impersonal values, and it may be better to criticize past changes in constitutions in the light of the values one at present entertains than to consider them in relation to 'national character'. 'National character' can only be a name for one's ideals and if one judges by it one is still judging by present values, only more blindly because less explicitly. Mr Ludovici would have made a more convincing case if he had not dragged in the Saxon character, as everyone must feel on reading 'The Study of Celtic Literature' that Arnold would have made a more serious attack on his contemporaries had he not used the clownish abstractions of Celt and Saxon. The changes Mr Ludovici deplores are not peculiar to England, and his case has much in common with the case which for many years M. Maurras has been making out in France.

Mr Ludovici's belief that our history is a struggle between the particularist natives and the rulers who cared for the common interests causes him to observe our present conditions erroneously. He desires for the worker a status which only the possession of property can give, but he none the less overlooks the fact that people are now forced to do more for the state than before and that the life of the ordinary worker is regulated by the state as never before. 'Particularism' is a vice few can now afford to practise.

I have written chiefly about what I consider to be the faults of Mr Ludovici's pamphlet, but the reader would do well to expend sixpence to discover the virtues for himself. In the course of the pamphlet Mr Ludovici raises many of the questions which must be considered by anyone concerned about the future of England, and he raises them with the right intentions.

The Civil Service

Emmeline W. Cohen, *The Growth of the British Civil Service* (Allen & Unwin)

This history of the Civil Service in the last hundred and fifty years is a record of improvement, and improvement is always suspicious. I certainly would not deny that the civil service is hard-working and honest, but a story of progress is almost always a story with something left out. One could write an account of a number of social and political institutions and show that they had improved, much in the same way that one could give an account of the development of the steam engine. The discovery and development of the steam engine is a thing to wonder at; obviously good, if considered by itself, for the modern railway engine has more steam than Watt's kettle, and it uses it more effectively. But the history of the technical development of the steam engine is not the history of the last hundred and fifty years, and an insulated account of the steam engine is a story which none but an imaginary abstract technician could call wholly a story of good. That engines are better than they were is undeniable; that we are better off for having better engines is a thing to be disputed about. In matters of government it is equally easy to abstract, and abstraction is even more surely a falsification. One might say that Parliament has improved because it represents more people than it did; one might assert that it has improved because each member represents a more or less equal number of voters, and places (which are not human) have no representation. Those cases involve evident presuppositions, but the development of the civil service is much more obviously akin to technical development. The civil service is a machine for governing. But it has grown more virtuous and industrious, and although virtue and industry are likely to make it work better, and, so regarded, are technical improvements, are they not also moral qualities and must not an improvement in them be pure gain? Whether so laudable an improvement may save souls from damnation I am not theologian to prognosticate, but I should not expect to find a civil servant in heaven because he had done his job thoroughly. Civil servants have improved by becoming more diligent and less corruptible, but their newly acquired virtues are not valued for their own sake. To value them so would be to adopt a partisan attitude, and it might lead one into controversy. The virtues are prized because they make their possessors impartial. Impartiality is sought in a servant of the state because it makes it more easy to govern by means of him, and to render a man impartial, and nothing more, is to denature him. It is a means of using a part of him only as one uses part only of a technician. If honesty and diligence are desired in a servant of the state, it is because those virtues are subject to utility. Utility is the principle by which one evaluates the servant; and the servant on his part has to consider only expediency. He is given the frame of things; into it he fits his actions; if his master is lucky he fits his moral notions into it, too, and then his contentment is complete and he is little likely to give trouble. He has completed the work his master proposed for him, and more than submitted to his master's demands, in his inward heart regarding as an honour what it was only proposed that he should do well for his wages. But that is a refinement; what is demanded is that the servant's action should subserve utility, that he should look at things, not as one conversant with taste and morality – if taste and morality are to be independent of his master's designs – but as one seeking the expedient. To do a thing because it is the thing that does is to be the sole guide. To wash up with a moderate amount of Rinso, just the amount needed to remove the spilt egg-yolk from the egg-cups, and to be as incorruptible as your master's affairs demand, are equal and equivalent demands made upon servants. Both demand a self-control and an objectivity which are only the result of discipline and which represent improvements of the mind that do honour to the human spirit. Both are a training of the whole person; they involve a just appreciation of the facts which is necessary before considered and useful action, and, philosophically regarded, both may be said to guide one through truth to virtue. But in this world, where one has to act on inadequate knowledge and where one serves not an omniscient God but a fallible master, merely to ascertain the facts before one is not complete virtue. For the facts appear disproportioned; the

master's will, like a grotesque shape on the wall before one, is
likely to dominate, and before one has surveyed the universe it is
time to take a decision. Some other quality besides the faculty of
appreciating the truth is required: the ability to spring back from
the dominating shape, to detach oneself, to reconsider, and
perhaps after all to take a leap in the dark. And this other quality
is the vital basis of all morals; it is perhaps the undisciplined and
primitive essence of all life.

The praise accorded to the civil service, that it is impartial,
cannot therefore alone signalize it as laudable. Indeed, the
complete and abject submission to the will of a political master,
although now so much and so easily praised, would scarcely have
appeared praiseworthy to any of our reputable forebears. In the
seventeenth century, unquestionably the time of the florescence
of the English mind, it would have been unthinkable to praise a
man for submitting to a civil power simply because it was a
power, and it is unthinkable for any whole and independent
minds at present. The impartiality of the civil service cannot be
justified to any free person merely as presenting the politician
with the perfect instrument. It is valuable as a detachment from
the rivalries of politicians, but it can have merit only in relation
to some more fundamental loyalty. It is only the Crown that gives
meaning to the virtues of the civil service. Complete impartiality
with regard to one's political masters is not distinguishable from
complete indifference, and if there were not more permanent
elements in the constitution than the changing governments the
civil servant's impartiality would be mere servility.

It is with these reflections that one admires the creditable
history recorded by Miss Cohen, and watches in her pages the
civil service growing in industry, virtue, and efficiency. *The
Growth of the Civil Service* is a valuable book, and if Miss Cohen is
not herself a civil servant, she ought to be, for she writes clearly
and colourlessly in the style of the best official memoranda. She
sees her facts without appearing to understand more of their
implications than her limited subject-matter requires, but she has
mastered her subject-matter to perfection. Everyone who is
ambitious to understand the present state of the commonwealth
should know something of the way in which the civil service has
developed, and there could be no better introduction to the
subject than Miss Cohen's book.

Charles Péguy

Daniel Halévy, *Péguy et les Cahiers de la Quinzaine*, translated by
Ruth Bethell (Dennis Dobson)

> *He never wanted for anything. They say he was poor, but it's not
> true. All that he wanted, he had; a book, a box of paints.*

A pride that is almost savagery must have dictated those words,
spoken by Péguy's mother to M de Poncheville and preserved for
us by Barrès. Pride for her generation, savagery perhaps for most
of ours, whose greatest social effort has been to make dependence
respectable. Madame Péguy's claim to her own son is established
by her words. For if she was a peasant, of a family that for generations had cut wood and tended vines, his merit is to have
introduced into letters an individuality tempered as it could only
have been by peasant virtues. Laborious and frugal, – and these
are adjectives that sound harsh in the England of today – the years
served merely to expose the stamp of his beginnings: is not every
sincere life, in a sense, a journey to the first years? 'There is
nothing more mysterious', and it is with these words of Péguy
that M Halévy opens his story, 'than those dim periods of preparation which every man encounters on the threshold of life.'

Charles Péguy was born and brought up in the shadow of
Orleans, in the faubourg Bourgogne. His father had died before
Charles was born, and the boy was brought up by his mother,
who earned a living by mending rush seats, and by his grandmother, through whom he had contact with the (dare one say it?)
vivid and irreplaceable world of illiteracy. 'We didn't even know
what school was', his grandmother would say, 'I can't even read
the names of the streets. I can't read the papers.' This deprivation,
like others, brings its rewards.

'A child brought up in a town like Orleans between 1873 and
1880 has literally touched the old France', wrote Péguy, 'the
people in the old sense, the people in fact, he has literally had his
part in the old France, in the people.... The break-down came,
if I may say so, all in a rush and covered a very short space of time.'
The break-down came, though it was so much less complete
when Péguy died than it is now, and it is Péguy's distinction to
have carried certain virtues of the old France into the new; not in
an actual, social form (no one man could do that), but in letters,

in such a manner that they can nourish and inform those living in a world where human dignity is less respected.

Péguy started his education, as was to be anticipated, at the primary school, and it was a piece of good fortune that he encountered, among the early directors of his studies, M Naudy, who determined that he must learn Latin. He learned Latin; he learned Greek; and became a master of both languages, and although he was too hard-worked ever to become what is called widely read one cannot doubt that, in what he did know, he had read deeply. His studies took him to the Lycée Lakanal, then to Sainte-Barbe and to the Mont Ste-Geneviève which was to be, in a sense, the central stage on which his industrious and provocative life was played. At Sainte-Barbe (which Jaurès had recently left) he encountered the brothers Tharaud, and a number of others who became his friends, including Marcel Beaudouin whose sister he later married. He went then to the École Normale, where his studies were broken and never brought to their anticipated conclusion because, before the end, he had married (in order to know at once all the responsibilities of life) and turned printer, publisher and bookseller (in order, mainly, to print, publish and sell his own works). His life after that date was outwardly little varied; two weeks each year with the army by way of training and for all his holiday; a pilgrimage in time of need to Our Lady of Chartres; the war which was for him a conclusion. Péguy's life was not gaudy with honours or events; it was the negation indeed of such a life and a proof that renunciation is also a form of fulfilment.

At the outset of his work as a writer we find Péguy associated with unlike and unlikely figures – Jaurès, Léon Blum: men who were, in Péguy's phrase, *capitalistes d'hommes*. A motion of the Socialist Congress of December, 1899, is quoted by M Halévy:

> There is entire freedom of discussion on all matters regarding doctrine and method; but as regards action to be taken, the [Socialist] papers must conform strictly to the decisions of the Congress as interpreted by the General Council.
>
> Furthermore, newspapers are asked to refrain from all statements of a polemical nature likely to incur the displeasure of one of the organizations.

Now after nearly fifty years, we know more about this 'displeasure

of one of the organizations'; but Péguy's attitude to this sort of
thing involved something deeper than mere dissociation from a
party line. His portrait of Jaurès, lightly drawn, is yet damning;
not merely for Jaurès but for all his kind. Between that which is
genuine and contracted, and what is false and inflated the difference is absolute. Péguy divides men (in *Jean Coste*) into two
classes, in the one men 'whose care is work, and whom we should
call classical', in the other men 'preoccupied with representation'
and whom he called romantic. The terms may be changed at
pleasure, but nothing can change the division. There are those
who work, and there are those who fuss after something more
impressive.

It is impossible to give here any adequate idea of Péguy's
work. That work is bulky; none but a specialist or a man of leisure
would read it all. It has been called diffuse and repetitive, and in
a manner it is. But it is integrated as only the work of a man who
has found himself can be. And it is a certain spareness that strikes
us in Péguy's sentences, which are all bone and muscle. M Suarès
has said: 'For him there are no synonyms. There are none for the
artist, but the artist decides. Péguy could not. He wants to contain
in his thought all the twists and inflections of conscience. He does
not choose. So he gives us all the variants. And scruple completes
the system of digression.' The characteristic of his style (or styles)
could hardly be better defined. There is no question of perfection.
Much, it must be admitted, is unsatisfactory. Only the rhyme,
often, reminds one of the order of the lines of some of Péguy's
quatrains. Of the most famous M Gide has said that they are '(to
speak moderately) very mediocre'. Maybe, though no technical
fault could rob them, as they stand against the background of the
whole *oeuvre*, of their significance. But Péguy's circuitous
method, his tact in approaching a subject, giving an indication,
receding, then trying again by a slightly different approach, is
perhaps found at its best in such prose as that of *Notre Patrie*.

That book is a marvel. For that precious writing which is also
discovery Péguy's style is a perfect instrument and here, under the
German menace of 1905, Péguy discovers the *patrie*. To that
discovery he added another – had he ever really forgotten it? –
that of catholicism. That brings us to the completed man in
whom, but without any of the trappings of antiquarianism, the
old France was resuscitated. The voice he had carried with him

from the cradle spoke; the word was made flesh. His death on the Marne in 1915 was so much a fulfilment as to seem almost an indulgence. Those most famous verses which, M Gide warns us, are imperfect, cannot be trite from such a man nor, one may add, from France.

Heureux ceux qui sont morts pour la terre charnelle,
Mais pourvu que ce fût dans une juste guerre.
Heureux ceux qui sont morts pour quatre coins de terre,
Heureux, ce qui sont morts d'une mort solennelle...

Heureux ceux qui sont morts pour des cités charnelles.
Car elles sont le corps de la cité de Dieu.
Heureux ceux qui sont morts pour leur âtre et leur feu,
Et les pauvres honneurs des maisons paternelles...

Car ce vœu de la terre est le commencement
Et le premier essai d'une fidelité.
Heureux ceux qui sont morts dans ce couronnement
Et cette obéissance et cette humilité.

He was found face-down among the beetroots.

Ruth Bethell has done a signal service in translating and Dennis Dobson in publishing this book, which is an enlarged and re-written version of M Halévy's earlier essays (never published in this country). There could be no better introduction to Péguy's work – except, perhaps, as many pages of Péguy himself.

Epitaph on Nuremberg

Montgomery Belgion, *Epitaph on Nuremberg* (Falcon Press)

'Je me demande', said Henri de Montherlant after listening to the French official broadcasts of 1940, 'pourquoi il est si rare que les hommes parlent à leurs semblables un langage humain.' And it is alarming indeed how seldom any real voice is heard in discussion of public affairs. The reasons are easy to find. For it is, after all, a somewhat rare talent to be able to speak one's mind at all; it is perhaps a still rarer one to be able to speak it on subjects distorted by the stress of rival interests which include one's own. But Mr Belgion's voice, it goes without saying, is a real one; he writes a prose which follows the conformation of a subtle and sensitive mind. The subject of the Nuremberg trials was treated with ugly relish by the popular press, and by many of us it is regarded with nothing but weary repugnance. Neither of these two attitudes is likely to produce observations of any value. Mr Belgion, however, has somehow preserved through the corruptions of the last eight years a sensitive conscience, and it is this uncommon faculty which, in this little book, is to be observed agitating among the lies and prevarications of the Inhuman Voice.

Mr Belgion starts from the observation that there has been no convincing explanation of the Nuremberg trials, and that 'the absence of one is significant. An explanation fails to convince', he goes on,

> when it is not true. If the public of the world has not been given the true explanation of the Trial, it is not to be supposed that the lack of this explanation was accidental or aimless. The true explanation was kept back for a reason. I suggest the reason to have been that it was of the very heart of the real object of the Trial, and essential to its attainment, that it should not be disclosed.

Evidently the author of this pamphlet is a man who has smelt a rat and is determined to go after it. Mr Belgion proceeds to a critique of the thesis that the trial was the outcome of a 'demand' for 'justice'. He concedes that the 'demand' was made, but demonstrates with a wealth of detail the equivocation in the use of the word 'justice'. There would be no point in recapitulating here all the stages of the argument; it is to be hoped that the reader will get hold of the book and follow them for himself. It may be mentioned, however, that Mr Belgion thinks that there was a deliberate desire on the part of the authors of the Charter '*to pretend* that no persons except Germans could commit, or be suspected of deeds defined as "war crimes" or as "crimes against humanity"'. He goes on to show (what is obviously not difficult to show) that the Allies, and one ally in particular, did commit such crimes. 'There was not one kind of deed specified in the Nuremberg Indictment as a "war crime" which one or more of the chief victorious Powers, who arrogated to themselves the task of punishing so-called "war criminals" among the defeated, was not open to being accused of.' From this it is an easy step to the statement that the trials and condemnations, which ignored 'the principle of equality before the law', were 'in accordance with the official morality of the defunct National Socialist Government of Germany'. The object of the trials was to establish the guilt of Germany 'in the eyes of the whole world, and also in the eyes of the German people themselves'.

This conclusion is a commonplace and would, I believe, have been readily accepted by nine out of every ten English people at the time when the trial was first mooted. It is the merit of Mr Belgion's little book that he shows, with a brilliance of exposition that holds the attention from the first page to the last, what dangers lurk behind this simple and commonly accepted belief. The ordinary man would be very astonished to hear that the object Mr Belgion discovers behind the trials is an improper one for any proceedings that aim at justice. Yet of course Mr Belgion is right.

He is right but.... In the present state of public morality, it is doubtful whether politicians in states ruled by the popular will could in fact have acted much otherwise than as the allied leaders in fact did act. The 'demand for justice' was there, however equivocal the justice it asked for. The error goes back to the root of our troubles, of which the Nuremburg trials were perhaps no uglier a fruit than were the false ideological 'line-ups' of the 1930s, without which.... But it is useless to speculate.

T.S. Eliot on Culture

T.S. Eliot, *Notes Towards the Definition of Culture* (Faber & Faber)

When Mr Eliot first presented himself as a writer of prose, it was in the character of a literary critic. The essays collected in *The Sacred Wood* changed the course of literary criticism in this country, so far as it had a course; and so far as it did have a course, it was time it was changed. The stream started by this whang of the magician's rod is still flowing – if the analogy of a stream can properly be used at all for anything that has become desiccated. For Mr Eliot, however, *The Sacred Wood* was only a partial statement; he quickly became uneasy, like a man who has made a remark that has been overheard out of its context and so feels obliged, not to take back what he has said, but to qualify and expand it. The first major public demonstration of Mr Eliot's reservations was made in *For Lancelot Andrewes*. In the preface to that volume Mr Eliot spoke of a wish to dissociate himself 'from certain conclusions which had been drawn' from *The Sacred Wood*: he also spoke of a wish 'to indicate certain lines of development', and from this one may gather that there had been a widening or at any rate a deepening of certain interests since the publication of the earlier volume. It was in the preface to *For Lancelot Andrewes* that Mr Eliot introduced the ghosts of three unborn books which haunted his readers for some years. *The Principles of Modern Heresy* was the happiest of these ghosts, for it found embodiment, perhaps in slighter form than was originally intended, in *After Strange Gods*. *The School of Donne* had, in a sense, been written already. No doubt, had Mr Eliot carried out the work as he intended in 1928, he would have made a number of distinctions, and we should have found that the school of Donne was not quite what we thought he had meant, in his earlier essays, to indicate to us that it was. But that ghost was less haunting because we thought, with whatever imprudent assurance, that we knew the sort of form she would take. *The Outline of Royalism* was as near to being a figure of fun as a ghost could be; at that time, and for some years afterwards, it was generally known that marxist socialism was the only manifestation of government that one need take seriously and that monarchy was merely part of the monstrous opposite – called fascism, capitalism, imperialism – by which socialism then, even more than now, defined itself. Those who had ventured beyond the permitted fields, or asphalt pavements, of marxist socialism, and read some pages of Charles Maurras, could generally only regret that Mr Eliot was plotting to resuscitate an outworn political philosophy; outworn, for to them it was evident that people who enjoyed a free and pacific life under the stable protection of the Third Republic could have nothing to learn from the *ancien régime*. The point about the announcement of the three books in the preface to *For Lancelot Andrewes* was that it involved a declaration of unpopular loyalties. There was widespread regret that Mr Eliot had gone wrong. When I became aware of these things in 1931 people told me that I might read the poetry and *The Sacred Wood* but that I was to consult *The Left Review* before believing a word that was said in Mr Eliot's later writings in prose.

After Strange Gods appeared in 1934, and bore witness to Mr Eliot's theological preoccupations and, more important and more characteristic, to his determination to take these preoccupations into studies to which they were, at that time, more often than not thought not to be relevant. To apply the word heresy at all to the writings of ordinary irreligious people, who had put forward fallacious propositions without considering their relationship to Christianity, was by way of being an innovation. The introduction of the term 'heresy' in this context is an example of that confrontation of ancient and modern, or rather of the modern and the permanent, which every sound critic of letters or manners must make, and which Mr Eliot himself has on numerous occasions made so singularly well. Mr Eliot was driving back further into the roots of our culture without losing – and indeed while gaining – in awareness of the contemporary scene.

A more significant book, from the point of view of our approach to Mr Eliot's new study, was *The Idea of a Christian Society*, which appeared in 1939. By contrast with what was adumbrated in the preface to *For Lancelot Andrewes*, the book savoured less than one might have anticipated of practical politics, or of a close application of principles to the particular needs of this country. Perhaps it may seem a little absurd to talk of practical politics – which are, among other things, more long-winded – in connection with the somewhat rarified little books I have been speaking of. But one certainly got the impression, from *Lancelot*

Andrewes, that Mr Eliot was taking a stand in something other than, or in addition to, a theoretical sense, and there are few of his writings in prose after the date of that book that do not show, as the Commentaries in the *Criterion* showed, a growing sense of the urgency of public affairs, and of the relevance of the permanent values which Mr Eliot was concerned to uphold to the day-to-day goings-on of politicians and other public men. The extent to which *The Idea of a Christian Society* falls within the world of theory or the world of practical politics, however, hardly matters. What does matter is that during the last ten years Mr Eliot's pronouncements have had a simultaneous force and relevance in both worlds. The development that has brought Mr Eliot to his present position looks like an organic growth.

The *Notes Towards the Definition of Culture* are, in a sense, a synthesis of various interests which have been exhibited in Mr Eliot's earlier writings in prose. Characteristically, he tells us, in the first lines of his Introduction, of some purposes he had *not* in mind in writing the book. He did not, he tells us, intend to outline a social or political philosophy, nor to make the book merely a vehicle for his observations on a number of topics. His aim was 'to help to define a word, the word *culture*'. In short, he is concerned to make the thing look as little like a synthesis, and as much like an analysis, as possible. In the course of the book he does the things he disclaims the intention of doing, and several other things as well. But the words of the Introduction serve to warn us that Mr Eliot is here airing only such of his views on social and political philosophy as are relevant to the definition of culture, and no one, therefore, should suppose after reading this book that he has more than partial indications of Mr Eliot's views on these matters. The book goes beyond its nominal subject-matter only in the sense that it is impossible to talk sociology without talking several other things at the same time.

In the first chapter of *Notes Towards the Definition of Culture*, Mr Eliot endeavours 'to distinguish and relate' the uses of the word which differ according to whether one has in mind 'the development of an *individual*, of a *group* or *class*, or of a *whole society*'. 'It is part of my thesis', he says, 'that the culture of the individual is dependent upon the culture of a group or class, and that the culture of the group or class is dependent upon the culture of the whole society to which that group or that class

belongs. Therefore it is the culture of the society that is fundamental.' Mr Eliot then goes on to 'try to expose the essential
relation of culture to religion', and here he comes to a point
which is original in more senses than one, and somewhat abstruse.
He wishes to 'make clear the limitation of the word *relation* as an
expression of this "relation"'. Mr Eliot conceives 'culture and
religion as being, when each term is taken in the right context,
different aspects of the same thing'. Therefore neither can culture
be preserved or developed in the absence of religion, nor religion
preserved and maintained without reckoning with culture. But,
if there is question here of the unity of religion and culture, there
is no question of their identity. Hence 'aesthetic sensibility must
be extended into spiritual perception, and spiritual perception
must be extended into aesthetic sensibility and disciplined taste'.
It is true that Mr Eliot speaks as if religious standards and aesthetic
standards were ideally identical; or, to report him more accurately, as if to judge by either of these standards 'should come in
the end to the same thing', but he is careful to add that that 'end'
is one 'at which no individual can arrive'. The whole of the
passage from which this is taken must be studied in Mr Eliot's
own words – in all his own words and not merely in summary,
comment or even quotation. It is, I think, the central point of the
book and, incidentally, it is the point at which Mr Eliot's prose
exhibits the maximum of suppleness, passion and refinement. In
these pages Mr Eliot seems to be struggling to express the perception which is the basis of all his subsequent ratiocination, and the
writing shows at moments almost an excess of its own essential
quality, just as a paragraph of Sir Thomas Browne may seem, even
when the intensity of the writing is at its greatest, pleasurably
over-burdened with its own very different self.

After explaining his theory of religion and culture, Mr Eliot
goes on to discuss three of the conditions for culture. 'The first of
these', he says,

> is organic (not merely planned but growing) structure, such as
> will foster the hereditary transmission of culture within a
> culture: and this requires the persistence of social classes. The
> second is the necessity that a culture should be analysable,
> geographically, into local cultures: this raises the problem of
> 'regionalism'. The third is the balance of unity and diversity in

religion – that is, universality of doctrine and particularity of cult and devotion.

The first two are conditions that were evidently likely to strike a man whose political philosophy was of the kind to which Mr Eliot was supposed to belong, but it would be unfortunate if readers who do not share the views that they imagine to be his were thereby distracted from a careful study of the relevance of the persistence of social classes and regional differentiation to the persistence of culture. The reception Mr Eliot gets as a sociologist is bound to suffer from the fact that he has long ago declared certain loyalties, contrary to the practice of the typical modern intellectual, who looks up from his books or his test-tubes and announces that his long sojourn in the world of thought has taught him that he should join the party, and that he advises other chaps who want to be thought thoughtful to jolly well hurry up and do likewise.

It is the later chapters of this book, I think, and particularly the notes on education, which are likely to receive most immediate attention from the public at large. There would be no great harm in this, if people were thereafter and thereby coaxed into a consideration of the more fundamental matters with which the book starts. That may not always happen, however, for Mr Eliot's remarks on education are not only of great intrinsic interest but of great emotive force. There are several wholesome but unpopular truths in this final chapter, and it is unfortunate that Mr Eliot's presentation of them has in it an element which is bound to alienate certain readers more than the truths themselves would do. Mr Eliot's long residence in this country has not, one might guess, enabled him to see the country's social structure otherwise than as an outsider. The result is, one suspects, that he has an unduly simplified notion of what constitutes the governing classes, and perhaps attributes undue weight and value to the upper and upper middle classes. It may not be altogether extravagant to suggest that the fact that he tolerated – even from a collaborator – the sort of 'working class' dialogue that appears in *The Rock*, shows that his perception of what goes on in the working classes is or was somewhat blunted. In a note to the *Idea of a Christian Society* which is of special interest to the reader of the present book, Mr Eliot says: 'Britain will presumably continue to be governed by the same mercantile and financial class which, with a continual change of personnel, has been increasingly important from the fifteenth century.' That was hardly perspicacious, even for 1939, and a man of much less remarkable gifts, born and brought up in this country, would have avoided such a presumption. A similar defect of social perception marks some of the comments on education in this chapter. It is difficult, in the context of present society in England, to attach much meaning to being 'educated above the level of those whose social habits and tastes one has inherited', at any rate in the cases where the education has had any appreciable effect on the subject. And it is a pity that, in discussing the case against equality of opportunity in education, Mr Eliot has, as it were, looked at the problem from the top side only and spoken of the educated being unpleasant, or merely too numerous, and not concerned himself with the lot of the underdog, who would be deprived of his natural protagonist in the person of the man of lively wits who remains in the subordinate classes. One wonders, too, what Mr Eliot considers constitute advantages of birth in present-day England. The idea is not a simple one at any time; one might always ask whether a high degree of literacy in several consecutive generations may not deprive the heir of those generations of more than it gives him.

Without any major questions of principle being settled, or even more widely agreed upon, much that is done in this country might be better done if certain assumptions were less lightly made. Mr Eliot's approach to a definition of culture might be recommended to politicians, but for the fact that politicians are rarely of an age or temper to be persuaded to abandon their assumptions. To Mr Eliot's ordinary public, recommendation of any of his books is superfluous, but one may say that this one has a special interest for those who follow the elusive line of this paper. It is, by the way, inscribed to Philip Mairet.

Ego Scriptor: The Pisan Cantos *of Ezra Pound*

Ezra Pound, *Pisan Cantos* (Faber & Faber)

If one remembers, after eighteen years, the time, the weather and the exact place of one's first encounter with the work of a particular writer, it is safe to say that that writer produced an initial effect. If, after that time, one is still reading him with pleasure as well as admiration, it may be that the total effect has been one of those real adjustments of mind which even the most omnivorous reader can expect from only a few writers. At any rate, a sense of special benefit derived from the early works of Mr Pound is my excuse for the somewhat personal tone of this notice. The first lines by Mr Pound that came my way came as a quotation in an essay or article:

> For three years, out of key with his time,
> He strove to resuscitate the dead art
> Of poetry; to maintain 'the sublime'
> In the old sense. Wrong from the start –
> No, hardly…

It at once became imperative to read 'Hugh Selwyn Mauberley', which meant, incidentally, waiting until my next birthday for seven and sixpence to buy the elegant dark green volume of *Selected Poems* with Mr Eliot's preface. The most prominent element in the immediate response was the excitement induced by the rhythm of the verse: it was as if a kettle-drum were being played somewhere near the base of the thorax, left side. When I acquired the volume of *Selected Poems* and read 'Hugh Selwyn Mauberley' in its entirety, I was again delighted by unfamiliar rhythms; and when I read backwards to the poems of *Cathay* and *Personae*, there was the pleasure of tracing the process by which that personal voice had disengaged itself. One who is neither a maker nor a critic of verse must speak of these matters with diffidence, but as a reader one may record an impression that rhythm is the ligament that binds together the body of a poem; without vitality of rhythm, vivid images, pretty sounds and fine thoughts look as if they were sewn up in a bit of old sacking instead of a skin. There are many contemporary verse-writers who are bores because they can give you only a rhythm made originally for another poem, or worn by scores so that one doesn't know to whom it belongs. In Mr Pound's mature verse the rhythm has such vitality that I could read him with pleasure if I understood him no more than I do the Chinese ideographs with which his pages are embellished. I hope, however, that the situation is not quite so bad as that.

This is no place to add my mite to the confusion that exists on the subject of what is meant by 'understanding' a poem. 'Understanding' is something that people more respectable than myself assure me that they burn to apply to everything. If they look, for example, at a picture, and are in danger of feeling pleasure from it, they either declare that 'they don't understand it' or they apply their understandings to some object which, but for their assurances to the contrary, I should have suspected wasn't the picture: in either case, it seems, they feel better for having avoided submitting to the indignity of pleasure. With a poem, the same sort of difficulty arises. There are readers who have scarcely read a page of the *Cantos* before they have abandoned the verse to ask about the logical structure of a whole that is not yet completed. Luckily, one can refer them to *A Packet for Ezra Pound*, where Yeats tells how Mr Pound scribbled on the back of a postcard various groups and combinations of letters to indicate the fugal structure of the poem. That is one kind of answer, and it should be explained that the structure was so designed as to permit, or even to demand, the inclusion of records of some contemporary events, so that events which have occurred since the *Cantos* were originally planned can find reflection in them. One may add that, if it is still too early to judge of the structure of the whole, every page gives evidence of the effectiveness of particular juxtapositions and consequently proof of at least skill in designing the pattern in little. And if the design of the whole seems unlikely to embody dogmatic conviction any more than consecutive narration, that may be because 'States of mind are inexplicable to us' and 'Le Paradis n'est pas artificiel' and 'Nothing counts save the quality of the affection.' But this is hardly the place to pursue the traces of the philosophy of the *Cantos*, with which Mr Eliot expressed his disagreement before the first of them were published in this country.

The most useful thing the reviewer can do, by way of introduction to a fragment of a work not yet completed, is to show that the fragment is in itself rewarding, without reference to

considerations beyond it or to the completed work to come.
Quotations should induce readers unacquainted with the *Cantos*
to start on that voyage which begins with: 'And then went down
to the ship, / Set keel to breaker'; and they should satisfy those
who have read the earlier volumes that Mr Pound's hand has not
lost its astonishing skill. No quotation, however, can convey an
impression of the continuous readability of these *Cantos*; and
continuous readability, in a long poem, is much more rarely
achieved than the prominent place given to numerous long
poems in the histories of literature would lead one to suppose.
The readability is produced, I think, largely by the rhythm, which
is as varied and vigorous as the rhythm of many well-spoken-of
long poems is soporific. The rhythm forces one to attend, and in
some manner justifies the elipses and other terenesses of expression which, by cutting out what is inessential for immediate effect,
themselves promote readability. Mr Pound can tell in four lines a
story which would fill a page – perhaps more profitably to the
author – in a book of reminiscences:

> and the navvy rolls up to me in Church St. (Kensington end)
>   with:
>   Yurra Jurrman!
> To which I replied: I am *not*.
> 'Well yurr szum kind ov a furriner.'

Or, for those of more refined humour, there is Uncle William,
who made a great Peeeeacock and

> who would not eat ham for dinner
> because peasants eat ham for dinner
>   despite the excellent quality
> and the pleasure of having it hot.

In a line Mr Pound can convey a reminiscence and a lament:
'Orage, Fordie, Crevel too quickly taken', or a reminiscence and
a critical reflection of general validity: 'Fordie / never dented an
idea for a phrase's sake.' He speaks plainly, and he can use allusion
to reinforce his own plainness: 'and that day I wrote no further'.
If you want 'poetical' subject-matter:

> Here are lynxes   Here are lynxes
> Is there a sound in the forest

of pard or of bassarid
or crotale   or of leaves moving?
Cythera, here are lynxes
Will the scrub-oak burst into flower?
There is a rose vine in this underbrush
Red? white? No, but a colour between them
When a pomegranate is open and the light falls
half through it

And I do not know in what terms to commend these verses from
the eighty-first Canto:

Pull down thy vanity, it is not man
Made courage, or made order, or made grace.
Pull down thy vanity, I say pull down
Learn of the green world what can be thy place
In scaled invention or true artistry,
Pull down thy vanity,
Paquin pull down!
The green casque has outdone your elegance.

'Master thyself, then others shall thee beare'
Pull down thy vanity
Thou art a beaten dog beneath the hail,
A swollen magpie in a fitful sun,
Half black half white
Nor knowst'ou wing from tail

Pull down thy vanity
How mean thy hates
Fostered in falsity,
Pull down thy vanity,
Rathe to destroy, niggard in charity,
Pull down thy vanity,
I say pull down.

That is magnificent poetry: it is also plain speaking that might
serve as a model for any writer, in prose or verse.

Order and Anarchy: An Essay on Intellectual Liberty

Introduction

The relation of the free mind and person to the state is at present a chief concern not only of writers of every kind, from the low and high journalists to our half-a-dozen men of genius, but more obscurely, of everyone whom an extraordinary fortune has not politically neutralized. The subject has often been treated explicitly; more often it is an implicit part of some subject itself of more or less importance. It has acquired the quality of an obsession as the problem of morals did in Arnold's day. And it is, for moralists, itself a problem of morals.

This essay is concerned with the relation of the individual and politics, but the subject is limited in several ways. It contains no recipe for preventing any political or unpolitical person or group from starving or maltreating the reader or depriving him of his goods. It is concerned with the relation of the independent mind with society. Certainly I do not pretend that there are not practical conditions which must be satisfied before any complicated thinking can be effected. On the other hand, those conditions granted, whether the thinking is fruitful or sterile depends to a considerable extent on the methods of thought employed. This essay is a study in method.

The subject is further limited by the fact that, in writing, my eyes have been on British democracy. Other forms of government have not been forgotten; it would have been an act of genius to forget them and to think for a moment of England alone. For my present purposes the difference between British democracy and the fascist and communist régimes is insignificant. I shall not treat of morals, but that does not mean that the difference between the several kinds of states is necessarily insignificant for morals. My subject is the method of thought which best solves the question of the relationship of the free intellect with politics to the advantage of the intellect. Politics too may, I believe, derive some advantages. Naturally I do not suppose that I have added much to what better writers have said.

The future of Europe is to wars and military governments, but this essay is written with the gaiety which is obligatory in an intellectual.

I. Motives and Subject of the Essay

There have been of late many books on political matters, but few among them in which the principles of politics are enquired into. Enquiry into principles is not perhaps publicly discouraged, but anyone who turns his attention from certain popular questions is likely to be accused, in one manner or another, of inhumanity, as tomorrow he may be accused of lack of patriotism. This essay does not deserve to be called an enquiry into political principles, but it may be regarded as a demonstration made in favour of such an enquiry. In it certain questions are asked which, if they were truly answered, would make ease of mind more attainable, and all its inhumanity is there. I am aware that there are persons of good sense who believe that one should immerse oneself as fully as possible in the torments of the age, and who will therefore be out of sympathy with the motives of the essay. The motive of the essay is not, however, its subject, and the humane reader will not be shocked by an account of the virtues of the serene life. He may, I hope, be induced to consider by what gentle roads one may come upon fanaticism.

The essay concerns the state of the free person. Most of the words in our English vocabulary have become debauched and depraved, and it is difficult to speak unironically of 'liberty' or to use the word with much conviction that one knows its meaning. It will be necessary to define at the outset the manner in which the word is used here if the whole of what follows is not to be hopelessly misunderstood.

II. An Account of Freedom

We are to consider intellectual liberty. I am not concerned with the liberty of lives or properties or with the freedom of the body from hurt. The reason for my unconcern is certainly not that I think these matters unimportant, but that in order to say one thing one must keep silent about others. And my reason for keeping silent on the matter of civil freedom is that I think one can have nothing of interest to say about it until one has proposed a solution to the more obscure question of the freedom of the mind, for if the civil freedom one devises is to be freedom at all, it must first allow the mind to be independent.

Freedom, whether of body or mind, is independence, and it assumes the existence of something on which one might, but does not wholly, depend. The freedom of man in a state is independence of the state. It is evident that one cannot be completely free; it is even evident that complete freedom would be meaningless, but, supposing the reader to agree that some measure of independence is possible, we may examine the principle of independence, leaving the question of the degree in which the principle might or should be realized to politicians and their theorists.

III. The Definition of Freedom is Negative

It may be objected that the definition of freedom we have adopted, having no positive content, is meaningless or in some manner valueless. To that we must reply that a positive definition of freedom would contain something besides the idea of mere freedom; the question of what liberty is is not the same as the question what liberty is for. The definition of freedom as independence has, it is true, no meaning until one has defined the thing of which one may be independent. It implies a definition of the state, which is not the same thing as a political theory.

IV. The Principle of Government

There are several kinds of state, but we are not in this essay interested in distinguishing them. We have not to describe the mechanism of particular states but to identify the principle of government.

Statesmen talk so much of liberty that it is forgotten that the state is a machine that governs us independently of our wills. If it governed us according to our wills – supposing such a thing to be possible – it would become invisible and die because there was nothing for it to do.

It may be argued that the state need not govern independently of our wills and that in a democracy the government merely organizes the wills of the people and may in fact be in accordance with them. The answer to this argument is that the work of organization is the work of suppressing those whose wills appear not to coincide with that of the state. Further, the state should for our present purposes be looked at not from the point of view of the 'people' – an abstraction so nebulous as to be meaningless – but from the point of view of the free person, an abstraction less difficult to apprehend because it is realized less or more in every reader. And it is clear that in a democracy it is impossible that the will of the free person should become the will of the state, for if it did the state would cease to be a democracy and would become a tyranny. In a tyranny the wills of the members, other than the tyrant, are by the definition of that state incapable of realization.

It may still be objected to our account of the state that the members of at least democratic states may pay their taxes and perform their civil duties of free will. One performs these duties, however, in the knowledge that the state may force one to comply with its polite requests, and when therefore one acts in accordance with the will of the state it is hard to be certain that one is not acting because of the state's threat of force.

V. The Relationships between Person and State

If the state is to be regarded as independent of our wills and capable of constraining them it will not be improper, from the point of view of the free person, to identify the principle of government with force. And if government is the exercise of force, the person will not be free so far as he is subject to it. The delimitation of the frontiers of government is a matter of some difficulty which will be attempted in succeeding sections of this essay, and it may at present be sufficient to say that, as the means of compulsion are many and people commonly succumb to them, we shall assume the relationships between state and person are affairs of force wherever it is not evident beyond doubt that they are free.

VI. The Impossibility of the Citizen being Free

One consequence of the accounts we have given of government and of freedom is that it becomes necessary to regard the citizen as in a condition of servitude. There can be no such thing as a free citizen in the sense in which we are using the term free, and a person is free in so far as he is something other than a citizen.

It should be understood that in this section the term citizen is used in its most limited sense, and the duties of citizenship are taken to be not those which a private taste or conscience imposes but solely those which the government exacts for the reason that it is a government.

VII. The Notions of Civil Liberty Compatible with Intellectual Ability

We have said in an earlier section that it is not possible to devise a satisfactory theory of civil liberty until one has solved the question of intellectual liberty. It may, however, be of assistance in understanding the limits of government if we now say what kind of theory of civil liberty will be in accordance with the account of intellectual liberty we are giving in this essay.

It follows from our account of the state as the embodiment of the principle of force that civil liberty will be the freedom of life, person, property and action from the control of the state. And it follows that this freedom will exist only so far as the state tolerates it, or so far as the principle of government is inoperative in the state.

In what manner may the state tolerate the existence of civil liberty? In so far as it embodies the principle of government, it will do so by allowing apparent disorder which it has force to reduce to order. Persons will appear to be outside its system of force when in fact they are not so.

This idea is implied in the definition of liberty given by Montesquieu and others as liberty to live according to the laws. The state may change the laws, and in any case one did not choose the laws which have already been made, but one has liberty in the sense that one will suffer no violence so long as one acts in accordance with the pronounced will of the state.

The extent of one's freedom, according to this definition, may be small, and one may be much at the state's mercy. The content of certain of the laws may, however, be such as to give an appearance of more liberty under certain conditions.

The chief method of giving an appearance of greater liberty than the naked person could have in the face of the laws is to legislate for the security of property. This is the matter of interest in Locke's otherwise dull book. The position of the owner of property may in practice be more secure than that of the man without property, but his position before the state is fundamentally the same. The law may be changed and the privileges his property gives him may be suspended or destroyed.

The idea that civil liberty may depend on property is of interest in this essay for another reason. Property means force and a man with property may be more free than a man without because he is temporarily able to resist the state's force with force and to obtain civil liberty by making a local disorder.

VIII. The Mind as a Force in Public Affairs

Unlike the body, the mind does not secure its liberty by force, although the body may, of course, obtain certain of the conditions of liberty for it. The conditions the body obtains for it will, however, be the conditions in which the mind may be free, and it is to succumb to a delusion of the most dangerous kind to suppose that there are physical conditions (and in particular, political conditions) in which the mind will inevitably enjoy independence. Its freedom is a result of its own act or attitude.

In speaking of the mind, I have attempted to give no definition of it. I am aware that this may lead to difficulties. It would have been possible to give a definition, but I am not sure that it would have been possible to give a satisfactory one, and I have preferred to take the word with all the looseness with which it is commonly employed and to allow the sense in which it is here used to appear gradually as the context exhibits it. The reader is asked to remember this in reading the present and the following sections.

Although people often speak as if the mind was, or could be, a power in the conduct of public affairs, they often do with a notion even vaguer than the one we entertain of what the mind is. It is obvious that they cannot mean that reason, as the mere power of observing contradictions, in any way governs. They may often be thinking of the part of morals in politics. It is not necessary to understand the philosophical notions of the state which their view of morals may imply to discuss the part of morals in politics, so long as one discusses it from the point of view of politics and not from the point of view of morals. From the point of view of politics, morals are sentiments whose political function depends on the fact that they are common to a number of people, and usually more nearly identical in people grouped together in one state than in people in different states. The function of morals, as well as the distinctions between different kinds of morals, will be the subject of later sections of this essay. What is important here is that these sentiments may be used, as physical objects are used, as the weapons of a directing mind, and that it is not the mind as director, but the weapons, which constitute the force. The question whether the force can exist without the directing mind is a separate question which we need not discuss.

The mind as governor must on our account of government be the utilizer of force. Its function is, in the simplest terms, the employment of violence, and fraud, ruse and treachery are methods proper to it.

IX. Propaganda

We are little concerned, in this essay, with the effects of physical violence on the free person, but much with the manipulation of sentiments. The latter method of exercising force supplements the method of physical violence and government is complete only when both methods are used. As literacy has spread, the manipulation of sentiments has taken a larger part in government, and it may be said to have replaced some physical violence.

All propaganda has this characteristic, that it tends to make of one opinion those to whom it is directed. The opinion is not necessarily that of the person who is responsible for the propaganda, but it may be assumed to be an opinion which he desires for good reason that people should hold. Propaganda unites the people in such a manner that they are more useful to the propagandist.

It is only the people influenced by the propaganda who are united by it, and propaganda diffused by people of opposed interests is likely to form hostile groups. Propaganda in favour of a race and propaganda in favour of a class have the same effect in this: they unite some people only to divide them more sharply from others. It may be said, I think, that, *ceteris paribus*, the more propaganda there is in any group the less physical violence there is, but propaganda tends to intensify the feeling of difference of one group from another and therefore causes more hostility and probably more violence between them.

It follows from what has been said of the unifying effect of propaganda that liberal propaganda, which none the less claims to exist, is a contradiction in terms. The propaganda invites one to abandon one's individuality, and propaganda pretending to be in favour of individualism really serves some other cause. It forms a compact mass of minds which tends, when it moves, to move as a whole. Even if the propaganda which united the mass was not consciously directed, its effect is to form a mass which may with ease be directed. The mass may, moreover, be directed by persons whose sympathies are not at all with those (supposing, what is not difficult, a case in which they exist) who originated the propaganda because they believed in it. The great efficacy of liberal and individualist propaganda lies in the fact that it denies that it is propaganda. The innocent individualist, by helping a work of propaganda, produces a result which is the opposite of his intentions. With great enthusiasm and good will he plays into the enemy's hands.

The battle of the individualist in politics must in the nature of the case always be lost, and in the nature of our case the battle must today be more than ever completely lost. That may of course not be a reason for declining to fight it, but the matter of this section should provide reasons for not fighting it with the enemy's weapons.

X. *Public Displays of Sentiment*

The efficacy of propaganda depends on the persons to whom it is directed sharing certain sentiments. The common sentiments will before the intrusion of the propagandist be among the things that hold the group together, but the propagandist will make them more efficacious for that end in several ways. He will upset the organization of sentiments which before his intrusion was related to the people's factual environment, and he will overdevelop certain of them so that, finding no satisfaction in their immediate environment, people project a fantasy on the state and live vicariously. The sentiments are no longer directly related to the people's activity.

It is impossible to distinguish neatly between these detached sentiments and those directly related to private life, and it is with some reluctance that I attempt it. It is necessary, however, to remark that the increase in public displays of sentiment marks some change in the function of sentiment. The change is not, however, a complete change of kind, nor is it entirely recent. It is merely that we have the privilege of observing detached sentiments in a more than commonly inflated condition, and we have that privilege because our public life is more than commonly disgusting.

XI. Democratic Morals

The moral sentiments which are prominent in British democracy are detached sentiments of the kind we have been describing, and the amoral spectator may think that they are part of a moral method different from that of La Rochefoucauld and Pascal. One of the differences may appear to be that Pascal and La Rochefoucauld observe, whereas the morals commonly displayed in British politics appear to be the work of a prophet rather than of an observer. It must not be thought that I am accusing my country in particular; I am describing, in local terms, a political mechanism which is also to be seen elsewhere. The mechanism happens to work particularly well in England because we are politically so mature.

On closer enquiry the public morals of England may appear to be after all the work not of a prophet but of a statesman. It is notorious that to continental observers it appears that our moral indignation subserves some end of imperial policy. They imagine our public men hatching plots with an entertaining duplicity of which certainly not all of them are capable. That the duplicity is sometimes conscious I would of course not deny, but more often it is the effect of political tradition. The successful policies of the past have left behind them a sediment of feelings which indicate the way statesmen should behave in certain circumstances.

That the phenomenon is not a new one may be understood by a reading of *The Idea of a Patriot King*. Bolingbroke invites the king to be moral because, in a country where the people have a mind to be free, it is for his safety.

XII. The Modern Popular Governor and the People

In modern popular states, whether they are called democratic or fascist, the governors appear to be at one with the will of the governed. They appear not only to be part of the same system of force as the governed, but to be the same kind of part. They share, or appear to share, popular feeling, and act as they do because of, or apparently because of, those feelings. They do not stand above the people and direct it: they usually like it to be thought that any other man (of the same race or nation) would have done what they did, had he been in office and had he had the wits to think of it. The directing will be supposed to be the people's. I am aware that this description may appear to be inapplicable to Germany and Italy, but it must be remembered that I am talking of the matter as the leaders intended it to be viewed by the common person and not as it may appear to the wary reader of the more conscious and acute pages of *Mein Kampf*. The description I have given is, however, in some ways more obviously relevant to the democratic states.

The local democratic statesman is one who is merely a part of the sentimental system of the whole people. It has already been demonstrated that a democracy cannot express the will of the people composing the state, and a corollary of this proposition is that the ideal democratic statesman cannot exist.

XIII. The Common Man of Action

The common politician is half governor and half one of the governed. He does not exercise force in such a manner that his will embodies completely the principle of government; he is partly sentimental and acts partly at the orders of sentiments which he shares with the governed. I am not speaking now of the governor who takes account of and makes use of the sentiments of the governed; that procedure, as we have shown, is perfectly in accordance with the principle of government. I am speaking of the politician who is partly deceived by his own propaganda.

The unconscious politician is the type of the common man of action. The ordinary man at his work takes the floating propaganda about him and makes it his own. He uses it, unconsciously, and he is deceived by it. Within a system of force, he brings himself to believe that the floating ideals are the reasons for his action. And in a manner they are, for he is sustained by the illusions created by the propaganda.

It is more often vanity than avarice or the desire for any tangible good which is the motive for action. The common man of action cannot bring himself to believe that he is merely part of a system of force, as he most often is, or that the motives of his actions do not deserve to be called by exalted names, as they most often do not. He cannot think any action he engages in unimportant, and appears to reason at the back of his skull that he engages in it and *therefore* it is important.

It will be seen that the error arises because he believes himself to be free where he in fact is not so.

XIV. The Machiavellian and Popular Sentiments

The machiavellian prince is the opposite of the democratic statesman. He stands apart from the people and he does so not only because he is the source of physical power in the state but because he is highly conscious of the moral forces at work in it and is therefore able to manipulate them. He is not sentimental, and observes popular prejudices only so that he may use them to bring the people more entirely within his system of force.

The machiavellian dissimulates because the objects of the persons composing the state are not the same as his own, and he has to appear to share their prejudices in order to render them patient. Dissimulation is necessary in manipulating both the sensible and the moral interests of the people. It is necessary for the people to think that the prince's ambitions will not make impossible the realization of their own, and it is necessary for them to find the prince a man tolerable to their consciences so that they will feel no moral discomfort in living under him, and so that they will be able to trust him not to lay hands unjustly on their goods.

XV. The Special Position of the Machiavellian in the State

The position of the machiavellian governor in the state is unique. He is as it were the point of intelligence in the system of force: the people, so far as they are deceived by him, are the blind parts. They pursue, as they think, their several ends, and he in every act perceives the mechanism of the state.

It is evident that the machiavellian statesman comes nearer than any other to embodying consciously the principle of government. He is the utilizer of force, physical and moral. For what purposes he may utilize it does not in this essay concern us.

XVI. All Government is Machiavellian

The machiavellian differs from other governors only in the degree of consciousness with which he exercises his function. All politicians, so far as they really govern, are utilizers of physical force and manipulators of sentiment. None is entirely in sympathy with the people and the distinction of the machiavellian is merely that he understands that he is not in sympathy.

XVII. The Freedom of the Governor

Having defined the position of the governor in the state, we may enquire whether the privileges of his special position include freedom. Freedom we have defined as independence, and it is clear that the governor cannot be independent of the state for the reason that he is the state. We have seen that the subject's civil liberty is made by the creation of a condition of disorder and this disorder is only apparent so far as the state really governs. The 'freedom to live according to the laws' is conditional on the will of the governor. We saw also that real disorder may be created by a man who has sufficient force to resist the demands of the state, and this, so far as it is maintained, is real civil liberty. The liberty of the governor is of the same type as the real civil liberty of the subject: it is obtained by the exercise of force against whatever threatens it. Only it is not the state, but other forces which are potential governors, which threaten the liberty of the ruler.

The liberty of the governor and that of the disorderly subject are both liberties of action, and it is by action that they are maintained. It is therefore useless for us to look here for intellectual liberty, although a political theorist might look here for certain of the physical conditions of some of the free activities of the mind. It may be added that in any system of force few can take part in government, and few can be disorderly subjects. If liberty of practice were the only kind of liberty we could enjoy, we should enjoy very little of it: and only few would enjoy even a little.

XVIII. The Free Activities of the Subject

The free activities of most persons in the state are made possible by apparent or conditional liberty. By free activity we mean here any activity which is irrelevant to the state's system of force. It may be expected that people will not in all cases be in agreement as to what activities come within the system of force, and about one kind of activity people are particularly likely to disagree. That activity is the reading and writing of literature.

XIX. Literature and Intellectual Activity

It is not my intention to attempt, in a section of a brief essay, to propound a new theory of art, nor have I one to propound. But because any conception of intellectual liberty which is of any interest must allow for the free production of works of literature, and because I was stimulated to write this essay partly by a feeling of dissatisfaction with the verse of certain of my immediate seniors, it may be well to make a few observations on the relations of literature and government. I should perhaps add that these remarks are not made in the belief that political criticism can replace literary criticism, but in the belief that the two are complementary. The uneasiness one feels in reading faulty political verse is due to literary faults, but political criticism may be able to account, in part, for the manner in which the faults arise. And this may be of use to the common cause which literary and political criticism serve.

The political critic would have nothing to say about the verse of Mr Herbert Read (although he would no doubt have something to say about Mr Read's recent theorizings). The faults of the verse, which give most of it, interesting though it is, too low a degree of tension for poetry and make it fall without impact on the mind, are faults which can be explained satisfactorily without going beyond the limits of literary criticism. Mr Auden's work is different: its method, no less than its subject matter, invites one to examine its author's political position.

The position of Mr Auden is well known. Expensively taught, and then an expensive teacher, he professes socialism. I am not sure that a purely proletarian communist movement could exist, and I am aware that there are theories which justify the position of the bourgeois instigator of revolution, but I do not understand the virtue of a socialism whose vital parts are bourgeois. It looks extremely like the usual politician's game of liberating the people for the politician's advantage.

In this essay it is not the virtues and vices of Mr Auden's socialism as such which concern us, but the effect which the contradictory position he stands in has on his writing. Because he is a communist, Mr Auden must appear to oppose the bourgeoisie, and because he is a bourgeois he cannot do so by having the sentiments of a proletarian. Every writer in a manner opposes his class when he sets his original perceptions beside the popular and sentimental productions which embody the prejudices of the class. This opposition would not, however, suffice for Mr Auden and his friends, because it would not be a political opposition. For a political opposition it is necessary to pit one body of prejudices against another, and because the prejudices of the working class are not his to use, Mr Auden had to make an artificial opposition. This is the function of the group of friends whose names appear often on the poems and dedications. They form a band which fights a harmless and often imaginary battle against our rulers. The

prejudices of the group are a variety of the prejudices of the bourgeois proper, and they are in fact part of the sentimental means by
which we are governed. It will scarcely be denied that Mr
Auden's best work is that in which these prejudices have least part,
and in which he merely records his perceptions. The bad part of
his work is the sentimental and political part.

This distinction between public sentiments and private
perceptions appears to me to be fundamentally the same as the
distinction between good writing and bad. If this in fact is so, it
may be said that bad writing is writing which expresses the politically manoeuvrable sentiments and is therefore part of the system
of force which is government. Good writing alone may be
described as independent of government, and one has intellectual
liberty just so far as one has the capacity to distinguish between
valid work and invalid.

XX. Methods of Political Thought

If popular sentiments are to be regarded as part of the instruments
of government, and if one is to be regarded as free only so far as
one is not at their mercy, it follows that thought which takes them
as its premises will not be independent of the state. The position
of abstract thought is not radically different from that of art. Its
starting point is the perception of the thinker, and if the thinker
sees nothing for himself his work will be valueless.

It follows from what has been said in the preceding sections
that free judgement on political events is not common. It is rarely
that people are able to judge without becoming part of the instruments of government, for it is only when they abandon the usual
categories of thought and protest as an act of art that their judgement is free.

It is not, however, my intention to recommend that we should
replace political thought by intuition; the example of the surrealist
politicians effectually warns us against that. Attempts to think
about politics in a manner appropriate to artists ends in the same
manner as attempts to think about it in moral terms. One must
persuade, and one finds that one has therefore abandoned one's
personal perceptions and is speaking in terms of the popular sentiments exploited by propaganda. One becomes a fanatic.

It is evident that in our account of literature and of government political thinking must be anarchical if it is to be valid as
thinking, but that is not to say that it must be such as will tend to
reduce existing governments to a condition of anarchy. There are
two kinds of political thought compatible with our idea of intellectual integrity. One is that of the person who criticizes the state
in terms of his private tastes (as distinct from the popular prejudices he entertains). This will be a kind of protest against the
conduct of politicians, but the anarchical thinker will hardly hope
to have a notable effect on them. He will understand (what M
Benda has pointed out) that ideas have political effect only when
popularization has denatured them. The other kind of political
thought compatible with intellectual liberty will consist not in
protesting against government but in understanding it. It will
consist in considering every political situation in terms of force,
and it will seek to discover in any situation how far the influence
of force extends. In some cases it will at that point come near to
the frontiers of literary criticism.

XXI. The Method Appropriate to Intellectual Liberty

Art, and protest of the kind that is akin to it, are uses made of
freedom, and a definition of them is not a definition of the
method by which freedom may be attained. It is not now difficult
for us, however, to give an account of the fundamental condition
of free intellectual activity. The method of thinking which makes
free intellectual activity possible is to look in the state, as in all
organization, for the principle of order, which is force, and to
detect the action of that force on actions and opinions. The
present essay is a modest illustration of this method.

XXII. Conclusion

It may be well to state, in conclusion, several implications which
this essay has not, and to give an opinion on another resolution
of the difficulties which are the subject of it. In doing so certain
of my own preferences, which I have so far tried to suspend as the
writing of a critical essay demands, may become evident to the

reader. The preferences do not, however, affect the validity of the method described in the essay, and the reader who has understood, and who has no taste for the tastes of others, need read no further.

It is not my intention to conclude in favour of political anarchism, nor of any form of government. As for political anarchism, I do not know whether the conditions which would make it possible could anywhere or anywhen obtain, so the question whether it is desirable is of no importance and perhaps of no meaning. As for the various forms of government, none for itself commands my loyalty, but I think that one may be justified in having a strong preference for one or another in a particular time and place. I admit the practical necessity of government, and my interest is to see that the form of it I live under is as little as possible offensive to my taste. But I should not expect to find my taste satisfied by any state.

Because the method of thought we have described includes a method of political thought which comes near to that of the machiavellian, it is in a manner a resolution of the opposition between the practical and the speculative intellects. The politician will almost certainly not be a complete machiavellian, and in any case he will be concerned to act, but the anarchic thinker will understand his function and we have shown that he will not be a fundamental political agitator. There is no reason why a man should not both enjoy a certain intellectual liberty and be a political actor, but if he does so he will be conscious of his duality. The mind will not go waving its arms with the body.

I am aware that this solution will not be satisfactory to those who entertain belief, and for them this duality will not exist. It exists for the unbeliever because action is inevitable and in any case for the pleasure of life proper, and because the tastes are not satisfied in action, and so long as they are only tastes and not beliefs there will be no motive for unsuccessfully trying to satisfy them. It is to my liking to recall in my final sentence that several of the most profound minds of England in the last hundred years have been believers: but to recognize them is not to be converted.

Charles Maurras

Charles Marie Photius Maurras was born in 1868, two years before that Third Republic whose enemy he was to become. The place of his birth was chemin de Paradis, Martigues (Bouches-du-Rhône) and it was there that he was domiciled when, seventy-seven years later, he stood on trial for his life on a charge of treason.

Scattered here and there in the writings of Maurras are indications enough to satisfy the imagination, if not the more popular faculty of curiosity, as to the conditions and circumstances of his childhood. His parents had three sons, of whom he was the second, but the eldest died before Charles was born. For several years Charles enjoyed the privileges of an only child, and soon after his younger brother came into the world his father left it. The father was a minor official, punctilious in the performance of his duties but with energies and interests left over for ideas and a mind on which Racine, La Fontaine and Voltaire had left their traces. Above all the father was, in the recollection of his sons, the source and embodiment of songs and dances. 'Sacred, profane, whatever is sung in church or at the opera, French, Latin or Provençal, or a mixture of the three, he knew everything, forgot nothing and ... he conveyed the movement of his resonant soul to the ear of his wonderstruck child.' That was not without significance for the journalist whose passion for letters was second only to his passion for the doctrine he taught and who was to say, in the course of a superb apology for his supple and lucid prose, that 'reason may convince, but it is rhythm that persuades'. Madame Maurras was of a different temperament from her gay and ingenious husband, and Maurras claims to have inherited from her whatever he has of will and seriousness. The two parents differed in political outlook as in temperament. Madame Maurras never had the slightest faith in the republic: 'but your father', she would dutifully tell the young Charles, 'took the opposite view.' She would recall how, when she was a small girl, the Prince de Joinville had visited her parents' house; she had expected a prince out of a fairy tale and met a young man whose naval uniform associated him with the forces that govern the world. If there was this reminder in the recollections of Madame Maurras, that royalty has a modern dress and function, there was in the popular aspirations that centred round the comte de Chambord an imagination that lifted contemporary politics into the timeless and pastoral world: '*S'Enri V deman venié!*' An old servant, Louise Espérandieu, had seen the King and Queen pass over the bridge at Avignon on their way to Paris. Maurras carved on his school-desk again and again V.H.V. (*Vive Henri V*). Then, at the age of twelve or thirteen, these loyalties were swept away by that philosophy of liberty which, in one form or another, has had to be encountered by every youth since at any rate the eighteenth century, and which indeed represents a persistent illusion to which local philosophies and aspirations have perhaps at all times given shape. The form the illusion took in the mind of the young Maurras was determined by Lamennais, a reading of whose *Paroles d'un Croyant* was the occasion of its inception. Maurras became a theocratic republican. Absolute justice demanded community of goods, equality of parents and children, masters and pupils. Maurras had swallowed all the claptrap. He was, however, unlike those who go mumbling mouthfuls of it all their lives, able to digest it. The period of rumination was one of that lofty and sceptical indifference which is a common feature of adolescence. It lasted roughly from Maurras's sixteenth until his twentieth year. Meanwhile, objective studies supervened, and he was drawn to consider the relationship between laws and institutions and the strength and weakness of states. He discarded the idea, essential to the romantic insurrectionism of Lamennais, that there is an irresolvable opposition between the interests of governors and governed. He began to reflect on the function of élites, which serve the multitude whether they will or not. His scorn for the 'many and absurd opinions' of the multitude grew at the same time as his passion for 'a small number of coherent and reasonable propositions'. This development marked out the shape of the finished man.

Maurras had taken his baccalaureate at the Catholic college of Aix-en-Provence, and in 1885 he had taken up residence in Paris. It was in the capital that he pursued those studies of history, philosophy and the social sciences which first enabled him to define his position. He was not, at first, much interested in practical politics, but the ideas that were ripening within him were bound to bring him, sooner or later, to take his stand in public discussion of matters affecting the government of France. Inseparable from the Provençal revival with which he had contact through the Ecole Parisienne du Félibrige was an aspiration towards decentralization and the revival of the provinces. The stories which Maurras wrote in the early years and collected in his first book, *Le Chemin de Paradis*, were dominated by a concern, somewhat general and theoretical in character, for the public good as well as for the purity and clarity of the abstract idea. The book, under the influence of a contemporary fashion and, perhaps more intimately, of Dante, was allegorically or analogically constructed so that, when one meaning was stripped off you were left, like the reader of a palimpsest, with others. These ingenuities have faded, and it is unlikely that anyone now, unless it be some student burrowing for a doctorate, will disengage from these stories more than is to be got at a normally attentive reading. But that much attention will show with what sort of man we have to do, and the author, as if already, in May 1894, doubting the efficacy of his allegorical method, made the main outlines of his mind clearer in the preface he addresses to Frederic Amouretti. He laments that in his generation even those young men who seem to love ideas love them 'as dead beauties'. There is a touch of romantic and melodramatic gesture about this, but in retrospect there seems to be still more of the impatience of one for whom ideas are heavy with personal consequence. 'The doctrine of the *Chemin de Paradis*', he says, 'is that the good life consists in misprizing nothing ... and then ... creating interior harmonies.' Knowledge and self-discipline are enjoined, and the two points at which it is possible to achieve a little discipline and agreement are said to be science and the love of one's country. Those who try to weaken those two supports of a public and objective reason are treated with the same contempt or disdain as those who waste their energies in an absurd pity for themselves or others, and those who seek to awaken concupiscence in the brains or bowels of merely instinctive people who might blessedly have died without having lived. The preface contains also the germs of those ideas about the Roman church which were to cause such scandal. Maurras describes his chain of ideas as 'sufficiently pagan and Christian to deserve the fine title of Catholic which is that of the religion in which we were born'. He speaks of 'the odd Saint-Simonian Jesus of eighteen-forty' to whom he opposes the Jesus 'of our Catholic tradition, who was on earth crucified for us'. 'Divinity is a number; everything is numbered and limited.' He has in mind particularly, in this part of his plea for harmony and measure, the Germans with their passion for the infinite. 'I am horrified above all by these Germans.' At this point his most abstract studies are touched and enlivened by his deepest passions. For he belonged, as he had occasion to recall at Lyons in 1945, to that generation which the socialist Jules Ferry reproached for being 'hypnotized by the blue line of the Vosges'. The defeat of 1870–1 had made 'revenge the Queen of France', and Maurras was not the man to fail to pay her a proper tribute.

The seedling ideas springing in the work of Maurras at this time showed that the moment was about to come when he could take his full and active part as a political controversialist. The year in which, in the little essays of *Trois Idées Politiques*, he extracted and defined the political sense of Chateaubriand, Michelet and Sainte-Beuve with a dexterity and firmness which showed him to be the complete master of his method, was the year when the Dreyfus case broke upon France. It is difficult, in the battered and bludgeoned Europe of today, with its inattention to ideas and its hebetude under repeated crises, to make present to oneself anything of the impact which the allegedly false condemnation of a single army officer had on the France of 1898. It was, however, not the fate of the mere individual officer that interested and impassioned the public. The case was something which, dipped into the politics of the day, caused the ideas therein held in solution suddenly to take shape and cluster about it. Dreyfus was a Jew, and it was alleged that he had been condemned on account of his race. The Minister of War affirmed that Dreyfus had been properly and regularly convicted. Those who put the safety of France before the rights of an individual were content to leave the matter there. Those who thought that justice must be done though the sky fell sought a revision of the case. No doubt it was possible for a patriotic Frenchman to take either view of the matter, and ranged with the Dreyfusards were such men as Péguy. It was not patriotism merely, but his understanding of certain principles of state, which put Maurras on the anti-Dreyfusard side of the discussion. Justice as well as patriotism, he contended, were on that side. There was much fevered discussion as to whether Dreyfus was innocent or guilty. Maurras did not concern himself much with this question. His view first and last was that 'if it happened that Dreyfus was after all innocent, by all means make a field-marshal of him, but a dozen of his principal defenders should be shot for the triple wrong they were doing to France, to Peace and to Reason'. Maurras, already himself convinced of the necessity of the monarchy, drew a moral from the *affaire* in an article entitled 'What good would a king be?' In the disquiet of the fully developed *affaire*, Barrès had said: 'There is no possibility of a restoration of the commonwealth without a doctrine.' His words must have reflected a need of which many patriotic and thoughtful Frenchmen were beginning to be aware. Maurras was, among the young nationalists of his day, the man equipped to indicate a doctrine and to give it precision. The original members of the *Action Française* group, which came into being under the shadow of the *affaire*, were not royalists. But they held like Maurras that the *patrie* was above everything, and it was inevitable that their views should give way to the more precisely formulated views of the latter. The *Action Française* was the movement of 'nationalisme intégral'. It was Maurras who showed them that that doctrine required objective embodiment in a king. The *Enquête sur la Monarchie* began to appear in 1900.

And so, at the beginning of the century, the stage was completely set for singularly coherent action which Maurras was to lead for fifty years. The paper, which became a daily in 1908, already existed in 1899. Names which long appeared in its pages were already associated with the movement. There was Vaugeois, the founder, Maurice Pujo who was at Maurras's side at the trial in 1945 and who was condemned with him, and Jacques Bainville whose lucid analytical mind commanded respect in quarters which viewed with suspicion or dislike the more polemically-minded members of the group.

The Ligue d'Action Française was founded in 1905. The declaration which had to be signed by its adherents contained, as was proper, a sufficient abstract of the doctrine Maurras was teaching. 'A Frenchman by birth and spirit...' it began. The doctrine was not one for all comers. It was not designed to correspond with an emasculated, Kantian reason. It was of France, and for the French: '...in mind and in will, I undertake to conduct myself as a patriot conscious of his duties'. The *ligueur* was expected both to understand and to act. Then came the declaration of enmity to the Republic.

I promise to fight against republican rule. The Republic in France is the rule of the foreigner. The republican spirit disorganizes national defence and favours religious influences directly inimical to the traditional Catholicism. France must once more be given a system of government that is French.

Our future therefore lies in the Monarchy as personified by His Grace the Duke of Orleans, heir of the forty kings who, in a thousand years, made France. The Monarchy alone ensures public safety, and making itself answerable for order, prevents the public ills which are denounced by anti-semitism and by nationalism. The Monarchy is the indispensable organ of the common interest, and enhances authority, liberties, property and honour.

I associate myself with the task of restoring the Monarchy. I promise to serve it by every means in my power.

One hears there echoes of the Dreyfus affair and of the current controversies which centred around the Christian democrats of the time. The monarchy was the means whereby alone could be secured the safety of those things to which the 'Frenchman by birth and in spirit' would be devoted.

Maurras had three main subjects of study and polemic in the years preceding World War I. They were: the weakness of the republic and the correlated strengths and benefits of monarchy; the religious question; and the German question. All three left their traces in the declaration. The references to the German question were, it is true, not explicit, for the declaration naturally kept to generalities, but it was that question which gave urgency to the other two. The *Action Française* grew up under the shadow of the German menace.

The doctrine of monarchy which Maurras conceived was determined, like every branch of his doctrine, by an acute sense that his beloved France was without adequate protection either from external enemies or from the enemies who weakened and denatured her from within. 'Yes or no, is the institution of a traditional, hereditary, anti-parliamentary and decentralized monarchy a matter of public safety?' Yes, ran the answer, put in a thousand forms as opportunity and occasion arose. France must have a central power which is strong, independent and essentially national. A traditional monarchy can provide this because by definition it gives perfect continuity, and independence of the popular storms and prejudices of the day. It is something to be accepted without dispute, an institution beyond the control of subjects, something handed down, *given*, like an indestructible monument or the original proposition of a geometry. It must be hereditary, because inheritance obviates those struggles about succession which are the weakness and distress of states under the hand of a mere Caesar or lifelong dictator. Moreover, the continuity of heredity binds the ruling family to the fortunes of the country for an immeasurable future. The hereditary monarch cannot conceive any future either for himself or for his family which is not dependent on the future of the country. The monarchy must be decentralized, so that people can go about their business and their business can be something that they know about. It must be antiparliamentary, for the king must be a king who governs, and the meddling of a parliament could only weaken the unity and continuity of royal power and hamper the identification of the king's interest with the national interest which is the guarantee of the efficacy of monarchy. The king has the whole cake, and is likely to guard it jealously. The members of an elected assembly, no less egotistical, will quarrel over the size of their slices. The king's egotism will serve the common good; that of the members of an assembly will be hostile to it. Moreover, an elected assembly is driven hither and thither by the claims and complaints of those who put it in power, but 'a cry, even a loud one, is worth just as much as its cause is worth', and the independent government of the king will judge of things as they are and not as the people or their tribunes make them out to be. Maurras respects the people, vehicles of ancient traditions and the arms and legs of France, but he might say with our Charles I 'as for government, it is nothing pertaining to them'. He was fully aware of the difficulty of 'any reform that is a little noble', and did not expect to rally the mass of the populace to his side. The scheme of revolution he favoured was the revolution from above. Monck and Talleyrand were the models he admired. He conceived an action discreet, economical and effective, carried out by a handful of determined men. The means of communication in the hands of a government of the twentieth century make it possible for a competent government to resist insurrection, but also make it possible for insurgents who have seized a few key points to exercise an instantaneous and powerful influence over a wide area.

The treatment Maurras accorded to the religious question, no less than his treatment of monarchy, was determined by his concern for the safety of France. His writings on this matter had, he said, no other object than 'to unite the separated members of the French nation'. He declared himself an atheist. Differing from Catholics as to what is true, he sought reconciliation and agreement on what is useful. The useful was sufficiently defined for him by the idea he had formed of the needs of France. He had no concern for the truth of the revelations the Church teaches; he was concerned to support her merely as a vehicle of a Latin tradition. '*I am a Roman* because Rome, from the time of the consul Marius and the divine Julius ... sketched the first outline of my France. *I am a Roman* because Rome, the Rome of the priests and the popes, has given the eternal solidity of feeling, manners, language and worship to the political achievement of the Roman generals, administrators and judges.' You could not have a more complete Erastianism of principle. Maurras maintained that 'societies of higher type exclude all forms of religious difference. The city-states of antiquity did so, and with very good reason. With very good reason too, the Roman Empire did so.' Maurras would have been on the side of Julian the Apostate. He would have shared the horror of those Roman men of letters for whom Christianity appeared as the substitution of a barbarous and formless semitic literature for the measure and order of the classical texts. In the twentieth century, he defended the institution of the papacy because he thought that, but for the Pope, 'the written monuments of the Catholic faith would necessarily acquire whatever religious influence was taken from Rome. The texts themselves would be read, and read literally. The literal text is Jewish and if Rome does not explain it, it will exert a Jewish influence.' Maurras was giving a new, anti-semitic twist to the counter-reformation. It was the influence of the Jewish spirit, not merely the undisciplined voice of the individual conscience, that he wanted to suppress. He regarded the language and the poetry even of this country as 'infected, for the last three centuries, by dishonouring hebraisms'. At this point his treatment of the religious question touches his criticism of literary romanticism. He stood, as in the days of the *École romane*, for 'the restoration of classical taste and of feeling for tradition in letters'. The safety of France, for him, was the safety of these traditions: armed defence and literary criticism were complementary.

One might say that Maurras, with a habit of mind so unlike that most commonly and complacently admired among Anglo-Saxons, believed in the effect and force of ideas. If a man holds ideas that directly or by long implication, threaten the state, beware of him! It is not merely Maurras's taste as one for whom Paris is the unique surviving and the third in historical order of the capitals of the civilized world, that is offended by the protestant and judaising elements in the French thought of the time. Whatever weakens a man's loyalty and subordination to Latin traditions makes him a less reliable Frenchman. The criticism of ideas is at one with the hostility to those foreigners, often Jews, who drift in and out of the country at the call of interests and conveniences which have nothing to do with the welfare of France; who enjoy civic rights, but exercise them with regard to sectional interests. For them Maurras employed the designation 'métèques'; we might say, after Blackstone, 'denizens'.

Maurras, the devoted servant of his Latin heritage, execrated the Germans. He attributed to them, and to the Jews who had worked like a leaven in their country, everything that is formless and crude in the thought of the time. The northern barbarians who from time to time came, in Montesquieu's phrase, 'to break the chains forged in the south', according to Maurras came to destroy an order and harmony to which they were insensible. The marks in their behaviour of an immature civilization – so acutely noted by Barrès in *Claudette Baudoche* – their passion for gazing inwards, where there is no measure, instead of outwards into the world of shapes and colours, the tactless elaboration of their metaphysical systems, all evoked his contempt. He feared the 'servitudes … threatening to weigh upon Gaul', and feared that France would let herself be overwhelmed by the barbarians. Later, when the barbarians had in fact come, as he had foreseen, and had been turned back at the Marne, he addressed them thus:

O toi, plus basse que les terres
D'où sont vomis tes combattants,
O dans ta paix et dans ta guerre
Singe inutile des Titans,

Race allemande qu'enfle et grise
L'impunité de la traîtrise
Et l'ignorance de l'honneur,
Aucun reproche ne te presse
Comme du manque de sagesse
Qui de tout temps souilla ton coeur.

But if Maurras held Germany and Germanism in abhorrence, he did not fail to make that dissociation, failure to make which has, in this century, led to such wide aberrations, on the part of statesmen and public, from political courses obvious to plain reason. Loathing Germany, he could yet admire the mechanism whereby unity of power at the centre gave strength to the periphery. Why should the civilization of France, so much better worth preserving than that of Germany, be denied a similar source of strength? The principle of absolute rule was, anyhow, a Latin principle. The Germanies had been distinguished until the ideas of the Revolution had awakened them, by a fissiparousness which found expression in the innumerable principalities of the old Empire.

It was in the light of national struggles which they to some extent concealed that Maurras understood the progressive movements of the century. He did not particularly admire nationalism, preferring in principle the international orders of the Roman Empire and the Middle Ages. But no such order exists in our century, and meanwhile it is nonsense to talk about the brotherhood of workers. The socialism of France weakened and divided her; the socialism of Germany was made to serve the cause of national unity on which its survival depended. There were only two ways of bringing about the political unity of the world. The first was by a universal and simultaneous outburst of goodwill, which an educated man, or any man with his head properly screwed on, could see to be an impossibility. The second had the advantage of having been tried already. 'The people of Rome seized the world and imposed on it by force or by ruse its language, its laws, its manners. Catholicism repeated the same fortunate and spiritual effort.' The fearful question that recurred in the writings of Maurras was: what if the same success should come 'to the power of Germany? to German thought? to both at once?'

If Germany was the primary menace, it was not only against

her that the interests of France had to be defended. England was in those days also something of a power. A sentence Maurras wrote in 1921, in elucidation of his views of 1905–14 on the foreign policy of France, carries its echoes to a date much nearer us. 'A country like ours, placed physically between Germany and England, does not have to choose one or the other; it should first of all love itself.' The alliance with England was *necessary*. Maurras had no doubt about that, because the interests of France and England, so different in certain respects, were in other respects identical.

When the war broke out in 1914, Maurras who, while Jaurès had been dreaming of brotherhood with German workers, had been announcing 'une épreuve que tout prépare', made a truce in his hostility to the Republic and supported the successive governments which undertook to lead France to victory. No one seems to have doubted Maurras's patriotism during those years – no one, that is, except M Paul Claudel, who took the trouble to testify to the court in 1945 his impression that the enemy had during World War I found Maurras's articles useful in compiling his own propaganda. A moving dedication dating from 1915 shows in what spirit Maurras addressed himself to the tasks of that time: 'With you, if my body had had the worth of my mind, I should have armed myself and fought…' One need not envy those who, having read anything of Maurras's work, can doubt the sincerity of that dedication.

The judgement of Maurras on the treaty of Versailles is summed up in the title of the volume of his contemporary writings on the subject: *Le mauvais traité*. The treaty was bad because it failed to encourage German particularism and left the country more united than ever. It was bad because it failed to resuscitate the Austrian Empire and so facilitated the course of Pan-Germanism. The basic error, which Maurras attributed in particular to President Wilson, was to regard the struggle in Europe not as one between Germanism and civilization but as one between the lily-white principle of democracy and the evil demons of autocracy. This false antinomy has persisted ever since in the minds of the statesmen and publics of the western powers. If it were possible for all the international disasters of the last thirty years to be due to a single intellectual error, this would be it. For Maurras, it was a matter of indifference whether or not Germans

were allowed to drop little bits of paper into ballot boxes. Nor
was the complexion of the alleged principles of the governments
resulting from this or some other procedure of primary importance in his eyes. What mattered was whether a German
government was put in a position from which it could control a
unified national machine. If it could do this then it would, sooner
rather than later, give expression to the historical Pan-
Germanism. The Second World War was implicit in the treaty
which had ended the first. This was not, as was the identical,
though differently motivated contention of practical Germans and
of the more unpractical Anglo-Saxons, because the treaty was too
harsh. It was because it was mechanically wrong. It did not
arrange the forces in play in such a way that the balance could
remain stable. Behind this error was Wilson's false antinomy.
There was the ingenuous faith that nothing much could go wrong
with a Europe where every person had a vote and every nation a
House of Commons.

The recovery of Germany between 1918 and 1933 was what
Maurras had anticipated. He supported every move which, like
Poincaré's initiative of 1923, tended to improve the relative position of France at the expense of Germany. Such moves were rare
and inadequate enough. Moreover, the treaty which had sanc-
tioned the Weimar Republic had completed Bismarck's work of
unifying Germany. It had provided the machinery for a national
action. The republican form lasted as long as it served any national
purpose. Under its tutelage the German army survived and was
re-formed. At the same time, the conduct of German democratic
politicians under various pressures from their electors and from
the western powers inevitably provided matter for criticism
which was exploitable and was in fact exploited by the nationalists. Maurras did not see 1933 as another stage in the imaginary
battle between democracy and autocracy. He saw it as an act of
resolve by the barbarians, who now once more felt sure enough
of themselves, and of the weakness of their prey, not to trouble
themselves any longer to hide their intentions.

It was a sign of weakening national consciousness and growing
befuddlement in the west that this obvious interpretation of
events commanded little interest. Indeed, in the thirties the old
false antinomy of principle, in a slightly modified form, became a
popular obsession. The term 'fascism', which should properly

have been reserved to denote a certain Italian nationalist movement, enjoyed the success of the century in a widely extended
sense. Such coherence of meaning as it possessed derived from
Marxist theory, and its popularity served no one but the communists. Meanwhile, there was increasing confusion as to the
meaning of 'democracy', the other half of this precious pair.
There was an increasing tendency to suppose that the more left-
wing a party was, the more democratic it was. This delusion
likewise served the interests of communism.

Maurras disdained the false antinomy in the new form as in the
old. It was indeed beneath the attention of a literate man. He
continued to see the conflicts in Europe as national conflicts. Italy
and Germany in turn had had national revolutions. One did not
have to suppose that they must necessarily be permanently in
league because both had disposed of the anti-national, including
pro-Russian, elements within their borders. The old national
differences would remain and perhaps become more marked. It
would be one of the objects of a prudent foreign policy to distinguish the differences and to profit by them. Moreover, if one were
able to allow oneself the luxury of a preference, there was no
question but that the preference would go to the country whose
civilization was the sister of that of France. It was these considerations which led Maurras to oppose action against Italy at the time
of the Abyssinian war. No action must be taken which would
jeopardize Italy's participation in the Stresa front and perhaps
throw her into the arms of Germany.

When civil war broke out in Spain, Maurras at once recognized the independent and national character of Franco's
movement. An independent Spain was to be preferred, in the
interests of France, to one under the influence or direction of
Moscow, Maurras supported Franco and did what he could to
discredit the Reds.

In 1938, Maurras counselled against a war which he knew
France was not ready to fight. He thought the declaration of war
in the following year ill-advised. A rational foreign policy, in his
view, must be based on force: the foreign policy of France must
be based on force in the service of France. No doubt war with
Germany, some time or other, was inevitable; no one had
watched its approach with more open eyes than Maurras. But
France should not, in Maurras's view, do anything to provoke

war while she was weak and Germany was strong. That was to invite a disaster which might be mitigated if it were deferred. To those who said: But if you let Germany go on unchecked, she will consolidate her position in central and eastern Europe and be stronger than ever, Maurras replied: Even if you declare war, you can do nothing for Poland; do not threaten what you cannot perform. If France herself is attacked, then there will be no help for it. Then you must fight.

The pact between Russia and Germany which was the curtain-raiser to the war can have caused Maurras little astonishment. For years he had been saying: In certain matters the interests of Russia and Germany go hand in hand. Russia aims at provoking a war in the west. It is odd to recall that in the thirties there were respectable, even eminent, people in England and France who imagined that Russia was burning to defend the rights and interests of the common people of the west. Surely Stalin had read all the Marxist pamphleteers, and knew about the menace of fascism?

Hitler and Stalin were, of course, looking after the interests of their respective countries as they conceived them. That was what one expected of a head of state who had real power. The laws that govern the strength and weakness of states are the same for Roman and barbarian. Meanwhile, who was looking after the interests of France? The answer, Maurras was convinced, was: Nobody. A congeries of politicians at the centre of things was no substitute for a king.

Once war had been declared, there was no further room for debate on the merits of the declaration. France must be defended. Maurras did not support those who called for displays of non-existent strength against Germany. The trial of strength would come. Meanwhile, France must try belatedly to make herself strong. When the trial of strength came it was settled according to the immutable laws that govern such matters. The government was handed to Pétain by the President of the Republic which had had its day.

Maurras left Paris when it was known that the city was not to be defended. The *Action Française* re-appeared on 1 July 1940 at Limoges and then, in October of the same year, the office was moved to Lyons, where it stayed until the allies arrived in 1944. In those four years Maurras was the brilliant apologist of the

Pétain régime. He did not think it necessary to approve or disapprove the Marshal's acts. Obviously Pétain would be subjected to various pressures from the enemy; obviously he would not be able to speak his whole mind in public. But he could be trusted to serve the interests of France with honour and discrimination. Maurras had long admired Pétain, and had perhaps considered him as a possible General Monk. However that may be, 'the worst of our defeats has had the good result of ridding us of democracy'. The assumption of power by Pétain gave Maurras the hope that some possibility of future greatness for France might still be saved.

From the days of Limoges onwards, the *Action Française* daily carried the *manchette* 'France, and France alone'. The words were a summary of the policy of the paper, indeed of Maurras's whole thought. France should love herself first, Maurras had said years before. What made people in England assume that, if Frenchmen showed signs of unwillingness to serve England, it must be because they wanted to serve Germany? It was probably that the question was put in a form which excluded the third possibility. In spite of the Russo-German pact, which should have enlightened the dullest, thought was still conducted in the obfuscating categories of Democracy and Fascism. Maurras was not a democrat, *ergo*, he was a fascist; he would flock with birds of a feather, *ergo*, with the Nazis. Yet 'France, and France alone' was a reasonable policy for (to employ an antiquated phrase) a man of honour.

France had suffered military defeat, which is inexorable. In these hard circumstances, Maurras no doubt recalled that France had rejected an armistice in 1870 only to be forced to accept harder terms in 1871. No doubt, in 1940, France was at the mercy of Germany. But even such a disaster as 1940 was not to be treated as if it were the end of the world. France must go on. And for this there must be a French government on French soil. This government would do what it could for the people of France. In the face of the powerful barbarians this might not, physically, amount to very much. None the less, a French administration would do what it could to mitigate hardships which could not be avoided. The people would not be abandoned. The head of the state, watching over the fate and interests of France, would be able to seize opportunities of improving her position. The war would not go on for ever. Had not the very enemy who had overrun France herself been a defeated power in 1918?

It is not to be supposed that Maurras approved the actions of all those about the Marshal. He did not. Some, including Laval, he considered to be traitors. Only those who, with complete loyalty, served the French interest, were to be tolerated. No doubt it was not, in the conditions of 1940–44, easy or indeed always possible to distinguish those people, but the principle was clear. When the Militia was formed to defend the will of Vichy, it was 'Oh what happiness'. But when Maurras discovered later that organizers of the Militia were in contact with the Germans, he took them for traitors. He opposed the *maquis*. If the government which he thought essential to the future of France were to survive, it must govern. It must not permit dissident elements to take the law into their own hands. If it did permit disorder, the Germans would inevitably intervene and French government in France would be at an end.

'France, and France alone.' To a German officer who repeatedly saluted him in the hope that the salutation would be returned, Maurras at last said: 'It is useless, Monsieur, I do not even see you.'

Maurras was arrested on 8 September 1944. On 27 January 1945 he was condemned to imprisonment for life for intelligence with the enemy.

The *Action Française* has failed. What Maurras did during the war was no doubt, as he said, 'a form of resistance like any other, less romantic, perhaps', but it would have served its purpose fully only if the democratic régime in France had been permanently overthrown. On the desirability of that we, who are not French, have not to pass judgement. Our British interest is merely that France shall be strong. Pétain is in prison, and de Gaulle is at large in France, a restless critic of the Fourth Republic. We have not to suppose that, in the eyes of history, the two will be held to have served different causes. And history will record that among the *maquis* were many communists, who were only temporarily and provisionally the friends of France.

But although Maurras and his movement have failed, for his lifetime at least, to bring back the monarchy to France, it would be rash to say that even that practical objective has been brought no nearer by their action. At the trial, when Maurras confronted the representatives of the Republic in what was almost certainly the last of his many encounters, the moral victory was his. The reader of the trial, now or a hundred years hence, is unlikely to envy the role of '*Monsieur l'avocat de la femme sans tête*'. The record remains, and crowns the work of a lifetime. It may yet operate as the record of the trial of 1649 operated in 1660. At least it will work as the trial of our Charles I has done to form and direct minds applied to the issues, rarely enough considered, on which the health and fate of states finally depend.

The work of Maurras has its point of departure in the Revolution of 1789. The work of Hooker perhaps contributed to our being spared a disaster similar to that of the French, but the rebellion of 1642–60 has left upon our history and in our minds scars that go deep, and 1789 and 1917 were salt in these old wounds. No doubt Maurras is not the man to set all to rights for us. He is a Frenchman, speaking for France. But he can help us, inasmuch as a preliminary to any satisfactory synthesis of our political ideas must be a re-statement of that side of the case whose apologists have so miserably defaulted.

Fervet opus.

Reflections on Marvell's Ode

I

It is rarely that a crucial event in our national history is adequately celebrated in verse. When this does happen, the national consciousness is enriched by something more than the mere event and something more than the mere poem. The Dalai Lama, who saw the film of *Henry V* and then, a studious boy of fifteen, turned to the text, received, there can be no doubt, something more valuable than a diplomatic assurance. Heroic verses, the property, so far as any can be, of a living nation, quicken a stranger's sympathy and enhance the nation's stature. So much for the man who gives permanent form to the courage expended in a battle. But what shall we say of that rarest kind of poet who, standing at an intersection of times, declares his position so truly that, after three hundred years, we can still thereby find our political orient? I would not like to have to name two such poets in our literature, but one was Andrew Marvell, in turn tutor to Cromwell's ward and Fairfax's daughter, assistant to the Latin Secretary, and Member of Parliament for Hull, to whose electors he most discreetly avoided speaking his mind.

The 'Horatian Ode' was written in the early summer of 1650. Cromwell had just returned from the visit to Ireland which is still popularly remembered and mythologized in that country. He was made captain-general and commander-in-chief of the parliamentary forces in place of Fairfax, who had scruples, and he was about to enter upon a campaign in Scotland. With this campaign, and with the return from Ireland which was the nominal subject of the poem, Marvell was only incidentally concerned. He could spare wit to say:

> The Pict no shelter now shall find
> Within his party-coloured mind;
> But from this Valour sad
> Shrink underneath the Plaid:
> Happy if in the tufted brake
> The English Hunter him mistake;
> Nor lay his hounds in near
> The Caledonian deer.

On the subject of the Irish campaign itself he is almost perfunctory: 'And now the Irish are asham'd / To see themselves in one year tam'd.' The embarrassment his subject gave him is shown by the only lines in the poem which smell like the official praises of a laureate:

> They can affirm his Praises best,
> And have, though overcome, confest
> > How good he is, how just,
> > And fit for highest trust.

But the real purpose of the poem was, or became, something different from the celebration of a military triumph. In the previous year, 1649, an event had occurred which left a wound in the mind of the country and shattered her political constitution. It was not merely that the execution of Charles I was such as to be apostrophized in contemporary prints: 'O horrible murder!' It was not even that, perhaps of all forms of murder, the judicial is the most repugnant. The people that let out an unearthly groan in Whitehall were, so to speak, having an inhibition removed. Other kings had been knifed and poisoned, but one might say that that was not in itself serious. In Charles the taboo of kingship was violated, and the execution made way for a new race of men. The process of enlightenment was slow, and it still took two hundred and fifty years to produce Mr Kingsley Martin. The death of the king was the true subject of Marvell's poem, and he indicated remoter consequences than could follow in his own time.

Marvell proceeded at first by way of an analysis of Cromwell's personal character: 'So restless Cromwell could not cease / In the inglorious Arts of Peace'. It is this restlessness, and not to the nature of any national task in hand, that Marvell attributes the fact that the captain-general 'through adventurous War / Urged his active star'. And to emphasize this odd subjective element in Cromwell's action, he points out that the general first 'Did thorough his own side / His fiery way divide'. One cannot miss the irony of the comment: 'For 'tis all one to Courage high / The Emulous or Enemy.' He goes on:

> Then burning through the Air he went,
> And Pallaces and Temples rent:
> > And *Caesar's* head at last
> > Did through his Laurels blast.

> 'Tis Madness to resist or blame
> The force of angry Heavens flame:

Cromwell is the scourge sent from heaven. 'And, if we would speak true, / Much to the Man is due.' It is to miss the point of this comment, which belongs to the lines immediately preceding, to replace the full stop after this couplet, as at least one popular edition does, by a comma. This 'Man' is also a scourge in his own right. The sympathetic portrait that follows merely prepares for a further irony.

> Who, from his private Gardens, where
> He liv'd reserved and austere,
>   As if his highest plot
>   To plant the Bergamot

It is this harmless character who 'Did by industrious Valour climb / To ruine the great Work of Time'. The lines are of great and elegiac magnificence. Cromwell's work appears to Marvell primarily as one of destruction, not of liberation. 'Though Justice against Fate complain, / And plead the antient Rights in vain'. There is no suggestion that the new order is just or right; on the contrary, justice and rights are on the king's side, and Cromwell is merely an irresistible fate. The rights 'do hold and break / As men are strong or weak'. For rights must be defended, and the eviction of the weak by the strong is the natural law of the world. Marvell's couplets suggest something in the nature of a scientific demonstration:

> Nature that hateth emptiness,
> Allows of penetration less:
>   And therefore must make room
>   Where greater Spirits come.

Charles is presented in a very different manner from Cromwell. This is no doubt in part because there is a sense in which Cromwell is the 'greater Spirit', and in part because Charles, as a tragic actor, plays an objective and symbolic role. But it is also because, as the representative of the old order of supra-personal rights, he has less need of mere personality. His dignity is above it. He is a king, not a film-star or a Hoover salesman. By the old rule, he was to be accepted without reference to his personal qualities. But those qualities were in fact, as his trial and speeches show, of a very high order. He performed his final part in a manner which served the royal cause. Lionel Johnson's verses, fine as they are, are flaccid beside those in which Marvell cele-brated the scene:

> While round the armed Bands
> Did clap their bloody hands.
> *He* nothing common did or mean
> Upon that memorable Scene:
> But with his keener Eye
> The Axes edge did try:
> Nor call'd the *Gods* in vulgar spight
> To vindicate his helpless Right,
> But bow'd his comely Head,
> Down as upon a Bed.

And the commentary goes on: 'This was that memorable Hour / Which first assur'd the forced Pow'r.' The rest of the poem defines the nature of the 'forced Pow'r' that was, after the execu-tion, the indubitable government of England. It was a personal rule, the rule of a man of character, as no previous government had been. Cromwell had not 'yet grown stiffer with Command, / But still in the *Republick's* hand'. The 'yet' is perhaps not prima-rily an adverb of time, but it gives a warning of what was to happen, and what must happen in all dictatorships not tied to an objective order superior to themselves. The prophecies of libera-tion will not stir more than a rueful smile in the twentieth century, which has seen some:

> A *Caesar* he ere long to Gaul,
> To *Italy* an *Hannibal*,
> And to all States not free,
> Shall Climaterick be.

But one has, after all, only to consult the first two lines to under-stand the sense of 'free' in the second two. The final apostrophe contains the final judgement:

> But thou the Wars and Fortunes Son
> March indefatigably on;
> And for the last effect
> Still keep thy Sword erect;

> Besides the force it has to fright
> The Spirits of the shady Night,
>   The same *Arts* that did *gain*
>   A *Pow'r* must it *maintain*.

The forced power must be maintained by force. The context
suggests something stronger: by force alone. It is no longer a question of a primacy of rights merely *supported* by physical strength.
The old sanctions have gone.

II

It was not unnatural that, when the old rights were threatened,
they should have produced their apologists. In the thirties of the
seventeenth century a gentleman of Kent had written and circulated among his friends a little treatise that had the odd fate of
remaining unpublished for nearly fifty years and, not long after it
had been published, being remembered for the attacks it excited
rather than for itself. The attacks were, naturally, from those who
were in effect the intellectual fathers of Whiggery, and the writings of these fathers triumphed with their cause. But the most
broadminded might surely admit that, if Locke saw fit to devote
his first *Treatise* to a criticism of Sir Robert Filmer, and Algernon
Sidney saw fit to attack him throughout the whole of his
Discourses, which are much longer than Filmer's own book, it
might be because there was something in the *Patriarcha* which the
promoters of Whiggery had cause to fear.

Filmer, in his main work, had the advantage of not writing for
publication. It is true that Algernon Sidney might claim to have
been in the same situation but it is hard to see what purpose his
polemical, even vituperative book could have served if it were not
intended for publication. It might possibly have been the lonely
work of a man who liked to dramatize himself. It was certainly
not, like the *Patriarcha*, designed primarily for the instruction of
the author and a few friends. The unusual circumstances of the
generation and birth of Filmer's book together, no doubt, with
the aristocratic cast of the author's mind, gives the *Patriarcha* an
honesty which, even after more than three hundred years, is
bound to hurt a little.

The first chapter of the little treatise has the accommodating title 'The Natural Freedom of Mankind, a New, Plausible and Dangerous Opinion', and Filmer gives the tart warning that the desire of liberty was the cause of the fall of Adam. The new opinion alluded to in the title is, of course, widely received. 'The common people everywhere tenderly embrace it as being most plausible to flesh and blood, for that it prodigally distributes a portion of liberty to the meanest of the multitude, who magnify liberty as if the height of human felicity were only to be found in it.' Filmer's refusal to indulge the people in their preference for liberty, that is to say for themselves, has no doubt helped to keep his name in obscurity. But this unpopular attitude is not the main reason for his work being so little read. Hobbes held out little enough hope to the aspiring democrat, but our young men have long been encouraged to sharpen their teeth on the *Leviathan*. The real cause of the neglect of Filmer lies not in his opinions but in the kind of reasons he gave to support them. And in this he differed widely from Hobbes. Hobbes was an atheist, and men of the most liberal opinions have long felt for the atheist a kindness they could not extend to men of Filmer's stamp. Filmer not only supported the odd notion that the 'greatest liberty in the world... is for a people to live under a monarch' at a time when the ghosts of the age were beginning to head towards democracy. He grounded himself in a religious historicism at a time when the minds of men were beginning to hanker after a kind of explanation that could be called scientific. Almost everybody still believed in the authority of the scriptures and in the scriptural account of the origin of the world. It was not easy, therefore, for anyone to deny arguments evidently in accordance with the history presented by the Bible. None the less, people were ceasing to feel that a demonstration of accordance with scripture was an explanation. They sought something of a kind which, whether scientific or not, could be stated in the abstract terms of scientific study. It is this situation, no doubt, which accounts for Locke's and Sidney's uneasiness about Filmer, and for the ignoring of him by subsequent writers. Filmer used a type of argument which was still officially recognized, if not found altogether satisfactory, by men of his own and even of Locke's generation. Later, when the prejudices of science and democracy had widely replaced the prejudices of religion, Filmer's reasoning could be treated as insignificant.

It was not so, however. The truth is one and, if enquiries are taken far enough, discordances disappear. Even from a point of view generally empirical and scientific we should now be disposed to give more credit to Filmer's political ideas than to Locke's. Whether or not we felt able to follow point by point his demonstration that 'the subordination of children is the fountain of all regal authority', and his derivation of all monarchy by descent from Adam's kingship, we should certainly be inclined to attach more importance to the traditional development of society than to what Filmer denounces as 'such imaginary pactions between kings and their people as many dream of' or than to Locke's 'state of nature' with a 'law of Nature to govern it'.

Adam ruled as a father, and 'there is, and always shall be continued to the end of the world, a natural right of a supreme Father in every multitude'. This right was properly by descent and ideally every contemporary king was a remote heir of Adam. Filmer did not, however, make the fantastic and untenable assumption that all actual kings were in the right line of descent. 'By the secret will of God', he says, 'many set first do most unjustly obtain the exercise' of supreme power. But these acts of violence did not upset the divinely appointed order of the world. Filmer was not of those who see in every unfortunate event or evil action a denial of God's providence. His view of the world was more penetrating and more entire. 'God doth but turn and use men's unrighteous acts', he says, 'to the performance of his righteous devices.' The divinely appointed principle of government remained, come what might of its application in the rough-and-tumble of history. All 'subordinate and inferior fathers', the ordinary fathers of families, in short, derived all their rights and privileges from the act of sovereignty of the monarch, whose power is absolute. Similarly, Filmer insists that 'in such kingdoms as have general assemblies for consultations about making public laws, it must be remembered that such meetings do not share or divide the sovereignty with the Prince, but do only deliberate and advise – their supreme head, who still reserves the absolute power in himself'.

This notion of the absolute nature of the final power in the state is out of tune with the work of most English political theorists since Filmer, though not with that of Hobbes, but it has a logical vitality which cannot easily be repressed. Whatever practical consequences may be drawn from the proposition, it is undeniably the nature of government to govern and, unless one escape with a sophism, to govern must be understood to include constraining the wills of others. 'So that they that say that the law governs the kingdom, may as well say that the carpenter's rule builds the house and not the carpenter, for the law is but the rule or instrument of the ruler.' Filmer sees this irrefutable but unpalatable principle of government as embodied in a mere tangible person, a king. This honest proceeding has given offence to the many who have preferred that the seat of authority should be in a concealed place or even that the fact of an inevitable constraint should itself be so far as possible concealed. To talk of the 'superiority of Princes above laws' may not please the ears of the people, but the discreet student must recognize that such language represents the facts. It is one of Filmer's sober and realistic objections (borrowed from James I) to all doctrines of contract between king and people that 'a contract ... cannot be thought broken, except that first a lawful trial' determine the matter; and against the king 'no writ can go'. The doctrine that the king can do no wrong does not mean 'that it is right for kings to do injury, but it is right for them to go unpunished by the people if they do it'. If the king offend, the people's remedy is 'by petitioning him to amend his fault'.

These observations are relevant not only to traditional monarchy; they apply to the supreme repository of power in any state. They apply to the 'forced power' of Cromwell as to the rightful power of Charles. They are to be understood as an analysis of the very nature of government. So far as a 'forced power' and a rightful may, on Filmer's view, be distinguished, it is by the traditionary element in the latter. No voluntary act of man can create a right: all rights are from a source independent of his will. Filmer would have treated with contempt those vulgar doctrines of our age which seek to derive rights from alleged personal merits or even from the meanest wants and appetites of the common man. The dignity of the 'great work of time' which Cromwell destroyed was in its objectivity. That work stood above the people of England as a manifestation of a super-sensible order. It required obedience without trading any advantage for it.

III

These are not notions that would win an election, but with Algernon Sidney, Filmer's detractor, we are in the modern world. 'Who will wear a shoe that hurts him?' he asks, ignoring the obvious answer that we all do. 'Kings and all other magistrates', he writes, 'are constituted only for the good of the people.' 'We ourselves are judges how far it is good for us to recede from our natural Liberty.' We have here the prim reader of *The Guardian*. 'If the Multitude may institute' (as is supposed by Sidney) 'the Multitude may abrogate', and subjects are every bit as good as their king. 'If disagreements happen between King and People, why is it a more desperate Opinion to think the King should be subject to the Censure of the People, than the people subject to the will of the king?' Filmer had given an answer to that, but Sidney has not understood it. 'How can it be possible', he says, 'for one man born under the same condition with the rest of Mankind to have a Right in himself that is not common to all others, till by them confessed.' And what may lead people to admit superior rights in others, if no man is born with rights above others? The answer Sidney gives is the classic answer of democratic theory: 'Virtue only gives a natural preference of one man above another.' Filmer had spoken of 'a necessity upon every People to choose the worst men for being the worst, and most like themselves'.

Sidney has most of the essential prejudices of a modern democrat, but neither his station in history nor his rank in society would allow him to draw the final outrageous conclusions. He may describe himself defensively as 'being no way concerned in the defence of Democracy', and the theoretical position he intended to hold against Filmer was that 'there is no Form [of Government] appointed by God or Nature, those Governments only can be called just, which are established by the consent of Nations.' But the 'consent of Nations' evidently implies some leaning towards a form of government relying on democratic principles, and in another place Sidney says that 'Democracy, in which every man's Liberty is least restrained, because every man hath an equal part, would certainly prove to be the most just, rational and natural.' He even holds up Filmer to ridicule for having discovered in 'Popular Government' the faults of 'Ignorance and Negligence' 'that were never', he says, forgetting his reading, 'found by any man before him'! But although it is not very clear what Sidney means by 'Popular Government', it is clear that he did not favour any government so popular as to leave no room for great families like his own. Indeed he may be said to have favoured an aristocratic republicanism which was, as it were, the ideal precursor of Whig oligarchism. The common people were in Sidney's view still 'the rabble', among whom, even in popular governments, you might find some 'aiming only at the satisfaction of private Lust, without regard to the common Good'. 'It is neither reasonable nor just', he says, 'that those who are not equal in Virtue should be made equal in Power.' Like some left-wing intellectuals of our own day, he seems to have assumed that *true* equality would leave himself and his like socially superior to the masses. Sidney stopped short of conclusions which were implicit in his doctrine and which, since his day, have been demonstrated.

Sidney's apology for popular government has been so far superseded both by later theorists and by events that it is of little more than historical interest as showing how a true if querulous patriot could come to hold the views that Sidney did. A more interesting line of thought in his book is his justification of sedition. In this matter he was, on his own principles, perfectly right. Kings are 'purely the creation of the people', he says, '… from hence it may rationally be inferred that he who makes a thing to be, makes it to be only what he pleases.' And elsewhere: 'Why should [kings] not be deposed, if they become enemies of their people?' Sidney's system, if his loose agglomeration of prejudices and ideas may be so called, did not provide an answer. He is able to talk of 'Seditions' and 'Tumults' 'upon just occasions'. For when he talks of a king he talks not, like Filmer, of one with traditional and sacred trust, but of a placeman of the people. Why should such a monarch not be kicked downstairs?

IV

With the second half of the twentieth century we are once more in an epoch in which a political theory must include a theological reference. The lay state, for which Locke's *Letter on Toleration* is an early and classic apology, hovers uncertainly for a little while

longer in the world of political reality, but from the world of
theory where historical changes first occur it has already disappeared. There is Christian theology, and there is the barbarizing
claptrap of such men as Professor Bernal. However little we know
about these things, we know enough to feel ourselves within the
orbit of one or other of these systems of thought. Or rather,
within the orbit either of the Christian and European system of
thought or of that obfuscating terminology which is designed to
make thought impossible.

At the moment in 1650 when Marvell conceived his 'Ode' the
old theological order had been struck a blow in the person of
Charles I, and the new world of a 'forced' and lay power was open
before him. It was opened by men who emitted more mouthfuls
of religion than any governors of England before them had ever
done. It is by no means clear how far Marvell, in later life, pursued
the consequences of his own prophecy. Nor is it easy to say what
course of speech and action would have been followed, during
the Commonwealth and Restoration, by a man conscious that the
times had been divided by the events of 1649. Marvell was a
fastidious man, but he lived in the world of the possible. He was
a patriot, and no Englishman worth his salt would not have been
pleased by the victories of Blake and infuriated by the naval disasters under Charles II. So far as can be ascertained, Marvell was a
constitutional monarchist, desiring to see the King of England as
'the only intelligent Ruler over a rational people'. It was the
language of the new age.

I hope that we are all constitutional monarchists. But the question remains: What is the constitution? The authorities give their
accounts, and the thing they describe changes slowly as they
describe it. Often there has been a tendency, among people at
large, to think of the constitution in terms of certain time-
honoured institutions which had lost much of their real power
and to ignore or underrate those newer institutions in which
power was running strongly. Now we perhaps see more of a
tendency, equally misleading, to emphasize the importance of
whatever is most crudely vocal in our polity at the expense of the
less strident elements which may count for more in determining
the country's fate over a stretch of centuries. And if we consider
this country, with its thousand years or more of recognizably
English history, we shall not be apt to discard any element in our

constitution which has served our unity and so our continuity. We shall rather consider whether and how these elements may, in the turn of time, once more be strengthened. It cannot even be taken for granted that a king of England may not one day, in place of the *Le roy le veult* with which he signifies assent to statutes, return, in the 'gentle language' in which refusal was formerly given, the answer *Le roy s'avisera*.

As *Ceres* Corn, and *Flora* is the Spring.
Bacchus is Wine, the Country is the King.

The Nature of Public Administration

What is this operation which is the life of the great bureaucracies? The administration which is the *raison d'être* of the multifarious offices clustered around Whitehall has been much denounced, sometimes admired, on odd occasions even studied. But in the main it has been denounced or admired for its effects and studied in its structure. The effects of government administration are an aspect of the history of a people, and the structure is a diagram of the channels of the more formal communications within it. Neither brings us close to the working of the bureaucracies. We are more likely to be brought close by some such personal account as that given by Sir Edward Bridges (*Portrait of a Profession*, Cambridge, 1950) a year or two ago. There we read of work which provides, 'and provides to a considerable degree, an intense satisfaction and delight in the accomplishment of difficult tasks, a delight which has much in common with that felt by scholars or even on occasions by artists on the completion of some outstandingly difficult work' (p. 32). We find also an emphasis on the 'strong corporate life' of the civil servant. We find him portrayed as the exponent of a departmental philosophy, 'the resultant of protests and suggestions, and counter suggestions, from many interests', which represents 'an acceptable middle point of view after the extreme divergencies have been rooted out' (p. 17). Thus we are told two things by Sir Edward Bridges. One is about the affective character of the civil servant's work. A man may take pleasure in it because it is difficult. It is not altogether clear why the pleasure, or the difficulty, should be compared with that encountered by the artist or the scholar, who are certainly not the only other people to be confronted with difficult tasks, or to take pleasure in overcoming them; while the corporate character of the civil servant's work does not give him any obvious affinity with the artist of modern times, or with the scholar *qua* scholar and not *qua* member of a learned institution. The second thing we are told is about the opinions the civil servant is likely to hold and to contribute as occasion arises to the solution of his Minister's problems. These opinions are not his own. They are a mediocrity arrived at not because they are likely to be true, though sometimes they may even be that, but because in a system of protests and objections a man may hold them and escape without too many rotten eggs plastering his head. Neither of these two points made by Sir Edward Bridges describes the nature of the intellectual operation, if there is one, that the servant of state performs. One must in passing note in Sir Edward Bridges, as in other only less eminent authorities, a conviction natural enough in those who have spent a lifetime in the Service and have emerged a long way up, that the Service has not only changed beyond all recognition in recent times but has improved to an almost equal degree. Miss Emmeline Cohen (*The Growth of the British Civil Service*, London, 1941) is struck by the improved industry and integrity of the civil servant in the last hundred and fifty years. Sir Edward Bridges sees an abatement of departmentalism (pp. 22–3). Mr C.K. Munro (*The Fountains in Trafalgar Square*, London, 1952, pp. 22–5, *et passim*) sees men less intent on giving orders and more anxious to serve. None of these observations, not even the last, is entirely without foundation. But none of these improvements, most probably, has been without compensating drawbacks. All of them appear to have been in something subsidiary to the operation of administration. The fact that the improvements are supposed to have been so great suggests that they cannot have been in anything permanently essential to the conduct of government. For government has been going on for a long time, and if so much improvement had taken place in its essential procedures we should not have to go far back in history before we came upon a complete anarchy. And looking the other way, we should be uncomfortably near the millennium.

We may take comfort, however. In fact, if we look back three hundred years, we see Samuel Pepys transacting the King's business as aptly as it has generally been done in this century. When we read him our temporary peculiarities, such as the size of our bureaucracies and the quality of our honesty, are seen as such and we catch a glimpse of whatever it is that enables governments to persist at all. The constitutional changes since 1660 have not been of such a nature as even much to alter certain relations of Parliament and the executive. The modern civil servant will recognize himself in this: 'This month ends with my mind full of business and concernment how this office will speed with Parliament, which begins to be mighty severe in examining our accounts, and the expense of the Navy in this war' (30 September 1666). He will recognize the tactician's satisfaction at the diversion caused by the Great Fire: 'He says he hath computed that the rents of houses lost by this fire in the City come to £600,000 per annum; that this will make Parliament more quiet than otherwise they would have been' (15 September 1666). And he will know the feelings, which are in the very marrow of the profession, described in the words: 'Reckoning myself to come off with victory, because not overcome in anything, or much foiled' (3 October 1666).

It has no doubt often been remarked that Frontinus exhibits all the qualities of a good civil servant. It was his task and pleasure, about the year AD 97, to reform the administration of the water supply borne into Rome on the great aqueducts. The task had just those characteristics which caused Sir Edward Bridges to reflect that he is almost an artist; but the reflections of Frontinus were different. There were disparities between the records and the facts which no one had bothered to check; there were false measurements which made it impossible for the authorities to balance their books. In these matters Frontinus set order, and he pauses in his record only to notice the superiority of these works of utility over works of mere beauty such as the Greeks were proud of. *Otiosa sed fama celebrata opera Graecorum.* Frontinus recognized that his modest function was to serve in matters that could be commonly appreciated. He was the man from the water company. But he was not particularly modest about the manner of his performance. He speaks of 'my natural sense of responsibility' and 'my fidelity', and pompously insists 'Those who sought the Emperor's pardon, after warning received, may thank me for the favour granted' (*De Aquis Urbis Romae*). His was a typically useful and uninteresting mind.

What are the qualities of mind most needed in the public servant? As his subject-matter must always be a good that is not only common but is commonly recognized, he had better not be in the habit of seeing things with his own eyes, unless he has an abnormal disinterestedness which enables him at once to set aside his own vision. Perhaps it is to be preferred that reality should appear to him exclusively in that form which is capable of preservation in a number, a name, a date – verbal forms which are references and not presentations. His concern, like any philosopher's, is with relationships, but he must always avoid all those questions of value to which philosophic study of relationships is apt to lead. He should have a mind tenacious of his limited sort of fact, and exclusive of other sorts, and such a delight in the play of relationships that the question of value never troubles him. Since great disinterestedness is not always to be found in combination with the primarily required ability to perform juggleries with the rigorously limited fact, he had better be provided with a vanity like that of Frontinus, or one more ignoble. If his most desperate concern is to thrust himself onwards to the top, so that he subscribes in good faith to Montherlant's formula of 'le combat sans foi', he will not be deflected by a temptation to examine values. If he can blow himself up like a bullfrog with thinking of the organization that happens to move under him, he will not seek to inquire whether that organization has any merit apart from the service it performs to his pride.

If Pepys, with his victory over the Accounts Committee, and Frontinus, with his pomposity and his virtues, display the facts of administration, neither brings us face to face with an explicit theory. They are, however, possibly nearer such a theory than the contemporary writers I have quoted, who seem self-consciously to wish to set on the operation of administration a value which does not belong to it. Miss Cohen with her moral improvement, and Sir Edward Bridges with his artistic delight, have fixed on matters more relevant to other fields than to the one they profess to be describing. The comments which both Sir Edward Bridges and Mr C.K. Munro make about the corporate nature of the civil servant's work look more hopeful. That indeed is a genuine characteristic, but it could not be pretended that it is peculiar to the work of government officials. What J.B. Yeats (*Letters*, London, 1944, p. 239) stigmatizes as the 'collective mind, dull as the House of Commons and serious as the Bank of England' is common to all business transacted in great organizations. It is by an abdication of the individual vision that such organization is possible. There may of course be an individual initiative within such an organization, as there may be an individual initiative or valour within an army, but in so far as an organization exists by meanings rather than by acts there is little place for the sort of individual adjustment of accepted categories which constitutes thought in a properly intellectual field. The adjustments, and the associations and dissociations, which are made are made to suit the necessities and opportunisms of action and not to fit the truth which, in any philosophical sense of that term, is irrelevant. 'The practical man', to quote J.B. Yeats again (p. 276), 'cannot afford to be sincere.' He must, not only on all questions of value but even on matters of fact, share the provisional delusions of his fellows. It is a discipline, but it is not a discipline of truth. It requires the muscles and obedience of an acrobat rather than the patience of a philosopher.

But because these things are characteristic of all work in a great organization they cannot provide us with a description of the characteristic operation of the official. To find that, we have to look at what distinguishes the administration of government from other forms of collective organization. There is a tendency more or less plausibly to blur this distinction. It is sometimes even taught that government and industrial organization are closer together than they ever were before, or that government, as Mr C.K. Munro contends, now provides services rather than regulations. No doubt it is true that industry presents certain analogies with government, in so far as it requires, as a subordinate purpose, the government of its employees, but an industrial or commercial organization exists for ends of production or commerce which stamp it with its own characteristics. The suggestion of the kinship of industry and government administration is made with the *arrière pensée* that industry will be less hostile to what is said to resemble itself; and so far as the suggestion is believed we have, not an approximation to the truth, but the success of an act of government comparable to the successive acts by which, throughout history, the governor has claimed kinship with the governed in order to secure that he is himself tolerated – a principle which attains its greatest refinement in a complicated modern democracy. This might be called the sympathetic fallacy. Mr Munro's way of describing certain developments in contemporary administration by saying that the official provides not regulation but a service might be called the philanthropic fallacy. This too, so far as it is accepted, represents a triumph of government, but not of the truth. For if a government provides a service, it does so for precisely the same reason as it applies a regulation. It does so because it thinks that that is the best way of governing. If you can keep your kingdom quiet with a few policemen armed with battle-axes, your administration can be of the simplest, but if the people will not be quiet without regulations about how it is to pay for its false teeth then even that detail becomes important for the conduct of government. Administration in the present age is characterized by the necessity the administrator may be under of taking notice, because they may become matters of public concern and ultimately of public order, of the most personal concerns. That does not indicate any change in the nature of government; it merely reflects the habit of an urbanized and literate population.

The essential character of government, and so of the administration by which alone it is effective, is a process of maintaining the unity of a political group by yielding to the governed enough to keep them quiet and not enough to damage irreparably the fabric of the state. This description covers equally the primitive administration of three policemen and the complicated organization of the welfare state. That is to say, it is a description of the operation of the administrator in both kinds of state as well as in all intermediate kinds of state. Evidently the subject-matter that is put before the administrator may be of the most diverse character, but not the subject-matter but the method constitutes the essence of administration. The administrator steers what may appear to be a craven course among the various pressures of public and still more of semi-public opinion and the opinion of groups, and his concern is to come off with victory, not in the sense that his opinion prevails, for he has no right to one, but in the sense that at the end he is still upright and the forces around him have achieved a momentary balance. Professor Laski (*Reflections on the Constitution*, Manchester, 1951, p. 199) regretted that in this country civil servants are not to be reckoned among the experts on the subjects with which they deal, that for example no official at the Home Office 'has ever made a contribution of importance to the study of penology or criminology'. That regret shows a mistaken view of the sort of animal the official is. He is, in fact more akin to the criminal than the criminologist. He is the man who has been trained to a practical operation, not to the exposition of a theory or a search for truth. The operation, in his case, is nothing less than the preservation of the state. He is, no less than any soldier, a man who must give his life to the Crown. That is what gives his task a permanent sense amidst the mutations of party policies.

There is no need for the administrator to be a man of ideas.

His distinguishing quality should be rather a certain freedom from ideas. The idealisms and the most vicious appetites of the populace are equal before him. He should be prepared to bow before any wisdom whose mouth is loud enough. It is the negative character of the official's role which makes him, while admitted to be honest and trustworthy, an object of distrust. It is clearly undesirable that his cynical method, beneficent in its proper field, should be applied beyond that field. People who, from the official point of view, are mere trifling forces at the periphery of things may, from the point of view of the truth, be at the very centre. The fact that to the administrator they may be of less weight than some well-organized pack of fools should strengthen and not weaken their determination. The acts of the administrator are, in effect, mere acts of recognition. It is the business of those who think they hold the truth in any subject to make themselves recognizable to the administrator's deliberately commonplace vision.

Anything alarming there may be in this description of the administrator's work is due to the generality of the description. Governments differ as countries differ, because the facts to be recognized by them are different. It is the state of society which colours the government much more than the reverse. Yet government has a certain positive role, and those who understand what is being done should use their efforts to secure that the officials are men who might, in the last desperation, exhibit a scruple.

A Note on the Monarchy

There is no danger of our forgetting that we live in a democracy. The fact is repeatedly mentioned, usually in the course of a reminder that the democracy we live in is one of a number. Moreover, it is usually supposed that the common elements by virtue of which the democracies constitute a nameable class are more important features of the governments concerned than are the elements by which they differ. Although every literate person must have had cause to doubt this in particular cases, the ordinary supposition so far has force that the patently undemocratic element in these governments, and most of all in our own, are obscured. It is true that, in a democracy we suddenly have cause to dislike, the undemocratic elements will as suddenly walk abroad like skeletons from a cupboard. In the case of our own country, certain undemocratic elements are inescapably visible even to the most friendly eye; they have to be laughed off or explained away as 'survivals' (as if democracy itself were not that) enjoying, in comparison with the real works of government, only an inferior degree of reality. So Trooping the Colour must be regarded as a leg-show of guardsmen, the crown as a bauble, and the Coronation itself as something for the illustrated papers.

It is a common state of mind to suppose that, in matters of government, the more obvious a thing is the less it is to be believed. Bagehot was of this mind. He was a publicist, and the dearest professional hypothesis of such people is: Things are not what they seem. The outward show, what you, poor fool, take to be real, is something they whip away to show you the cleverly constructed machinery behind. The typical publicist is like Berkeley's minute philosopher, putting a logomachy in place of the visible world. With such people, the very patency of the monarchy tells against its significance being recognized. Bagehot attributed importance to the monarchy, but it was an importance of an inferior kind. The Queen was 'dignified', in his phraseology: that meant she was not much good. She was for fools to goggle at. As there were a lot of fools, that counted for something. Indeed, Bagehot seems to have estimated the number of those who were not fools as being, in his day, not more than ten thousand (*The English Constitution*, World Classics, p. 6). These read the *Economist* and formed a freemasonry of republicans.

Bagehot has had a prolonged success, so that one might be tempted to think that the Constitution, so sensitive to everything that is said about it, has adapted itself to him. At any rate we find Ivor Jennings, whose book *Cabinet Government* is so sober that it might have appeared as a serial in *The Times*, saying without turning a hair that 'the existence or absence of a monarch does not in itself make a fundamental distinction in a Constitution' (p. 303). This outbids Bagehot's statement that it is a 'fiction that Ministers are, in any political sense, the Queen's servants' (p. 11). Jennings can even say: 'The functions of the head of the state, be he King or President, are ancillary' (p. 303). For Jennings, as for Bagehot, the cabinet is really the head as well as the guts of the commonwealth.

Observe that the place assigned to the monarch is a matter of theory. It is not directly dependent on the facts about the day-to-day exercise of her powers. We can accept what Jennings says on that point. He says, among other things, that in that matter Bagehot was wrong, and that the monarch may in fact have considerable influence on the decisions of the government (p. 303). For all that, his view of monarchy is, in principle, the same as Bagehot's. The monarch is ancillary, she is not part of the main function of government. Bagehot and Jennings agree in this matter in spite of their differences as to the facts because such conclusions are the children of faiths, valuations and predispositions as much as of observation. Do not be deceived by Bagehot's boasting that he looks at the 'living reality' and not at the 'paper description'; that he is for 'rough practice' and not for 'the many refinements of literary theory' (p. 1). All that is merely a flapping of the robes of the wizard and diviner. It is a glimpse of the role Bagehot liked to think of himself in. The author of the biographical note prefaced to his *Literary Studies* says that 'it was a satisfaction to him to show that he understood the world far better than the world had ever understood him' (R.H. Hutton, 'Prefatory Memoir to Bagehot', 1898, p. 1).

Against Bagehot and Jennings we can set Clarendon, for although 1688 may have altered some practices of government (even if to a less extent than is sometimes supposed) it could not alter the principles. Clarendon says: 'Kings having still all the power remaining in them, that they have not themselves parted with, and released to their subjects, and their subjects having no pretence to more liberty or power than the King hath granted and given them' (*A Brief Survey of the Leviathan*, 1676, p. 89). It is a weakness of writers on politics in our days that they have to pretend that what they write is pure observation. Clarendon's remark is pure theory. It contains an assertion or principle about the final source of power. What the kings have 'released to their subjects' is of course a variable matter of fact, but a variation, as between Clarendon's day and our own, in the quantity of what has been released, does not affect the principle. If we start with an unlimited power, whatever is given away something will remain. To quote an authority more likely to be tolerable to modern opinion than is the historian of the Rebellion, here is D. Lindsay Keir: The king's 'prerogative, however circumscribed by convention, must always retain its historic character as a residue of discretionary authority to be employed for the common good' (*The Constitutional History of Modern Britain 1485–1937*, 1946, p. 491). The monarchic principle is not that the king should have all power, but that he is the legitimate source of all power.

Look at our present constitution by the candle of this principle. We shall deny Bagehot's assertion that it is a 'fiction' that 'ministers are, in any political sense, the Queen's servants'. We shall say, on the contrary, that the Queen rules through her Ministers, and that she does not rule any the less for that, just as Ministers are not the less Ministers because they exercise their functions in the main through officials. But the Queen, you will say, does not attend to the details of her country's administration. The Minister does not attend to the details of his Department's administration. It would be a true anachronism for him to do so. It would be a true anachronism for the Queen to express her preferences in the million and one topics that come before her government. The Minister has one inalienable function, which is to secure the coherence of his Department. The Queen has one inalienable function, which is to secure the coherence of her country. The Minister performs his function more by taking advice and bowing before facts than he does by giving advice and making the facts bow before him. And so with the Queen. Her quiescence is the very principle of order. In the course of her duty of securing the coherence and continuity of her realm, the controversies which overturn parties are of no account. 'The Queen's service must be carried on', now this way, now that, to please the whim of party and populace, but that is only because, if those whims are not appeased, there will be disorder and the service will be broken or at an end. The Queen's duty perhaps demands any submission except what will break the realm.

In this scheme of things, the reins of authority meet in the Queen's hand. All the other authorities are subordinate and derivative from her. If the Commons unseat a Government, she takes other advisers because her duty is to govern in a manner that will be tolerated. Jennings makes much of what he calls a new principle. He says that a fundamental change came with the Reform Act. Before it, the government reposed in the Sovereign's confidence; afterwards, in the people's. There are historical refinements, evidently, in the position before the Reform Bills and after. But there never was a time when a Government had not to be tolerable if it was to endure. James II's popery made his power crumble under his feet. It is not the Reform Bills themselves, but the urbanization and literacy which produced them, which made it necessary latterly for the monarch to listen as attentively to the murmurings of the people as formerly to the growls of the nobility. It is the notorious complexity of a modern administration which has caused the monarch to 'release to his subjects' (in Clarendon's phrase) so many powers.

The maxim that the Queen's service must be carried on means, among other things, that it is of greatly more importance that there should be a government in England than that its complexion should be that of one or another party. It is of the nature of party politicians to exaggerate and exacerbate their differences. They present their policies, which are merely an aspect of things, as the thing itself. The thing itself is the great *res publica* whose continuance the Queen wills. She wills, all the time, all those laws which, by and with the advice of the Lords Spiritual and Temporal, and the Commons, she or her predecessors have enacted and have not repealed. She wills the continuance of all those rights she has protected without enactment. While she broods over this body of laws and institutions, and her servants daily perform the acts which constitute the life and continuance of that corpus, the party managers come along with their medicines and their scalpels to purge or trim some corner of it. The activity of the most fevered session of the House amounts to no more than that. Much is made of these adjustments, and much ought to be made; but more ought always to be made of the great work of time which is the subject of these meddlesome but necessary treatments.

It is recognized by all theorists of government that their problem is to find and define the executive, and it is recognized by Bagehot and Jennings that recent times are (to put it no higher) not marked by any weakening of the executive's powers. Bagehot and Jennings, however, have in effect chosen to place the head of the executive at an intermediate point in the chain of command. They have said virtually that the Cabinet is the beginning and end of government. They have done this partly, no doubt, out of a Whiggish or Progressive horror for the supreme though not for the penultimate heights. Partly, however, they are motivated by an inability to admit a principle of government to which the most exalted advices on our day-to-day affairs would be subordinate. They both have the publicist's touch, and for the publicist day-to-day affairs have a final dignity. Moreover, these matters are those which the popular will, whether of ten thousand or ten million, is supposed mainly to busy itself about and by which it is mainly evidenced. And the Cabinet, even if at a couple of removes, reflects what the people are supposed to think about these matters.

But if the recognition of the importance of the executive means anything at all, it means that the fact that the Cabinet reflects in some measure a popular will of some sort is the least important thing about it. The Cabinet is a government not because it is an outcome of certain electoral procedures but because it governs. It is government not in so far as it obeys the people but in so far as it constrains them. What a government loses when it ceases to be regulated or modified by an electoral procedure is not the power to govern but a certain advisory force which tells it what the people will stand. It can go on governing, but henceforth it has to rely exclusively on other means of informing itself when the worm will turn. Politicians are apt to make something tragic out of electoral procedures which may result in their losing their jobs. But an electorate which votes in such a way that an existing Cabinet is overthrown is not saying that it will not continue to be governed substantially according to the same laws as before. It is, in effect, not objecting to the things that in general are done, but in a greater or less measure to the way in which

some of them are done. The Crown in short remains; the Constitution remains; the officials, who are the Queen's servants and not
the politicians', raise their eyebrows and continue as before, only
noting that certain emphases must be slightly changed – and in
general Oh how slightly!

The constitutional development of recent times, and still more
the spread of literacy and the frequent allusions to acts of government in even the most widely circulated of the papers called
news-papers, have obscured the fact that the so-called popular
character of our modern governments is an historical accident.
Popular institutions are – to use a word which Jennings misapplies
to the head of the State – ancillary. It would be perfectly possible
to govern England without Parliament or elections. At first there
would be merely a prolongation of the administrative peace of the
parliamentary recess. Then, when new legislation was required, it
would take the form of Orders in Council. The Departments,
carefully consulting the outside world, would produce the material for these enactments as they do for enactments of any kind.
Ministers, appointed by the Crown at its own full choice or on
the nomination of the Civil Service Commissioners or the
Treasury, would come to their offices to decide important
matters. Briefed by the officials, they would continue to explain
things to the press, to their correspondents, and to those who
came to see them in deputation. They would meet from time to
time in committees, which would be the Cabinet and its committees. There would be a chief among them, who would be Prime
Minister, and they would look through him to the head of the
State who would give unity and continuity to their miscellaneous
acts. Elections, and an elected House of Commons, do not
produce a government. They merely modify it. They inform it
with life and even with information, and it would be, in the strict
sense, an imbecility for a government to dispense with these
resources. None the less, a government conducted without
them would be less ill-informed than is commonly imagined
about the impact of its proposals. Even at present, with the extra-
parliamentary consultations that take place, 'many wills', as Keir
rightly says, 'mingle with that of Parliament in the making of a
law' (p. 463).

Plain words about the nature of government have always been
offensive to the people and to all but the most intrepid of those

whose career depends on being elected by them. Whatever Charles I may have meant by the phrase, there is a sense in which the assertion that government is 'nothing pertaining to' the people is not controversial but a statement of inescapable principle. A government must be a compact body with a central point and capable of rational communication between the parts. It must be capable of acting as an entity on the larger body of society and compelling that larger body to act as an entity, but an entity more loosely knit than the government, and not necessarily with any rational communication between its parts, so that the government may divide and rule, cajoling one section of its society with one argument and another with another. It may of course try to persuade the governed that it is so responsive to their wishes that it is really hardly a government at all. But that is a kind of ballyhoo, practised, incidentally, with most thoroughness by governments like Hitler's or Stalin's, which enforce their wills most ruthlessly and in the most intimate departments of their subjects' lives. The essence of a government consists in being obeyed, and we learn this quickly enough if we refuse to pay our income tax or decline to present ourselves for military service. The part of the people, in contradistinction to that of the government, consists in obeying. Naturally the fact is not much advertised by politicians who are allowed to share in the governing only on the pretext that they represent us. Charles I, who was not interested in this aspect of the matter, could speak more freely, even if only at the price of his head.

The general horror with which the pure theory of government has always been regarded – well illustrated in the *succès de scandale* of Machiavelli – is by no means without foundation. It is obscurely felt that to talk too openly of these matters is likely to have an unfortunate effect on the way in which government is in fact conducted, just as it is felt that too public a recognition of our private lusts may end in an intolerable disorder. But just as it is salutary not to deceive ourselves about our sexual appetites it is salutary to remember that, politically, we live in a system of force modified, as the expression of our appetites is modified, by traditions as ancient as our race. It is, roughly speaking, the claim of political parties that they stand for this modification and not for the system of force that is modified. In our own Constitution, there is a certain truth in this. If the elected elements influence

and inform a permanent executive rather than themselves constitute it, and influence and inform it in such a way as to render it
more tolerable, they may plausibly claim to be on the side of civilization rather than of the naked appetite. None the less, in so far
as they tend, through the necessities of the electoral system, to
exaggerate their own benign influence and to conceal the extent
to which the executive is not so much changed as given new force
by their election, their influence is obscurantist. There is a
tendency to contrast a wicked past, when terrible things were
done behind the back of Parliament, with the present Golden Age
in which, because actions of State are in general the subject of a
vote in the House, nothing really wicked can be done. It is as if
the executive had been touched for a sort of King's Evil by this
formal contact with the public will. This way of looking at things
is a little less than honest. As to the nature of what happens in
Parliament, one must at least take into account such views as those
of a very perspicacious observer who wrote:

> Members carry on a ceaseless mock debate with one another,
> inside and outside Parliament – a debate that has little relation
> to any of the real issues of the day, and all real political discus-
> sion is outside Parliament and between people who are not
> members. It is only the man who is not handicapped by the
> letters 'M.P.' after his name who is free to tell the truth about
> politics. (Christopher Hollis, M.P., 'Can Parliament Survive?'
> *Everybody's Weekly*, 12 January 1952)

While the politician, by his insistence on his *representative* character, tends to obscure the fact of the separateness of government
and people, he tends also, by suggesting that his is the only legitimate creative role in the State, to denigrate the State which exists
independently of the politician's role. The orthodox theory may
be said to be that the State, starting with the Queen at its head
and descending to the humblest clerk behind a government
counter, is neutral. In a certain limited connotation of the term,
that is true, and is, moreover, an excellent thing. Neither the
Queen nor her officials are to be associated with any political
party; they work independently of all, because their functions
demand that they take a view in which the most hotly-contested
policies of parties can be seen as parts of a longer perspective. But
the neutrality of the Crown neither is nor should be absolute. An

absolute neutrality would involve a policy of individual self-interest in which the State itself would quickly dissolve. A less absolute form of neutrality, such as is much more likely to develop, and may be said in some measure actually to have developed, would consist of making a religion of bowing before *force majeure*. (There is a sense in which this has always been the religion of officials. Cf. Winston S. Churchill on the character of Sunderland: 'a competent official, one of those dangerous beings who, with many gifts of mind, have no principle of action; who do not care what is done, so long as they are in the centre of it'. *Marlborough*, vol. I, 1933, p. 276.) The forces would be assumed always to be tolerable on the grounds that the permanent State must always look outside itself for its regulative force. This view of things has a certain charm, because it seems to promise a government responsive to the changes in society, and if a State is to endure it must show a large responsiveness. None the less, there are evident limits to the tolerance the State can properly exhibit. The most obvious limitation is that it cannot tolerate, to the point at which they become a real menace to its existence, suicidal tendencies in its society. It cannot tolerate treason. That will in general be readily conceded, and it may be said to fit into the logic of *force majeure* if one assumes (what may, however, be doubted) that treason can only be of the minority. But that is surely not all. Unless one maintains the right of an executive to exercise any bestiality on its subjects, it must not evade the responsibility of making a positive contribution to society. For all the horror of what is called ideological government, a government having no principle but self-preservation must surely, in the last analysis, be worse.

The limitations of the tolerance of the State are expressed primarily in the sovereign. There are no doubt persons who can recite the Oath of Allegiance and regard it merely as a form of words conveying a reality which they might not well explain but which they vaguely hope is more popular. None the less, any conception of treason as being something other than, in the last analysis, infidelity to the Queen, is bound to prove a form of evasion. The final safeguard of our unity is a point of unity in a single Person present on the throne by hereditary right and form of law. If we depart from that, we admit the legitimacy of faction. No doubt it is only in the most desperate troubles, such as we pray we shall be preserved from, that that Person would present herself to us so directly. But it is well that we should not allow sloppy ideas to obscure what would be our duty in such an emergency. We have in our generation seen in Europe such national divisions as can leave no doubt that it is not desirable that, in a final crisis, the choice of guide should be left to our individual whims. What Keir calls the monarch's 'final responsibility for the national interest' (p. 491) can mean only, in the last desperate case to which no precedent is equal, that the Queen must be the judge of the fate of the nation. And if treason is not the only thing the State should decline to tolerate, other positive elements must find expression in the Queen as head of the executive, and in appropriate, more partial, forms in her various servants. No doubt, in the public mind, the conception of the Queen can contain no more than that mind contains. That is to say, the monarchy will be seen through the only explicit ideas that the largely secularized and press-fed populace has access to. But the sovereign of England is an Anglican, and only those ignorant of the superior force of a coherent and comprehensive body of ideas over an incoherent and partial, can suppose that this fact is without a national significance which will end only with the monarchy. The Queen adheres to the only religion possible in the West, and to that form of it which is most surely embedded in our millennial English traditions.

The ultimately religious character of the monarchy is to many a matter of derision. We have Kingsley Martin sneering at the suggestion that the Coronation 'would in some way be rendered inefficacious if it were not exclusively solemnized by an Archbishop' (*The Magic of Monarchy*, p. 9). Such persons should distinguish between their own incredulity and the nature of the thing. Their smiles are in imitation of Voltaire who, after all, lived before Frazer and even before Fustel de Coulanges. Do what we will, religion moves our secularized society as the appetites of sex move none the less the man or woman who denies them. If we deny our ancient motives, it is out of a will to frustrate ourselves and bring our country to ruin. The monarchy, perfectly adapted to the needs of a modern society, is so in part because it can draw its loyalty from the deepest wells. So long as we have the Queen, her heirs and successors, England could remain conscious of herself and give play to her deepest energies even after the most appalling national catastrophes. If the mechanical civilization of the West should one day break down, and we can no longer ignore the possibility, that nation will most readily re-assert itself which can re-establish, around the indubitable leader to whom a thousand years of history point, a compact and simple administration.

Autobiographical Reflections on Politics

When, at the age of seventeen and in 1931, I started my studies at a provincial university, I do not suppose I had any interests that were specifically political. My view was, roughly speaking, that literature was the only thing that mattered, and the light at the centre of all was poetry. It was therefore in terms of esthetics that I expected the world to be explained, as I was of course convinced that it could be. But I had, also, a certain social knowledge the importance of which could only become plain to me when it was tested against a different knowledge. I knew the working classes merely as people, because I had been brought up among them, and I knew also some of the myriads of small independent persons who lived among them, enjoying as little security or less and living sometimes even more modestly. It was at the university that I first encountered the working classes in the field of theory. Even within the central field of my interest they were not to be avoided, for it seemed that they had taken possession of poetry. It was the day of Auden, Spender and of a Day-Lewis who had not yet become a professor. It seemed that to be a poet you had to feel the woes of the working classes more than anyone else's. These classes had woes, for it was a time of great unemployment and poverty. But I could not help noticing that it was not from a world I inhabited – which actually contained working people – that these three Saint Georges came riding to the relief of the poor. They came, it seemed, from what they represented as the closed middle class of 'majors, vicars, lawyers, doctors, advertisers, maiden aunts' (their maiden aunts, not mine) whom they made a special point of denouncing. They taught that one should be ashamed of being well off, and I felt that I was invited to be ashamed too, because though I was not well off I had to admit that I was not a proletarian. About the same time I began to meet people who belonged to the social world of the three poets and who, like them, were beginning to drip the tears of socialism. I could not help noticing that when they spoke of the workers it was as if they were speaking of people in some far-off fairyland or alternatively of a remote race of South Sea Islanders or of a favourite breed of beetles. None the less they had, it seemed, the only language in which one could speak with indignation of the lot of the unemployed.

Moreover, it was taken as of course that they alone had those treasures of intellect which, rightly spread around, were bound to result in a cure of every economic and social evil. Their hearts were so soft that these troubles took precedence over every other care that might have touched them more nearly. Indeed every other care was merely an invention of the exploiters to turn one from the remedy one knew and was, at an early opportunity, going to employ. Any thought of religion was clearly of that kind. So too was any anxiety about the perils of war of which a few people were trying to make out that the world was full. The Union of my university had the distinction of declaring, even before the Oxford Union more notoriously did so, that it would not fight for king and country. That would have been quite an unreasonable thing to do.

It was a piece of good fortune that the works of T.E. Hulme fell into my hands about this time. Here was somebody, intellectually *vornehm* if anyone was, recommending one to consider the fallacies not merely of humanitarianism but of humanism. It seemed that that doctrine had been invented just like any other. It had been invented, and its day was passing. Moreover every philosophy, according to Hulme, was made up of a rational super-structure and a *Weltanschauung* with the selection of which reason had not much to do. Whatever conclusions one might draw from that, one of them might well be that a certain distrust would not be out of place when one listened to even the most plausible of persuaders. There were, of course, several known members of the Communist Party among my acquaintances at the university. They smiled the smiles not only of a powerful organization but of an arcane knowledge. But whatever my sympathies with the practical part of their programme I was, though lightly armed, able not to understand their appalling theory. It was a victory for the voice which, Socrates said, never told him what to do but told him what to desist from.

My academic studies at this time happily included some atten-tion to the philosophers and poets of our seventeenth century. I suppose the basic notion behind academic teaching about this period was that between the death of Elizabeth in 1603 and the Revolution of 1689 which was still called Glorious, this country, in common with most of western Europe, shook itself free from theology and began to think real thoughts of the kind that logical

positivists allow. Although none of my teachers was of the latter
school, in the matter of political theory most attention was paid
to writers who could somehow be held to be in the empirical line
that stems from Bacon. I think I even then understood, with the
help of Hulme, that that tradition favoured not only scientific
methods but a group of preconceptions and prejudices which
were as unargued as those of the religious tradition which, it was
supposed, was being abandoned. I have the impression that
Winstanley and the communist diggers who took part in the
debates at Putney under the Commonwealth were, for all their
wide-eyed innocence, thought to be more relevant to contemporary politics than so fruitful a thinker as Filmer. Filmer was so
old-fashioned as to think in terms of a divine society and the patriarchal group, and had been the butt of Locke and Algernon
Sidney, so that his unpopularity was not to be wondered at. I
have, however, no cause to complain about the time I spent in
those studies. An early introduction to the fissiparous political
idealists of the Commonwealth is something an Englishman may
be grateful for; and there is no eccentricity of idealistic socialism
that will astonish him thereafter.

When I graduated in 1934 the unemployment we had talked
so much about seemed to await me as it did all but the luckiest of
my contemporaries. Employers preferred to take from the older
universities the few exponents of useless subjects they wanted.
Nobody answered the applications I made for various jobs, but as
it turned out I was given a travelling scholarship which enabled
me to go to Germany, a country chosen less for its intellectual
attractions than for its rate of exchange, which was such that I
could keep alive even on the little money I had. The Nazi revolution had not long taken place, so my journey had an unusual
interest as a political excursion. I should put it on record that, at
the moment of my departure, I might be said to have attained
what was, for my years, a fair degree of political agnosticism. It
was as if my mind had been reduced to a blank sheet. What was
drawn on it in the following months were the first lines of a new
pattern. I stepped into another country as soon as I left
Southampton. We were travelling on a boat of the North German
Lloyd. As we went aboard the band played God Save the King,
and two young Nazis exchanged grins over my head. A year
before I had sat down in public when the same tune was played,

but the incivility of these young men impressed me unfavourably. I was beginning to know that I was English.

The first impression of Germany, to a young man who had read the newspapers of 1933, was of a disappointing calm and order. Outward signs of menace were not, however, lacking. There, true enough, were the squads of storm-troopers marching about the streets, and once I looked down on a parade of the Arbeitsdienst with their gleaming shovels and perfect military formation. When soon afterwards I visited an Arbeitsdienst camp it was to read in the eyes of boys who were merely unused to discipline a resentment against the whole philosophy of Hitler. Gradually, as my peaceful days ran on, I detected small and genuine signs of oppression. The young men who collected for the Winterhilfswerk were received with a kind of respect I did not like and there were well-attested stories of people who had been taken away for six months and had said very little about it when they came back. I was not quite in the fantastic world which the popular press in England had represented as being that of Hitler's Germany, but I was in a world where certain political nerves, in England still well covered, had been exposed. It was possible to feel the pull and thrust of force in a way that could hardly be done at home. It was not only in encounters with the patently Nazi that this was to be felt. Onkel Willi and Tante Else, with whom I lodged in Hamburg, were too old for political conversion. One day, however, Tante Else came in with radiant face and a newspaper bearing the great headline

DER KOENIG ALEXANDER UND BARTHOU ERSCHOSSEN

I did not know much about either gentleman and did not care, but I could not help being impressed by the indecency of Tante Else's joy. 'They were the enemies of Germany', she cried in the face of my puzzlement. It was supposed to be a sufficient explanation. It was evident that my hostess felt towards Germany quite differently from the way in which anyone I had known at home felt about England. It had been a dogma with my more enlightened friends that only capitalist intrigue kept the nations apart. Impressions such as these strengthened my suspicion that this was not so.

My next stopping place was Berlin, and it had been arranged that I should live in a little flat which turned out to be shared between the editor of a Labour Front journal, a Herr Doktor of some speciality or other who did something in an office of one of the heavy industrial enterprises, and a boy who was learning to be an actor. All three were from Saxony, and their talk together was in that dialect. It struck me as odd that, minute though my resources were, I was well off in comparison with them. I could occasionally eat jugged hare in the Kurfürstendamm or drink coffee with *schlagsahne* in the Potsdamer Platz. If I went out with one of them at midday it might well be to Aschinger's, where you could have soup for a few *pfennige* and the bread was free. That poverty and violence might go together I well understood, for that I had learned from the Communists who accompanied the hunger marchers entertained by my university friends before I left home. The structure of Germany seemed to be made up of hunger and rapacity.

The purposes of my being in Berlin were vague, but centred around the university. My by now fading suspicion of impending rebellion was momentarily pricked into life by the finding of a bomb in the cloakroom and the offer of a reward to anyone who could identify the criminal who had left it there. But the deepening impression was of a ruthless imposition of order, met from below by a response that had needed only to be released. My friend the Herr Doktor was anxious to go off for a course with the Reichswehr and spoke gleefully of the conspiracy by which it was growing beyond the limit allowed by the treaty. A young man I knew had been a member of Roehm's Storm Troop and, when the shooting began, had made for an island in one of the lakes around Berlin and had lain on his belly in the open till he thought it safe to steal back. This world was not that of my student friends at home who preached a violence they had been protected from.

From Berlin I went, by way of Dresden and its delicious Baroque, to Prague, where my German met with incomprehension until it was discovered that I did not speak it as a native. I had come armed by my friends in Berlin with introductions to Nazi agents and I was taken to see an aged and charming German lady who, I suppose as part of a programme, told me that the insolencies that the Germans suffered at the hands of the Czechs were nothing new, for in her day the Slavs had been the object of Hapsburg favouritism. For Germans in Czechoslovakia the only solution – not an immediate one, of course, they could not hope for that – was union with Germany. When I left the country I was loaded with literature to prove the point, and the rigours of the customs official at Eger relaxed when he found what I had in my baggage. It was thus that I first crossed a frontier with a feeling that the guns might be loaded.

The rest of my vacation took me by way of Nuremberg, Munich and Stuttgart to Freiburg where I spent as much of the second semester as my vanishing resources allowed. It was a pleasure to be in the Rhineland, and by the time I first looked across the river to the line of poplars that was France I had learned to hope that the fortresses there hidden were strong enough to withstand the armies that must soon surely move once more in that direction. By this time there was no longer any question of wondering, as I had done a year or two earlier, whether war was indeed possible between modern states, or whether the talk of it was not rather a political invention to keep the peoples amused. I knew that modern states could go to war and that one intended shortly to do so. And it was clear to me that any international comity was an unreal cover for the belligerent nationalisms of Europe. It was not a question of whether one wanted to be a nationalist. Nationalism was what was; and an appreciation of European affairs in any other terms was more or less a misrepresentation.

One final enlightenment awaited me in Freiburg. While I was there, Goering came and made a speech with allusions to the Church which were stonily received in that so Catholic country. And I attended a lecture to see Theodor Haecker, with grave dignity, turn over page after page of what he had intended to read while in the front row before him students in brown shirts stamped their jack-boots. These events made me aware of the existence of people who deferred to a principle that was not mere force and wished their unquestionable loyalty to Germany to find some more complex and balanced expression than in the thrust of aggression and oppression. Ecclesiastical history was not among my interests at that time, and I had no means of pursuing these reflections very far.

A large part of the following year I spent in Paris. There were still no jobs but there was, on the other hand, a travelling scholarship large enough this time for me to be able to live there for a while in spite of the high cost of francs, provided that I exercised the strictest economy. If it was in Germany that I first learned to see Europe's nationalisms as plainly as my hand before my face, it was in France that the subject first acquired theoretical importance and the pattern of my future thinking about politics was determined. Already in Freiburg I had laid hands on a volume of Daudet and one of Maurras, and when I first encountered the *Action Française* in the streets of the Latin Quarter I had to buy. From the paper day by day I learned, as a conscious method, what was already becoming a habit as a result of my observations in Germany, namely, to think of politics in general, and foreign affairs in particular, as matters of force. But it was less on the daily articles of the commentators, however, than on the great volume of the *Enquête sur la Monarchie*, on *L'Avenir de l'Intelligence* and other volumes of Maurras that I began to sharpen my mind. Everything that democracy believed in was called in question and, more important, *reasons* were given for the survival of hereditary institutions which I had assumed could be tolerated only by stupidity or inertia. If the nation was indeed the true unit of government in modern Europe, and the history of that Europe was so largely a battle of national interests, a royal house was more likely than any other political invention to secure a nation's coherence and persistence from generation to generation. The monarchist doctrine of Maurras I took, no doubt with a little over-enthusiasm, as explaining most things in France, but it can have had little influence on such vague thoughts as I had about the government of England. When George V died, I believe my French host and hostess were more affected than I was. After all George V was only a real king, and I was still young enough to feel the superior attractions of theory. I suppose any general conclusions must have been stored up for future use. I returned to England and my first article was published in the *New English Weekly* early in 1937. In this article, which was entitled 'Charles Maurras and the Idea of a Patriot King', I used an idea that I had picked up in France to illumine what was to me an otherwise uninteresting page of Bolingbroke. This exercise turned on the identification of the king's interest with that of the nation, and that has been a *point acquis* with me ever since. I have never since been tempted to regard the monarchy as an accidental or auxiliary part of the constitution, as is done by such writers as Jennings.

My main efforts at this time were necessarily directed to something very different from so conscious a manipulation of ideas as my article represented. I had now to earn my living in a great organization, a type of activity for which nothing in my life hitherto had at all directly prepared me. Any administrative work necessarily involves the handling of material of little intrinsic interest, and the same might no doubt be said of the use of the productions of academic scholarship. But owing to the tolerance of my tutors and my habit of going after my own game I had not used those productions very much. Still less had I been accustomed to that abstinence from one's own intellectual preferences without which work in a great organization cannot be carried on. This made me perhaps excessively conscious of the contrast between what seemed the infinitesimal force of the individual thinker as compared with the tremendous power of the public world in which money is earned. There were two worlds, which I had to bring to terms, not merely as a theoretical exercise but because I had necessarily to live in both. My conclusions at this stage were set out in what were grandly called 'Extracts from an Essay on Intellectual Liberty' published in 1939 [= 'Order and Anarchy']. The central idea of this essay was an opposition between public sentiments and private perceptions, and the assimilation of the former to the system of force by which states are governed – the latter being of course a conception grown out of my travels and reading in Germany and France. 'There are two kinds of political thought compatible with our idea of intellectual integrity', I wrote.

> One is that of the person who criticizes the state in terms of his private tastes (as distinct from the popular prejudices he entertains). This will be a kind of protest against the conduct of politicians, but the anarchical thinker will hardly hope to have a notable effect upon them. He will understand (what M Benda has pointed out) that ideas have political effect only when popularization has denatured them. The other kind of political thought compatible with intellectual liberty will consist not in protesting against government but in understanding it. It will consist in considering every political situation in terms of force, and it will seek to discover in any situation how far the influence of force extends. In some

cases it will at this point come near to the frontiers of literary criticism.

For my notion of literary criticism was that:

bad writing is writing which expresses the politically manoeuvrable sentiments and is therefore part of the system of force which is government. Good writing alone may be described as independent of government, and one has intellectual liberty just so far as one has the capacity to distinguish between valid work and invalid.

I must have been helped towards these formulations by some reading of Proudhon, but no doubt they record the shock of an intellectual, briefed in the machiavellian theories about the world of public action, on encountering the world which those theories purported to represent. And conscience, you will note, I still thought of as the private conscience of the literary man. Nothing in the outer world could correspond to his preference. Incidentally there was in all this more than a touch of Manicheeism, of which I first became conscious some ten years later on reading Saint Augustine.

I became rather contemptuous of those who expected any correspondence between their preferences and the outside world. The people I thought of in this connection were mostly thin-skinned intellectuals like the egregious Mr Spender. They were people who, when the war came, were very cross because it might stop them producing what were supposed to be their masterpieces, and because national war was not, so to speak, part of their theory of things. For me it was part of the ordinary deplorable conduct of nations, and I did not expect any attention to be paid, when it came, to my peculiar aptitudes. I had already in peacetime submitted to what amounted, for a man of independent and philosophic tastes, to a considerable discipline. The discipline of war would merely be more of the same. The modern state, with its elaborate and centralized administration, was really yearning for war, whatever pacific sentiments might be entertained in a particular country. War merely completed the integration to which the state aspired in peacetime. It made it possible for the state to control everyone's movements and, having achieved the perfection of its methods, to trundle the whole weight of a people against an enemy.

The distastefulness of this process was perhaps viewed even with a certain relish. Whereas to a humanitarian the war appeared to be not merely a disaster but a thing against nature, to me it seemed, though no less a disaster, one which was merely a realization, in a form which everyone had to admit, of a reading of politics which I had already admitted. There was, in principle, nothing to disturb oneself about. Moreover I must confess, though no doubt it shows me in a disagreeable light, that I watched with a certain malicious pleasure the squirms of those who had scruples about the war. For me there was no room for doubt about England's credentials. It was not that I was sanctimonious about her rightness. Certainly I *felt* England to be in the right; but as an intellectual matter I hardly admitted the categories of right and wrong in politics. All that counted was that England had been there for a long time and was my country. The windbags who invented ideals for her to fight for were wasting their time, or would have been, had it not been necessary to feed some such stuff to the people to keep them happy. I preferred the mere animal stubbornness of those of my unthinking fellow-countrymen who, protected by a fortunate history, assumed that they would go on. I preferred such people not only to the professional publicists and idealists but to both the supercilious writers of the *Horizon* group, who (one might honour some exceptions) were too good for the war, and the unimportant but sinister group who chose this most inopportune moment to brood publicly on the fall of the Roman Empire.

The simple dogma that we, the English, would and should go on acquired a new complexity during the army service which took me to India. At any rate my notion of who the English were there acquired a new dimension. In Bengal one could feel 'the oppression of a tradition backed by centuries not of Christianity and respect of the human person but of superstition, torture and even (not so far away) self-immolation and human sacrifice.' (I quote from some unpublished notes of 1943.)

The sacredness of kites, monkeys and cows became a nightmare; it was possible to watch these creatures moving among human beings and to see the human beings as of less account than they, and this transvaluation made them grotesque and frightful. One imagined one could feel the air heavy with the self-satisfying doctrine of reincarnation (men are born unequal and they deserve to be), one caste spitting on another. In Calcutta restaurants one could see rich Hindus treating servants with a contemptuous impatience of which a European would hardly have been capable because he could not have entertained such feelings unmixed with shame.

It seemed to me then that a country like mine, which had been Christian, and seemed still, for all its diseases, healthy compared with Hindustan, need not tread lightly on the corns of India. 'But the British were leaving India because they lacked conviction. They no longer knew what they wanted in the country. If they still had a function to perform, the statesman who could inform them of it had not appeared.' Amidst the evasions of a Hindu world it was possible to see something of what was meant by saying that Europe had been affected by Christianity. When on the way back we put in at Gibraltar it was not merely the Rock that stirred me, though no Englishman, I hope, can see that for the first time without emotion. The coast of Spain was the frontier of the Latin and Christian west and England was, in its odd and insular way, part of that. After my stay in India I knew better than from Massis what there was to defend.

Finding my way in England after the war I had two main threads to follow. One was my political education in France in the thirties and the other was my earlier studies of our seventeenth century. My thoughts turned naturally to Maurras, his support of Vichy and his imprisonment as a traitor. I had never taken the view, common in England in 1940, that any Frenchman who did not love us must love the Germans. There was the third possibility, that they might love themselves. But there remained something in Maurras that needed apology. He had never come to terms with the world as it is. With the exception of the four years of the first war, and the brief period at the beginning of the second before it became physically impossible to speak for a united France, he devoted the whole of his long and profoundly moving career as a writer to the destruction of the political form which, whether he liked it or not, was the form of France in the modern world. He believed that France must cure herself of democracy as of a disease, and re-adopt political forms which, in the long movement of thought by which France was best known in the outside world, she had decisively rejected. With such conviction, he was forced to become the exemplar of several of the vices he spent so much energy in attacking, and this made him in some respects a confused and confusing guide. He conceived of civilized man as giving allegiance to the state, a juridical and objective body, and not to any such vague conception as the 'people'; but he had been drawn to exemplify the very romanticism he opposed when he set the *pays réel* against the *pays légal*. He thought of affairs of state as a practical business, and jeered at the pretensions of *philosophes* and intellectuals to meddle with such matters. Yet what was he himself but an intellectual who did not like the world of his time, and hacked his way through the unpleasant facts around him with a chopper constructed out of principles he had got from books? He pretended that politics should be not an affair of sentiment but a calculation of interests, but when he said 'a cry is worth what its cause is worth' he forgot that, in a modern popular state, a cry itself and the sentiment that goes with it are forces to be reckoned with. When at last he confronted at Lyons the advocate of the 'femme sans tête' – the Republic which had given so absolute a demonstration of its incompetence – he was a candidate for martyrdom for an idea, not a political force to be reckoned with. One does not imagine the Cardinal de Richelieu standing in such a position. One does not imagine so truly political a mind making such an apology. Maurras was, indeed, not a man of action. In an apology for some delicate but still published words about the strength of France he once said in the *Action Française*, as if *sotto voce*, 'One would prefer to say such things in the king's chamber', but such is the practical world that Maurras would probably have been as far from the centre of advice in an absolute monarchy as in a democracy. When he spoke of the king's chamber he was dreaming. A different sort of capacity from his is wanted in cabinets. He spoke of 'being right' as 'still being one of the ways of immortalizing oneself'. But it is the philosopher's way to immortality; the practical man's way is to be successful.

A clue to the difficulty I now felt about Maurras's position was to be found in some words of Barrès in his journal of 1903–4. It is there set down that Barrès had not expressly joined 'the movement of Maurras and Bourget against the Revolution' because, 'when one is a traditionalist one cannot escape the necessity of

taking things in whatever state one happens to find them'. The
Revolution of 1789, as event and as myth, had entered the blood
of the people and had become part of France. It was not enough
merely to react against it. A man concerned about the government of France must take account of it in a more comprehensive
way. For the Englishman it is no doubt easier, owing to the acci-
dents of his country's history, to take a comprehensive view and
to accept things in the state in which he finds them. He is helped
by the fact that the Great Rebellion took place in the seventeenth
century and not at the end of the eighteenth when it would have
been a revolution. At that later epoch the current of a rising indus-
trialism would have joined the current of constitutional
innovation and the combined force of the two streams would
have swept away all before it. In the seventeenth century the
people of England, having tried and been tried by the engineers
of a revolutionary and military republic, turned to the king as if
they were re-entering the order of nature. No Englishman,
consequently, can be driven into the sort of opposition in which
Maurras found himself.

When I had taken stock of the Maurras who had been tried
and imprisoned as a traitor, it was natural to turn again to my
seventeenth-century studies, and this time to Filmer and
Clarendon rather than to the writers who had been most recommended to me as an undergraduate. Whoever considers, in the
light of what such writers say, the events of the Rebellion and the
Restoration, is driven in due course to consider the English
Church. For the king of England is a Christian monarch, not
merely crowned but consecrated, and the English Church may
claim to be what the Roman Church was under Constantine, in
a relationship to the state which, in principle at any rate,
continued for centuries with the Holy Roman Empire. The
execution of Charles I was a blow to Christendom, and the
Commonwealth prepared the way for the lay state of modern
times which rests on the equality of all opinions and consequently
can offer no ultimate justification for itself beyond the force that
it is able to exercise. This characteristic of the modern state had
been evident to me for too long to retain anything of the attractions of a discovery, and it repelled me for the brutal thing it is.
The new if still somewhat dim perception of the nature of Christendom which my Asiatic residence had given me no doubt made

me readier than before to pursue the theological and ecclesiastical implications of what happened in the seventeenth century. It may well be that other causes too, of which it would not be proper to speak here, led me in that direction. However that may be, I found myself considering the role of the national church outside as well as within the context of the Rebellion and Restoration.

The English Church received in full measure the shock of the Reformation, and was a forum for all the doctrinal arguments of the time. Under Edward VI the English rite prevailed, under Mary the Roman rite was reintroduced and was practised indifferently by priests ordained under either. In this way the succession was continued and under Elizabeth the problem of comprehending all Englishmen within the national church took precedence over the problem of the reunion with the Roman Church which political as much as theological considerations had now rendered for an incalculable future impossible. This effort of comprehension did not entirely succeed, for the English liturgy was not palatable to extreme Protestants, but the settlement had enduring consequences of great political importance. England was given what might be termed, borrowing words from Barrès who regretted that France had never had any such thing, a 'national Catholicism'. Anglicanism, it has been said, is a loyalty not a doctrine, and it was a Catholicism coloured with this loyalty which formed so many of the best minds of the seventeenth century. Hooker, who more than anyone else, devised the theoretical basis of the Anglican polity, died in 1600, and one need only evoke the names of Donne, Herbert, Vaughan, Traherne, or of Lancelot Andrewes, Fuller and Jeremy Taylor to suggest for anyone acquainted with our literature the power this tradition had to bring the English mind to its full flowering. It was the extreme Puritans, who had not been contained within this tradition, who in time grew powerful enough to overthrow both Crown and Church, and in the Commonwealth the English Church lived under oppressions that must have seemed likely to bring it to extinction and which did indeed reduce it to a mere remnant. The succession was maintained, but multiplication of sects under the Commonwealth had been such that the notion, very strong on all sides a hundred years earlier, that there could be only one Church, had been weakened, and when the Church was restored with the monarchy, it once again failed to contain the whole nation. James II may have toyed with the idea that the national church could be reunited with Rome by a royal act, but the time for that had gone with Mary Tudor. Apart from the theological intractabilities which had recently been armed and knew their strength, there was the fact that, through a century's experience, the Pope had come to be looked upon as the inveterate associate of England's enemies. The increasing toleration of the next hundred years looked less favourably upon Roman Catholics than upon nonconformists of our own growth because the former, with their foreign connections, threatened the integrity of the nation as the latter did not. The English Church suffered almost as much, though differently, in the eighteenth century in its prosperity as it had done in adversity in the mid-seventeenth. It was so much the nation, or at any rate the ruling part of the nation, that the deism and even materialism of fashion began to eat into it, and it numbered among its prelates men who were content to explain away or merely ignore the meaning of the liturgy they used. There were, however, such men as William Law, Christopher Smart and Samuel Johnson who still had their fingers on the thread of the main Anglican tradition. The thought of such men, so much of the eighteenth century and yet with longer memories and deeper roots, helps one to understand the force behind the doctrines which Coleridge, himself following a thread from Hooker, developed in *Church and State*. 'In relation to the national church, Christianity, or the Church of Christ, is a blessed accident.' He conceived of an *enclesia*, a clerisy, a learned order of men 'chosen in and of the realm', and an *ecclesia*, 'the communion of such as are called out of the world'. Grievous errors arose if the functions were confounded, and 'fearfully great and grievous would be the evils of the success of an attempt to separate them'. The national church should be, as it had been in Elizabeth's day, 'a great and venerable estate of the realm', and not 'reduced to a religion', one of a number of warring sects. It was 'an essential element of a rightly constituted nation ... religion, true or false, is and ever has been the centre of gravity in a realm, to which all other things must and will accommodate themselves'. The catholic truth within the national church will fecundate it, and it in turn will fecundate the nation. 'Allegiance to a foreign power, or the acknowledgement of any other visible head of the Church but our sovereign lord and king' was an absolute disqualification for trust or function in that church. Coleridge was restating what had been the fundamental *political* position of the *Ecclesia Anglicana* since the break-up of mediaeval Europe had given the Papacy the problem, which it had never satisfactorily solved, of conducting relations with sovereign national states.

The development of Methodism, which was the major social and religious movement at the end of the eighteenth century, marked, once more, the failure of the English Church to accommodate all the king's subjects in England. But it was a child of the English Church, and the national sap ran into it as it could never have done into the Roman Church when a second hierarchy was introduced as a foreign mission in 1850. It is worth remarking that Wesley, as was to be expected from his original High Churchmanship, was firm and clear in telling his followers to respect their duties to the Crown. It had indeed been Wesley's contention that 'whoever separated from the Church [of England] separates from the Methodists', and this was his position until the end. But his own impatience caused him to falter and his successors broke away. None the less Methodism did in fact bring a form of Christianity to the proliferating masses of the industrial revolution who would otherwise have been pagan, and did so in a manner which contained at least the possibility of reintegration within the national church.

It is the monarchy which, in a thousand years of history, has made it possible to speak of England as one country, and it is the Church which, for an even longer period, has been the source of the nation's persistent renewal. There is no reason to suppose that, in these matters, the future will differ from the past. Indeed I believe that England will lose her identity if she does not maintain her historic monarchy and church, and it is in the light of the service it renders to these two causes that whatever is said or done in the name of England must be judged. We must maintain, to guide our conduct, the conception which Hooker had so clearly in mind of a country in which to be a subject of the Crown is to be a member of the national church. This will seem an unpractical objective only to those who do not understand that the very neutrality of a modern administration makes it in the end responsive to any idea that is widely enough held. In the very complexity of our present entanglement there is hope. For we have not to do with a country where a political atheism and a political Christianity are set against one another in a deceptive battle, but one in which a fragment of our heritage is to be found in each of the parties.

It is not the writer's function to invent anything in the nature of a programme. He has only put down his thoughts as best he can, and for their own sakes, knowing that the statesman's material is the popular experience and feelings which the ideas of philosophers and the perceptions of artists have already affected. What the writer proffers does not, in a healthy society, act on the statesman directly but by mingling with the ideas of thousands of other people, most of them dead.

One may believe, indeed, that so great is the weight upon us of other men's thoughts, most of them not finding conscious expression in us at all, that what we are is many times more important than what we think. But if we can catch a glimpse of our enduring needs at all, it will be in the most permanent of those institutions which have shaped our history. A man born in England can hardly be more faithful to his country than when he uses, in one of those parish churches where it has been used for so long, the magnificent Prayer for the King's Majesty or the Queen's: 'O Lord our heavenly Father, high and mighty, King of kings, Lord of lords, the only Ruler of Princes…'

Natural History

I

I can remember, in my young age, sitting at the table in the breakfast room, trying to make a poem about sleigh bells while my
mother made the Christmas cake. I have no doubt that she was
more successful than I was, and that my despair was justified. In
adolescence I often knew in advance – sometimes the day before
– when a poem was coming on, and I had not to think about it
in case I should spoil it. It may be that the prohibition was no
more than the superstitions which have always readily attached
themselves to pregnancy, but there is probably something in the
nature of poetry which makes it necessary to avoid conscious
premeditation. The beginnings of poetry are hopelessly imitative,
and it is difficult to see how the gathering burden could unload
itself in rhymes which were nothing but John Drinkwater or
Robert Louis Stevenson. But that was how the ecstasy in the coal-
house ended when, later, I pressed my heart against the edge of
the table and wrote the lines which appeared in the Children's
Corner of the *Bristol Observer*.

It is no doubt a sense of the inadequacy of the vehicle that
makes one discard one's models with fury one after the other.
John Drinkwater gave way to Rupert Brooke, Rupert Brooke to
Edith Sitwell and to Dante Gabriel Rossetti. Finally John
Drinkwater and Robert Louis Stevenson had to be got out of the
house, it shamed me so to see them on the shelves. Need I say
that it was the first intimation of sexual love, as for Beatrice, which
filled out my sequence of sonnets in the manner of the House of
Life? It could be said that that represented a progress, for the
model was at least a little nearer what I had to put into it.

At this time, naturally, Thomas Stearns Eliot put in a grave
appearance and bade me desist from these excesses. I was about
seventeen. Shortly afterwards I was pounded by Pound. I had my
Weltanschauung adjusted by T.E. Hulme. Public-schoolboys
invited me to admire the working classes. From all this I never
recovered. At intervals for the next year or two I wrote poems
which 'showed awareness' – that would have been the expression.
For about a year (*circa* 1932) I must have been contemporary.
How I got over this is mysterious, but it was not all done by liter-

ature. I was struck down by an appalling adolescent grief, as is not uncommon. René Béhaine identifies the very moment when he left behind him 'le sens du bonheur et le pouvoir d'être heureux' (the reference is to be found on pp. 132–3 of *Avec les yeux de l'esprit*, vol. VI of the *Histoire d'une Société* – surely one of the best books of the century). It was something of that kind.

At the same time, my learning grew. Do not be alarmed, ignorant reader, it was never very great. But were not Thomas Stearns Eliot and Ezra Pound learned? And, although I have not told you, I had been – oh, on a much more modest scale than those two thought indispensable – a not unlearned boy. For in the Rossetti period I had already read through the *Britannia's Pastorals* of William Browne of Tavistock, Robert Greene, the *Hero and Leander* of Christopher Marlowe, besides many other poets recommended or unrecommended in schools. I read them aloud in the lavatory in those days. But now the obligation to acquire culture became grave. I advanced through the seventeenth century looking for strange creatures, but more especially for those who had earned a mention in the works of my masters. I too could evaluate poets then. I despaired of being a poet myself (I was despairing of everything at that time, you will remember). I believe I must have aspired to be an educated man. So I gave up the exercise of verse.

This was in the year of our Lord nineteen hundred and thirty-four, and the twentieth of my age. The muse took her leave of me in Berlin, at a time, appropriately enough, when I was supposed to be writing a thesis on the translation of poetry, though no such work was ever produced by me. Instead, I gawped at marching columns of young men in jack-boots, at blond prostitutes in the Kurfürstendamm, at paintings by Klee which could still be seen at the Kronprinzenpalais, at anything that could be gawped at, and at four o'clock in the morning lectured on a particularly abstruse sentence from *Ulysses* in the waiting-room of the Friedrichsstrasse station. It would not repay you to follow me to Prague, Nuremberg, Munich or the several other cities I honoured at that time. My preoccupations were political, and when I reached Freiburg I was looking for books by Léon Daudet.

I do not wish to say more about these days than will indicate what I was up to while the Muse's back was turned. The next year

I was in Paris, a passionate reader of the *Action Française* and of everything of Maurras I could lay my hands on, from the *Enquête sur la monarchie* to the *Conseil de Dante*, partly because I had already had the left-wing part of my education, and partly led on by the seductions of his prose. Everyone had had enough of educating me by then: it was the public authorities that did it, though they were less free with their money then than now. The young will have heard, and their elders will have learned more forcibly, that in those days you either fought your way to a job or rotted on the dole. I already knew about having no money. And I was acquainted with no one who could conceivably help me to a job. So I became a civil servant. You had only to pass an examination and they could not refuse you, even if you said (as I did at the interview) that you chose the Civil Service because it was remote from everything that interested you.

It was remote. Most of my contemporaries struck me as rather Oxfordy young men and, meaning to be friendly, everyone asked me what college I came from and of course I came from none. I was put into a room with a man of experience who was doing things about unemployment insurance. I had read Kafka so I understood all this perfectly, but the working of the Civil Service was a mystery to me. It was possible to read bits of the *Decline and Fall of the Roman Empire* in between times. I acquired habits of diligence, however, though not the applause of the more influential of my betters.

My first article appeared in the *New English Weekly* in 1937. It was called 'Charles Maurras and the Idea of a Patriot King' – with allusion to Bolingbroke. Others followed. In 1939 I wrote for a review called *Purpose* a long essay which asserted 'that the distinction between public sentiments and private perceptions is fundamentally the same as the distinction between good writing and bad. If this in fact is so', the essay went on,

> it may be said that bad writing is writing which expresses the politically manoeuvrable sentiments and is therefore part of the system of force which is government. Good writing alone may be described as independent of government, and one has intellectual liberty just so far as one has the capacity to distinguish between valid work and invalid.

It was an assertion which did honour to the Muses, but the one

we are talking about did not visit me during these years except to
say

> Here lies a civil servant. He was civil
> To everyone, and servant to the devil.

It was only in the immense, prison-like leisure of a troopship
moving southwards through tropical waters that a few lines were
squeezed out, to define my condition.

It did not occur to me to amuse the boredom and oppression
of military life by continuing this exercise. I kept an intermittent
notebook, and three or four times during this exile the lines broke
up, and stresses and rhythms took charge, I like to believe because
of an involuntary concentration of attention. I had sweated for
months and years for those poems: not in the writing of them, but
literally sweated, travelled vast distances, protected my bread and
jam from the kite-hawks. If I had set out to provoke myself to
poetry it would not have been in that way.

My most deliberate attempt at writing at this time – to keep
my wits alive and vent my spleen – was the translation of some of
the political poems of Heine (*Versions and Perversions of Heine*,
London, 1955). The value of such performances is that they
provide technical exercise without conscious meddling with the
writer's own experience. After the war I had the good fortune to
be asked to translate some stories of Supervielle, which loosened
the muscles of my prose and gave me hints as to how I might use
it for narrative and imagination. I did not use it, and when the
muse of verse rhythms popped up again – it was not until the
nineteen-fifties – it was to prefigure in twenty lines what became
a long work in prose. I do not mean that these verses were any
sort of a deliberate sketch of the prose work, but when I had
written that work I could see that it had been prefigured. The
twenty lines with which I resumed my writing of verse had been
ground out, much as the lines on a troopship had been, without
wilfulness and out of an accumulated pressure. The springs went
so deep that I had only to get up at six every morning for a year
and put a bucket into the same well to draw up my sixty thousand
words of prose.

From that time the practice of verse has been intermittent but
has never been intermitted for immense periods, although 'on
voit le style d'un homme qui a toujours commencé à écrire, et

qui n'a jamais écrit'. That was said of a man of affairs – of Richelieu and his *Testament politique* – by Montesquieu (in the *Cahiers*)
and, because scale does not matter I may be forgiven for thinking
that I know what is meant. The pressure of affairs, by which one
earns one's living, is at a barely tolerable enmity with the needs of
the writer, yet it may not be wholly unproductive. Certainly the
conduct of affairs is, by the standards of the writer or artist, for the
most part a frivolous business. There is more genuine difficulty in
the ordering of material, the simplification of complex problems,
than the writer who has been spared these horrors is apt to give
the man of affairs credit for. But ideas are frowsy by the time they
come to be used for action. The language of business is stale. It is
the mechanical faculties of memory and logic which have most
play in it. The men are vivid, however. This is the world, and the
gamut of the classical moralist – ambition, fear, dissimulation – is
not to be exhausted without some experience of it.

One should not write more poetry than one must, and some
formula has to be found for passing the time between poems. The
conduct of affairs is one, though probably not the best. While one
is seeing this world, what worlds is one not seeing! But at least
these avocations prevent one from thinking of oneself as a poet,
which for most writers of verse must be very salutary. The anni-
hilating pressure of work seems an enemy, but so many times of
idleness, as a student and in the army, have produced nothing that
one cannot say with certainty that relief from this treadmill would
produce more, though I think it would. The writing of poetry is
a matter of personal economy, but it cannot be treated as such,
for one does not know what one wants to discover. One can only
go on living, and be grateful for this by-product if it comes. It may
be just pleasure, or it may be the truth peeping out. 'Un homme
qui écrit bien' – to quote Montesquieu (in the *Cahiers*) again –
'n'écrit pas comme on a écrit, mais comme il écrit, et c'est souvent
en parlant mal qu'il parle bien.'

II

The poet has problems which you can call technical, if you like
the word, but when he is at work all his problems are one, which
is to keep what he is saying within the limits of the perceptible.
The words of most of the communications which pass between

people cannot be seen, smelt or tasted; they can barely be heard. They are (what is called) understood, by which is meant that they have certain practical effects, as the turning of switches or the movement of gear levers. It is this skeleton language which is used, almost exclusively, in the conduct of business, so that you have the absurd spectacle of people – fine figures of men, perhaps well-dressed and otherwise covered – talking to one another as if they were constructions of wire, watching for answers on a number of dials and occasionally blowing one another's fuses. The ordinary document of business has no existence apart from the use of the moment. It *does* a particular job: it establishes certain very limited connexions, but try to look at it apart from that particular purpose and you will see what is meant by saying that it has no existence. The poem exists less contingently, and you could make an esthetic theory (no doubt someone has) on the basis that the more the poem succeeds in living independently of time and place the better it is. But that would be tautological like most esthetic theories. The point is that the poem exists as a natural object exists, so that you can look at it, hear it, smell it, as you can wind, waves or trees, without asking why you are doing so. The poet literally feels his way forward, and when the moment comes when he is no longer touching something he has either finished his poem or is left with a broken piece in his hands.

Perceptible literary objects come in all kinds of shapes, and the work of a particular writer, taken chronologically, is likely to show a series of shapes related in the same way as the shapes you might expect to see emerging one after another from a painter's studio. The changes in the series pass for being the poet's development, but how does it look to him and why does he pass from one point to another in the series? He is not ordinarily thinking of developing (to give the professors something to write about). He is thinking – so far as he can be described as thinking of anything apart from the subject-matter – of making a poem which will not be the same as the last one. The development of the series is in one sense the result of a negative rather than a positive effort. If the familiar presents itself as he feels his way through the poem, he discards it, knowing that it would not be part of the poem, but would be a 'soft' bit. What, through its familiarity, can no longer be attended to, is of no use for his purposes. The unfamiliarity ought to be continuous but it is not absolute. Unfamiliarity is a relative thing. It is related to what is familiar; there is a background of expectedness to all that is unexpected. The poet may change things, but he starts from somewhere.

In the matter of verse forms, where he starts from may be more or less firmly dictated. The volumes of Johnson's poets show how obsessive a form can be. They also show what variety can be produced within a single form and how the attention flags if nothing new comes up. The difficulties of the twentieth century are not those of the eighteenth. We are not too narrowly dictated to but, like our architects, have now such a variety of possibilities that we can easily think ourselves original when we have not attended enough even to familiarize ourselves with a pattern that we could depart from.

It is an absurdity to try to be original. You might as well try to be beautiful or intelligent. But the complementary process of ridding yourself of obsessive influences can possibly be assisted by some conscious effort. A young man, however, cannot shrink back at the first touch of an alien hand. He has to live through his Eliot, his Yeats or whatever it may be. For a time he must wear fashionable clothes. Then he must discard them, and be prepared to find, not merely that he is naked, but that under, those clothes he simply was not there at all. Those who are simply not there at all do not hesitate to fill the poetry pages of respected journals, or even whole volumes, but silence is better. (Tarr went round persuading his friends to give up art.) Indeed silence is an admirable thing, nearer to poetry than the chatter of literary apes.

Because of the negative aspects of unfamiliarity, the fact that what is new is recognized by being different from something that is known, people may have difficulty in distinguishing a genuine variation from a mere copy of the theme. There is no sure way of making the distinction except by being able to do so. Some people can look and listen but more, it seems, can not. It is generally claimed that this is difficult only for contemporary work and that anyone can tell that *The Splendid Shilling* or *Cyder, a Poem* are superior (in their modest way) to most Miltonic blank verse of the eighteenth century but I think this phenomenon must be due to some other process.

The idea of the poet as a maker of novelties sets some puzzles. Is the difference that must exist between one poem and another by the same hand, of the same kind as that which must exist between the work of different poets? I do not know whether it was the same Anon. who wrote 'The Oakerman' and 'Tom o' Bedlam', 'From the Rugged Ile of Orkney / Where the Redshanke walkes the Marish' and 'I know more than Apollo, / For oft when he lies sleeping'. I find it hard to believe that it was not, but I do not see how one can say that it could not have been one man picking up another man's tune and making his own variation on it. This is easier, perhaps, at times when there are fewer tunes to be heard than in our day when we are deafened by polyphonies and on every hand the libraries give up their dead.

One readily thinks of the poet's problem as being that of learning to speak with his voice, but there is a lot of metaphysics as well as history behind this apparently innocent view. It raises all sorts of questions as to what this self is which is said to have a voice of its own. When I think of bits of writing which echo in the mind as *personal*, it is often of bits which are more obviously of another time and place than of another person. Thus it is England still climbing out of the Middle Ages which speaks in this from *The Life of Lord Herbert of Cherbury*, written by himself:

> And certainly since in my mother's womb this Plastica or Formatrix which formed my eyes, ears, and other senses, did not intend them for that dark and noisome place, but as being conscious of a better life, made them as fitting organs to apprehend and perceive those things which should occur in this world: so I believe since my coming into this world my soul hath formed or produced certain faculties which are almost as useless for this life, as the above-named senses were for the mother's womb; and those faculties are Hope, Faith, Love and Joy.

And it is the sixteenth century – though seen under the modus of action rather than of philosophy – which speaks in these verses of Sir Walter Raleigh:

> Although to give the lie,
>   deserves no less than stabbing,
> Stab at thee he that will.

But probably it makes sense to say that these authors sound real because they are telling the truth, as it seems to them, which is the only form of truth anyone can tell, except inadvertently.

As a piece of technical advice to the writer: Tell the truth and hope for the best is, however, inadequate. Some good writers have been quite extraordinary liars, along certain lines, as for example Ford Madox Ford. The truth is interesting if you can tell it, but the writer will feel a need to simplify his problems by abridging it in some way. What is not so good is putting in phoney bits. This also everybody does more or less, but the better writers less. The advice one might give – if any advice were of any use – might be to write about something about which you have some truth to tell. For the poet the truth is what he can perceive. This is the point at which the technical problems and the problems of subject-matter become the same. But is rhythm a part of the truth? It seems odd to say so. One feels for the subject, and if one finds it one finds the words. But the rhythm? The fact is that you cannot find the words without the rhythm, and what you might call your words, in a borrowed rhythm, would not be your words. So evading other people's rhythm is part of finding your own words, though you might help yourself by a preliminary decision to use or eschew certain forms, as the Pound of 'Mauberley' and the Eliot of 'Sweeney among the Nightingales' are said to have opted – with what reservations the products show – for the metric of the Bay State Hymn Book because free verse 'had gone far enough'; or as one might decide that it is too dangerous to attempt satire in pentameters of Dryden, Pope or Crabbe.

To know when one has some truth to tell is in a way the whole tact of the poet – a sort of slyness he has to use within his own mind. Rilke talks about 'Tausende von Liebesnächten' going to the making of a single line, and the poet's choice of a subject is no doubt related to his physiology and to the succession of his outward circumstances. One imagines that Shakespeare could turn anything to account because his receiving apparatus was as nearly perfect as could be, but most writers can manage only a few scratchings on the limited subject-matters of which, amidst the general obscurity of their lives, they manage to apprehend something more or less concretely. Why their gropings should sometimes succeed and sometimes not is about as explicable as why love and liking turn up how and when they do. Though I could not find a subject-matter by saying: That has been much in

my experience, looking at my poems after the event I recognize
that many of them are the small visible pinnacles of apperceptive
icebergs.

III

When Charles I saw some of Denham's poems he advised him
'that when men are young, and have little else to do, they might
vent the overflowings of their Fancy that way, but when they
were thought fit for more serious Employments, if they still
persisted in that course, it would look, as if they minded not the
way to any better' (The Epistle Dedicatory, in Denham's Poems).
'Whereupon', says Denham, 'I stood corrected as long as I had
the honour to wait on him.' In some sense poetry is secondary, a
series of glimpses on a journey, which you would not have had if
you had taken another journey. Nonetheless, most of the business
of life is trivial by comparison. The stockbroker, the businessman,
the civil servant, the commentator, and such-like figures of the
popular imagination, are generally easily replaced by other
despatch cases with the same contents. We are more like one
another than one might suppose. But what the poet does is not to
be replaced by the work of anyone else, and the capacity to
produce even a few bits of poetry is incomparably rarer than mere
ability to transact business. As to whether that makes the poet
incomparably more valuable than the man of affairs I know
nothing, but it is hardly for the disciples of the price mechanism
to say that it does not, unless they maintain that no one wants the
stuff anyhow.

The Study of Affairs

I

It is a far cry from the world in which Denham was advised by Charles I to give up writing verses if he wanted to be 'thought fit for more serious employments'. There are several scandals, for the modern *littérateur*, in this curious dialogue between the poet and his master. What business had the King to tell Denham to stop writing? And what business had Denham to listen to him? Here are the mutual vices of autocracy and abjection, indulging one another! And of course, for modern mythology, the poet is superior to the King, so the whole relationship is upside-down. But the matters on which Denham was to be engaged were not without a proper seriousness. The conversation took place after the delivery of Charles I into the hands of the army, and 'he was pleased to command me', says Denham, 'to stay privately in London, to send to him and receive from him all his Letters from and to all his Correspondants at home and abroad, and I was furnished with nine several Cyphers in order to do it: Which trust I performed with great safety to the persons with whom we corresponded.' For the modern mind the poet, or more generally 'the artist', is someone for whom the state ought to do something, and the ages of patronage are recollected, and beautified in the recollection, to justify this position. The poet, in this conception, is a lolling beauty for whom all kinds of things should be done. May it not be, however, that if a correct tension is to be established between the poet and the great world of the majority, the poet, who is after all a man and not an object of literary criticism, has first to understand that he is not a romantic exception but a member of the commonwealth? No doubt if he thinks when he writes of serving the commonwealth with his pen he will serve it badly, and his works will deserve oblivion; but why as man should he regard himself as excused the duties of the world? – and if that is not a suitable expression let him choose another. It is after all the poet, and not that abstraction the commonwealth, who can feel the tension, and who can understand, if there should be a relationship between the public and private worlds, what it could be. The merely literary writer fades, but we carry in our minds the words of those who have expended themselves in the ordinary life of mankind: 'Le contemplateur, mollement couché dans une chambre tapissée, invective contre le soldat qui passe les nuits d'hiver au bord d'un fleuve et veille en silence sous les armes pour la sûreté de sa patrie.' (Vauvenargues: *Réflexions et Maximes* CCXXIII.) No doubt the poem, the book, has a peculiar social role about which treatises might be written, but the poet, the man, surely has not and the less airs he gives himself the better. It is indeed in so far as he manages to enter upon the life of the world at large that he is able to produce a book which has a social function to perform. Of course the world at large is far from being concerned only about its public functions, so the poet living for himself may enter upon concerns of the most profound importance. Still, it is a romantic fallacy which proposes as his special field his bed, his favourite seat by the canal, or some other private pleasure. There was something in the classic notion that the best poetry would be about the fall of princes – great events, at any rate, which drew to themselves deep stocks of the energies of mankind, though much bad verse has been written by people who were by no means equipped to write the best poetry trying to make this dream come true.

II

The time of Denham's scandalous conversation with Charles I was also the time when the English language was at its most resourceful and was the vehicle of our profoundest insights. But now, 'American is already a language of exclusively external relationships, a tradesman's tongue' (Ananda Coomaraswamy, *The Bugbear of Literacy*, p. 24), and English is not far behind. There has been a deterioration, in the lifetime of men now in the public service, of the language in which affairs are conducted. If one goes back a little further, to the mid-nineteenth century, when a report was more likely to have been the work of one or two able men, unimpeded by a committee and a secretariat, the human voice may occasionally be heard in official documents. It is worth comparing Northcote and Trevelyan's report on the Civil Service, of 1854, with the report of the Royal Commission which reported in 1956. The obfuscations of the latter document are, however, nothing to those of the characteristic pronouncements on economic policy which are emitted by Whitehall at short intervals. While it is still, happily, true that in the arcana of the service men who are capable of it may communicate with one another in nervous and informal prose, the official utterance, as such, is slithering into unintelligibility. The remedies proposed by Sir Ernest Gowers, of improving the English of the lower and middle orders, are nothing to the point, because the trouble has its root in a systematic detraction from the human mind which is built into our system of government and commerce. For the purpose of government and commercial policy a grotesque simplification is accepted. There is a determination to see all human activity in terms of production, and not of the production of a diversity of goods, but production *tout court*, which is summarized and valued in terms of money. This service of quantity which is the most readily recognizable value in a technological age, has ultimately no need of the human mind at all. At any rate, it has no need of that human mind which has laboriously crept out of pre-history, with the help of cave drawings and stone circles, and achieved itself in Dante or Shakespeare. A very mean instrument, comparatively speaking, will provide the consciousness needed to set the production targets or to plan the machinery to go to the moon. All this effort is collective, not in the sense in which, perhaps, the primitive drawing was so, as expressing a rising individual consciousness which would be that of *man*, and not just of the artist, but in the sense that it is made up of bits, no one gives to it more than a part of his mind.

The poet is the natural enemy of all this because the nature of his activity is such that he clings to the conception of man. Admittedly this conception is becoming increasingly tenuous, because it is increasingly difficult to postulate a special importance to that category. It is not merely that, for science, man is an object rather than a subject; it is that there seems to be less and less point in attributing importance to this particular biological grouping. Consciousness could classify what it perceives in innumerable other ways, each just as relevant for a number of technological purposes. It may well be that we are approaching the end of history, reaching out into an age which will not understand the past of the human race, and which will, accordingly, have nothing in it that could interest us.

It is not to be assumed that the human consciousness we have is a permanent acquisition. It seems to me not improbable that a psychic change may be happening, not unlike the physical change which overcame the Neanderthals in the last days of that race, but more rapid.

> Before the Neanderthals died out during the advance of the last ice sheet, a change of structure ensued. The body of the later Neanderthal became more massive and heavy, the head became even lower and more bulging and the dental arches heavier. The later Neanderthals were barrel-chested and bull-necked and there is some indication of bowed limbs. In all these features they are unlike modern man; thus we see again the extraordinary evolutionary phenomenon of a very recent and distinctively man-like form progressing away from the condition of modern man during the same time that modern man was arising from his ancestors. (Hampton L. Carson, *Heredity and Human Life*, p. 130.)

III

The mythology of progress which dominated the nineteenth century has given way to another which, being still in fashion, is of course not regarded as a mythology at all. The current doctrine recommends *change* as being a good thing. In its origins this doctrine is (as the doctrine of progress perhaps was) technological. People in industry 'ought to be' infinitely adaptable, in order to make more and more goods, and more money, more rapidly. Whatever the inventions of technologists demand of them, they should be prepared to do. Even supposing a doctrine of maximum adaptability is a good one for the individual to adopt (and consider, for example, what this means in terms of sexual behaviour), the doctrine that *other people* should be indefinitely adapted to whatever the new world requires of them is certainly tyrannical. It demands changes in consciousness otherwise than as a function of individual growth. Of course this deformation of consciousness in the interests of organization is no new thing; no doubt the whips of Egyptian slave-masters operated a little in this direction. But in a technocratic world the devices for treating people as things are much more subtle and far-reaching. The very kindnesses of the great organization are done without any conversation between consciousnesses. The sick man is taken into hospital and modified as one might modify an engine. The somewhat unfashionable idea that a plague is a visitation of God's wrath respects the being of the sick man in a way which the successive transformations of William Smith into William Smith, Mark II and Mark III, does not. The social sciences, as yet inept and uninstructive, aim at a similarly high-handed treatment of the social group.

In this violent world the man of letters plays a benign and conservative role. He sees himself as one with the animal creeping out of pre-history. If he produces new work which shocks and startles, it is precisely because he is not being destructive as the surgeon or the publicity man aim at being destructive. It is because he is opening up a new area in consciousness, indicating a point to which you may go from the point you now occupy. While the technologist puts something over on you, the poet offers to take you with him, if you feel able to go, which admittedly most people do not.

IV

It is hard to realize how many more paid intellects we now have than we had a few years ago. The universities are overflowing, at public expense, with people who, in addition to talking to and examining other young persons of both sexes, are actually supposed to think for their money. Among the many (numerically) flourishing disciplines – as even the most accidentally demarcated group of subject-matters loves to call itself – the study of literature and the study of politics are not among the least. So much that is authoritative is written about literature and public affairs by people without experience of either that it is with the greatest diffidence that one who happens to be both poet and public official opens his mouth to suggest points at which these two studies may touch one another. The social and political background of literature are understood, with more or less acuteness. But what about the literary background of political studies? It is hardly too much to say that much of the energy of dons whose speciality is politics is expended on putting to rights politicians and officials who merely have to do what the dons talk about.

Perhaps it would be fairer (and I hope not disrespectful) to say that
these dons are kept at public expense rather as licensed fools at the
court of a prince, so that they may say things which those who
have responsibility for action are too prudent to say, and sometimes be right against all the advice of prudence – sometimes, of
course, not. We should be grateful for all this help. There is,
however, another possible study, less akin to that of the mere
publicist. It is possible only for the man of humane learning, the
man with a sense of poetry and theology as well as of, say,
economics. This is to consider the impact of government and its
devices on the governed. There is of course a sociologist's way of
doing this. But possible modifications of consciousness will in fact
only be perceived and expressed by the man who himself has a
consciousness of unusual depth and an unusual measure of literary
cultivation. It is perhaps unreasonable to expect that people
should display these qualities in exchange for a salary.

William Barnes

William Barnes came of the best blood in England, being the son of a small farmer in the West Country. Like many another in that countryside, the family was 'downstart' – in his own language – being an offshoot, or so he thought, of a gentleman's family of Gillingham in Dorset. That matters little enough, one way or the other. What does matter is that Barnes came from a stock neither high nor low, grown into the country like a tree-root. All distinctions of origin are on the way to being effaced, but there are still those who understand the intense pride of such birth, the furthest possible removed from pretension. In rural society it was a middle station; the gentry were above it, the labourers below, and its members no more aspired to be taken for the one than they feared being mistaken for the other. Snobberies are the product of an urban confusion, now spread too over an urbanized countryside. But before that happened the classes were an order of nature, worth nobody's while to question; a barrier of sorts, but not one that obscured the sottishness or other quiddity of the man on the other side – rather a setting against which his qualities could be shrewdly estimated and tartly commented. The tendency of social distinction to obscure personal worth is a phenomenon of dissolution, when members of different classes find themselves in competition in a world of supposed equalities.

The place of Barnes's birth was Bagber in the parish of Sturminster Newton, where his father had a poor farm and his uncle and aunt, across the common, a better one, until the fortunes of rural life turned against them and they had to sell up. The language spoken in this little world in 1801 – the year of Barnes's birth – was a Dorset untroubled by the mobility of populations or an excess of reading matter: 'the speech of our forefathers', as he is recorded as having said eighty-four years later, which in time would 'be scarcely remembered' and none would 'be found to speak it with the purity' he had heard it spoken with in his youth. He did 'some little to preserve the speech', but while we are considering origins, rather than directions, it may be well to reflect that it was some such speech – in different but related dialects – that Shakespeare and Raleigh spoke as boys and there will have been more than a trace of it even in the speech which Raleigh used at court. The Vale of Blackmore, whose capital

Sturminster Newton is, must in 1801 have been a remote pastoral valley, the life of which was nearer to that which the Elizabethans knew – and which in the sixteenth century ran to the fringes of London itself – than to the almost universally suburban life of our own time. In Sturminster Newton things were still made by hand which elsewhere were already being made more numerously, and worse, by machine, and the equipment of farms and cottages was the stools and pots and pans and benches of an earlier age. These things matter the more, in Barnes's growth and development, because he was not one who was sent away to school at Eton or Winchester, or to college at Oxford or Cambridge, but found his education on his doorstep. A world of selection tests and scholarships may be surprised that he found it at all. There was, however, a good church school, and the curate at Sturminster Newton was one of those illustrations – which do not always spring to light when one scrutinizes the countryside of the time – of Coleridge's thesis as to the benefits conferred by a Church which sought to put a scholar and a gentleman in every parish. Barnes was fortunate in his clergy, both in Sturminster Newton and later, in Dorchester, and it was under these benign auspices that he grew up. He left school at thirteen to go into a solicitor's office. As things went in his world, he was favoured.

Although his studies had made a fortunate start in Sturminster Newton, Barnes needed a more metropolitan scene and at the age of seventeen he moved from the capital of the Vale of Blackmore to the capital of Dorset itself. In an age when every illiterate youth has to be transported to Paris or Barcelona before he has left school the movement may seem a modest one, but it answered to the natural need of a boy of Barnes's age to turn his back on his origins. Dorchester was the right field of force. It showed Barnes a little of what is called the world, but against a background which he perfectly understood. It was the resort of farmers on market days and the Tunbridge Wells of the local county families. Once again he had a sympathetic employer – another solicitor – and a clergyman who helped him with his studies. It is extraordinary how the vigour and range of these studies grew. Barnes was not put in for examinations but had a natural taste for learning. He made progress in classical and modern languages. He became a highly competent engraver, for he was a man of his hands as well as of his head. He also fell in love with an exciseman's daughter whom he was not to be able to afford to make his wife for nearly ten years. One would give a lot to be able to meet the Barnes of those days. The evidence is that he was a young man of great charm and eagerness of spirit. By the time he was twenty he had printed a pamphlet of verses (in Dorchester of course); one of these published poems celebrated a Julia (the actual name of the girl who became his wife) whose father 'he lik'd the pecun'ary ore'. That must have caused a titter in the town. He went through a normal adolescent comedy with Julia's parents; he was snubbed when he tried to write or visit, and ignored the exciseman in the streets. At twenty-two he was no nearer an income he could marry on and went off to Mere in Wiltshire to take up school-mastering. E.M. Forster charges Barnes with a lack of sentiment about the Labourers' Revolt of 1830. The lowest middle classes have always lacked sentiment about the condition of the workers. They understand the troubles of poverty too well. It is the Schlegels (of *Howard's End*) and the Shelleys of real life who get excited. Barnes could be accused of lack of sympathy with the labourers only by someone with a very politicized notion of sympathy.

Barnes was to go on schoolmastering for nearly forty years. He had not, by the move to Mere, acquired a salary. He was trying to collect pupils and to get fees out of reluctant payers. The society he lived in was not one that readily offered security. Going to Mere meant turning his back on the intellectual stimulations of Dorchester. He had few social diversions, and used his leisure for study – mathematics as well as languages – and he continued to engrave. He was an ingenious and original schoolmaster, and gentle in an age when gentleness in schoolmasters was by no means to be taken for granted. He unaffectedly tried to impart something of his own diversity of interests. The school at Mere did at last enable him to marry, when he was twenty-six. In 1835 he returned to Dorchester and opened a school there. The success of the boarding establishment depended quite largely on Julia, and when she died in 1852 a certain listlessness set in. But the inter-vening years were years of active poetical production. His verses appeared in the *Dorset County Chronicle* and the first volume was published in London in 1844. Barnes says that he wrote for recre-ation in the evenings after his days of school-mastering. He certainly did not organize his life for poetry. His most conscious

efforts were for the support of his family and the pursuit of a
remarkable variety of studies, linguistical, philological, mathemat-
ical and archaeological. The poetry came 'naturally as the leaves
of a tree', as Keats said it should. But it is not unrelated to his more
time-consuming studies, and tricks from the Welsh and the
Persian are concealed in his indubitably spontaneous verses.
During these years in Dorchester he also collected pictures – a
Gainsborough and a Richard Wilson among them – excusing the
expense which he felt should rather have been on his numerous
family by saying that he spent nothing on wines or tobacco. He
was not what you could call *maudit*.

It is characteristic of the slow but persistent movement of
Barnes's career that at the age of thirty-six he put his name down
at St John's College, Cambridge, in order to be able, under a
statute then in force, to take his degree of B.D. ten or more years
later. He was ordained in 1847 and was given the care of the tiny
parish of Whitcombe, detached from another for the purpose. It
was not a living; it brought him thirteen pounds a year and he
walked out from Dorchester to serve it. He would have liked, but
did not get, the headmastership of Dorchester Grammar School,
and the diminution of his own school in Dorchester after his
wife's death made him seek employment elsewhere. It is of
interest that, with all his intellectual attainments, some reputation
as a writer, a public and impeccable rectitude and intense application to whatever duties he undertook, he obtained none of the
employments he sought, perhaps because his ferocious spirit of
independence allowed him to take none of the steps that are
normally taken in these matters. It was not until he was over sixty,
at a time when his financial anxieties were acute, that he was
offered the living of Winterborne Came, the parish near Dorchester which included his old church of Whitcombe. It was this
that made possible the patriarchal flowering of his last years.

Few men could have been better suited to the work of a parish
priest; it is hard to conceive of anyone better suited to that work
in the Dorset of that time. In temper and in learning, Barnes was
Herbert's 'Country Parson'; he had the super-added advantage of
an intimate sense of the ways of his flock which the years at
Bagber had given him. Though the bibliography of the last
twenty-five years of his life shows a continuous literary production, particularly but by no means exclusively prose, he was out

every morning visiting his parishioners, with his prayerbook and his pockets full of sweets for the children. Travelling on foot in a widely-scattered parish, he reckoned to visit everywhere once a fortnight. The muse came to him less frequently as he grew old, and he never pretended that she was there when she was not. She never withdrew her favours. Barnes could have said with Malherbe, 'Je les possédai, jeune, et les possède encore / A la fin de mes jours.' At eighty-five, in the year before his death, he dictated the lovely verses of 'The Geäte A-Vallen To'. On the very eve of his death verses escaped him, in the same breath as the Third Collect at Evening Prayer.

II

Such was the life and death of William Barnes, a figure of the sixteenth century rather than the nineteenth, not through any literary affectation but because his social origins, and his absolute truth to them, made any such affectations unnatural to him. E.M. Forster says that Barnes's 'prose-intelligence was provincial', which may be admitted, if we admit also that his attention to his subject, and his ignorance of cultural drifts, remind us of Selden or Camden.

The list of prose works is formidable – perhaps thirty books, to say nothing of papers and essays not collected, on philology, grammar, applied mathematics, archaeology and social matters. Most of them are odd little books, such as no publisher would look at now and few wanted then. They are home-made things, with a complete lack of pretension. In a sense they belong to the Barnes who kept school in Dorchester rather than to Barnes the poet – a few because they are schoolmasters' books, if not school-books, but more because they show what were the day-to-day workings of the mind of one in whose ordinary life poetry appeared, to those who knew him, to play only a small part. Yet they are certainly not without relevance to the work of the poet. It is not merely that passages here and there confirm the facts on which the poems are built, as this account of a sale:

> My uncle was a farmer in the West of England, but became insolvent from the depression of the agricultural interest after the French war. My aunt had a numerous family, and her long

exercised solicitude as a mother, and her continual struggles against misfortunes, had nearly brought her with sorrow to the grave; she was calm, and it was only when either of her daughters passed her, that a tear rolled down her sallow cheek. The young men were in that severe and reckless mood in which young men are frequently thrown when assailed by misfortunes they can still resist. The girls were bewildered, and scarcely knew what happened to them; then were driven away the cows under which the weeping milkmaid had so often sung the simple songs of the country; then went the waggon in which the merry haymakers had so many times ridden in to the feast of harvest-home; and in short, then every thing that was dear from familiarity was taken away, and my uncle, as he looked on the fields he had so long cultivated with hope, and of which he had taken the produce in grateful joy, sighed and dropped a tear as if he had said 'Dulcia linquimus arva'. (*Labour and Gold*, 1859, p. 146.)

Nor is it merely that the prose works illustrate the learning and industry of the author, though the reader of the poems may well reflect that the author's acquaintance with the sixty or seventy languages from which the 'principles and forms' of the *Philological Grammar* were drawn does not suggest that Barnes wrote in the Dorset dialect through any narrowness of linguistic scope. He wrote in it because he was celebrating the virtues of the ordinary population of a fortunate countryside. If he did not notice the Labourers' Revolt (as the social historians see it) he noticed the labourers, and cared in his writings as in his life for the families which grew up around him on a bare subsistence. If like Herbert's parson he makes 'a hook of his charity', saying 'I give you this for the good you have done or followed', he also cares that every family shall have a house, denounces the long hours, lack of holidays, and the restrictions of industrial life which deprive a man of the chance of 'a break for half-an-hour's talk with a welcome friend'. He is acutely aware of 'the tyranny of a great working capital' and of the damage done by excessive division of labour, which may make a girl 'a fitting companion only to the frame and the bobbin'. He exhibits the prejudices and loyalties of a race untouched by liberal delusions, and introduces his note on the 'Character and Intelligence of the Britons' (*Notes on Ancient*

Britain, 1848, p. 79) by saying in reply to Horace's accusation that the Britons were cruel to foreigners, 'most likely we English, though we may deem ourselves men of a more refined life, should be found quite as warlike and bloodthirsty … if another race were to bring the sword against us'. He might be that yeoman in Fuller's *Holy State*, who 'goes not to London, but … seeing the King once, he prayes for him ever afterwards'.

The most interesting of Barnes's prose works, to the reader of his poetry, may be thought to be the grammatical and philological works, though a certain dryness and laboriousness of analysis is to be expected. Different versions of *The Glossary of the Dorset Dialect* were produced in 1844, 1863 and 1886, and the subject matter of the book was throughout his central preoccupation, even if not always in the analytical form in which it is there presented. In a sense Barnes's books on language are a disappointment; it is as if they were always approaching a point they never quite reach. But they are genuinely thrown up by his life-long meditation on language as he had found it used, and they express by implication a profound dissatisfaction with the thinner speech that the multiplication of means of communication and the mobility of populations were already making. The language Barnes spoke in his boyhood was a genuine common store, made to express what those who spoke it could understand. Each man took as much of it as answered to his share of the world, what he had directly by sight and hearing and touch. It is as far as possible from the meretricious speech of public and commercial media which all but the most sophisticated are now ashamed not to talk. In taking the spoken Dorset speech for the solid base of his work, Barnes was turning his back on the literary effects of 'the money-making mind, which looks on the work of God mainly, if not only, as sources of wealth'. His translation into Dorset dialect of one of the contemporary Queen's Speeches to Parliament (see the preface to *A Glossary of the Dorset Dialect*, 1886) is a piece of social criticism as well as literary criticism. His radical approach made him a literary innovator of the most unselfconscious kind. He did not merely react against the increasingly pervasive influence of commerce, as some of the best urban minds of the century did; he was moving surely, on his own, in a direction which would be seen to be a right one when many more blatantly advertised paths had ended in nothingness. Certain Scotch writers of our own day have had recourse to dialect as a means of detaching themselves from the corrupt speech of the time, and the exercise has enabled the best of them to return to current English and renew it. Some of Barnes's later English poems are in a tone and manner which he might never have attained if he had not first acquired sureness in a speech that the more sinister contemporary influences could not touch. But his dialect was not synthetic. More fortunate in his birth than MacDiarmid, he inherited a speech and was not driven to invent one.

It must be admitted that Barnes's exercises in the purification of language led finally to ludicrous excesses of Saxonizing, of which *English Speech-Craft* (1878) contains instructive illustrations. But the theoretical aberration never upset the balance of the language he used in his verse, for which he had a true touchstone in his early memories. In any case, Saxonizing is not the only, nor perhaps the most important aim of Barnes's linguistic studies. The *Philological Grammar* (1854) is nothing less than an attempt to analyze the essential content of all language; to define, for example, the series of relations which grammatical cases convey, whether indicated by case ending, by preposition, or in some other way. It is the essential movements of the human mind that Barnes is seeking to define. This objective is perhaps most clearly seen in *Tiw or A View of the Roots and Stems of English as a Teutonic Tongue* (1862), which is said to have been a favourite with him among his books. In this book he tries to reduce the English language to 'about fifty primary roots', reached 'through English provincial dialects and other Teutonic speech-forms'. The roots are given in the form of the initial and final consonants, as for example 'Pring', which is said to mean:

> To put forth, in a striking form, to any sense or to the mind
> as to –
>
> The feeling – in upstickingness;
> The taste – in sharpness;
> The sight – in prinking gaiety of colours or clothing;
> The mind – in mind-striking action, or upstickingness of behaviour.

Various terminations, such as -nk, or -k or (more remotely) -m, -d or -n, are substituted for the final -ng, and this brings into relations such words as 'prang' (western dialect, 'finely clad'), 'prong' (as used in haymaking), 'prick', 'perk up', 'prim' (eastern dialect for 'the spindle tree'), 'prune' (as of trees). The result is to reduce all speech to a small number of basic physical apprehensions, a conception which throws great light on the language of the poems, and on the prominence in them of physical movement, sometimes of a boisterous kind.

In his study of archaeology Barnes prided himself on 'a careful use' of his 'little knowledge of the British language, which ... Antiquaries have too often neglected', and there is no doubt that for him an appreciation of language was a *sine qua non* of such understanding as we may have of human life. But the study of language took him back to physical apprehensions, and an esthetic ideal of the physical man and woman was never far from the mind of this majestic parson with long beard and flowing cassock: 'the beautiful in nature', he says in his 'Thoughts on Beauty and Art' (an article in *Macmillan's Magazine*, 1861, printed as an appendix to Giles Dugdale's *William Barnes*, 1953), 'is the unmarred result of God's first creative or forming will, and ... the beautiful in art is the result of an unmistaken working of man in accordance with the beautiful in nature'. Barnes had spoken in *Labour and Gold* of feeding like squirrels and exercising like monkeys, and in his 'Thoughts on Beauty and Art' he spoke of the beautiful in man being the state in which 'there should not be a spot on his body where ... an insect or prickle might hold itself, so that it could not be reached by the fingers of one of the hands'. As for animals, so for man, beauty is 'fitness for the good continuance of the animal as such'.

III

Barnes called his poems 'of rural life', whether they were in the Dorset dialect or in common English, and the label has been read by an urbanized literary world to mean that they are of a limited and specialized interest. Barnes wrote about rural life because his life was in fact rural, and he used the material that came to hand as much as Baudelaire did when he wrote about Paris. What is disconcerting, because it was so rare in poets of his century, as indeed of ours, is his contentment within the order of nature, an order of nature capped by grace, for the church is as much part of his countryside as the 'wide-horned cattle' and the 'cracklen waggon', 'a pleäce, where we mid seek / The gifts o' greäce vrom week to week'. Barnes celebrates the life of the English country-side as Shakespeare in *Henry V* celebrated our national wars. There is more to be said about both than is contained in Barnes or in Shakespeare, much of it less agreeable than what is to be found in those writers, but that does not detract from the truth of the elements they presented, one might say created. Barnes's theme — so far as a poet can be said to have a theme apart from the poems he writes — is nothing less than what is fit 'for the good continuance' of the human animal. His personal griefs — and they are as poignantly expressed as those of anyone who has written in English — are felt against a larger background of natural growth and decline, with this world — however unpalatable the notion may be — completed by the next. Children occupy a prominent place in his scheme of things, not as beastly little Peter Pans but as people setting out on the journey others are already far advanced in, their needs providing a motive for their elders' continuance, while 'livèn gifts o' youth do vall, / Vrom girt to small, but never die'. It is not the 'individual', that insecure inven-tion of liberal romanticism, that is here in play. What William Barnes does is part of the action, not only of his contemporaries who crowd in to Shroton fair, but of the 'vorevathers' and descendants. His view of things is far removed from that typical contemporary mixture of extreme subjectivism and mechanism — of overweening awareness of one's own wants and rights and smartness about the operation of determinism in others. He is not solipsist and mechanical but one of a company, natural and theo-logical. By the same token he inhabits a more permanent world than that of modern politics, and for him the first meaning of 'our own free land' is the few fields a man may manage to own, as in his Dorchester days he bought a few symbolic acres of Bagber.

The best known of Barnes's poems are some of those lyrics he wrote after the death of his wife. These verses are not the simple product of the emotion of that time. Barnes does not present his grief in the setting of a school in Dorchester, in the running of which his wife gave him the most practical help, but identifies himself with the countryman taking 'the bit he can avword' out under the beeches, so that the predicament is no longer merely his own. No distress could darken his sense of the existence of

others, and the scrupulousness which made him lug the most
inconveniently shaped purchases back to his rectory rather than
trouble the Dorchester tradesmen to deliver them, enabled him
to enter into the feelings of labourers and small farmers, whether
as the subjects of his poems or as his parishioners. The transference
of his observations into verse was made easier by the use of dialect,
for he was a listener and it is in the turns of language that people
most plainly reveal themselves.

> Good morn t'ye, John. How b'ye? How b'ye?
> Zoo you be gwain to market, I do zee.
> Why, you be quite a-lwoaded wi' your geese.

It is the very inflection of ordinary speech, and where else would
you look for that in the verse written in England in 1833? It is not
in the odd line or two that Barnes has caught it; all the eclogues
in his first volume of Dorset poems have it throughout, combined
with an utter sureness in the handling of metre. This represents
an immense technical liberation, and the poetry of the nineteenth
century suffered a progressive softening through lack of attention
to it. It should not be supposed that an achievement of this kind
would come inevitably, and as it were in the course of nature, to
anyone writing in dialect. A glance at the Dorset verse of William
Holloway (1761–1854) will show that that is not the case; or you
may look at the 'Northern Farmer', which Tennyson is supposed
to have written, after seeing Barnes's poems, to see what could be
made of the speech of the north. Barnes was always happy with
the eclogue as a form, for it suited his sense of the plurality of lives
about him, and it is marvellous what differences of tone and
manner he catches – a girl with 'sca'ce a thing a-left in pleäce'
when she comes out of the crowd at Shroton Fair; two men
discussing the advantages of a 'little bit o' land' beside one's house;
waggoners arguing about a load. For sheer technical proficiency
in the handling of dramatic variations the last poem in the
collected volume of Dorset poems ('A Lot o' Maïdens a-runnèn
the Vields') is incomparable, though the material of it is slighter
than that of some of the others.

Had Barnes merely achieved lucidity and variety in dramatic
dialogue that would have been one of the more notable achievements of the century, more particularly since he showed in the
1868 volume that he could do the same thing in common English

when he chose, and if some richness is lost in that speech it is only because it was less his own than the language of Bagber. But Barnes could carry his conversational tone into the most intense lyric and into the most elaborate rhyme-scheme, and combine it with a sweetness of refrain which is almost painful, like Spenser's refrain in 'Prothalamion'. For sheer verse-craft, you will scarcely find in the nineteenth century the equal of 'Shaftesbury Feäir' or 'The Wold Wall' – 'To Paladore. Aye, Poll a dear, / Vor now 'tis feäir', or 'Ah! well-a-day! O wall adieu! / The wall is wold, my grief is new.' Such is Barnes's skill that the reality of the voice is enhanced, not lost, amidst intricacies of rhyme and metre, as in 'Grammer a-crippled':

> 'But oh! though low mid slant my ruf,
>   Though hard my lot mid be,
> Though dry mid come my daily lwoaf,
>   Mid mercy leäve me free!'
> Cried Grammer, 'Or adieu
>   To jaÿ; O grounds,
>   An' bird's gaÿ sounds
> If I mus' gi'e up you,
> Although 'tis well, in God's good will,
> That I should bide 'ithin a wall.'

IV

That Barnes has been undervalued many people are now willing to admit. It may be a long time before the Dorchester Museum does more than exhibit his buckle shoes and a school-desk in a corner of Hardy's room, but there are poets who look on him as one of the great masters, and the critics will follow. It will not be in a resuscitated dialect that his influence will be shown. He was not a local poet except by accident. He did not seek out a language to give himself idiosyncrasy, but exploited the natural speech of his boyhood. This enabled him to escape from the literary foibles of his time more quickly and completely than he could otherwise have done, as a comparison of the poems in the 1846 volume in 'national English' with the Dorset poems of the same time shows. His use of dialect probably enabled him to maintain his liberty of feeling amidst the uncomprehending pressures he must have faced from his social superiors. Barnes is not there to encourage a factitious oddity, but on the contrary to demonstrate that the poet has to develop in a straight line from his origins, and that the avoidance of literature is indispensable for the man who wants to tell the truth.

Sevenoaks Essays/Native Ruminations

Introduction

The conduct of government rests upon the same foundation and encounters the same difficulties as the conduct of private persons: that is, as to its object and justification, for as to its methods, or technical part, there is all the difference which separates the person from the group, the man acting on behalf of himself from the man acting on behalf of many. The technical part, in government as in private conduct, is now the only one which is publicly or at any rate generally recognized, as if by this evasion the more difficult part of the subject, which relates to ends, could be avoided. Upon 'the law of nature and the law of revelation', Blackstone said, 'depend all human laws.' This quaint language, which would at once be derided if it were introduced now into public discussion, conceals a difficulty which is no less ours than it was our ancestors'.

It was reasonable for Blackstone, using this language, to use also language of a certain nobility in describing the functions of Members of Parliament:

> They are not thus honourably distinguished from the rest of their fellow-subjects, merely that they may privilege their persons, their estates, or their domestics; that they may list under party banners; may grant or withhold supplies; may vote with or against a popular or unpopular administration; but upon considerations far more interesting and important. They are the guardians of the English constitution; the makers, repealers and interpreters of the English laws; delegated to watch, to check, and to avert every dangerous innovation, to propose, adopt, and to cherish any solid and well-weighed improvement; bound by every tie of nature, of honour, and of religion, to transmit that constitution and those laws to their posterity, amended if possible, at least without derogation.

This is so unlike the language we should use, in relation to Members of Parliament, that it has an air of comedy. Honour and religion are – many would say, happily – subverted, and nature has become uncertain, so it is not clear what binds the Members. Are they there after all merely 'that they may privilege their persons'? They would for the most part shy away from that explanation. Many might say they were there to make innovations, as Blackstone thought they were there to avert them: and while for Blackstone 'dangerous' was the adjective which went naturally with 'innovation', for our Members other, more approving, qualifications would come more readily to mind. They might well be so busy about change as not to catch sight of the fundamental problem, which remains, however. What are they there for, if not merely to 'privilege their persons'? If not tied by honour or religion, they are perhaps tied by nature, which science may study, and their innovations are in her service. It is a possibility.

A Possible Anglicanism

I

The real difficulty of the Creed is the first word – I – the number and person of the *Credo*. The *ergo* of Descartes, like many others before and since, now looks like a confidence trick.

This is a difficulty which is least in youth, when the force of desire makes a certain animism easy. Surely a spirit must dwell in that body which is the object of nascent desires? But later the reflection comes that that spirit is like one's own, which is less impressive. A more wholesome reflection, perhaps, is that one's own body is like another's. That is to say, one can explain one's own spirit in terms of another's body, and so of one's own; reassure oneself that, however uncertain it is to be oneself, one must at least be like other bodies, which seem plausible enough. This is a pagan reflection, but it may also be a Christian one, though it is self-regarding, perhaps, in a way that the young man's animism in relation to another body may not be – but that is only perhaps, too.

Whichever way one approaches the subject, one arrives at the identification of the self and the body, whether or not the two are coterminous. There is nothing but the body, its actions and manifestations, that has any claim to be thought of as a self. Is spirit something different? If it is, I am quite without understanding of it. Unless of course it is a hallmark, set on the body by God, or a sort of standard pattern, the image of the Creator. But that must be an object of faith, because it cannot be perceived – believed in if at all in sheer despair at what can be perceived, and out of need for a reassurance of one's identity, not so much with oneself as with other creatures. It therefore looks like a metaphysical projection of the common need to be like another body, and to be reassured that the other body contains consciousness, or whatever it is that one perceives in oneself. I have always slid over these difficulties to the resurrection of the body, so little believed in, incredible certainly, but more understandable than any other apology for the life everlasting – the only understandable one, I would say. It is that or nothing.

That, as distinct from nothing, is, it seems to me, what religion is. There is nothing but God to choose. Apart from that, which we properly call Him, not on account of sex but because of an identity with ourselves, there are only the miscellaneous performances of the human body, of any sort of body – not merely that of a cat but of a stone, for if consciousness has to be inferred from external appearance stones have their performance as well as those who are more usually thought of as our neighbours. If He does not exist the miscellaneous performances of the human body are not *sui generis*, the sums you do are no more than the sums done by a calculating machine, your punch is like that of the boulder that falls on you. Indeed I am afraid we believe in Him in order to be *sui generis*, in order not to perish. And if our faith is right He chooses us – we are a mirror and there really is someone looking in.

The Christian faith is that God was made man. And what is man? Why, he is the image of God – there is no other meaning I can attach to the expression. He is the broken image which was remade at the Incarnation, for our reassurance. There is a circle there which may be a deceit. If we believe it is because we want to choose and be chosen. If our belief is true it is because we must so choose. Otherwise the desire to choose and be chosen is the illusory appearance of something else, a mere accompaniment of being driven on by forces which indifferently drive everything. One cannot say that that alternative is improbable.

There is a trick in the abstraction of language which could deceive us either way. Because there is nothing of us but our bodies and their manifestations, the language which reminds us least of them seems most promising of a truth beyond them. But in fact what we say is said in words which have their start in the operations of the body. Words are not ours but the words of a myriad, having point only because of their history, ultimately of their prehistory. The man who speaks, if there is Man, is the same who (I think it was Frobenius who put me on to this) at some stage of prehistory – and it may be in some of contemporary consciousness – could have sexual intercourse without being aware of it, as I might scratch my head without knowing it. We speak as historical persons – well, to say persons is to beg the question, but we do not speak as ourselves. If we are selves, it is by virtue of other selves that we are so. And our speaking is that of a race, of a tribe, of a time. There is no speech which is not of a here and now and it is nothing except in terms of other times and elsewhere. That is why the historical church is so apt to our needs and meaning. It is a congregation of meaning and there is no meaning without congregation.

There is no meaning except in terms of a time and a place. If one could understand it would be at one altar, in a stone building, in such a place, at perhaps eight o'clock on a Sunday morning. If there were no sacraments there would be nothing. If there were not England there would be no church, for me who happen to have been born here. I am an Anglican.

II

If the *ecclesia anglicana* is the vehicle of meaning for me, it is the centre of England, however little it seems to be regarded. That is to say, it is so so far as England enters my consciousness – to which word I prefer *conscience*, and consider the French are more fortunate (and more exact) than we in having only one word for the two (English) conceptions. The *ecclesia anglicana* is the centre of the political England no less than of the others, and the political conceptions which omit it are not merely incomplete; they are without middle. It is no less true, however, that any consideration of the Church which ignores the vulgar exterior of doing and intriguing – the ordinary behaviour of men – is an abstraction of an individual mind, the invention of a non-imagination – a partial, protestant mind like Kant's, trying to elevate our thinking above the world of sense. The truth is that churches have their politics, in the most vulgar sense, no more deserving of pity than other politics. There is no reason to adopt a soppy, Christianish way of talking about these things, as if everything to do with the church demanded the manners of a Ladies' Working Party. This soppiness is of course a new thing, the product not of sweeter and more gracious ways of thinking but of the progressive realization that the Church is socially unimportant and can (nearly) be ignored. It was not very nice that people should burn one another for their faith, or that archbishops should be executed for their political devotion to their sovereign, but these things were done because, at the time when they were done, there was not the present facility in extracting from theological conceptions all trace of practical meaning.

The progress of democracy – for which Locke's *Letter on Toleration* is an early apologia – has been a process of laicisation. It has succeeded in driving religion into the recesses of a thing called the individual conscience, which has to be less than the *consciousness* people have of their physical environment, including themselves, so that it bothers nobody. Then, it is said, we can ignore people's beliefs, indeed the proprieties of our politics demand that we should do so. We will debate in parliament about the things we can really agree about – what we all want, food, keeping the enemy away, never mind who we are or what form we give to the food we eat. The end of this is a material world which there is no-one to observe. There is the food secured for us by our governors, the fuel that warms our bodies, the machines which carry us around or replace our labours. All this system is to be promoted and no questions asked, for *conscience* has nothing to do with it. It is the Neanderthal man, with his mind closing upon him as he reaches the end of his path. Of course the conception is muddled. If politics are planned as a system of doing things to people (which, so far as it ignores consciousness, is the same thing as doing things to things) it assumes a supreme political group who do the doing, who are not merely some *thing* but some *bodies*, not merely some bodies but bodies with consciousness. There could be a new serfdom which would make this possible, but it is an oppression which would so much impoverish the human race, the conception of what man is, that even for the governors it would in the end be of little interest.

Under this negative debate of our public affairs, once excused under the name of liberty and now, more often, under the name of economics or production, the conscious, including the ecclesiastical, groups still stir. Not only stir, but exhibit all those political symptoms which are admitted to exist only in relation to groups concerned with the matters the consciousness of the commonwealth admits. Just as, in westernized Africa, black habits are likely to break out and disrupt the internationally admitted plans for a century ahead, the suppressed political forces of ecclesiastical politics are likely to irrupt one day, amidst profound misunderstanding, on the surface of our political life which denies them. The forces are, in the last analysis, only those of the *ecclesia anglicana*, with its tail of protestant sects fading imperceptibly into the great mass of what might be called the *prejudice of disbelief*, and the Popish non-conformity which has its political centre else-where. Meanwhile, so far as a residual theory of establishment is still admitted, the *ecclesia anglicana* is inhabited by (its own and others') belief that it occupies a seat of political influence, while the Roman conspirators, unhampered, plan the destruction of the whole edifice, political and social. Coleridge, so far as I know, was the last man of first-rate intellect who took this possibility seriously.

III

Does it matter an awful lot? one might ask. I will not here enter upon the doctrine of papal infallibility, which is an absolute bar to liberty of conscience, as it used to be called, or to the free admission of all that comes to our consciousness, as one might more lucidly put it now: except to say that it is also an invention, in its final form, of the democratic 1870s, the earliest moment at which it became politically possible for the Curia to get the explicit endorsement of its long-nurtured, but hitherto always partially thwarted, ambitions. The essential thing is whether we want, in this country, a Roman *imperium in imperio*; as to which I agree with Coleridge that we do not. Rome has since the Middle Ages understood the necessity of government, and she has progressively insisted on the superiority of her own. But her government is like other people's, as was well enough understood in the old Catholic monarchies and given rational form in the Reformation conception of the sovereign as governor of the Church in his own dominions – a conception of greater antiquity, it could be claimed, than the notion of papal infallibility; it is, indeed, much the conception of Constantine. It has often puzzled people, in recent times, that in the sixteenth century men should have attached so much importance to the subject following the religion of his prince. What we may think of as mere tergiversations, however, conceal a profound sense of the identity of the Church and the commonwealth, as aspects of the same body, so that a failure to follow the prince in his religion partakes of the nature of schism. And as for the theology of it, given that the Church is one, but is torn, is our Catholicity more injured by being out of communion with the Bishop of Rome than by being out of communion with our prince and those among whom we live? Note the *non-conformist* quality of the papists among us.

Of course the identity of Church and commonwealth was never more shadowy than it is now – or never since, say, the days of Constantine. But one cannot be complete without the other, and the notion of the solitary catholic is ridiculous. We are a broken-down lot, whichever way you look at it. If you look at it from the point of view of the ordinary non-Christian subject – he is not now even legally called that, he is a citizen, if you please – is there any point in monarchy at all? There is because the truth is not a matter of his or of anyone else's opinion. He cannot help being human, poor devil, if that is what we are. Therefore he exists as we (the obscure Christians) do, in virtue of the existence of others. And if Man exists only by God, the fact is not altered by Mr Jones thinking otherwise. And if he does not think – a better and happier condition than being all the time in exacerbated error – he may still feel that a King or Queen can stand for us as policies and the ministers who promote them cannot. Already in the Cabinet, with its score of ministers, whose policies are the subject of analytical discourse, the human mind – which is the same as the human body – has begun to disintegrate; but it is one in the crown, which is as mysterious and unknowable as we are ourselves. It is by virtue of that that we are one. The need for this identification is not likely to become less, in the future, whether the future lies in an abstracted world of international organizations or in a physical devastation which sends us back to our primitive concerns. It is probably only for the local group that this can have any meaning. Others should not be discouraged from shedding the burden of loyalty. It may well be that the Crown will end, as it began, as the Crown of England.

An Essay on Identity

I

It is, indeed, very hard to understand what makes up 'I'. And the mere existence of the pronoun should not at once persuade us of the existence of the thing.

There is, of course, a sense in which 'I' is self-evident. But it is a pretty silly sense, a sort of tautology. 'I' is the fact of the assertion being made. It does not get one out of the prison of solipsism, but when we say 'I' exists, what we are really hoping is that there are other 'I's. If we do not mean that we do not mean anything, indeed there could hardly be such a thing as meaning.

We are therefore talking about the existence of 'Man', and this is a very difficult conception indeed. Moreover, it is a conception rich in history; it is history. It is also biology. To discuss 'Man', in fact, one can only proceed by taking some traditional universe of discourse, and defining him in terms of it. There is nothing else.

The answer to 'what am I?' can only be that I am one of those two-legged creatures of which we see so much. Biology and history tell us something about them – their relations with other species of animal, their relations with one another. 'I' becomes at once a term for a variant, though it could also mean one of two identical twins, identically brought up, if that were possible. In any case what makes 'man' is not the fact of 'I', the individual, but the fact of the species. Unless one can say 'I am a man', i.e. one of a kind, 'I' does not say anything. Yet what is meant by 'I', the individual, is something more overweening than that. The something is historical and conceptual. It has been invented by man, I suppose as a comfort. It is a reason why you should not kill me – which is something living creatures seem to be constitutionally against, though few take it as hard as man.

Taking it hard, however, is merely a function of consciousness. And consciousness – as is not perhaps widely understood –
is purely traditional. Adam did not know what he was doing. That
was his innocence. There was a point at which consciousness
emerged, presumably out of the frustration of wishes. It has
grown and been handed down. What it amounts to is determined
by the traditions of particular societies. A 'culture' is partly a style
of consciousness. It can however be more easily studied as a style
of behaviour. Behaviour and consciousness are two related aspects
of 'Man'. They are not identical; there is plenty of behaviour
without consciousness. But the style of one affects the style of the
other.

The individual 'is', or may certainly be identified as, a sub-style
of consciousness and behaviour. The variant is not important,
except in terms of a tradition which says that it is. Tradition, once
developed beyond a certain point, has to say something about
'Man'. The subject is so difficult that it usually starts by saying
something about gods. These are projections, which is not to say
that God might not be there all the time, watching all this. But
mythology is about man, the first sketch of a difficult subject.

The individual is nowhere in this. And what did God become,
in Christian history? He became Man, one for all. The meaning
of the first Adam was Man, and so with the second. His incarnation was like the descent of a Platonic form into physical shape.
It was a reaffirmation of the kind. Every bit of the kind was
important. In the end the bits thought they were important as
'individuals'. The claim is ill-founded.

II

The incarnation is a tall story. But of course if you believe in God
you can believe it. If you do not believe it, you can still believe
that the kind is important, though without giving a reason for it.
Is the difference between the importance attributed to kind by the
Incarnationist and that attributed to it by the rest of the world of
any significance in relation to the 'individual'?

The matter is not free from difficulty. Is every 'individual'
included in the Christian salvation? It has generally been supposed
not. The saints are a sub-kind. Those who believe in Christ shall

not perish, but have everlasting life. The rest shall perish in some sort. Cowper thought himself one of these: ACTUM EST DE TE, PERIISTI. The saints are, as it were, a wealthy class, those to whom, having already, more shall be given. The Christian looks for a more precise identification by hoping to approximate to this class, he is a kind of snob. His 'I' is not merely the two-legged animal; it is an 'I' with paraphernalia, more or less realized. The rest of the world no doubt has its own snobbisms, their 'I's are variants of sub-kinds, more sharply defined on that account. Is there any possibility of an 'I' which is not, as it were, redefined by a snobbism?

It is in fact impossible to conceive it. Is an idiot a man? Yes. A monster? Yes. A man in a long coma preceding death? Yes. I give the answers of fashion. At other times it might have been said that the idiot was possessed, and so out of kind. And so on. But in fashionable terms where does the man begin? At the mouth of the womb? How premature must a foetus be to be disqualified? Are the ovum and sperm constituent parts of a man? You must choose your snobbism rather arbitrarily. And when you have chosen it, you say to those outside it: Periisti. Identity implies the election of a sub-kind, and henceforth a course of conduct which may be described as the management of the sub-kind. The object of this management is to collect the sub-kind into some ark or paradise. For the Christian it is theologically prescribed. For the self-justifying abortionist – as distinct from the abortionist who is willing to murder for money, who belongs, of course, to a species with wider terms of reference – it is the group of healthy people, as contemporaneously conceived. The two-legged may be handled without scruple in relation to those outside the group. This health is something which can be ascertained in relation to other people. Medicine and surgery at large are the treatment of other people. They are the technics of humanist management. Its objects are the preservation of a kind. It ought not to be too scrupulous about incidental 'individuals'. The Christian should not be too careful with the damned; the kindness so often exhibited is a symptom of weakened faith.

Is there a Christian management of the sub-kind? Since God became Man, would it not be reasonable to seek an objective salvation for the holy, to attempt a kind of eugenics for God's people? 'Not one of these little ones should perish', to be sure, but what about these and these? The ones not yet born? The ones whose parent orgasm is being mounted at this moment? Those who will tear one another's eyes out, in a hundred years' time, for the last food in Asia? Is every bit of mankind important? What does number mean in relation to holiness? Would it not be a kindness for old men to kill themselves?

III

What makes up the 'I'? If the separate parts of our kind are 'individuals' there would have to be identifiable minds in the separate bodies. But are there? 'Creation's matter flows through us like a river.' It flows, but the question is whether there is an 'us' that it flows through. And so with consciousness. It flows, but its contents are historical rather than individual. It is a matter of 'culture' what we are conscious of. The 'thought' is a common thought; only so could it be understood. A stream loaded with old bottles, the vegetation of several countries, rags of clothing perhaps, flows around the world. It makes no sense to talk of the individual mind. The individual body, perhaps. That is made of matter that flows in this changing form, comes from and goes to other things. But for its limited history of growth and decay it is defined by its skin, it is one in the clear sense of being separable from other things. The individual, if anything, is this, without regard to consciousness. It begins with the egg and the sperm; it ends, not with certified death but with the disintegration which follows. In the end it is not there, as an identifiable thing. There is no 'personality' apart from it. If that were ever collected again, it could only be at the resurrection of the body.

'Call No Man Happy Until he is Dead'

I

Conduct is supposed to be of the individual. And so, it is supposed to be directed from the inside, for that is how the individual is conceived of as being directed. That is what used to be called being a 'rational creature'. There are no such creatures nowadays, but the conception of being directed from the inside persists. Indeed it was never so popular. The preferred theory is now that not only the direction, but the rules of conduct themselves, come from inside.

There is something in this. Man, like other machines, moves according to the laws of his construction. There may be question as to how absolute those laws are, but nobody doubts that there are limits within which he must operate, whether or not those limits are held to be fully known. The limits are the range of human conduct, and it is generally held that the individual has to choose points within that range, and that this is called freedom.

It may be so. But, whether or not freedom is an illusion, there is at any rate an apparent question of how I should act. And so of where to look for the rules. Or what motives to admit, which is the same thing. Those in search of the individual usually prefer the motives of non-conformity, or motives said to be so. If the differentiation goes far enough, whom may they not find? Them 'selves', no doubt, as the unattainable end; meanwhile in observable particulars their conduct resembles that of other people. At best they contribute to the fissiparousness of groups; more generally merely share in the popular fickleness, which heaves to and fro between accepted opinions.

It is better, perhaps, to accept the external direction of one's conduct. There is then no nonsense about one's 'self', no attention to the pathology of the moment. The mind can be used to reflect the outside world, as is the case with the best animals. There is a duty of discrimination, which cannot be avoided, but one makes as little as may be of internal doubts and hesitations – the flaws in the mirror, the ripples on the surface of the reflecting water, or the unidentified objects lying below the surface.

One should be glad to find social conceptions one can conform to. They represent possibilities of one's nature, and the most one can hope to do is to embody certain of these possibilities.

II

The person who takes this orientation finds a kind of renewal. The 'individual' sinks from sight and is extinguished; in exchange, one has all the benefits of history, not as an emporium to choose from, but as they bear down upon one at a particular point of time, like a column of air. The famous 'conflict between the individual and society' – that Byronic conception – is resolved, because one term is lost. One enters, as a negligible quantity, on a vast playing-field and has all the possibilities of the game being played there. One chooses roles and tries to perfect them – not one role, but as many as one can discern. Instead of the 'problem of conduct' there is the matter of discernment. The attention is shifted from the subject to the object. Indeed one does not bother about the subject; perhaps it is not there.

'Call no man happy until he is dead' is a paradigm of this conception of things. The happiness is not an affective condition, it is a state of prosperity, judged as such by others rather than by the subject. Or if the subject judges of himself, he judges as he would of another man, because it is of a man that he is judging, not of a 'self'. Health, wives, children, cattle or other riches according to the custom of the time, the marks of honour accorded by other men – these are the constituents of this happiness. In all this there is room for a large discrimination. One need not keep many cattle to be sure of one's milk, in a society in which it comes to the door in bottles. One may not get an honour one cares for by owning a bigger car than one's neighbours. Diogenes is an early example of sophistication in this kind. He sought an objective condition, as much as any patriarch in the Old Testament, but he was on the brink of the terrible discovery of him'self' which would ruin everything.

III

The roles one chooses – the husband, the father, the soldier, the man of affairs – one plays them more or less well according to the richness of one's inherited conceptions. There is no way of acquiring such conceptions except by inheritance, but of course whereas any fool can inherit money the ability to inherit conceptions depends a little – though less than is usually thought – on the capacity of the heir. The capacity of the heir is, however, a small thing compared with the capacity of the society he lives in to remember and transmit, in short to embody. You cannot be

Plato in Bechuanaland or George Herbert in Connecticut. You cannot be in the Italy of the twentieth century a man of the first century A.D. So in fact you are largely directed from the outside, however little you like to think so, and it is not so much a recommendation I am giving you as a short view of the nature of things.

To seek to discriminate among your inherited possessions, to understand more profoundly the roles it is your chance to be called upon to play, is more than enough to occupy anybody. Of course there are wilful persons who imagine that they stand outside society and change it, but it is merely that they have struck a not very rich vein of tradition. Their ideas of changing come from where other people's ideas come from; they cannot be got from anywhere else. And if those who talk most of changing society also talk most of individual liberty, it is merely that they are confused. To make a change is to make other people bend. If one can do that at all it is only by putting them in the way of a current. And what is the meaning of acquiescence, to the reed the stream catches?

<h1 style="text-align:center">IV</h1>

Acquiescence is perhaps a joke. At any rate it is clear that, for the most part of our lives, there is no more in it than is involved in going quietly. What opinions do you hold about being born, growing, declining, and dying? You will do these things even if you are against them. And how? You will do them as they are done in these parts, at this time. How much less acquiescence is involved in being compelled by someone who says he understands your role better than you do yourself? Is there really much difference between persuasion and compulsion? The mythologies of the moment say that there is, and they have to be obeyed. In the very act of obedience to them the man who understands his role will see that there is no freedom of choice, that a compulsion underlies all our persuasions. But if it does, should we deny it?

The word 'democracy' is now so full of air that it is about to burst. Its bursting will not be the end of everything but the recognition, in passing, of a truth. There is reason to believe that it may mitigate the boredom of our society. If hunger does not drive us, do we not need more than ever those who will put us in a corner

and make us fight? The ease of technology will, in any case, in the
end produce a race of diminishing consciousness, for whom the
only persuasion is by force. The triumph of technology would be
to leave people with so little consciousness that they did not
notice the change.

On the Eros of Poetry

I

Ernst Robert Curtius says, in *Europäische Literatur und lateinisches
Mittelalter*, that most of the themes employed by modern lyrical
poets, 'out of their own experience', are to be found in late classical antiquity, where they appear as the themes of rhetorical
exercises. It is uncertain how much is swept away by this observation. Certainly most of what has been thought about poetry in
the last two hundred years, at any rate in the form in which it has
been thought. The poet was after all not expressing *himself*. The
very existence of the conception of *self* may be in doubt, from
other causes, and what Curtius says comes to demolish the notion
of expression.

Certain literary curiosities fall into their place. It would generally be said that Shakespeare, in his sonnets, was expressing himself
in some more personal sense than in his plays. But this is an
absurdity, from several points of view. In the first place, it is ludicrous to suppose that the author of the plays was the helpless
victim of his own biography when it came to inventing material
for the sonnets. And secondly, if the notion of self-expression is
fundamental to the notion of poetry, how does it come that
Shakespeare is expressing himself more radically in the sonnets,
because of their supposed biographical reference, than in *Lear* or
the great plays of his maturity?

II

It would usually be thought that Spenser and the other Petrarchans wrote lyrics of a more 'artificial' character than, say, Donne,
because they are more evidently the coherent members of a group

– those who succumbed to the 'Petrarchan tradition'. They might well not be expressing 'their feelings', because their sources are known to be literary. Because Donne is outside this tradition, he is often thought to be not only 'more original' but writing more directly from his own experience. It is the very notion of experience which Curtius is, by implication, questioning. The difference between Donne and the Petrarchans is perhaps not the closeness of the relationship between the subjects of their verse and what actually happened to them, but the degree and nature of the psychological insight which these authors respectively brought to their themes which, like 'experience' itself, are merely traditional.

It is too readily supposed that there is a 'personal experience' which can be conveyed in words. In fact, the consciousness we have is a product of history, and we think we feel as we do as much as feel that way. We can only feel as we do, because only so will our forms of words and thoughts allow us to feel. There may be some uniformity between the feelings of men who have their legs cut off, whether in the forests of hundreds of thousands of years ago or in London now, but certainly even in so patent a matter there will be differences. But when it comes to the feelings of a woman abandoned by her lover, the whole force of a civilization is in play. There is no original feeling of such a situation, and no overlay of tradition. The whole is an invention of thousands of years, places, times, religions, cultures. The individual variant which could be 'expressed' – if we admit the conception – must be negligible by comparison.

III

The fact that our thoughts are not our own does not mean that there is no distinction to be made between the thoughts of one and another. There are degrees of relevance of thoughts to situations; there is variety in the capacity of different people for assimilating and applying what they have assimilated. The first symptom of a wide intelligence is its receptivity. The colour-blind who cannot distinguish red and green are the type of imperfect awareness – imperfect that is within the possibilities of a particular culture. The depth, coherence and relevance of what one person has to say will immeasurably exceed those qualities in what another says, and the poet has his place in this scheme of things. In a sense he will be less concerned than other people to be original, because he will be seeking among forms of thought long current for the formulation which will apply most exactly to the new situation.

IV

The prominence of the erotic in the thought of the twentieth century is not the mark of any increase in the activity of the erotic organs, or even of the reverse. It is a result of the desuetude of other thought-forms which are recognized as being of general interest.

The problem – which was perhaps one of the problems of Catullus – is how much weight the contemporary Eros can bear. It will clearly not bear very much unless it is reinforced by streams coming from more profound sources. There are only two – the stream of classical mythology and that of the Christian faith. Both are erotic, though they have proceeded side by side through the centuries, burbling at one another like quarrelsome water-gods.

The poet who can still draw on these sources will not merely illustrate the contemporary Eros. He may revivify the popular apprehension of the Christian and pagan worlds, so that, for example, in fifty years' time, people might sing hymns of which the imagery did not seem grotesque. But it would need more than a few bedraggled poems to have such an effect.

A Note on Morality

To say purpose would be to beg the question, but the effect of moral rules is to produce coherence – and from one point of view, perhaps an important one, it does not matter what the rules are so long as the coherence is there. Of course coherence is also a word that begs some questions. There are modes certainly, but the essential thing is that everybody should think the same, or same enough. When that happens you have a culture in which, typically, all the vases are the same shape. The importance of the sameness, from the individual's point of view, is that it provides expectations. It is immoral to disappoint this expectation, roughly speaking. The sameness also produces conventions about the meaning of actions, which again is reassuring. For it is above all meaning that actions are in need of, if we are to be human. This means attaching actions to traditional patterns of thought, preferably the general view, at any rate a view which enough of us hold to make it respectable. In an evolved society it seems that everything has been thought about, and everything has a meaning. In a disrupted one the meanings are inadequate.

Are there any morals apart from those of particular societies? 'Thou shalt not steal', 'Thou shalt not commit adultery', are already notions with a particular sort of society in mind. This 'thou shalt not' is not absolute; it related to an existing idea of what is the done thing. It is dependent on the form of property and the form of marriage established. If there were Christian morals would they go beyond the need of particular societies, and what would their relationship be with the laws of a particular society, formerly seen as the law of God? The first Christians solved this question, in relation to Jewry. Having burst into the Gentile world, they then found another question. Was there a Christian social form (sc. morality) to be imposed? The answer was yes, but it has never been an entirely satisfactory one. It is least satisfactory in the less stable societies. In the Middle Ages, and long after, Christian morality had taken the place of the Law, and the finer breath of Christianity blew over it, as it had over the Law. In an unstable world, Christian morals have to justify themselves, a task for which they are not altogether equipped because, like all morals, they prefer to be taken for granted.

Take the famous morality of marriage. It could not be said that the gospels do more than bless the morality of a society in which, by that time, monogamy had become general. Certain dicta may even be held to equate adultery with the ordinary thoughts of man. If there is a pattern of behaviour as well as the dicta, it is not of monogamy but of abstinence. The only family exemplified is strictly inimitable.

Is it then the duty of Christians to establish a certain relationship with the morality of the day, whatever it may be? This is not antinomianism but it may be held to come too near to it. The alternative is to wage a war of Christian morality against whatever

else is current, as if an agrarian or even a sheep-rearing society
could replace a society of contraceptives and euthanasia.

On Poetic Architecture

I

There is no reason to suppose that the state of mind of the poet,
when he writes a poem, is reproduced in the mind of the reader.
It has sometimes been said that the poem represents an 'organization of impulses' which is transmitted – it is generally supposed
with beneficial effects – to the reader, who in this way manages
to live for a moment with the sages. If you believe that you can
believe anything about the relationships existing between
members of the human race.

In the first place, one should try to be clear – or as clear as one
can be – about 'the state of mind of the poet, when he writes a
poem'. What sort of correspondence has it with the poem
produced? The poem is, of course, some of what is passing
through his mind. It is certainly not all, even though he is likely
to be more nearly absorbed by this activity than by many others
that he engages in. And 'passing through his mind' is not an easy
conception either. The only proof, really, is that the words get
written. What accompanies the act of writing may be various.
The poet may be exalted or he may be merely numb. He is just
as likely to feel the emotion he is (as they say) 'conveying', *after*
he has written it as at the time of writing. He may be frozen as it
comes to consciousness. In any case he is using words which are
not his own (words are not a man's own), though his organization
of them owes something to his own physiology and, of course,
history. He speaks with the voice of a civilization and if anyone
understands him it will be people who 'understand' what he
'understands', whatever that may mean. But what does it mean?

II

Does it make sense to talk of 'understanding' a person as distinct
from 'understanding' a thing? There probably is no distinction,

except in so far as affinity between the subject and object (the same sort of animal, the same civilization) give a peculiar quality to one's relationship with things like oneself. That people share states of mind is obviously true in the sense that consciousness is historical and within a particular civilization there will be commonly accepted explanations of various classes of event. But the only proof of your understanding of a person is your ability to adjust yourself to him or her, or her or him to yourself, just as the only proof of your understanding a motor-car is your ability to handle it in various ways and to do what it wants to do (if it is to go at all). The more complex the machines the wider the range of mutual adjustments, but one is usually more stupid than another, as a car is more stupid than a man and will normally come sooner to the point of exercising its will, i.e., refusing to adjust itself any further.

III

'The poem' is words on a piece of paper, or spoken, just as 'the building' is erected before you and you must make of it what you can. Nobody supposes that you feel what the builder or architect 'felt', as he sweated through his work, even in cases where there is one man to whom a 'feeling' or an original creative act could with any plausibility be attributed. Of course buildings are in styles as well as being in materials, and many people have a hand in them. And so have poems although one man will, these days, put his name on the title page. Take no more than a due amount of notice of it; it is to get the money, or the reputation, or in hopes of the same.

Le Roi Soleil

I

Does consciousness of one's own body differ from consciousness of other things? 'One's own body': an expression already heavy with metaphysic. At first it seems obvious that it must. 'One's own body': the one that is always there; the least interesting of bodies. If consciousness is the centre, or perhaps the maggot, then that body is the nut and the surrounding world is the shell. Most of what goes on in our own bodies we are unconscious of; it is the microcosmos. The macrocosmos is hardly more mysterious, or unknown; its size alone is impressive.

What we see, what we touch, we do with our own eyes, our hands, parts of our bodies. But it is also our eyes which see what we see of ourselves, our fingers which touch our skin or our tongue which touches our teeth. What of our consciousness of what goes on inside our bodies? The bellyache, the sudden lesion? These pains are not external to our bodies, but they are as external to our consciousness as events we perceive in Mars. Is not consciousness a convention, more or less, a matter of history? Could not an animal have a bellyache without being aware of it? It would not be an ache, no doubt, but there would be the visceral disturbances, the vomiting would follow, and then quiescence. How much we perceive of the convulsions of the macrocosmos is a matter of the tradition we have inherited. But so it is, surely, with the bellyache. If two states of consciousness could be compared (as they cannot, with any accuracy, because only one is known) the neolithic pain would differ from our own, for there is no pain, certainly no located pain, without meaning.

II

But if the relationship of the consciousness to the microcosmos and the macrocosmos is the same, what becomes of the notion of personality? It is more extensive. Instead of trying to conceive of a consciousness which corresponds to a physical person, as if such a person could float out of space and time, one takes the consciousness *de facto*, with all there is in it, which is something of the world as well as of a single body. A person becomes, not what he thinks he is, but what he is, or at any rate what is. The 'what is', like the person in other conceptions, can be seen from inside or outside; the more or less of correspondence there is between these two views is a commonplace of morality.

Who was Louis XIV? He was what he was seen to be, or if he was not, it was because there was more to be seen and not because a 'reality' was hiding in Versailles behind an appearance. Subjectively, he was what of his world he was aware of, and in building Versailles he was to some extent building himself. A whole skein of connections met in his hand, and it matters more whether a king dies than whether a beggar does. What profound sense has it that not a sparrow falls without the knowledge of your father which is in heaven? It is supernatural.

By Way of Explanation

I

About a month before George Herbert's death (according to Walton), a conversation took place between him and a Mr Duncon, who had been sent by Nicholas Ferrer:

> 'I desire you to pray with me.'
> 'What prayers?'
> 'O, sir! the prayers of my mother, the Church of England: no other prayers are equal to them!'

The point needs no illustration, but when he prayed, daily, 'Lighten our darkness, we beseech thee, O Lord', it was 'Illumina, quaesumus Domine Deus, tenebras nostras'. The prayer is in the breviaries of Sarum and York, in the sacramentaries of Gregory and Gelasius. The *mother* of George Herbert was the Church, looking on him with her English countenance. It was 1633, the year in which the King first greeted Laud, then Bishop of London, as 'my Lord's Grace of Canterbury', adding, 'you are very welcome'. It was only eleven years before the Archbishop, on Tower Hill, said: 'Cupio dissolvi et esse cum Christo' and passed through 'a mere shadow of death, a little darkness upon nature', as he said in his prayer.

II

A less austere character, Robert Herrick, who welcomed the king into the west when he published his *Hesperides* in 1648, looked towards death through the ordinary sensualities, and hardly distinguished the sacred from the profane:

Holy waters hither bring
For the sacred sprinkling:
Baptize me and thee, and so
Let us to the Altar go.
And (ere we our rites commence)
Wash our hands in innocence.
Then I'le be the *Rex Sacrorum*,
Thou the Queen of *Peace* and *Quorum*.

Herrick had been deprived of his living before his book came out; and he is not heard of again till he goes back to Dean Prior in 1662, aged seventy-one. In this year was issued the edition of the Prayer Book we now have, the use of the Elizabethan book, as it more or less was, having been illegal from the Ordinance of Parliament, Die Veneris, 3 Januarii, 1644, for the taking away of the Book of Common Prayer, and for the establishing and putting in execution of the Directory, until the Restoration.

III

Roger Clark, rector of Ashmore in Dorsetshire,

> When the Rebellion broke out … adhered Immovably to his Majesty's cause, and betook himself to the army under my Lord Hopton; for which he was Plunder'd of all that he had, the Soldiers Tearing a broad the very beds, and Scattering the Feathers out of the Ticking: … they took the Two Young Sons, being Twins, the Elder named Roger, and the Other, Richard, and laid them stark-naked in a Dripping-Pan before the Fire, with a design to Roast them: but a certain woman, whose name was Pope, came and snatched them away in her Apron. (Walker, *Sufferings of the Clergy*, 1714)

It happens that the minute-books of the Parliamentary Standing Committee, which sat in Dorset during the Rebellion and interregnum, have been preserved: perhaps the only ones of their kind; there was good reason for destroying such books. 'Whereas we are informed that Leonard Snooke of Stower pvost, one Combe of Fifehead and Thomas Dowden of Kingston have been in armes against the Parliament, it is therefore ordered that you seize, inventory and secure their estates…' It is a matter of taste, or perhaps something more, whether you sympathize with these men or with John Hampden, that model of the bourgeois who makes a virtue of not paying his taxes. Somebody gained by the losses of such men as Leonard Snooke, one Combes and Thomas Dowden: 'shall hold and enjoie the farmes called Grange and Waddam, beeinge part of the sequestred estate of Robt. Lawrence, Esqr, for delinquencie'. And instead of ecclesiastical discipline – 'It is hereby ordered that noe minister whatsoever shall psume to preach in the pish church of Blandford in this Country without leave first obtained from Mr Trottell, minister of Spettsbury.'

IV

At the Restoration, Jeremy Taylor was consecrated bishop – to an Irish see – and some other reparations were made to tired men.

Thomas Ken, whose sister Anne was married to Isaac Walton, was ordained in 1661 or 1662. He became Bishop of Bath and Wells in 1684. In 1688, with six other bishops including Sancroft, Archbishop of Canterbury, he submitted To the King's Most Excellent Majesty (James II) the petition which humbly sheweth

> That the great averseness they find in themselves to the distrib-
> uting and publishing in all their churches your Majesty's late
> declaration for liberty of conscience proceedeth neither from
> any want of duty and obedience to your Majesty, our holy
> mother the Church of England being, both in her principles
> and constant practice, unquestionably loyal ... nor yet from
> any want of due tenderness to dissenters, in relation to whom
> they are willing to come to such a temper as shall be thought
> fit, when that matter shall be considered and settled in parlia-
> ment and convocation; but yet among many other
> considerations, and this especially because that declaration is
> founded upon such a dispensing power as hath been often
> declared illegal in parliament, and particularly in the years
> 1662 and 1672, and in the beginning of your Majesty's reign...

The seven bishops were taken to the Tower 'for contriving, making and publishing a seditious libel'. But Ken would not take the oath to William; nor would Sancroft and seven other bishops.

Ken went to Wells and from his chair asserted his canonical right. The rest of his life he spent in Longleat, where he wrote two thousand pages of verse, as a form of laudanum, he said, which shows how dangerous it is for a man to have time on his hands.

V

One does not often think of Swift as a cleric, because his imagination was unbridled, and because he was Irish and the merits of a later (rebellious) nationalism are supposed to have washed away the stains of his loyalty. But Swift said: 'Might not those who enter upon any office in her Majesty's family, be obliged to take an oath parallel to that against simony, which is administered to the clergy?' And in 'A Letter concerning the Sacramental Test':

> As to the argument used for repealing the Test, that it will unite all the Protestants against the Common Enemy; I wonder by what figure these gentlemen speak, who are pleased to advance it.... 'Tis an odd way of uniteing parties, to deprive a Majority of Part of their antient Right, by conferring it on a Faction who never had any Right at all, and therefore cannot be said to suffer any loss or injury, if it be refused them. Neither is it very clear, how far some people may stretch the term of Common Enemy. How many are there of those that call themselves Protestants, who look upon our Worship to be idolatrous as well as that of Papists, and with great Charity put Prelacy and Popery together as terms convertible?

VI

Queen Anne died in 1714 and the country has been more or less given over to Whiggery ever since. In 1717 Convocation was suppressed so that it should not condemn the invisible Bishop of Bangor, Dr Hoadley, to whom William Law wrote (in the *Defence of Church Principles*):

> But, my Lord, as human nature, if left to itself, would neither answer the ends of a spiritual or civil society; so a constant

visible government in both is equally necessary; and I believe, it appears to all unprejudiced eyes that, in this argument at least, your Lordship has declared both equally unlawful.

VII

George Hicks, the non-juror who in 1694 was consecrated titular Bishop of Thetford, used the First (and more Catholic) Prayer Book of Edward VI, and in 1717 the Nonjurors published their own office, which was closely allied to it. Those who followed the latter book were called the *Usagers*, from the mixing of water with the wine, saying the prayer for the dead and other usages prescribed in it. 'What can be more heinously wicked', wrote Law, himself a Nonjuror, 'than heartily to wish the success of a person on account of his right, and at the same time, in the most solemn manner, in the presence of God, and as you hope for mercy, to swear that he has no right at all.'

From Johnson it is enough to quote the *Dictionary*:

TORY. One who adheres to the ancient constitution of the state, and the apostolical hierarchy of the church of England.

WHIG. The name of a faction.

Not wholly irrelevant are certain curious verses of Charles Wesley about Methodist preachers:

Rather than suffer them to dare
Usurp the priestly character,
Save them from arrogant offence,
And snatch them uncorrupted hence.

Omitted in the second edition. John did not like them.

VIII

The Tories of the nineteenth century are Samuel Taylor Coleridge and the Duke of Wellington, and the latter was already intent upon ruinous calculations: 'What I looked on as the great advantage of the measure' – for Roman emancipation – 'was that it would unite all men of property and character together in one

interest against the agitators.' Coleridge was intent upon fanciful
conditions:

> a declaration, to which every possible character of solemnity
> should be given, that at no time and under no circumstances
> has it ever been, nor can it ever be, compatible with the safety
> of the British Constitution to recognize in the Roman
> Catholic priesthood, as now constituted, a component Estate
> of the realm, or persons capable, individually or collectively,
> of becoming the trustees and usufructuary proprietors of that
> elective and circulative property, originally reserved for the
> permanent maintenance of the National Church.

But, on any terms, the emancipation of the Papists was the end of
even the possibility of that system which Coleridge himself
defined:

> the Constitution, in its widest sense as the constitution of the
> realm, arose out of, and in fact consisted in, the coexistence of
> the constitutional State ... with the King as its head, and of the
> Church, that is, the National Church, with the King likewise
> as its head; and lastly of the King, as the head and Majesty of
> the whole nation.

The political device of the latter part of the seventeenth century
was not the Restoration but the Revolution which is sometimes
called glorious, and indeed you might call it that by comparison
with the one which took place in France in 1789. From the time
Charles raised his standard at Nottingham, Toryism as defined by
Johnson has almost always been a doctrine of opposition, and so
it will remain.

The Politics of Wyndham Lewis

Wyndham Lewis was born on board his father's yacht. Perhaps it was thought safer for such an explosion to take place off shore. Yet that was in 1882, thirty-two years off from the first *Blast*. Lewis was not, as writers go, young when he exploded.

These facts are to be kept in mind. It matters greatly, in considering a man's politics, when he was born, where he came from, who his parents were. For politics is a science of the milieu, and there has to be a milieu before you can have the science. The considerations of *locus* and *status* are among the determinants, if not of the political philosophy itself, at least of its presentation as well as of its subject-matter. It is to be set down that his father came of a well-to-do New York family; that his mother was an Englishwoman of Scottish-Irish extraction; that the couple separated when he was about eleven; and that the main parental influence on him, as on Coriolanus, was his mother. His schooling, which was mainly at miscellaneous private schools, ended with two years at Rugby, but he was bottom of the form and Arnold would have been ashamed of him. Then he went to the Slade. After that, there were seven years in continental Europe, mostly in Paris. The Lewis who resettled in London, in 1909, was therefore a man of independent stock, largely self-educated, perverted moreover by gallic and other foreign notions. The man who met the war of 1914 was no Rupert Brooke, Sassoon or Rosenberg (to compare small things with great) but a man armed *cap-à-pie*. When he reached the dark wood of the western front he was, appropriately, thirty-five, a man who could say to his battery commander: 'I am in your battery, not in your Sunday school', and to Ezra Pound: 'I am truly not sanguinary except when confronted by an imbecile: not, thank God, from lack of stomach. Too much sense. Alas, too much sense.'

It does not take a Lewis to identify the war of 1914–18 as a political watershed. Indeed there was too much vulgar apocalyptic talk on that occasion. The Lewisian apocalypse was a pre-war affair. It was not an excitement borrowed from events but an intellectual performance of its own. In essence it was a thing of the eye. 'Paul Cézanne', Lewis said in a much later pamphlet (*The Demon of Progress in the Arts*, 1954), 'can revolutionize the manner of painting of a generation or two of painters; but it is quite impossible for his canvases to have any effect outside the technique of painting.' Lewis was not the man to 'set men chanting with diabolical glee around the guillotines', like the author of *Saint Nicolas a trois clériaux*; he was not one who, like Jean-Jacques Rousseau, 'with his books ... tore up society by the roots'. He *saw* things differently, as indeed Jean-Jacques Rousseau did too, but with this difference, that that romantic figure did not think he had done his job until he had set the heart of Europe palpitating. Lewis did not care for palpitations, or rate them very highly. He was, notoriously, the man with the cara-pace; in considering his politics, it is more useful to think of events as breaking over him than of him rushing into the breakers to perform antics of great interest in themselves. It is what he saw, not what he did, which is of political significance. If it had been possible to use words which, by analogy with Cézanne's painting, had no effect outside the technique of thought, that is what he would have done. But words are not like that; they have their lower as well as their higher magic, and they are inextricably bound to action, which aspires to thought, and uses rhetoric, such is the nature of the human animal. Lewis did not avoid the misun-derstanding this situation gives rise to. He said – with a touch of Manicheeism – 'The game of government goes on, and it is a game that no philosopher has ever been able to interrupt seriously for a moment', and that was an ideal as much as a lament. But he could not keep out of trouble; he even, perhaps, itched more than a little to be in it, at times.

Not unrelated to the difficulties of using speech as the medium of political philosophy are the difficulties arising from those aspects of Lewis's writing which are called his personality. Not even Ben Jonson himself emitted a more obsessive penumbra. One is the presence of mannerisms, not unrelated to art, appar-ently as compulsive as the habit a woman might have of screwing up her handkerchief, or a swallow has of building, repeatedly, a certain sort of nest. V.S. Pritchett asserts that the first and last sentences of any of Lewis's paragraphs 'will rarely be found to have any logical connection', but a more striking characteristic of his work is that it is so intensely patterned that, starting from almost any sentence chosen at random, one could start an expla-nation which would not stop short of the completed *oeuvre*. It is this which makes it impossible to write about Lewis's politics without a consciousness of his work in other *genres*. Lewis has himself well defined the nature of the difficulty in some remarks on Shakespeare in *The Lion and the Fox* (p. 179):

> With the exception of Chapman, Shakespeare is the only 'thinker' we meet among the Elizabethan dramatists. By this is meant, of course, that his work contained, apart from poetry, phantasy, rhetoric or observation of manners, a body of matter representing explicit processes of the intellect which would have furnished a moral philosopher like Montaigne with the natural material for his essays. But the quality of this thinking – as it can be surprised springing naturally in the midst of the consummate movements of his art – is, as must be the case with such a man, of startling force sometimes. And if it is not systematic, at least a recognizable physiognomy is there.

Lewis's thought likewise arises out of and in the course of his art – a sufficient ground for its being ignored or misunderstood in an age when a certain sloppiness goes into the general conception of art, and nowhere more than in Anglo-Saxondom.

This dominant personality – to end the introductory part of my remarks – contained powerful antinomies. On the one hand the Socratic ('"the great market-asses" he used only as stalking-horses' – *Physics of the Not-Self*), on the other a figure not unlike his own Coriolanus (*The Lion and the Fox*):

> This scene between Coriolanus and his mother is the key to the play: it shows Coriolanus as the rigid and hypnotized schoolboy influenced in his most susceptible years by a snobbish and violent parent, and urged into a course of destruction which, the machine of an idea, he mesmerically pursues: it is now too late even for the master mind to pull him up.

It would not be difficult to pick out, in the early stories or elsewhere, sentences which characterize Lewis's approach to his political studies ('But I approached him with impassive professional rapidity, my eye fixed on him, already making my diagnosis', from *A Soldier of Humour*). There is a sense in which Lewis, for all his talk about 'Philosophy', never succeeds in disengaging himself from the habits of his carapace, so that it is no Descartes, exercising reason like a dog on a lead, but a dramatic personage, *called* a philosopher but half actor, who does the thinking. He is almost visible on the page, using his great eye, being 'strongly polar' in the matter of sex, claiming to love quiet but all the while bustling to attract attention. If *Time and Western Man*, as has been said, seems always on the verge of saying something important, there is the same air of promise about all Lewis's theoretical writing. It seems big with an idea which is never quite disengaged. What you do see, vividly, is the man who is about to disengage this idea. You see, moreover, a great deal of what he sees as he sets about his task. It is rather as a view of the society of his time than as a theory of it, that *The Art of Being Ruled*, as well as the slighter political books, are important. There is a sense in which Lewis's social and political work is more akin to (the under-rated) Captain Marryat's view of America than to de Tocqueville's, in spite of Lewis's affection for philosophical talk and his taste for destructive analysis. But of course Lewis's mind is infinitely more penetrating, subtle and elusive than that of the engaging seaman. And he is moving in a greatly more sophisticated world. It is a world in which persons and mannerisms are sharply seen but in which people are the servants and carriers of ideas more important than themselves, so that in the preface to *The Diabolical Principle* (1931) he can say: 'Paul and Jolas are the names of notions, associated with other (and far more powerful) notions. In the influence they exert it would, it seems to me, be foolish to deny their importance.' And there is, in *The Art of Being Ruled* itself, a tendency to see society as an interplay of ideas (which it also is) rather than as a collection of people harried or possessed by them. The habit brings carica-ture into the world of theory, as if Bunyan had turned from his visual account of the destiny of man to be expository. Yet in a profound sense Lewis lives up to Schopenhauer's account of the 'true philosopher' as one who 'is to be recognized by a constant sense of the *unreality* of the things by which he is surrounded'. The mean and shoddy suddenly appears as such, as Lewis approaches this or that aspect of our society or our intellectual life 'with impassive professional rapidity'. He is particularly adept at not sparing the rot that lives in the interstices even of major work, the seriousness of which, in its sounder parts, he would no doubt recognize. His relative contempt for Sterne is significant in this connection and moreover, when pondered upon, illuminating and right. The great fashionable idols come crashing down.

> The blood of the roman circus; the cheap pastry of stuffy and sadic romance, with its sweet and viscous sentimentalism, which was manufactured with such success by Proust; the highly spiced incestuous pastry of Freud; the *exaggeration*, emphasis, and unreality of all forms of common melodrama, are all in the same class, and are vulgar first, and evil because of that.

The criterion Lewis claims to use is the aesthetic; 'the ethical canon must ultimately take its authority from taste'. It is the 'soberness, measure, and order that reigns in all the greatest productions of art' that he fixes his mind on in his discourse on society. And against this canon may be seen this fundamental corruption at the root of society:

> ... had the Peruvian potters been accommodated with the resources of a Staffordshire factory for producing pots, they would immediately have abandoned their archaic wheel. Since men in the aggregate, however, are made by their occupation, both the potter and the hunter ('presented suddenly with machine-guns') would deteriorate, become parasitic on their machines, and upon the engineer and inventor. *But in neither case would that appear to them as a consideration of an order to appeal to a man or woman of the world.* (*The Dithyrambic Spectator*, my italics)

So on the stage of *The Art of Being Ruled*, as of the *Apes of God*, move the great, soft, pseudo-revolutionary figures who have taken their colour from the shoddy world of technological change which surrounds them, and as they drift with it they pretend to be resisting and changing it. This is the classic social and political scene, as set by Lewis. 'Everyone who has money enough today is a revolutionary; that and the dress suit are the first prerequisites of a gentleman.'

Times have changed since 1927. The fashions now well up from the lower orders, happily supplied with money to indulge their fancy in a world of mass-produced gew-gaws, and the revolutionary change is now seen as technological. Lewis in fact prognosticates that the 'revolution' so much in the air, and so suspiciously supported on all sides, must envisage 'the purification and ordering of the world from top to bottom'. Of course the reordering he foresaw is not one that the public thinkers, still using the language of individualism and 'democracy', overtly intended. It is a community 'working together under a centralized consciousness and despotic, or at all events very powerful, control', one in which, in Lewis's desperate remedy, mankind would at last be 'let down' to a level appropriate to their mass imbecility. And no one can say that, with television, this work is not going forward at commendable speed, so that the families of professional men, where the ordinary wits of a society ought predominantly to be found, think it natural to bring up their families in a welter of sensation to which, appropriately enough, Freud and Proust form part of the intellectual background; while they themselves suffer instruction in the affairs of the world at the hands of David Frost. These images are not a world of reality, but that is not where the great public wants to live. Behind this façade, or unobtrusively beneath it, the intellectual work of society has to be done. There seems to be a stage in the argument where Lewis passes, rather inconsequentially, to a new hope:

> it is easy to see how the passing of democracy and its accompanying vulgarities, owing to which any valuable discovery has to fight its way in the market-place – and the better it is, the bitterer the opposition – must facilitate this putting the intelligence on a new basis. The annihilation of industrial competition and the sweeping the board of the Small Man, commercially and socially, should have as its brilliant and beneficent corollary the freeing for its great and difficult tasks of intelligence of the first order.

This is, alas, an unproven conclusion. What Lewis was doing, in *The Art of Being Ruled*, was not so much indicating the lines of a new society as defining the position of the intellectual in relation to it. He saw this type of figure as not meddling in revolutionary talk or other tasks of power, but quietly getting on with his work. Despite some starts in the direction of reform, inevitable from the nature of language and from his own pedagogic instinct, Lewis saw himself as having 'too much sense' for action, 'alas, too much sense'.

In view of this conviction, it is remarkable – but less so because of a certain ingenuousness which he simultaneously maintained towards the world of affairs – that Lewis should find himself, in the thirties, embroiled in the most potent political controversies of the time. This involvement has perhaps done more than anything, since, to retard the popular recognition which, however, shows signs of coming at last, in the measure in which it could come to such a writer. *Count Your Dead: They Are Alive* contained salutary warnings about that dress rehearsal for 1939–45, the Spanish Civil War, which was otherwise so one-sidedly reported in this country. But it is the book on *Hitler* (1931), above all, which made its author suspect to the politicizing critics. No doubt incautious expressions are to be found in that book, viewed as a contribution to practical politics, but the real fault lay in the stupidity of its readers. Lewis set out his warnings clearly enough at the start: 'it is as an exponent – not as critic nor yet as advocate – of German Nationalsocialism, that I come forward. It seems to me very important that an unprejudiced and fairly detailed account of this great and novel factor in world affairs should be at the disposal of the intelligent Anglo-Saxon.' Was this controvertible, in the world of 1931? Or was Lewis so wrong in suggesting that Schacht was a more intelligent banker than Mr Montagu Norman? It was an offence no doubt to see Hitler 'as the expression of current German manhood', as indeed he proved to be, and not (in the inclusive language of sentimental Marxists) merely as a 'Fascist' and so by definition opposed by all the grand array of the virtuous German masses. A worse offence was to find some truth in a remark of Sir Oswald Mosley's and to go beyond him. That political clown had pointed out that 'there had never, in fact, been any "democracy" in England at all', on which Lewis's gloss was that he 'might of course have added that there had never been any democracy anywhere' – a gloss which, after all, puts Mosley's *boutade* in a proper perspective. The book on Hitler is, in the Lewis canon, a relatively unimportant one, a pedagogic pamphlet rather than a radical work. It should have been read with less hostility and more understanding. Its reception illustrates, after all, the weakness of Lewis's thesis that the intellectual can work quietly away, in a manner beneficial to the masses, without the masses taking notice of him or himself aspiring to a hand in the power-games of government. It is impossible for anyone, who understands Lewis at all, not to sympathize with the situation which led him to write *The Hitler Cult* (1939): 'Today, to be neutral is to be anti-British' and to recall that he had said in *Blast*, number 2 (1914) that 'it appears to us humanely desirable that Germany should win no war against France or England'. But these things belong to biography, and to the world of power, rather than to the world of enlightenment in which Lewis's major political writings moved.

After the war there were moments when the advancing shadow of Russian military strength seemed to bring him to a suspicion of a dangerous courtesy in that direction. But this, too, was no more than a brief inclination in the direction of a centralism such as seemed to him inevitable. In the meantime, a more significant change had come over him, of which *Self-Condemned* (1954) was the fruit at last. It was as if the explosion of *Blast* had been followed by an implosion. The man of the carapace disappeared. The unity of this development with Lewis's earlier work is demonstrated by the completion of *Childermass* (1928) by *Monstre Gai* and *Malign Fiesta* (1955). All that need be said here – and regretfully – is that this movement into a new level of reality has no counterpart in Lewis's political writing, except so far as a hint may be gathered, from those terrifying later volumes, of a view of man and woman which does not supersede, but completes, the earlier philosophies of the epidermis. If he had rewritten his political writings at the end, Lewis would, I think, have escaped from Manicheeism and from the indifference to the affairs of power which lay so uneasily upon him. He would have been driven from a politics designed to defend 'the intellectual' (that abstraction of liberal democracy) to one of profounder attachments.

From *English Poetry 1900–1950:*
An Assessment

W.B. Yeats

I

When William Butler Yeats died, at the beginning of 1939, he had had all the honours. The Nobel Prize for Literature had come his way sixteen years before, just as he had completed a year as a senator of the newly-established Irish Republic. The French government offered to bring home his remains in a destroyer, but they had no luck that year and it was not until 1949 that the bones were put in the shadow of Ben Bulben. The stone, by Yeats's direction, says:

No marble, no conventional phrase;
On limestone quarried near the spot
By his command these words are cut:

> *Cast a cold eye*
> *On life, on death.*
> *Horseman, pass by!*

Yeats was a great egotist, and frivolous enough to think it worth while cutting a figure even after his death.

The career which brought him to this final gesture started in a genteel, semi-detached house in Sandymount, near Dublin, in 1865. Three years later the family moved to London, where Willie attended a 'rough' and 'cheap' school – the Godolphin, Hammersmith. His father, who had started life reading for the Irish bar, was an artist, and he had relatives in Sligo with whom he spent holidays. With these advantages, he 'did not think English people intelligent unless they were artists'. He was thus provided, from an early age, with a situation which could give colour to the sense of apartness so exceptional a boy might naturally feel. The Irish must have suffered from a sense of inferiority

in those days, for there was an Irish master at school who made
him stand up and told him 'it was a scandal' he was so idle 'when
all the world knew that any Irish boy was cleverer than a whole
class-room of English boys'. When Yeats was fifteen the family
returned to Ireland, and he completed his education at the Dublin
High School, where he had to find other excuses for his dream of
superiority, and at an art school, for his father, who was a man of
great intelligence as his published letters show, thought that every
boy, no matter what he was going to do, should have a training
in art. Willie was already writing verses, and already 'composing
in a loud voice', and was to be a poet. In 1887 the family was back
in London, and Willie was cultivating publishers. *The Wanderings
of Oisin* appeared in 1889. It was, as Louis MacNeice says, full of
'the languor of late Victorian old age', but John O'Leary collected
subscriptions for it, presumably seeing the Irish bard under all this
old stuff.

The curious mixture of estheticism and dreamy nationalism
from which Yeats started has a parallel, it is not often noticed, in
the French nationalist movement at the end of the nineteenth
century, but while Maurras and his friends could find an esthetic
in Racine and André Chénier the Irish had only a load of old
fairy-stories and some improbable heroisms.

> A tall lanky boy with deep-set dark eyes behind glasses, over
> which a lock of dark hair was constantly falling, to be pushed
> back impatiently by sensitive fingers... – a tall girl with masses
> of gold-brown hair and a beauty which made her Paris clothes
> ... unnoticeable, sat figuratively and sometimes literally, at the
> feet of a thin elderly man, with eagle eyes, whose unbroken
> will had turned the outrage of long convict imprisonment into
> immense dignity.

Thus Maud Gonne, for whom Yeats broke his heart, describes
'John O'Leary, the master, and his two favourite disciples'. The
auspices were perhaps too poetic, for a serious writer. O'Leary
himself must have been an impressive figure. He held, as he says
in his *Recollections of Fenians and Fenianism*,

> that all agitating movements, however inevitable and neces-
> sary they may be, are at best but a necessary evil, involving all
> forms of self-seeking and insincerity, accompanied with

outrage and violence, and opening up the widest field for the exercise of that treachery and cruelty which lies latent in human nature.

He preferred the older methods of Wolfe Tone, an engaging character who, as he said at his court-martial, 'designed by fair and open war, to procure the separation' of Ireland from England, and to this end arrived off the entry to Loch Swilly, in 1798, with a French fleet, ending his life shortly afterwards in a manner which might be expected. Yeats, of course, was of Anglo-Irish stock – not of the Scotch Protestants of the North but Church of Ireland people like Swift and Berkeley and the builders of eighteenth-century Dublin. To the distractions of estheticism and romantic nationalism Yeats added that of magic. In 1885 he chaired the first meeting of the Dublin Hermetic Society and he dabbled in such rubbish on and off throughout his life.

II

The volume of *Last Poems* (1940) shows what was the terminus of Yeats's journey.

> You think it horrible that lust and rage
> Should dance attendance upon my old age;
> They were not such a plague when I was young:
> What else have I to spur me into song?

Yeats is of course here cutting a figure, as in his epitaph (1938), which is also in this volume. The lines are not merely a statement of what he thinks. His mind is also on the spectator whose eye is supposed to be on him, but he is speaking out. Only the last line, perhaps, betrays the romantic figure who had become half an encumbrance to him. The 'spur me into song' is draped language, it is not how people speak, and even if Yeats himself had spoken in those terms – as well he might – one would have felt he was overdoing it a bit, providing something for his lovely voice to say, something he could flash his eyes over and shake his hair about. The line does, of course, betray the enduring obsession about being a poet – as if this somehow took precedence over merely being a man, which is the subject of the most serious poetry. There is no doubt, however, that in these final poems Yeats is trying desperately to cast aside pretences and to get to the root of his mind. In a way the most impressive attempt – the most successful perhaps – is the brief 'Chambermaid's Second Song':

> From pleasure of the bed,
> Dull as a worm,
> His rod and its butting head
> Limp as a worm,
> His spirit that has fled
> Blind as a worm.

It is the chambermaid who speaks, but it is the old man she sees, and he is no longer in a position to give himself airs. In 'The Statesman's Holiday', where the speaker is obviously a *persona* of the poet's, he is strutting, but there is a desperate throwaway air, as if he wished to make nothing of himself. The tone is not far from that which is found in certain of the songs in the songbooks of the Restoration period – *Westminster Drolleries* and the like.

> With boys and girls about him,
> With any sort of clothes,
> With a hat out of fashion,
> With old patched shoes,
> With a ragged bandit cloak,
> With an eye like a hawk.

– and so on. He writes ballads with what appears to be a deliberate recklessness:

> 'Because I am mad about women
> I am mad about the hills',
> Said that wild old wicked man
> Who travels where God wills.

But there is a pretentiousness about this which shows up at once beside this from the seventeenth century:

> My Cozen Moll's an arrant whore,
> And so is her sister Kate,
> They kicked their mother out o' dore,
> And broke their Father's pate.

Yeats is not merely singing a tune, and not merely uttering the lusts of an old man; he is also protesting, in a sort of last will and testament, that the world of the senses is more real than those abstractions which the world of the thirties was always trying to ram down people's throats, as the world of the sixties does too, though with a change of tone. 'In our time the destiny of man presents its meaning in political terms', he quotes Thomas Mann as saying, and his commentary is:

> How can I, that girl standing there,
> My attention fix
> On Roman or on Russian
> Or on Spanish politics?
>
> … But O that I were young again
> And held her in my arms.

It is understandable, but it is too pre-conceived to impress us as poetry.

Yeats's politics, which were really a department of his obsession with the dramatic, were with him to the end. We get recollections of the more colourful bits of the history which produced, in the end, the rather drab Republic:

> Come gather round me, players all:
> Come praise Nineteen-Sixteen,
> Those from the pit and the gallery
> Or from the painted scene
> That fought in the Post Office
> Or round the City Hall.

Parnell and Roger Casement have their poems, and from the contemporary scene there are O'Duffy's Blue Shirts, who had attracted Yeats for a time. 'The Three Marching Songs' is better in the earlier version, published in *A Full Moon in March* (1935) as 'Three Songs to the Same Tune' – and Yeats often in fact composed and chanted to a tune:

> Grandfather sang it under the gallows:
> 'Hear, gentlemen, ladies, and all mankind:
> Money is good and a girl might be better,
> But good strong blows are a delight to the mind.'
> There, standing on the cart,
> He sang it from his heart.

There is a sort of 'dare' about this, among the humanitarian liberalism of the thirties, and although one could not deny the lines a
certain dramatic success, they are not the work of a man who has
faced reality very soberly. They strike a posture. Yeats was, in fact,
defying the mob of inferior beings he was always apt to imagine
around him, and he looked to O'Duffy's Blue Shirts to make
good, in some way, the destruction of the great houses of his
youth which of course, in Ireland, had been done physically by
his friends the Irish revolutionaries though it would have
happened, no doubt less dramatically, in any case.

> Down the fanatic, down the clown;
> Down, down, hammer them down,
> Down to the tune of O'Donnell Abu.

It is a sort of nihilism. Kipling is rather milk-and-water stuff beside
this: 'When nations are empty up there at the top, / When order
has weakened or faction is strong'. Yeats's weakness, as when he
sat at the feet of O'Leary, was for a little movement and colour in
politics, without caring too precisely where it was likely to lead.
But once again, it was an aspect of his distrust of abstraction:

> God guard me from those thoughts men think
> In the mind alone;
> He that sings a lasting song
> Thinks in a marrow-bone.

This is one of Yeats's most successful statements of his final position, though the two remaining stanzas of 'A Prayer for Old Age'
(also in *A Full Moon in March*) slip back into the inferior dramatics
of 'a wise old man', 'a foolish, passionate man' – figures of fun,
equally.

Although the *Last Poems* and *A Full Moon in March* have so
much interest as showing, with some bleakness, the point at
which Yeats finally arrived, the essentials of this last philosophy
are exhibited much more fully, and with more variety, in *The
Winding Stair and Other Poems* (1933). Here the tensions are far
better sustained. Old age still has for him something of the quality
of a discovery. He is no longer the 'sixty-year-old smiling public
man' of *The Tower*. Nor, on the other hand, has he yet been
driven to the desperate gesticulations of the *Last Poems*, in which
the voice is often more emphatic than the passion. The period in

which most of these poems were composed began with Yeats being 'staggered', as he wrote in a letter to Olivia Shakespeare, by his 'first nervous illness'. There was an illness in 1927 from which he 'hardly expected to recover' but then he did expect it and started to write, his sense of life much sharpened by the nostalgia for it which can come to sick people. This volume starts with what, when one comes to think of it, was an astounding piece of insolence, a poem 'In Memory of Eva Gore-Booth and Con Markiewicz', written while the sisters were still alive. These two friends of his youth had become old women; how could it be otherwise? It was long enough ago that they had played their part in his youthful frequentation of great houses. The poem has great charm but, viewed in this light, also a good deal of superficiality and some coarseness. It is a symptom of a general weakness in Yeats that, just as he himself struts and poses, except in his moments of greatest absorption, so he tends to see other people as archtypal figures, or masks, through his own preconceptions rather than for what they are. It is true that in this poem he gives colour to his attitude by asserting that it is their abstract, Utopian politics which have changed the girls to something 'withered old and skeleton-gaunt' but when one thinks of Yeats's own final fling, in *Last Poems*, in favour of politics of a different kind, one is less impressed. One might almost say that, in this dedicatory poem, Yeats is abusing his literary ability to strike an attitude of egotistical contempt. Were they more 'shadows' than he was? *He preferred them young*, of course.

The second poem in the volume, 'Death', starts as Yeats not infrequently does from a natural and truthful expression, only to find that the simple truth is not enough and so he takes refuge in rhetoric.

> Nor dread nor hope attend
> A dying animal;
> A man awaits his end
> Dreading and hoping all;

– but he cannot stand at this point. He fumbles for his hero's mask and becomes 'A great man in his pride / Confronting murderous men'. Should he not have known that, facing death, there are no great men, except for the spectator? Yeats has changed his ground and we feel we are being cheated. He was, after all, talking only to impress us. The 'Dialogue of Self and Soul', which follows, is hardly successful as a dialogue, because the characters are not sufficiently differentiated, but it contains lines which show Yeats painfully trying to look at the truth about his life, and to see clearly

> The ignominy of boyhood; the distress
> Of boyhood changing into man;
> The unfinished man and his pain
> Brought face to face with his own clumsiness;

but he steps aside for the attraction of 'The finished man among his enemies', which is comforting stuff, for it is the 'malicious eyes' of others that have got it all wrong and he is, as he sees himself, a hero. There are, as so often, magnificent gestures as he struggles: 'A blind man battering blind men', till, with a final dramatic assertion, he claims to 'cast out remorse' – 'When such as I cast out remorse'. The 'such as I' betrays him. There is more truth in the lines of 'Vacillation' which Eliot pointed to as showing how Yeats 'achieved greatness against the greatest odds':

> Things said or done long years ago
> Or things I did not do or say
> But thought that I might say or do
> Weigh me down, and not a day
> But something is recalled,
> My conscience or my vanity appalled.

In 'Vacillation', which is a series of eight short poems, Yeats is held in the tension of conflicting impulses and it is this situation which gives the poetry of this volume its strength. The figures he conjures with here are not Casement or the men of 1916; they are Berkeley, Swift and Burke – the great intellectual figures of what, after all, still remains Ireland's most productive period. He is still struggling, for some sort of intellectual solution which will hold the opposing forces in balance. 'Between extremities / Man runs his course' – between day and night, or some other set of antinomies. The fumbling for a solution is understandably confused, and Yeats, as ever feeling the need to speak out and to speak impressively, flings himself into a sort of moral discourse:

> Get all the gold and silver that you can,
> Satisfy ambition, or animate

The trivial days and ram them with the sun,
And yet upon these maxims meditate:
All women dote upon an idle man...

There is a curious passion for generality in Yeats which contradicts his declared hatred of abstraction. The types and masks with which his work is littered are really a form of imperfect abstraction. He is not content to rest on his own experience, as a poet more wholly of the century would be likely to do. No doubt the moralism he favours is one which has come to him through a long course of estheticism, but it is a moralism all the same and in this respect his attitudes are more akin than seems at first sight to be the case to those of the great Victorian poets. He is cut off from any fruitful tradition – from Swift, Berkeley and Burke, of whom in some ways he made so much – by the frivolous attitude to Christianity exhibited in 'The Mother of God' and in the references to von Hügel. At moments he seems to approximate rather to the Marquis de Sade, whose not very profound, and perhaps insane, view was that the first duty of women was to lay themselves open to whatever lusts he chose to exercise upon them. There are moments when Yeats drops his moralism, and all his airs. The fourth poem of 'Vacillation' shows him in a London teashop – Lyons, probably. For a moment one sees the poet without affectation:

My fiftieth year had come and gone,
I sat, a solitary man,
In a crowded London shop,
An open book and empty cup
On the marble table-top.

But even this attractive small poem ends with an assertion in which Yeats's egotism finds an outlet. He is 'blessed and could bless'; he sees himself as a source of power and puts the surrounding humanity in a different category. If we can provisionally accept Yeats's 'look at me' act, lyrics such as 'Acquaintance; companion' and 'I ranted to the knave and the fool' are impressive. They have great concentration and a spareness of diction which puts them, by any standards, high among the productions of the century. But when it comes, as he said in an earlier poem, to dining with Landor or John Donne, one can only conclude that though he may dine with Landor – no mean company – he will never dine with Donne, whose poetry is immeasurably nearer the bone.

The series of twenty-five short poems under the general title of 'Words for Music Perhaps' are among the most remarkable productions of Yeats's deliberate art. The themes of lust and youth and age are presented in a sort of Punch and Judy show. Crazy Jane and the Bishop are both puppets, attempts no doubt to externalize the argument of life and death going on under the skin of the ageing poet. While the impulse for the poems unquestionably comes from deep sources, there is a strong element of preconception in the subject-matter as, no doubt, in the form. It is in this paring down of language, in the later poems, that one suspects the influence of Pound, though F.R. Higgins, whether through observation or national loyalty, attributed the development rather to the influence of native Irish poetry. As to the subject-matter, the theme is set in the first encounter of 'Crazy Jane and the Bishop' – Yeats's senile passion, perhaps, and the Puritanism of de Valera's Republic. The mask Yeats wears is certainly that of the old woman recalling the lover of her youth, not that of the Bishop whose skin was 'Wrinkled like the foot of a goose'. It is as if, by choosing the more complete disguise of the female part, he could the more easily hide from himself the fact that his own skin is wrinkled and that he resembles the bishop more than the young lover Jack. The theme is developed with many variations and complexities, in the best of the poems with a new tone in which realism is caught up in the lyric impulse. But the realism is elusive, and is perhaps less realism than a mask of harshness and ugliness which gives astringency to the beauty of the whole. Indeed the exaggerated expressions of lust pass quickly into dream, to which world they belong:

> I had wild Jack for a lover;
> Though like a road
> That men pass over
> My body makes no moan
> But sings on:
> *All things remain in God.*

Those who think that realism should look up their Villon. The most successful parts of the series are perhaps those where

meaning almost disappears in a cry of exultation or anguish, and
the argument between Crazy Jane and the Bishop is lost sight of
in a general cry of old age.

> Those dancing days are gone,
> All that silk and satin gear;
> Crouch upon a stone,
> Wrapping that foul body up
> In as foul a rag.

The lyric pitch is maintained to no small extent by the masterly
use of refrain: '*I carry the sun in a golden cup,* / *The moon in a silver
bag*' – in which Yeats owned he had a debt to Pound, or

> '*I am of Ireland,*
> *And the Holy Land of Ireland,*
> *And time runs on*', *cried she.*
> '*Come out of charity,*
> *Come dance with me in Ireland.*'

The series ends, rather weakly, with some stuff about Plotinus.

There is, in the *Winding Stair* volume, a second, shorter series
of lyrics, 'A Woman Young and Old', matching 'A Man Young
and Old' in *The Tower* (1928), less desperate in tone than 'Words
for Music Perhaps' but with something of the same skill in
handling short-lined stanza forms. The girl speaks, but it is so to
speak the girl of a male observer. 'I admit the briar / Entangled in
my hair / Did not injure me'; still more in 'What lively lad most
pleasured me / Of all that with me lay?' There is nothing psychologically revealing about either series of poems; indeed the
psychology may be said to be strictly preconceived. What is
attempted rather is a sort of dogmatics of lust, not an easy subject,
nor perhaps one which is capable of sustaining itself without
support from elsewhere. Perhaps the chorus from the *Antigone*
with which 'A Woman Young and Old' concludes is intended,
like the reference to Plotinus at the conclusion of 'Words for
Music Perhaps', to indicate some support from a world of pagan
theology, but it is not very convincing.

III

Although the development of Yeats's verse is from a Victorian tapestry, with plenty of adjectives, and a romantic subject, to a spare line drawing, he never entirely moves into a world which is, as it were, continuous with the world of prose. It is not merely that, to the end, he regards himself as entitled to use inversions – such as 'all that with me lay'. It is not, certainly, that his language always bears evidence of being the product of the release known as inspiration. No important writer of the century has more of an air of deliberation than Yeats has, and it is well known that a number of his poems were written out first in prose, and then converted. It is rather that one feels that Yeats is claiming for his work a certain sort of protection. He is the man in the poet's mask. His prose is 'the prose of a poet', exhibiting in turn great intellectual force and silliness, both in the same portentous language, and intended to be taken with equal seriousness because the poet has so delivered himself. At the outset of his career, Yeats made a pronouncement about his intentions, in *The Celtic Twilight* (1893), which he lived up to to the end. 'I have desired', he says, 'like every artist, to create a little world out of the beautiful, pleasant and significant things of this marred and clumsy world.' Yeats's conception of the beautiful and the significant changed with fashion. In place of romantic love we have, in the late poems, the exertions of copulation. The world he made was still collected in order to impress. Yeats always seems to demand to be listened to on his own terms. The test of a poet, in the end, is, however, the extent to which he can be taken on other people's terms. With regard to his native country, Yeats's intention was 'to show in a vision something of the face of Ireland to any of my own people who would look where I bid them'. He would point to what was 'beautiful, pleasant and significant' to himself, rather than elucidate what was there. The contrast with Swift, whose companion he liked to think himself, could not have been more absolute.

A more illuminating comparison may be made with the great theorist of the theatre, Edward Gordon Craig. Craig was a man of great intelligence and invention who devoted himself, largely in vain one might think, to the revivification of the theatre by the application to it of the lessons of tradition, eclectically gathered in a manner which is reminiscent at times of Ezra Pound searching the classics of many countries for a modern idiom. He wanted an unnatural mode of speech, an unnatural mode of delivery, actors like marionnettes, disguised beyond recognition, conventionalized movements and expressions dependent on masks and formal movement. You might say that this programme which Craig intended for the theatre was adopted by Yeats for himself. One has only to put Yeats's work beside that of Hardy to be aware of the stiffness of his clothes. There is no psychology in Yeats, only magic. There are no people, only dolls – of elegant and dramatic appearance, very often. Craig went so far as to say that 'no matter what the work is to be, if it is to be called an art work it must be made solely from *inorganic* material'. It needs the satiric genius of a Lewis to apply this principle, even partially and intermittently, to the art of literature. Yeats was not the man for such ruthlessness. His portrayals are of conventionalized types – the beauty, the aged lecher, the hero and, of course, The Poet. We do not learn anything from them, but they amuse us.

IV

The Tower (1928) is usually thought the high point of Yeats's art, when *The Winding Stair* is not. It starts with an artifact of singular power and elaboration, 'Sailing to Byzantium'. It is the poet's most consistent attempt to give himself over to the intellect, as 'Words for Music Perhaps' is his most consistent attempt to give himself over to the body. Both are reactions to old age. Both represent a clinging to life, a determination not to give up in the face of failing powers, and have the *panache* of spirited old people who show a defiant energy. For the Yeats of 'Sailing to Byzantium',

> An aged man is but a paltry thing,
> A tattered coat upon a stick, unless
> Soul clap its hands and sing, and louder sing
> For every tatter in its mortal dress.

The 'soul' of this poem is an entity which can make itself more athletic by intellectual studies, which, as the title poem of *The Tower* puts it, can 'Choose Plato and Plotinus for a friend'. Byzan-

tium with its elaborate toys 'Of hammered gold and gold enam-
elling' is the destination of this non-natural, aspiring intellect. It
is a vanity if ever there was one, a conception which comes in
direct line from the Art for Art's Sake of the nineties. The artifice
breaks into what is certainly among Yeats's most telling poetry
with 'Sick with desire / And fastened to a dying animal / It knows
not what it is.' But the 'artifice of eternity' into which Yeats asks
to be gathered has no existence beyond the poem. It is part of a
gesture, impressive in the poet, but meaningless for common life
when one closes the book.

'The Tower', the second poem in the volume of that name, is
an example of Yeats's best rhetoric. The first section is, so to
speak, a mask of old age.

> Never had I more
> Excited, passionate, fantastical
> Imagination, nor an ear and eye
> That more expected the impossible –

That lively old gentleman – can it really be good for him to be so
excited and passionate? – supposes that he must abandon 'the
Muse' and give himself over to abstractions. One knows perfectly
well that he intends nothing of the kind, but the threat arouses
our sympathy. In the second part of the poem Yeats brings out all
his dolls. The great houses are evoked, with Mrs French and her
'serving-man'; 'a peasant-girl commended by a song'; 'the man
who made the song', blind, of course, like Homer who, although
Yeats did not read Greek, is readily brought out to mime the part
of The Poet; and so on. In the third and final part of the poem,
'It is time that I wrote my will', the poet works himself up into a
final resolution which is essentially that of 'Sailing to Byzantium':

> Now shall I make my soul,
> Compelling it to study
> In a learned school
> Till the wreck of body,
> Slow decay of blood,
> Testy delirium,
> Or what worse evil come –

– until the death of his friends, even of his girl friends, seems
nothing. All this is bravado. We learn nothing of the real old man,

who took to reading detective stories and, if he ignored the death of his friends, did so not because he had a fully-fashioned soul but out of selfishness, like the rest of us, and particularly the old.

'Meditations in Time of Civil War' is, similarly, a parade of conventional conceptions. Yeats broods on the great houses which fascinated him when he was a young man, and helped him to build up his grandiose conception of himself, or rather perhaps to provide a symbol for the isolation from inferior persons which he felt already. In prose terms it is rather absurd. There is a great circumlocution to come to the conclusion that merely to dawdle around the achievements of another age gets you nowhere. In the second part of the poem he describes his house – the tower of Ballylee he acquired shortly before his marriage, and which he had managed to buy for what must have been the very satisfactory price of thirty-five pounds. When Yeats had first known this establishment, years before, it had found a sensible contemporary use as a farm with a mill attached. Yeats turned it into a poetic house. In his poem, the farmer and the miller, and the other intervening nondescript persons, have disappeared. He thinks of the 'man-at-arms' who first lived there, a Norman no doubt, then presents himself as the second 'founder', though what he is founding is, of course, nothing so useful as a strong place to a Norman invader; it is somewhere where his heirs might find – as presumably they did not – somewhere 'To exalt a lonely mind, / Befitting emblems of adversity'. But of course in the twentieth century a refurnished Norman tower, so far from being an 'emblem of adversity', could only be a luxurious cottage for some well-to-do person to fill with antiques, something which Harrods, or some agent in New York, would sell at a better price than thirty-five pounds. As for the poet's work-room, '*Il Penseroso*'s Platonist toiled on / In some like chamber' – Yeats was, unquestionably, not a man for *Making It New* but for making it old. The scene he sets is a preconceived one. A sword given him by a visiting Japanese completes the *décor*. He might well be pleased with it, but there is more than a touch about him of the collector who wishes to impress you with a personal distinction which has rubbed off from his collection. The most convincing part of the poem is that in which Yeats describes a brief encounter with a Republican soldier, 'An affable Irregular / A heavily-built Falstaffian man' – for he too is described in conventional, literally *stage* terms rather than seen with the naked eye – 'Comes cracking jokes of civil war / As though to die by gunshot were / The finest play under the sun'. He is jealous at even this clouded encounter with reality.

> I count those feathered balls of soot
> The moor-hen guides upon the stream,
> To silence the envy of my thought;
> And turn towards my chamber.

Those lines sound authentic.

The impact of public affairs did, undoubtedly, have its effect on the development of Yeats's poetry. His romantic imagination was with the ghost of O'Leary, but he was himself a man of the English ascendancy. It is only when caught off guard that he speaks in this character, as he does in 'Sixteen Dead Men' (from *Michael Robartes and the Dancer*, 1921).

> O but we talked at large before
> The sixteen men were shot,
> But who can talk of give and take,
> What should be and what not
> While those dead men are loitering there.

It is borne in upon him that the Anglo-Saxon game of compromise is finished. He is appalled, and as a man with a foot in both camps explains his position. The shooting of the rebels in 1916 was a tactical mistake, one of those fatal martyrdoms of which more is apt to be heard. The whole poem has a clarity and directness which Years rarely achieves for long without a touch of marmoreal elaboration.

The Wild Swans at Coole (1919) contains some of the best poems in the plain deliberate manner of the second part of Yeats's career. With this plainness and deliberation comes a certain hardening of the perceptions, not unconnected, perhaps, with whatever desire to elude reality it was drove him to compress into a logically coherent system the odds and ends of visions and magic that he had always played with. There is also the influence of the theatrical doctrine of masks, unhappily translated to a place where it does not belong. Although one may come to feel forcibly these limitations, this decline in poetic candour at a time when Yeats's technical capacity was increasing, there is no denying the strength of the writing, in its kind. There is a sense in which the later Yeats is more rhetorician than poet, and a poem like 'In Memory of Major Robert Gregory' marks this development powerfully. Before he calls up Robert Gregory himself – the son of his friend and collaborator Lady Gregory, and killed in the war – he evokes other friends of his youth: 'Lionel Johnson comes the first to mind, / Who loved his learning better than mankind, / Though courteous to the worst' – those are nice things to say about a man, but they do not get very near their subject, nor probably were they meant to. Yeats is as it were creating a figure which will serve instead of Lionel Johnson in the eyes of posterity. He is making an historical mask behind which his friend can shelter. Lionel Johnson would probably have appreciated the kindness, but in the long run it must show up that it is not the truth that Yeats was concerned to tell. One could not be further from the *Nihil excipio, sed in omnibus te nudatum inveniri volo*, of the author of the *Imitation*. Yeats is peopling a story-book, and among these fustian characters he was, in the end, to be not the least. The method is a first, immensely talented sketch of the method of creating bogus personalities which has become one of the diseases of the age, with every scruffy talker seeking to pass himself off – on the television screen if nowhere else – as a fascinating personality. The stanza rises as a sort of *crescendo* of impressiveness, of a kind which is a characteristic weakness of Yeats's later work, to the vacuity of, 'A long blast upon the horn that brought / A little nearer to his thought / A measureless consummation that he had dreamed'. Then John Synge is called up, 'That dying chose the living world for text', and succeeded in hiding himself behind a stylized picture of the people of Arran, a race, Yeats says, in his best fustian vein, 'Passionate and simple like his heart'. George Pollexfen comes next, and then he turns to Robert Gregory himself, to dress him up as 'Our Sidney and our perfect man', and to account for his absence there is that precious phrase about 'the discourtesy of death'. These are things which, if said in conversation among friends, could only seem embarrassing and pretentious. Yeats gives a not dissimilar treatment to himself in a poem in the same volume on the doubtful theme of 'Men Improve with the Years', where he asks us to regard him as 'worn out with dreams, / A weather-worn, marble triton / Among the streams'. If anyone thinks that serious he should refresh himself with a course of Sir

Thomas Wyatt. Yeats is better, at this stage in his career, when he
is frankly playing, as in 'Solomon to Sheba'.

He makes a pretty thing with his two dolls:

> Sang Solomon to Sheba,
> And kissed her dusky face,
> 'All day long from mid-day
> We have talked in the one place,
> All day long from shadowless noon
> We have gone round and round
> In the narrow theme of love
> Like an old horse in a pound.'

Here there is no pretence; the puppets are puppets. The result is
that the poet, moving with a skill that comes of much training,
manages to convey, indirectly, a genuine, fleeting impression
from his own experience. There are a number of short poems in
this volume in which Yeats uses his immense competence unpre-
tentiously and with great effect. The accent of truth is in 'A Song':

> I thought no more was needed
> Youth to prolong
> Than dumb-bell and foil
> To keep the body young.
> *O who could have foretold*
> *That the heart grows old?*

The life of the sentiments transmits itself to the verse. There is the
short poem 'To a Young Girl' – presumably to the now nubile
daughter of Maud Gonne, who was the romantic passion of his
youth.

> My dear, my dear, I know
> More than another
> What makes your heart beat so;
> Not even your own mother
> Can know it as I know,
> Who broke my heart for her
> When that wild thought,
> That she denies
> And has forgot,
> Set all her blood astir
> And glittered in her eyes.

The best example of Yeats's more deliberately stylized presentations at this period is the poem 'Upon a Dying Lady'. The subject
was a perfect one for his method, and the scene and the properties
introduced are closely modelled on reality. The poem describes
how Aubrey Beardsley's sister Mabel entertained her friends, and
they her, when she was dying of cancer.

> With the old kindness, the old distinguished grace,
> She lies, her lovely piteous head amid dull red hair
> Propped upon pillows, rouge on the pallor of her face …

She conducted herself with great courage, torn between amusing
herself with improper stories and the rather pathetic 'O yes I shall
go to heaven. Papists do' – which Yeats characteristically elaborates into, 'Thinking of saints and of Petronius Arbiter'. There are
dolls about her, which her friends have made for her, and these
dolls help to give the scene the exterior qualities his dramatization
requires. He picks up the theme in:

> She is playing like a child
> And penance is the play,
> Fantastical and wild
> Because the end of the day
> Shows her that someone soon
> Will come from the house and say –
> Though the play is but half done –
> 'Come in and leave the play'.

For a moment Yeats's desire to make a pretty, formalized scene
and his feelings of pity in the presence of the dying woman
become congruent. It is not grief that the poem conveys; it is
hardly concern for the chief character; it is a sense of the propriety
of her having been so perfect a piece of furniture in the poet's
ambiance.

Responsibilities (1914) contains some short poems in the plain
emphatic manner which Yeats had not yet made his own, enough
his own, to write in at length. We get 'Toil and grow rich. /
What's that but to lie / With a foul witch' – and there are poems
which reflect Yeats's implication with the affairs in Dublin, the
affairs of the Abbey Theatre and of the Municipal Art Gallery. He
is showing already the scorn of what he regarded as the mob

which became so prominent in his later work. There are also more wavering lines not half-way from an earlier manner, such as, 'Poets with whom I learned my trade, / Companions of the Cheshire Cheese' – a reminiscence, of course, of the Rhymers' Club. But the emergence of the later from the earlier Yeats is seen more clearly in the preceding volume, *The Green Helmet* (1910). There are the lines, to which he had to give the rather grandiose title of 'The Coming of Wisdom with Time':

> Though leaves are many, the root is one;
> Through all the lying days of my youth
> I swayed my leaves and flowers in the sun;
> Now I may wither into truth.

Yeats was conscious of the change, which in *Responsibilities* had become explicit as 'there's more enterprise / In walking naked', though the later work hardly lived up to this resolution. The 'Fascination of What's Difficult' reflects the tension between the artist of the nineties, with his Pateresque sense of the status of the beautiful and the privileges of the man who invents a work of art, and the man bedevilled by the cares of a less insulated life – in Yeats's case the work of the Abbey Theatre: 'My curse on plays / That have to be set up in fifty ways, / On the day's war with every knave and dolt.' No doubt the dragging of his art into the public world made his tongue rougher, and gave him a certain sort of maturity. At the same time something was submerged – what, can be guessed at from 'His Dream', a curious romantic ballad which probably comes nearer to expressing his profound concerns than the more patently outspoken poems:

> I swayed upon the gaudy stern
> The butt-end of a steering oar,
> And saw wherever I could turn
> A crowd upon the shore.
>
> And though I would have hushed the crowd,
> There was no mother's son but said,
> 'What is the figure in a shroud
> Upon a gaudy bed?'

Here the poet is one of the ghosts; he is in a situation in which he cannot resist his dream. The crowd on the shore watched him, but he had to take up their song: 'The running crowd and gaudy ship/Cried out the whole night long.' The poem was the transcription of a dream, and the wilful attitudes which dominate the later poems were excluded.

Backwards from *The Green Helmet*, through *In the Seven Woods* (1904) and *The Wind among the Reeds* (1899) to *The Rose* (1893) and the beginnings, one comes upon the post-pre-Raphaelite who is a poet of the end of the nineteenth century rather than a beginner of the twentieth. There is much to be found in these volumes of a languid charm which has by no means entirely faded. Yeats began, so to speak, from a dead end, and the history of his development is the history of his struggles to get out of it. How far he climbed out into the daylight of natural speech is a matter about which there can be more than one opinion. Time will make the matter plainer, but it is possible that, in the long run, the best of the earlier poems, precious though they are, will seem a more direct expression of the poet's mind than what came later. At any rate, 'The Happy Townland', 'The Folly of Being Comforted', 'Who will go drive with Fergus now?', 'Innisfree' itself, are keys with which to unlock the later poems and are not more likely than they to be forgotten.

T.S. Eliot

I

T.S. Eliot was born in St Louis, Missouri, in 1888. He was the seventh child of Henry Ware Eliot, to whom *The Sacred Wood* was dedicated, posthumously, with the epigraph *tacuit et fecit*. What Henry Ware Eliot did – the *fecit* – was to be secretary, and ultimately chairman, of the Hydraulic-Press Brick Company, in which he made quite a lot of money, providing an affluent home for his children and benefactions for cultural and other institutions in St Louis. What he was silent about will never be known; perhaps the *tacuit* was Tom's translation of 'too much pudding chokes the dog', which is reported to have been his comment on the suggestion that he should go into the Unitarian ministry. The Eliots were a notable Unitarian family. H.W.'s father – T.S.'s grandfather – was a figure in St Louis: Unitarian preacher, civic mover, perhaps saint, and finally he became Chancellor of the University, with the foundation of which he had been associated. He was evidently a man of ability and charm. A friend speaks of his 'sweet plain-speaking' and calls him 'calm, quiet, kindly and sincere in his reproofs'. He must have contributed significantly to his grandson's heredity. Moreover, although he died before Tom was born, his ghost was powerful in the family. William Greenleaf Eliot had come from New England for the enlightenment of the Middle West, and it must have been as if Tom had grown up in the shade of a sort of Unitarian Clapham Sect. Good works, the perfectibility of man, and a distrust of ritual, must have hovered over the household. Charlotte Eliot, the poet's mother, was the daughter of 'a commission shoe merchant' who became a partner in the trading firm of Stearns and Bailey – her father was a Stearns. She was intelligent, well-educated, and a performer of good works. Her influence must have reinforced and continued that of William Greenleaf Eliot, whose biography she wrote. A Protestant piety surrounded Tom's cradle, and a serious literacy awaited him as he came to the age for it. Charlotte Eliot, who lived not only to see *The Waste Land* but to receive the dedication of *For Lancelot Andrewes*, followed her son's literary career with sympathy and hope. She was herself a poet, in the pages of *The Unitarian*, *The Christian Register* and *Our Best Words*, and towards the end of her life her 'dramatic poem', *Savonarola*, was published in London by Cobden-Sanderson, with a preface by T.S. Eliot. She thus attained at least a vicarious distinction as a woman of letters.

Tom was at Smith Academy, St Louis, and at this establishment, on Graduation Day, 1905, when he was seventeen, he recited a poem of his own composition in which he looked into 'the future years' and saw 'Great duties call – the twentieth century / More grandly dowered than those which came before.' He added, fairly enough, that 'If this century is to be more great / Than those before, her sons must make her so / And we are of her sons.' The recital must have been very pleasing to Tom's mother and to the headmaster. This 'queen of schools', as the poet called her, was to close down a few years later for lack of pupils, but Tom could not foresee this and apostrophizing her, proclaimed: 'Thou dost not die – for each succeeding year / Thy honor and thy fame shall but increase / Forever.' After this Tom went to Harvard, and at the age of twenty-two (Harvard Class Day, 1910) that establishment also was graced with an 'Ode':

> For the hour that is left us Fair Harvard, with thee,
>   Ere we face the importunate years,
> In thy shadow we wait, while thy presence dispels
>   Our vain hesitations and fears...

concluding with:

> And only the years that efface and destroy
>   Give us also the vision to see
> What we owe for the future, the present, and past,
>   Fair Harvard, to thine and to thee.

But by this time Eliot had also written, and published in *The Harvard Advocate*, mannered verses after Laforgue, which are interesting not only as showing how early this influence came to him but also that the manner, and even 'cats in the alley', came to him before the poetry.

At Harvard Eliot studied Greek and Latin, attended a course on Dante, did some French and German and some philosophy. After taking his master's degree in 1910 he spent a year in Paris. He then returned to Harvard and enrolled himself for a doctorate. By now his mind was turned resolutely to the study of philosophy – the philosophy not only of Europe but of India – and in 1911 he was enrolled for a course of Indic Philology. His preparation for his future mission, whatever it was to be, was as deliberate as Milton's. It looked at this time, however, as if his mission was to be not a poet but a Harvard philosopher. In 1914 he was in Marburg; it was the war which brought him back to London and to Oxford. He completed his doctoral thesis at Merton College. It was published nearly fifty years later: *Knowledge and Experience in the Philosophy of F.H. Bradley*. It is as if Eliot would not yield to the muse until he had tested all that rationality could do for him – a disposition unusual enough in the poets of this or perhaps of any other age. Eliot came in time to think that he had no gift for abstract thought, and no doubt he was no Berkeley or Coleridge, in whom such expression touched the roots of the mind. He was an able, acute, immensely conscientious man, whose training set him to work things out with the sort of thoroughness which gives merit to the work of, say, a James Fitzjames Stephen. The solid, evangelical background probably counted for something in the matter, as well as a genuine diffidence before, and respect for, minds of another cast than his own. There is no doubt that this was of great value to him; Harold Joachim, under who he studied at Merton, understood what his pupil wanted to say and 'how to say it'. But looking back towards the end of his life, Eliot found himself 'unable to think in the terminology' of his doctoral thesis, and there is little doubt that had he continued with his 'academic philosophizing' he would have left his real springs untapped.

Oxford provided the best teachers for Eliot's immediate purpose, but one may wonder whether it was the best initial point of contact for an American who wanted to understand the country. It must certainly have had limitations for the young man who had come from what Dreiser characterized as the 'newly manufactured exclusiveness' of the well-to-do quarters of St Louis and the self-conscious superiority of Harvard. From Oxford Eliot went for a year as a teacher at the Highgate Junior School; he was later employed in a bank. Meanwhile, he had not merely drifted into the London of Pound, but, more discreetly, as a no doubt acceptable recruit, into the world of the Spenders – before Stephen had pulled more than an apron-string – of the Gosses, the Garvins and the Sitwells. There were still drawing-rooms in Mayfair during Eliot's first years in London. When in 1922 he founded *The Criterion*, the money was put up by Lady Rothermere. When she failed him, there was Geoffrey Faber and, fruitful and profitable though that association was, one cannot but wonder whether the emanations of distinguished upper-middle-class Victorian family were exactly what Eliot needed. A sensitive ear cocked for the conversation of the lower orders never quite made up for the lack of immediate roots in this country, and Eliot became the imitation Englishman as Pound became the imitation American.

II

The position of a young American in London during the latter part of the First World War must have been odd. Most of the young natives had gone off to the trenches, and many of them were killed. In 1917 Eliot, aged twenty-nine, took over the editorship of *The Egoist* from Richard Aldington, aged twenty-five, when the latter in his turn went to France. There are no direct traces in Eliot's work of this sort of situation, but it must have left its mark on him. His social success cannot have been altogether unaccompanied by a growing sense of isolation from his contemporaries. There is an element of pre-vision in poetry, to the extent that it may uncover elements which have not yet begun to operate in the conscious life of the poet, but will do so in time, and 'The Love Song of J. Alfred Prufrock', which was brought to London in 1914 by Conrad Aiken, before the poet himself appeared, designates profoundly certain aspects of Eliot's situation in the late teens of the century. No doubt Eliot had contemplated London from St Louis, through the eyes of what he came to regard as the decadent genius of Dickens, and Dickens remained with him, distorting as well as sharpening his vision. He has told us that he was, between the ages of sixteen and twenty, a reader of John Davidson, and there are lines in 'Prufrock' which could well have come straight from *Thirty Bob a Week*. 'And time for all the works and days of hands / That lift and drop a question on your plate' is both the mood and rhythm of Davidson. So is this, with the characteristic eleven syllables packed into the line: 'To have bitten off the matter with a smile'. It was an attempt to reach beyond the prim circumference of a well-protected youth. But there are other elements in 'Prufrock', of a more directly autobiographical kind: 'Deferential, glad to be of use, / Politic, cautious, and meticulous'. The footman who held Eliot's coat as he made his first forays into Mayfair no doubt partook of 'the Eternal Footman', and no doubt 'snickered'. The polish which must have recommended the young American was a protection. 'There will be time to murder and create' means, perhaps, time to dawdle in ratiocinations about F.H. Bradley, time to finish the thesis, before giving way to the subterranean and insistent muse.

One can see, from 'Conversation galante' in the *Prufrock* volume of 1917, as well as from several of the poems published in the *Harvard Advocate* in 1909–10, the value to Eliot of French poetry, and of Laforgue in particular, as an aid to standing apart from the American scene and, more important, as an aid to speaking in something different from the current Anglo-Saxon tone. There is a note of irony which makes the casual reader – and must above all have made the first readers who were surprised

by the poem amidst the oceans of diluted Shelley and Keats –
think that he is in the presence of the self-conscious wit of ordinary clever conversation. But not at all: the irony of Laforgue has
been a lever, a crowbar to heave out of the way the literary
preconceptions of the time, so that the poetry can spring from
deeper wells. 'Prufrock' is an intensely confessional poem, and
what hope would there have been of using the language of John
Drinkwater to pour out the apprehensions of this taut, acute mind
which had been seeking for truth in Bradley and Bosanquet,
Moore and Russell, McTaggart and Meinong, to say nothing of
the Vedas? Under the transparent mask is the cerebral young man,
whose experience is not equal to his intellect, looking with
longing, not least, at the ordinary mysteries of youth. 'Arms that
are braceleted and white and bare / (But in the lamplight, downed
with light brown hair!)'. If he has 'known the arms already,
known them all', it is in the appalled imagination which sees the
end before it arrives at the beginning. Always, as long as Eliot is
developing, there is this acute spreading of antennae towards the
future, as when in the first poem of *Ash Wednesday*, not yet forty-
five, he is the 'aged eagle' who no longer has motive to 'stretch
its wings'. 'The Portrait of a Lady', the second poem in the
Prufrock volume, is in the same strain. The poet is pretending to a
sophistication which he possesses only intellectually. His airs of
superiority to the lady portrayed are, patently, the nerves of a
young man wishing to begin, but held by complicated strands. 'I
smile, of course, / And go on drinking tea.' What else would the
young academic philosopher, from a highly disciplined family
presided over by the ghost of William Greenleaf Eliot, attempt?
Or even think it best to do? Nor should it be thought, by some
idiotic dogmatist of the permissive, that that was not in fact the
best thing to do. It was a complicated ball of string that the young
Eliot was unwinding. In the charming, if slight, 'Figlia che piange'
– the subject of which is a statue – his considerations reach a
momentary stasis. The other two important poems in the volume
are 'Preludes' and 'Rhapsody on a Windy Night', in which the
lonely young man finds his 'objective correlative' in the scenes of
the streets he has wandered in at night. 'You had such a vision of
the street / As the street hardly understands' are words addressed
to a feminine *persona*, but there is little doubt that the poet is also,
and more particularly, addressing himself. He is

> moved by fancies that are curled
> Around these images, and cling:
> The notion of some infinitely gentle
> Infinitely suffering thing.

Precisely, and the sputtering street-lamps, the cat which 'devours a morsel of rancid butter', and *la lune* which *ne garde aucune rancune*, are there to conceal the need. There are, throughout this volume, hauntings which become more explicit later, the London scene of *The Waste Land*, the lilacs matching the hyacinth garden, just as Christ the tiger appears already in 'Gerontion', before the poet knows who has taken possession of him.

'Gerontion' is by far the best poem in the next, the 1920, volume. The epigraph now is from *Measure for Measure*, not from the grandiloquent *Jew of Malta*, which lends itself to dramatic attitudes, and the versification is now firmly modelled on that of the Jacobean dramatists, It could be maintained that 'The Love Song of J. Alfred Prufrock' is the more original poem. There is in 'Gerontion', for all its magnificence, a touch of writing up, in a Shakespearean manner, the hesitations and misgivings more rawly confessed in 'Prufrock'. This is true particularly of the crucial paragraph beginning 'After such knowledge, what forgiveness? Think now', which, however, ends with a sudden release from the depth of the poet's own mind: 'These tears are shaken from the wrath-bearing tree'. 'As to the problem of knowledge, we have found that it does not exist', as the doctoral thesis on Bradley says. The ratiocinations are the evasions. Where Eliot hesitates and reasons, he does so in order not to be lost, but he recognizes the vanity of the exercise, without concluding that we can or should give it up, the human race being what it is. It is this honest duplicity which makes it quite beside the mark to compare Eliot's intellectualism disadvantageously with, say, an alleged natural directness in D.H. Lawrence. Eliot has absorbed his civilization, not forgotten the apes. The rhymed quatrains of the 1920 volume – the counterpart of Pound's approximations to regular verse in *Mauberley* – are brilliant and, so to speak, suppress some powerful impulses, but despite a certain novelty of tone, a cleverness long absent from English verse, they do little to advance what Eliot has to say nor do they do much to liberate the language for new expression. The poetic triumphs of the poems are at bottom conventional:

> The nightingales are singing near
> The Convent of the Sacred Heart,
>
> And sang within the bloody wood
> When Agamemnon cried aloud,
> And let their liquid siftings fall
> To stain the stiff dishonoured shroud.

There is, in Eliot, an ever-present disposition to retreat, and the bastions of the quatrain, within which Pound could not contain himself, proved almost morbidly attractive to the slightly younger man.

III

The Waste Land represents an immense advance. It is, above all Eliot's work, probably the one to which one can confidently apply the analysis of the process of composition given in *The Use of Poetry and the Use of Criticism*,

> that some forms of ill-health, debility or anaemia, may (if other circumstances are favourable) produce an efflux of poetry in a way approaching the condition of automatic writing – though, in contrast to the claims sometimes made for the latter, the material has obviously been incubating within the poet... it seems that at these moments, which are characterized by the sudden lifting of the burden of anxiety and fear which presses upon our daily life so steadily that we are unaware of it, what happens is something *negative*: that is to say, not 'inspiration' as we commonly think of it, but the breaking down of strong habitual barriers – which tend to reform very quickly...

The poem was written at a time when Eliot had some sort of breakdown.

As is now well known, the original manuscript was sold in 1922 – the year of the poem's first publication in *The Criterion* – to the American collector John Quinn, and came to light only in 1968 when the New York Public Library announced that it was in their possession. The original chaos is therefore now emerging; the poem as published had undergone various excisions and revisions which left it a more impersonal monument than it might otherwise have been. There is, however, no question of the discovery at last of the whole of an original poem out of which the published version was carved. It may not explain how large the original work was. It is clear, however, even from the fragments reproduced with Donald Gallup's article on the manuscript in the *Times Literary Supplement* in November 1968, that the editing in 1922 – in which Ezra Pound played an important part – took the reader a little further from the poet's mind, a proceeding of which Eliot probably thoroughly approved. His defences were further strengthened by the addition to the printed volume of the Notes, which had a certain scandalous value of their own. They carried a suggestion that poetry could be erudite, a notion which seemed strange to a generation brought up on the Georgians, and ranked as a novelty or even an aberration. The careless reader was apt to think that erudition was impersonal. In fact, Eliot was able to make poetry out of *From Ritual to Romance* because his own sexual preoccupations gave life to the world of fertility ritual and legend. The ancient cities that fell about his ears did so because, as he walked through London, he was conscious of the sharpness of his own desires. The notes contain references to Ovid, Shakespeare, Baudelaire, Dante and others, as clues to some of the allusions or quotations in his text. This pointed Eliot's by no means novel practice of drawing on other poets and could be read as a sort of defiance of current notions that poetry was inspirational lark-song. Curtius had not yet revealed that most of the expressions in which the romantic poets claimed to pour out their souls had already appeared in late classical times as themes for academic exercises in rhetoric.

The decisive novelty of *The Waste Land* went far beyond these superficialities. The kaleidoscopic effect produced by the succession of contrasting scenes was no doubt enhanced by Pound's editorial aid; it might be expected from the man who was to pour his mind into the *Cantos*. But an ebb and flow of themes, and unexpected juxtapositions, are an original feature of *The Waste Land* as of the *Cantos* and indeed of much of the visual art of the century. The real proof of originality, however – if any could be said to be needed after *Prufrock* – was in the rhythm, where indeed it is always to be looked for in poetry. The opening of the first section, 'The Burial of the Dead', is superb:

> April is the cruellest month, breeding
> Lilacs out of the dead land, mixing
> Memory and desire, stirring
> Dull roots with spring rain.
> Winter kept us warm...

It is a drum-beat never exactly heard before. The whole section is triumphant in its masterly dawdlings, hurryings, alterations of pace. Eliot had a regurgitating mind, and he uses here not only Ezekiel, Webster, Baudelaire and Dante but his own earlier work. 'The Death of Saint Narcissus', which probably belongs to the period 1911–15, contains the lines

> Come under the shadow of this gray rock –
> Come in under the shadow of this gray rock,
> And I will show you something different from either
> Your shadow sprawling over the sand at daybreak, or
> Your shadow leaping behind the fire against the red rock:
> I will show you his bloody clothes and limbs
> And the gray shadow on his lips.

The version in 'The Burial of the Dead' is tauter, and the conclusion of the passage immeasurably more powerful:

> There is a shadow under this red rock,
> (Come in under the shadow of this red rock),
> And I will show you something different from either
> Your shadow at morning striding behind you
> Or your shadow at evening rising to meet you;
> I will show you fear in a handful of dust.

The opening section of *The Waste Land*, besides announcing in ringing lines the theme of fertility and death, adumbrates the London which is, in a sense, the scene of the whole poem because it was Eliot's scene at the time of writing, and one which he was still exploring with sympathy and horror.

> Unreal city,
> Under the brown fog of a winter dawn,
> A crowd flowed over London Bridge, so many
> I had not thought death had undone so many.

It is the hell of the commuter, that type figure of the unanimous crowds drifting around the over-populated world. Odd personages stick out of Eliot's London crowds. There is the cosmopolitan detritus – Madame Sosostris, or, in the third section of the poem, Mr Eugenides, the Smyrna merchant. There are other figures of low life, with whom Eliot appears to have a different relationship. Those in the second section: 'When Lil's husband got demobbed, I said' – are almost certainly figures from eavesdropped conversations, in pubs or elsewhere. One imagines the young Eliot with a powerful longing to acquaint himself with the cockney world to which Dickens had long ago introduced his imagination. Among the passages struck out of the published version of 'The Burial of the Dead' is one of some length which recalls a world which must be that of *Sweeney Agonistes*. One has the impression – it can be no more – of being in the presence of something more than the fruits of eavesdropping, perhaps an incursion into an unaccustomed milieu, with the poet something between a participant and a listener on the fringe.

> First we had a couple of feelers down at Tom's place,
> There was old Tom, boiled to the eyes, blind,
> (Don't you remember that time after a dance,
> Top hats and all, we and Silk Hat Harry,
> And old Tom took us behind, brought out a bottle of fizz...)

There is the brothel, which is surely akin to the scene of *Sweeney Agonistes*: 'I turned up an hour later down at Myrtle's place, / "What d'y'mean," she says, "at two o'clock in the morning, / I'm not in business here for guys like you."' The mention of a cabman 'who read George Meredith' perhaps indicates the autobiographical nature of this recollection; that is the sort of detail one does not invent.

The next section is 'A Game of Chess', labelled in the manuscript 'HE DO THE POLICE IN DIFFERENT VOICES, Pt. II' – a sub-title which points to the synthesis Eliot made of the underworld of Dickens and his own listening-in to demotic conversations. Lil and her husband fill the latter part of the section, with an episode which Pound thought too long for the quality of the verse but which Eliot perhaps preferred to the whole episode with Myrtle and Silk Hat Harry, in which he may have felt more implicated. There is a good deal of evidence in this section that Pound did not have it all his own way, *il miglior fabbro* though he might be. 'The wind under the door' is annotated in the margin with what looks like a warning: 'Beddoes'. Pound also seems to have had some objection to 'inviolable' voice, though one cannot believe that Eliot was wrong to retain the adjective. No doubt, however, he meditated deeply all the exceptions of his so highly qualified reader.

The third section of the poem is explicitly concerned, almost throughout, with the London scene. It was a sleight-of-hand characteristic of Eliot to call it 'The Fire Sermon' from the allusion to Buddha near the end. The London is the London of history and imagination as well as of current reality, which of course is thought of as more sordid. There is the quotation from Spenser – 'Sweet Thames, run softly till I end my song' – and the reference to Elizabeth and Leicester, looming larger on the London stage for a newly-arrived American, perhaps, than for the native. Eliot's own brief experience of an office where he had no business is in 'the violet hour, when the eyes and back / Turn upward from the desk, when the human engine waits / Like a taxi throbbing waiting'. Others beside the typist had felt that at the end of long, unwelcome hours in the bank. There is autobiography woven into the texture of the whole section. The bundle in the New York Public Library even contains hotel bills from Margate.

The fourth section, 'Death by Water', is apparently one of those which underwent important excisions. The surviving brief lines, which of course translate Eliot's own French poem, 'Dans le Restaurant', from the 1920 volume – 'Phlébas, le Phénicien, pendant quinze jours noyé' – were preceded by a much longer episode describing the voyage and shipwreck of a fishing schooner sailing past Dry Salvages to the eastern Banks.

> So the men pulled the nets, and laughed, and thought
> Of home, and dollars, and the pleasant violin
> At Maron Brown's joint, and the girls and gin.
> I laughed not.

The personal voice of Eliot the observer is unmistakably in those last three words, which come with sudden force. Eliot's recollections of the sea are implicated with Conrad and perhaps Coleridge, even more than his London scenes are with Dickens. No doubt his actual acquaintance with the sea was slight. For a poet a very slight experience may suffice. 'For an unfamiliar gust

/ Laid us down'. The schooner moves to shipwreck through a visionary horror. A quotation from *The Heart of Darkness* – 'The horror! the horror!' – was to have been used as epigraph for *The Waste Land*, but Pound persuaded Eliot that it was not 'weighty enough to stand the citation'. Eliot did, however, go to the same source in Conrad in 1925 for the epigraph to 'The Hollow Men'. The schooner passed 'the furthest northern islands'

> So no one spoke again. We ate slept drank
> Hot coffee, and kept watch, and no one dared
> To look into another's face, or speak
> In the horror of the illimitable scream
> Of a whole world about us.

One element in the vision is, unmistakably, a puritan apprehension at a first sexual encounter – whether in reality or dream – though it is not only that which is expressed by the 'three women' in the schooner's 'fore crosstrees' 'who sang above the wind / A song that charmed my senses while I was / Frightened beyond fear'. The schooner breaks on an iceberg with bears on it.

The fifth and final section of the poem, 'What the Thunder Said', is portentously annotated by the author: 'three themes are employed' – the word *employed* conveys a pretension to deliberation which is characteristic in the Eliot of this period, and doubtless deceptive – 'the journey to Emmaus, the approach to the Chapel Perilous (see Miss Weston's book) and the present decay of Eastern Europe'. A welter of memories and scraps from Eliot's wide-ranging studies fills the section. F.H. Bradley, the subject of the doctoral thesis, is there, and the Vedic studies. The whole does convey, powerfully, a groping after a vision to set against the squalor of contemporary London:

> Falling towers
> Jerusalem Athens Alexandria
> Vienna London
> Unreal

As he says in one of the more contrived parts of the section. The greatness of the poem, however, is in the very failure to present a coherent alternative. *The Waste Land* is a *Blick ins Chaos* – Eliot's most profound and veridical statement of his position.

IV

The prestige of *The Waste Land* was immense in the twenties and
thirties, not the less so for being, at first, the taste of a few which
spread more slowly than might be imagined by the generations to
whom Eliot has always seemed to be part of the English syllabus.
The achievement of this distinction was painful and contested. It
was likewise eight years – 1920 to 1928 – before what has certainly
been the most influential book of literary criticism of the century,
The Sacred Wood, exhausted its small first edition and went into a
second. The prestige of *The Waste Land* was not, as Auden
remarked in his broadcast at the time of Eliot's death, accompanied
by a comparable direct influence. 'When reading a poet who
found his own voice after 1922', Auden said, 'I often come across
a cadence or a trick of diction which makes me say "Oh, he's read
Hardy, or Yeats, or Rilke," but seldom, if ever, can I detect an
immediate, direct influence from Eliot.' The influence of Eliot
before the Second World War was, above all, that of the man, as
it became clear that this prestigious writer, *the* poet of the age as
Pope was of the first half of the eighteenth century, had attitudes
which the common prejudice of literary men or more generally of
intellectuals, had long ago assumed could not be those of the poet
or, indeed, of any intelligent and enlightened person. The razor-
cut of the verse, in its wit and rhythm, was not to be denied, but
surely the scholarly seriousness of the prose might be called in
question. When, in the preface to *For Lancelot Andrewes* in 1928,
Eliot made what he afterwards thought to be the injudicious
summary of his position in politics, religion and literature, the
ripple of scandal and derision so started ran on over many years. It
was a measure of the extreme ingenuousness, not to say ignorance,
of the professionals of the intelligence in those years. The publication of T.E. Hulme's *Speculations*, in 1924, should have helped for
those who came across it. At least that book made clear that a
simple progressivism was not the only possible point of view.
More generally, the slow pressure of *The Criterion*, from 1922
onwards, must have increased the general awareness of European
currents of thought and, belatedly, brought some notions of
Péguy, Sorel and Maurras into at any rate a marginal currency.
Before these could do their work, however, they were over-
whelmed by the liberal-marxist exclusiveness of the thirties, which
discredited Eliot's ideas before they had been understood.

Particular definitions apart, the general atmosphere between the two wars was hostile to an appreciation of the matter-of-factness of Eliot's more sombre mood, because it was assumed that reality must be otherwise and that Eliot was a *poseur*. Alternatively, he was just a poet and whatever he said, his critics knew better, as if what was said in poetry was not what the poet meant, but something with a special quality of doubtfulness. Eliot himself perhaps contributed to this confusion by bandying words with I.A. Richards about poetry and belief, in his essay on *Dante* (1929). Up to and including *The Waste Land*, the satirical note was sufficiently prominent for everything to be pardoned. It could be held that if Eliot introduced a more solemn note, it was only to make fun of it. With 'The Hollow Men' (1925) the situation changed. There is nothing very funny about this poem, unless you so account 'the prickly pear' or the world ending 'not with a bang but a whimper'. In some sense these apparent trivia did enable the poem to be swallowed, and concealed as much as they revealed its true nature. It was hoped this might be a joke poem after all. It was thought evident that it must have some kind of social reference. 'The Hollow Men' would be some sort of characterization of the age, as well as being a prank of the poet, exhibiting a yet more *outré* pose. The thought that men might be hollow, and that the poet might feel this as a matter of fact, about himself and others, was hardly digestible. Yet what Eliot was feeling his way towards was an attitude many generations had thought normal, and taken for granted as corresponding to the world they knew. The perfectionist hope, in which Eliot himself had been brought up, had eaten too deeply into Anglo-Saxondom for such gropings to seem other than extraordinary. There was another kind of silliness current in the twenties, which may be illustrated by Edith Sitwell's note in *Bucolic Comedies*: 'We are accused of triviality; but poetry is no longer a just and terrible Judgement Day – a world of remorseless and clear light.' But poetry had not changed; it was merely that there were, as always, people about who were trying to make out that the trivial is important. It is sobering, looking back over the poetry of the century, to see how soon the Judgement Day has come, for how many gaudy figures. It does not take much of the 'remorseless and clear light' of time. 'The Hollow Men' survives in this light, not least because it is an incomplete expression, a groping which proved to be preliminary to a Christian discovery, in whatever sense Eliot came upon one. It is a poem of holding back – which had always been a natural attitude with Eliot – but with a new, uncertain awareness as to what he was holding back from.

> Let me be no nearer
> In death's dream kingdom
> Let me also wear
> Such deliberate disguises
> Rat's coat, crowskin, crossed staves
> In a field
> Behaving as the wind behaves
> No nearer –
>
> Not the final meeting
> In the twilight kingdom...

He is in the 'dead land', the 'cactus land' – characteristic images of drought – but with an intense longing, which never quite attains its objective or even recognizes it:

> Waking alone
> At the hour when we are
> Trembling with tenderness
> Lips that would kiss
> Form prayers to broken stone.

The faint, interrupted echo of the Lord's Prayer – 'For thine is the Kingdom' – is no more than an echo, perhaps, or it may be a beginning.

By the time we come to *Ash Wednesday* (1930), Eliot had decided that it was a beginning. This poem is crucial for Eliot's subsequent development. The break with the tone of the earlier poems is now complete. A whole element has been subtracted. The moral duty to be ironical, which hangs over the earlier poems, is no longer recognized. It is as if the native earnestness had reasserted itself, and this time completely. What Eliot most wants he says he renounces. It is difficult to speak of the poem without entering rudely upon the man's inner integrity, which one cannot know. But all criticism involves this presumption. One ought not to put the question quite in the form of whether Eliot in fact accepted the Christian faith as he hoped he did, for that would be to assume that one knows what the manifestation of such acceptance would look like. The question for the critic is whether we have in *Ash Wednesday* an expression of belief that carries us with it. There is the impediment offered by: 'Consequently I rejoice, having to construct something / Upon which to rejoice', and the question what that construction amounts to, how *wilful* it is, for poetry is not wilful. An immense and difficult step has been taken. Has it been taken successfully? Certain traditional expressions of the Christian faith are used without irony: 'Pray for us now and at the hour of our death.' In what sense is this expression used? Directly, as Donne when he says: 'Batter my heart, three person'd God'; or in some way dramatically?

The second poem of the sequence is more successful, for the poet gives himself up to images – the 'three white leopards' and the Lady 'in a white gown'. The three white leopards convince us, because we do not understand them, and feel that perhaps the poet does not, completely. The Lady is identifiable with the Virgin, easily enough, but there is an ambiguity about this figure, not merely because of our unsleeping sexuality but because of the historical confusions with the pagan Venus which are unmistakable in the Latin world. This air of dubiety gives authenticity to the figure, in the poem, for we distrust any pretension to an unmixed adoration.

> End of the endless
> Journey to no end
> Conclusion of all that
> Is inconclusible

also has enough of doubt in it to convince that we are hearing the poet's voice, and not the voice he would like to have. The third poem, also, with its images of the stairway, and pagan scene through the slotted window – 'The broadbacked figure drest in blue and green / Enchanted the may-time with an antique flute' – likewise holds our attention, for it is an admission of the flickering world we know. With 'Lord, I am not worthy' the poetry seems to fall. The poet is again trying to case himself in liturgical expression. The words are used by Christians approaching the Sacrament, from duty or habit, but that is life. It does not follow that the poet has a right to use them here, in his poem, and the poem does not really comprehend them. In the fourth poem, too, we may catch our breath at the images – the 'blue of larkspur', 'The silent sister veiled in white and blue / Between the yews, behind the garden god, / Whose flute is breathless' – but the success of the attempt at a theological connotation is less certain. Has Eliot really restored 'With a new verse the ancient rhyme'? One does not feel certain, and the 'Redeem / The time' has the inadmissible effort of construction about it. The opening of the fifth poem, with its echoes of Andrewes's *Sermons*, is also dangerous ground. For Andrewes the case was different. He was expounding what was accepted. We are looking for an apprehension. What is the place of ratiocination in this dilemma? It is uncertain, but Eliot was always inclined to take refuge in it. No doubt he was conscious of being one of the 'children at the gate / Who will not go away and cannot pray', one of those who 'are terrified and cannot surrender' – in a situation not unrelated to that of 'Prufrock' or of the narrator in 'Portrait of a Lady'. The final poem elaborates the same situation. How far does Eliot succeed in giving it a theological context? The question is not unrelated to one's view of the success of a poem, as a poem. For if he does not succeed, then the glimpses of 'the dream-crossed twilight', 'the empty forms between the ivory gates' are lyrical moments held together by wilful manipulations. The literary skill of the operation is, of course, immense.

V

A poem of a very different character, which of course pre-dates *Ash Wednesday*, is *Sweeney Agonistes*. This is a crucial poem, the importance of which has to some extent been obscured by the later plays. The best introduction to it is probably the notes, which must have been written not far from the date of composition, which Eliot prefixed to the Cobden-Sanderson edition of his mother's *Savonarola* (1926):

> Dramatic form may occur at various points along a line the termini of which are liturgy and realism; at one extreme the arrow-dance of the Todas and at the other Sir Arthur Pinero – or at least the ideal Pinero of Mr William Archer, who has abundantly proved, in attempting to prove the contrary, the complete futility of complete realism. In genuine drama the

form is determined by the point on the line at which a tension between liturgy and realism takes place.

This is, evidently, the germinal thought from which the whole of Eliot's dramatic development springs. The next step the drama had to take was clearly to be in the direction Pinero did not take. At the same time, Eliot saw – as Charlotte Eliot could hardly be expected to do – that 'the recognized forms of speech-verse are not as efficient as they should be'. He added that 'probably a new form will be devised out of colloquial speech', coyly not admitting that that was exactly what he was then up to himself. Eliot probably approached his task in a very tentative and sceptical manner, uncertain what would come. He was to use Seneca as a model, no doubt in order to escape from the over-bearing influence of the Elizabethan and Jacobean drama – in the origins of which, however, Seneca also had his place. It was the London scene of *The Waste Land* that he walked imaginatively on the outside of, perhaps feeding his imagination by eavesdropping, which provided the material for the exercise. 'These are the gloomy companions of a disturbed imagination', he typed at the top of his draft – probably, we may say on his own authority, before the work itself was actually begun – 'the melancholy madness of poetry, without the inspiration'. The quotation is from Junius, but it perhaps reflects a trace of the 'ill-health, debility or anaemia' one associates with the composition of *The Waste Land*. Those who saw Peter Wood's production of *Sweeney Agonistes* (at the Stage Sixty Theatre Club, in 1965) will realize what a dramatist was lost when Eliot found himself, in his later plays, unable to follow the line here so promisingly begun. The characters are genuinely exteriorized, there is no suspicion that we can identify a *persona* of the author in any of them. On the other hand, the poem as a whole is a reflection of the poet's mind as we feel we have a reflection of Shakespeare's mind in the later tragedies and tragicomedies. There is about the verse a gaiety which was certainly an element of Eliot's mind but rarely enough got through to his writing. It is not unrelated, perhaps, to the distance he felt between himself and his characters and to what might well have seemed the hopelessness of the dramatic experiment. To the extent that Eliot found himself not only incapable of following up his success, but of completing *Sweeney Agonistes* itself, the attempt was in fact hopeless. The value of this work is, however, not only in the dramatic attempt, but in what strikes one as the extraordinarily veridical projection of the confusion of the poet's mind. The instinctive forces acquire a bleak objectivity in the persons of ladies who were not quite Mr Eliot's type. The male characters are Eliot's nearest approach to the man 'with talk clichéd for chat' of Wyndham Lewis or what one imagines is the Middle Western turn of Uncle Ez. It represents a facility of movement in this hard world which is far from Eliot's usual precise suavity. The very rhythms show an openness to the draughts of the great world which is attained nowhere else in the work of this poet. '*Under the bamboo / Bamboo bamboo / Under the bamboo tree*' is not a 'crude' rhythm; it is one that drums into the mind and answers to profound movements of the near-consciousness more effectively than anything except the most telling parts of *The Waste Land*. The poem is concerned not with trivialities but with unusually unguarded moments of expression:

> I knew a man once did a girl in
> Any man might do a girl in
> Any man has to, needs to, wants to
> Once in a lifetime, do a girl in.

Let nobody say that there is anything in the creeping verse of the later *Quartets* which is more 'sincere' than that. And to what conclusion could Eliot bring this theme? A mystery which he could only express as a riddle. The last scene, in the 'Final Version' published in the programme of the Stage Sixty Theatre Club's Homage to T.S. Eliot on 13 June 1965, ends with this:

SWEENEY: When will the barnfowl fly before morning?
               When will the owl be operated on for
                                            cataracts?
               When will the eagle get out of his barrel-roll?
OLD
GENTLEMAN: When the camel is too tired to walk farther
               Then shall the pigeon-pie blossom in the desert
               At the wedding-breakfast of life and death.
SWEENEY: Thank you.
OLD
GENTLEMAN: Good night.

There is at any rate a case for saying that *Sweeney Agonistes* is Eliot's best poem.

Sweeney Agonistes was not published in book form until 1932, when no doubt Eliot had given up hope of completing it. His subsequent attempts at drama were of an entirely different character. The thoughts which had accompanied the gestation of *Sweeney* have their bearing on this development, but what had been a groping became a deliberate effort. *The Rock* (1934) is not a play; it is a pageant. We look for – and find – something of the artificiality which appears in the seventeenth-century masque. But there is less sense of *rapport* with the audience than, say, in Ben Jonson's masques. Jonson was doing something expected of him; Eliot was springing a poetic surprise. The prose Eliot wrote or permitted to be written to fill the interstices is appalling, and exhibits a lack of tact which, for such a man as Eliot, represents a degrading retreat into the superficialities of nice people. The verse of the choruses is excellent for declamation, and no doubt Eliot felt that he was making a useful step in the direction of a language which would be tolerated by the public. In *Poetry and Drama* (1951) he says some revealing things about the effect on his verse of his essays in dramatic speech. He found that 'a different frame of mind' was required for dramatic verse. In other verse one was writing 'so to speak, in terms of one's own voice'. The test is whether the verse is right to the poet; if it is, it may be hoped that other people will come to accept it in time. 'But in the theatre', Eliot goes on, 'the problem of communication presents itself immediately…. You are aiming to write lines which will have an immediate effect upon an unknown and unprepared audience, to be interpreted to that audience by unknown actors rehearsed by an unknown producer.' These considerations had been absent in the composition of *Sweeney Agonistes*, which Eliot almost certainly regarded as a 'closet drama'. They offer an ingenious and incomplete apology for the change which was coming over the author. Shakespeare wrote for an ordinary stupid audience; Eliot would do the same. But the situation, at the end of a long decadence of the theatre, differs entirely from the situation in Shakespeare's time. And Shakespeare, skilled man of the theatre as he was, managed his plays with a panache which gave the groundlings the impression that they were hearing something of interest without, one imagines, thinking that he had better put the thoughts of Lear in a language which would ensure that there was no misunderstanding and that immediate communication was achieved. In his later plays, Eliot's effort was to make the verse unnoticeable, while he affected a certain abstruseness of subject. Shakespeare was more given to taking a common subject and making the verse what he liked.

There is, indeed, an ugly deliberation about Eliot's approach to the theatre. He was, after all, fifty when *Murder in the Cathedral* was published (1935). It was his first full play and it is late in the day for such an adaptation. No doubt the technical problems of the theatre – very special ones, however, until *The Family Reunion* (1939) when Eliot first entered upon the common stage – were a stimulus and an amusement; they certainly occupied him in a different way from the way in which they occupied the Elizabethan and Jacobean dramatists for whom they were part of the ordinary surroundings of their life, indeed of their profession. The choruses of *Murder in the Cathedral* are really words that a chorus can speak, and one should not under-rate the skill needed for that. But the dramatic verse is generally lifeless. The character of Becket is thought out in advance, like that of a character in an ordinary historical novel. The struggles of conscience are appallingly unreal, inexcusably so for a man who must have known what they could be. Eliot achieved a big social surprise – how astonishing that the Church could attract a poet, let us make the most of it – but no one who is moved by his earlier verse can doubt that the play represents a grotesque falling away.

Eliot himself quickly realized that *Murder in the Cathedral* did not solve 'any general problem' and that it was a dead end. He therefore turned, for his next play, resolutely in the direction of contemporary life. Why this conscious effort should have been needed, in the author of *The Waste Land*, is matter for speculation. One must suppose that the social tone of the Anglicanism of the time had been too much for him. There are those who have thought it too much for the Church. In *The Family Reunion* Eliot's first concern was the versification. He sought, as if it was a new problem – the matter is set out at length in *Poetry and Drama* – 'a rhythm close to contemporary speech'. He was, indeed, on a new and shallower level, going over the problem he must have faced at the outset of his poetic career. The excuse is the novelty to him of the drama, but one cannot but suspect that a profounder reason was that he had, somehow, turned his back on his earlier development. He found a verse 'in which the stresses could be made to come wherever we should naturally put them, in uttering the particular phrase on the particular occasion'. It is not unrelated to the verse of the later of the *Four Quartets*, which could hardly have been written as they are without it. The form continued to be used without essential modification in the verse of the later plays. The last play that could be thought to come in our period [1900–1950 – *eds.*] is *The Cocktail Party* (1950), which is surely already the verse of a dead man.

VI

Eliot's final, and some would say crowning, performance as a poet was in the *Four Quartets*. In a sense, the title is a sleight-of-hand, for the sequence as now printed consists of an original poem, published in 1936, and a group of three developments of the theme which appeared in the *New English Weekly* in 1940–42. The first of the *Quartets* is decidedly the best. The verse on the whole is tauter. The lassitude of the dramatic utterances has not yet overwhelmed it. Indeed it may be that, in 'Burnt Norton', the poet was trying to pull himself together. He must have been aware that *The Rock* and *Murder in the Cathedral* represented a slackening. Now he would get back to something which kept him ahead of the vulgar reader, as the earlier poems had done. He does achieve a certain novelty, but it is a novelty into which deliberation enters rather palpably. 'Time present and time past / Are both perhaps present in time future, / And time future contained in time past.' It is, at a lower intensity, the ratiocination for which, in the fifth poem of *Ash Wednesday*, he had turned to Lancelot Andrewes. As he develops the argument, another parallel comes to mind.

> If all time is eternally present
> All time is unredeemable.
> What might have been is an abstraction
> Remaining a perpetual possibility
> Only in a world of speculation.

The ghost behind this is the young Eliot labouring at his thesis on F.H. Bradley. Philosophy which, early, was a refuge against the

seductions of the muse, is clutched at as a raft to save the poet who
is swirling along in the wide Missouri. 'As to the problem of
knowledge, we have found that it does not exist', he said in a
triumphal moment in *Knowledge and Experience*. But other problems remained, the practical world, 'this real world, which is not
metaphysically the real world'. The self which was the product of
metaphysics had become, by 1929, the 'simple soul' issuing from
the hand of God. But the nakedness and simplicity of the
'animula, vagula, blandula' are difficult to accept for the sophisticated mind, and the 'world of speculation' retained its attraction
for Eliot even though he did not believe in it and he knew it was
one he could not move in with any great expertise. In 'Burnt
Norton' it quickly falls away from him and he is left with the ordinary nagging memories, 'the passage which we did not take /
Towards the door we never opened / Into the rose garden'. It is
a familiar theme in Eliot's poetry, but seen now from the perspective of age – 'to what purpose / Disturbing the dust on a bowl of
rose-leaves / I do not know'. There is a congeries of recollections.
The roses which 'Had the look of flowers that are looked at'
perhaps touch, in the bottom of his memory, the 'thousand /
Roses that grew in an enchanted garden' of Edgar Allen Poe, who
must have been one of the poets of Eliot's youth. 'Clad all in
white, upon a violet bank' – from the same poem, 'To Helen' –
must already have been not far below the surface when he wrote
certain lines of *Ash Wednesday*. 'The surface glittered out of heart
of light' recalls the much more impassioned moment of *The Waste
Land* – 'Looking into the heart of light, the silence'. There
follows, at the opening of the second section of 'Burnt Norton',
what is, for a poet of Eliot's accomplishment, just a piece of
poetry. 'Garlic and sapphires in the mud / Clot the bedded axle-
tree' – and so to 'the boarhound and the bear', regurgitated
detritus like the nightingales singing near the Convent of
the Sacred Heart. Then we move into a style of discourse of
which the later Quartets are full. It does not convince us as
poetic apprehension of something hitherto undiscovered. It is
not a 'raid on the inarticulate' but the articulation of an idea
already consciously accepted. 'I can only say, *there* we have been:
but I cannot say where.' It is worthy of the doctoral thesis. As the
exposition develops it is difficult not to grow impatient with it.
Of course it is the writing of a man of immense accomplishment,

but it is not the writing of a man impelled. The words come from a level where half-forgotten reasonings settle, not from profounder depths. Nothing new has happened to the poet, and he is perhaps determined that nothing shall. Where we return to a visible world — 'Driven on the wind that sweeps the gloomy hills of London, / Hampstead and Clerkenwell, Campden and Putney' — it is the world of *The Waste Land*, but again with the temperature lowered and the concentration reduced. One cannot withhold an inclination before the figure of this man, haunted by his former achievements, wanting death but not finding it available.

> Words strain,
> Crack and sometimes break, under the burden,
> Under the tension, slip, slide, perish,
> Decay with imprecision,

– precisely – 'will not stay in place, / Will not stay still'. Of course not. There is much to be said for silence, at the end of a long life, but if one speaks one must accept the movement of life and language. And Eliot had, when he wrote 'Burnt Norton', still thirty years to live – the years of his fame, indeed.

When he took up the themes of 'Burnt Norton' again the marks of decay were not less. 'East Coker' begins with a tired rhythm:

> In my beginning is my end. In succession
> Houses rise and fall, crumble, are extended,
> Are removed, destroyed, restored, or in their place
> Is an open field, or a factory, or a by-pass.

The first words are striking enough; the rest is weak, nondescript verse which, from an anonymous pen, would excite no interest. One gets the impression, however, that Eliot is anxiously trying for a new beginning. This was perhaps his mood at the time of the last three *Quartets*; only the impulse is lacking. He goes forward a few paces then changes his subject, or his image, not with the force of dramatic contrast, as in the edited *Waste Land*, but because it will not take him any further. There are passages which would not be negligible from a lesser hand, but which, from Eliot, horrify us with the superficiality of the impression. There are the figures in the deep Somerset lane 'Where you lean

against a bank while a van passes'. Should he not have been
content to give us these impressions of old age, without the
portentous frame-work of time and eternity which is not a poetic
apprehension, like Vaughan's 'I saw Eternity the other night', but
the worrying of an abstract bone which he has seen before. There
are more pieces of poetry – 'Comets weep and Leonids fly / Hunt
the heavens and the plains' – as if the poet wants to reassure
himself that his hand has not lost its cunning. But it has, as he
lamely admits: 'That was a way of putting it – not very satisfactory: / A periphrastic study in a worn-out poetical fashion.' Alas,
the 'wrestle' with words and meanings is no longer 'intolerable',
though he pretends it is, though no doubt in his own mind he is
thwarted and sick that he cannot do what he would. The
'autumnal serenity' and 'the wisdom of age' are a washout, but it
is of no use to keep on saying so. 'The Dry Salvages' and 'Little
Gidding' offer no novelties. It would have been harder, perhaps,
for Eliot to have written what he had to say in prose, but he
should have done, for he knew already what he meant, as far as
he was going to know. Perhaps indeed he should have done a full-
length study of Nicholas Ferrar, for he still had a better mind than
anyone else who was likely to apply himself to the work.

The conditions in which poetry can be written are not usually,
perhaps not ever, within the poet's control. Eliot's immense
literary skill could have been fruitfully deployed in the latter part
of his life. But the identification of the point of his failure, and its
nature, are of public importance because it is not for the health of
the literature of the English-speaking countries that attention
should be deflected from *The Waste Land*, *Sweeney Agonistes* and
'Prufrock'.

Edward Thomas

The path of literary history is crooked. While Flint and Pound,
both his juniors by seven years or more, were establishing themselves as poets of more or less repute in pre-First World War
London, Edward Thomas, born in 1878, did not write a line of
verse and did not think he would be called upon to do so. His
whole production as a poet appeared in the two and a half years
before he was killed by a shell in an advance in the German line

at Arras, in 1917. On the other hand, no poet ever lived more consistently in his role than Thomas, or prepared himself more thoroughly for the final explosion. His very blindness as to where he was going was a product of the intensity of his concentration.

Thomas was born in South London and the homes of his childhood were in Wandsworth and Clapham. His parents were Welsh, with a dash of the English West Country; there were ties with Arthur Machen's mysterious Gwent and Caerleon. His mother seems to have had some temperamental affinity with Edward Thomas, but his father was a staff clerk in the Board of Trade addicted in his spare time to considering the state of the nation. As to religion, both parents 'were sober reverent people without a creed, though their disbelief in Hell and the Devil almost amounted to a creed. My father and I', Thomas relates in the narrative published posthumously under the title of *The Childhood of Edward Thomas*,

> made merry over the Devil and the folly of believing in him as we supposed many did. He used to try different chapels or different preachers, sometimes taking me with him, more especially when he had become an almost weekly attendant at a Unitarian Chapel. Here from the prickly silence of two hundred or three hundred people I gradually came to feel a mild poison steadily creeping into me on all sides.

More to the point was a visit with his mother to Caerleon upon Usk. 'Then for the first time', he says, 'I thoroughly understood what wells, apples and snails were.' The exultation is unmistakably akin to that felt by Thomas Traherne. Few, as the years of boyhood went on, can have made more than Edward Thomas did of the commons and odd scattered fields of South London. He went to the local board school, and then to Battersea Grammar School, and somehow managed to finish with a short spell at St Paul's. He was a boy of parts, and by the time he was seventeen bits of his descriptive writing had appeared in the *Speaker* and the *New Age*. By the time he was nineteen his first book was published – *The Woodland Life*. Meanwhile, he had already attached himself firmly to the girl who was to become his wife, Helen, the daughter of a writer and journalist, Edward Noble. There was still argument about Thomas's future. His father wanted to hound him into the Civil Service. He himself wanted to go to Oxford, and in the end he did go, passing there, undoubtedly, the time of his life when he was nearest to ease and luxury. For his own pleasure he read the poets and naturalists; for his degree, which was mediocre, modern history. The idea of going into the Civil Service, no doubt with better prospects than before, was presented to him again, with the same reaction as before. Edward Thomas managed his own affairs, and felt no desire to manage other people's. He had proposed to himself two things: to marry Helen and to write. The marriage had taken place and his first child had been born while he was still at Oxford. When he came down, he took his wife and baby from his parents' house, where they were living, to a squalid half-house with a dirty backyard. His connections with editors and publishers were, for so young a man, already of long standing, but he did not find it easy to get the work he wanted. No one was ever less of a showman than Edward Thomas. If it was possible to give the putting-off answer to someone who might employ him he seems to have given it. Nevinson, on the *Daily Chronicle*, was intelligent enough not to be put off, and gave him books to review. After that book-reviewing became a main source of income – a depressive and miserable occupation for a man of Thomas's temperament, and one which certainly gave him a profound contempt for the poetry of the day, for he did not take poetry lightly. About this time he managed to move into the first of his houses in the country, and he was never more than a visitor to the town thereafter. This first house was near Maidstone. It was no beauty, apparently, but it gave Thomas access to a Kentish countryside more at peace than it now is. When he was not working he wandered about. As a boy he had already walked many miles in Wiltshire and else-where; roads, lanes and fields were a natural habitat and going on foot his ordinary means of progression. It is difficult, in a world ravaged by the internal combustion engine, to understand the nearness to the ground these habitats can give. A nearness to the past, too, it may be added, for this is how people lived until tech-nology insulated them. Thomas's walks were long or short, a few hours or days and weeks at a time. Often he did not know the name of the village he was passing through. It was not that which interested him. He was interested in the anonymous life of the country, animal or human, and the weather and vegetation which belonged to the same nature. He was not a refugee from town, but someone exploring the country because it gave him life. There were successive homes – for a time on the Weald near Sevenoaks and then, in order to be able to educate the children in an enlightenment Helen Thomas approved of, in Hampshire near Bedales. Ideas of enlightenment, as of reaction, were far from Thomas's mind. He was too close to reality for that. He had thought nothing of Helen's officially intellectual friends earlier; he thought nothing of progressivism. He was without perceptible ambition but he wrote his books and did his reviews, moving steadily from the influence of Oxford and Walter Pater to a prose without airs and graces, and all the time under the tuition of the reality presented to him by natural objects, including his wife and children. He seems intermittently to have wandered off, partly for the pleasure of wandering, partly to get material for his books, and partly because he felt the strain of domestic affections. At least once he loaded a revolver and went out to shoot himself. He suffered a good deal of real poverty, which it is easy to do with three children. He had difficulties with editors and publishers and wrote an immense number of books with, apparently, very modest financial results. His books were mainly either critical or topographical. He was a good workman, but it cannot be said that these books are profoundly exciting, or that much would have been lost if they had disappeared, though, as from such a man they must, they contain much that is sensible and pleasing as well as occasional turns of phrase and rhythms which prefigure the poetry. But for Thomas's own development the books no doubt had a great importance. When the time came for poetry there was an immense, unheated experience of words to draw on.

There are few stranger things in the history of modern poetry than Thomas's sudden outburst. From the point of view of the ordinary literary man, the extraordinary thing is that Thomas had kept silent for so long. All the talents were there, and an intimate knowledge of poetry to give him his technical starting point. Perhaps he had too high a view of poetry to think it proper for him to try. When he started the atmosphere was troubled by war, uncertainty about his own future, and perhaps more strain than usual in his domestic arrangements. More simply, he met Robert Frost, who told him to write verse, and he did so. The meeting with Frost was no doubt fortunate. Thomas was probably better equipped than any man to understand what the American was

doing. The low tone, the attentiveness to people, the straightfor-
ward language, were such as Thomas could take to naturally. It is
more than likely that Frost's suggestion was a mark of confidence
Thomas needed, and he could respect it from that source if from
few others. When he started to write verse he found it came
easily; he had only to be unbound in order to be able to walk. He
was thirty-seven, at what might have seemed the *mezzo del
cammin*, though in fact he was at the end. He wrote therefore out
of no ill-informed ecstasy but as one who had brooded on the
inside of life as well as watched the changes of natural phenomena.
It is the poetry of thirty-seven or thirty-nine years, not of two,
which is packed into Thomas's two hundred pages of verse. The
stimulus which occasions a poem does not overwhelm him; it
rattles a chain of connections which take him back into the depths
of his history. It is to be recorded that, with the gift of verse and
his engagement as an effective soldier, Thomas's melancholy
cleared. He seems to have been a good officer and his death, very
likely, is what he wanted.

It is difficult to speak too highly of the rhythmic variety and
aptitude of Thomas's verse. The break into cadences which are
virtually those of speech at its most poised and sensitive, which
seems in retrospect to have been the aspiration of the poetry of
the nineties as of the imagists, was achieved instantaneously. The
workmanship is completed by an extraordinary tact with external
reality. The physical concomitant of what Thomas has to say is
never absent; the wind rustles as he speaks of it. When he enters
a wood one enters with him:

> I have come to the borders of sleep,
> The unfathomable deep
> Forest where all must lose
> Their way, however straight,
> Or winding, soon or late;
> They cannot choose.

One is physically present at the occasions he chooses to
remember:

> And I can only wonder how much hereafter
> She will remember, with that bitter scent,
> Of garden rows, and ancient damson trees

Topping a hedge, a bent path to a door,
A low thick bush beside the door, and me
Forbidding her to pick.

It would be a shallow judgement on such verses to think of
Thomas as the poet of country places, as if that meant some easy
evocation of agreeable scenes. He is touched to the quick by the
human relationships he has known, and one function of the
natural background is to reduce people to a tempo in which they
can be observed. All passion for the truth is revolutionary and
Thomas's work is a critique of what the world thinks of itself, and
of its methods of thought:

Today I think
Only with scents...

Odours that rise
When the spade wounds the root of a tree,
Rose, currant, raspberry, or goutweed,
Rhubarb or celery;

The smoke's smell, too,
Flowing from where a bonfire burns
The dead, the waste, the dangerous,
And all to sweetness turns.

Thomas's impressions are vivid to the point that his own mind
gives before the reality, and he evokes what he remembers with
marvellous clarity:

I never knew a voice,
Man, beast or bird, better than this. I told
The naturalists; but neither had they heard
Anything like the notes that did so haunt me
I had them clear by heart and have them still.
Four years, or five, have made no difference.

All his years are in the poems in which past and present meet
together. It is work grown from a rich deposit: 'the dead that
never / More than half hidden lie' – as in 'Celandine':

the flowers were not true,
Until I stooped to pluck from the grass there
One of five petals and I smelt the juice

> Which made me sigh, remembering she was no more,
> Gone like a never perfectly recalled air.

Life and death come together as if even the trace of a dried carcase
was not yet extinction:

> But now that he is gone
> Out of most memories
> Still lingers on
> A stoat of his,
>
> But one, shrivelled and green,
> And with no scent at all,
> And barely seen
> On this shed wall.

Thomas went to the war without regret, above all without fuss.
Towards the end of 1914 he wrote: 'I have been thinking a good
deal from time to time, trying to decide whether to enlist or not.
I don't want to: only I feel that it is the only thing to do if a man
is able-bodied and has nothing else to do.'

> Now all roads lead to France
> And heavy is the tread
> Of the living; but the dead
> Returning lightly dance.

He did not care about causes, or what the newspapers said. It was
'no case of petty right or wrong'.

> But with the best and meanest Englishmen
> I am one crying, God save England, lest
> We lose what never slaves or cattle blessed.
> The ages made her that made us from dust:
> She is all we know and live by, and we trust
> She is good and must endure, loving her so:
> And as we love ourselves we hate her foe.

It was Thomas's nearest approach to political poetry, and he had
as much right to the words as anyone could have. But his real
world is below these clamours, with a profound humanity based
on an intense physical apprehension.

> Then past his dark white cottage front
> A labourer went along, his tread

Slow, half with weariness, half with ease;
And through the silence, from his shed
The sound of sawing rounded all
That silence said.

Or the shepherd's widow: 'And I think that even if I could lose my deafness / The cuckoo's note would be drowned by the voice of my dead.' He praises a man whom the common talk of respectable people had dismissed as worthless, because a gipsy praised him for having paid up his half-crown when her daughter had a baby. The ordinary perspectives are nothing to Thomas, except in so far as he has himself felt their reality. The animal world is as present to him as the world of people: 'Boys knew them not, / Whatever jays and squirrels may have done.' Or this: 'But far more ancient and dark / The Combe looks since they killed the badger there'. It was himself Thomas was pursuing in this terrible but beautiful world of scents, rain, thunder, sunshine and death. There is a poem, 'The Other', in which he becomes explicit about the pursuit:

The forest ended. Glad I was
To feel the light, and hear the hum
Of bees, and smell the drying grass
And the sweet mint, because I had come
To an end of forest, and because
Here was both road and inn, the sum
Of what's not forest. But 'twas here
They asked me if I did not pass
Yesterday this way. 'Not you? Queer.'
'Who then? and slept here?' I felt fear.

He follows the other until once, in a tap-room, the other derisively asks for him. Then he flees.

And now I dare not follow after
Too close. I try to keep in sight,
Dreading his frown and worse his laughter.
I steal out of the wood to light;
And see the swift shoot from the rafter
By the inn door: ere I alight
I wait and hear the starlings wheeze
And nibble like ducks: I wait his flight.

He goes: I follow: no release
Until he ceases. Then I also shall cease.

In another poem, 'The Long Small Room', Thomas records how
'When I look back I am like moon, sparrow, and mouse / That
witnessed what they could never understand / Or alter or prevent
in the dark house.' It is his own house he is speaking of.

Walter de la Mare claimed for Edward Thomas in 1920 that
'when the noise of the present is silenced ... his voice will be
heard far more clearly.' I would say that fifty years have not yet
given him his rightful place. He is, without doubt, one of the most
profound poets of the century. What did he say? He said what is
in the poems, and there is no message beyond them. But he
belonged to the underside of the world, from which renewal must
come, and he speaks with conviction of matters which may be
touched and felt. The irregularity and straggling rhythms of his
verse, and the happy invention of his language, are far beyond
what was achieved by more explicit innovators. And he understood as well as Ford Madox Ford or Pound that no poem could
be good at all that contained definite purple passages.

From *The Case of Walter Bagehot*

Chapter Four: The Art of Money

Having misdirected his youth towards the study of literature, for which he had no talent, and then towards the study of politics, to which he made a destructive contribution, Bagehot turned in his later years to wholly serious matters. *Lombard Street*, begun in 1870 and finished in 1873, is a paean in praise of money. We have the authority of Keynes [review of Bagehot's *Collected Works*, in the *Economic Journal*, 1915] for saying that, as a contribution to economics, it is of no great account. Keynes noted that it was one book which, at the time he was writing, every economics student could be counted on to have read; he attributed this distinction to the desire of teachers of economics to conceal from the young student the fact that the subject was, in reality, not so amusing as Bagehot made it out to be. Bagehot did not, however, pretend that his book was a work of theory. Indeed, he went out of his way to emphasize that it was a description of concrete realities, and that is why he gave it a local instead of an abstract title. It was a study of the men who made money in the city, written by one who had a close acquaintance with many of those who dominated that scene, and who was by heredity as well as experience in the heart of the money trade.

Bagehot was writing in the great bulge of Victorian prosperity, and was conscious of these advantages, if that is what they were. His tone is that of a man showing off his plush furniture for the benefit of less fortunate people. 'Everyone is aware', he says,

> that England is the greatest moneyed country in the world; every one admits that it has much more immediately disposable and ready cash than any other country. But very few persons are aware *how much* greater the ready balance – the floating fund which can be lent to any one or for any purpose – is in England than it is in anywhere else in the world. [*Works*, VI, p. 12.]

Money was economic power, and Bagehot never asked the critical question as to whether the unprecedented concentration was a good thing, or whether it was a proper use of the dignified parts of government, about which he had written so cynically in *The English Constitution*, to act as a screen for the *sub-rosa* activities of bankers.

There is an almost childish lack of moderation about Bagehot's approach to his subject. In what he blithely called 'the non-banking countries', including Germany and France, there was more cash out of the banks than there was in England. But the French people, notoriously, would not part with their money. The result, though he did not specify it, was that France remained a predominantly agricultural country – or a backward country, as Bagehot would have said – while England moved rapidly toward a state of swollen manufacture and over-population, with consequences which are still with us, for good or ill, while the rest of the world has tried with some success to catch up. The distinction of England at this time was that it had an abnormal – and, historically regarded, perhaps morbid – amount of borrowable money. The banker collected a great mass of other people's money, and the borrowers gathered round him because, as Bagehot accurately said, they 'knew or believed' he had it. With a million pounds you could think of building a railway; leave that sum in its constituent tens and hundreds and you had to be content with scattered horse- or donkey-carts. These technological benefits came less from the ingenuity of engineers and craftsmen than from the seminal virtue of trusting bankers. The system had a democratic tendency, but one that did not go too far. It eroded the power of hereditary wealth, but it did not go so far as to recognize the voices of those whom bankers did not trust. This was the *via media*, the *optimum* as far as Bagehot was concerned. He admitted that the new men created by easy credit and a wave of the banker's wand were, as a class, less honest men than those who depended on the continuity of trade, and so of reputation. He admitted also that the system produced inferior goods because it relied on mere saleability, which could be achieved by relative cheapness, without regard to quality. But 'these defects and others' were 'compensated by one great excellence. No country of great hereditary trade, no European country at least, was ever so little "sleepy" … as England.' [*ibid.*, p. 16.] To prove the indubitable supremacy of that excellence Bagehot relied upon Darwin. The propensity to variation was 'the principle of progress'. [*ibid.*]

What it really amounted to was that men like Thomas Bagehot and Vincent Stuckey, placed at a point of vantage in an unsuspecting country-side, collected together the money produced by agricultural persons, who had no political thoughts, and transmitted it by way of London to Manchester and such places where entrepreneurs could then afford to pay wages which, miserable as they might be, were enough to attract people from the country-side to the mills where the new manufactures were carried on. Lombard Street was the go-between between the 'quiet saving districts of the country and the active employing districts'. [*ibid.*, p. 17.] Bagehot admired without reserve the prompt way in which money flew to the places where it could produce most interest for the banker. The amount of profit being made was the sole thing that interested him; the fact that what is profitable to a particular entrepreneur may, on a wider or longer view, be uneconomic or even destructive, did not detain him for an instant. He would no doubt have sneered cleverly at William Barnes's distinction [in *Labour and Gold*, London, 1859] between real and commercial value. Barnes was a Dorchester schoolmaster, a poet and a philologist. He was also the son of a small farmer and had seen the peasantry despoiled by the saving that went on in 'the quiet districts'. Bagehot noticed the money that was made; Barnes noticed other things.

The peculiarity of the English economy, at this time, was that trade was conducted predominantly on borrowed capital. 'There never was so much borrowed money collected in the world as is now collected in London.' [*ibid.*, VI, p. 20.] Nearly all of it could be asked for any day the owners pleased, and if they did, the whole structure would come tumbling down. The ratio of cash reserves to bank deposits was unprecedentedly low. The whole system, therefore, might be thought, by the bystander who did not trust bankers enough, to be unstable. Bagehot himself recalls the 'astounding instance of Overend, Gurney, and Co.' [*ibid.*, p. 21] whose credit was almost as good as that of the Bank of England, but who none the less in a few years lost everything. 'And these losses were made in a manner so reckless and so foolish, that one would think a child who had lent money in the city of London would have lent it better.' [*ibid.*] No doubt Messrs.

Overend and Gurney none the less wore what appeared to be grown-up bankers' faces as they went impressively to and fro in the City. Perhaps there is some reason to doubt the efficacy of a system in which production stops or goes at the whim of money-lenders.

At the centre of this system was the Bank of England, which was conducted on much the same principle as other banks and which most people, including experts, believed to be essentially the same sort of institution. In a sense it was. Merchants kept their reserves at one of the lesser banks, which in turn kept their reserves at the Bank of England. On the board of the Bank of England they wrangled about how much money they had to keep idle, and complained that their dividend was low because they had to keep more than other people. In a manner the whole credit of the country depended on this ordinary commercial board. The wheels of trade and manufacture could stop because of the folly or misjudgement of these ordinary city characters. Everyone fortunately trusted the Bank of England but Bagehot obviously did not think that this trust was particularly well-founded. It was indeed persisted in in the face of evidence, for on various occasions the Bank of England had almost or quite suspended payment, or had had to be helped out in some way. What really distinguished the Bank of England from other banks was that, in the last resort, the government was behind it. That does, indeed, make a difference, not merely to the bank but to the nature of credit and, one might have thought, the standing of bankers. The whole system Bagehot describes is based on the assumption that money-lending is a private game, played by discreet men who, for reasons financial and personal rather than economic and public, could at any time interfere with the operation of the economy and regularly did so. This raises the question, which Bagehot did not pursue, as to how far such men are, for their private devices, operating in secret what should be regarded merely as part of the delegated authority of the state.

Bagehot does not pursue his enquiries in this direction merely because he has considered the matter and is so sure of his answer. 'No such plan would answer in England' – no such plan, that is, even as state management of the Bank. Bagehot's view is that the country could very well have done without the degree of intervention represented by the setting up of the Bank of England and by its special position. But for that, there would be a group of rival banks at the centre of things, as there are rival manufacturing interests, and this multiplicity would have given a greater security. But credit cannot be invented and since people trust the Bank of England it has to be left recognizably as it is. The political parallel Bagehot draws is characteristic. It would be easy, he says, to 'map out a scheme of Government in which Queen Victoria could be dispensed with … we know that the House of Commons is the real sovereign', for of course we have read *The English Constitution*, 'any other sovereign is superfluous'. [*ibid.*, p. 51.] But stupid people will trust the Queen. In the same way – not stupid but – shrewd men of business have confidence in things holding together round the Bank of England; better, therefore, leave it as it is. The whole plan of having political nominees 'would seem to an Englishman of business palpably absurd; he would not consider it, he would not think it worth considering'. [*ibid.*, p. 53.]

But Bagehot saw clearly that the government of the Bank of England was in fact a national function; he would have the Board of Directors turned from semi-trustees for the nation to real trustees, with a trust deed which made their responsibilities clear. The system he recommended was, really, that the country should be run by men of business looking towards a written republican constitution, in the trust deed of the bank, while the eyes of the common people were averted in the direction of the Crown, where there was no power but, for vulgar minds, much entertainment. The theory of *The English Constitution* is really the counterpart of the theory of *Lombard Street* and it is the latter which is at the centre of Bagehot's notions of government.

The development of banking as a sort of arcane government under the cover of the publicly admitted forms was a relatively recent affair. It takes a long time to establish public confidence in a form of government, and the most stable constitutions are those which are accepted rather than explained. The growth of deposit banking, recent and still local, involved a similar growth. The essence of deposit banking was 'that a very large number of persons agree to trust a very few persons, or some one person. Banking would not be a profitable trade', Bagehot goes on to confide, 'if bankers were not a small number, and depositors in comparison an immense number'. [*ibid.*, p. 56.] It was of course part of the mystique of this shadow republic, growing up within

the ludicrous monarchy of Queen Victoria, that you could trust
it more than you could trust the government. It was supposed to
represent the private interest of the depositor, though like all
government it in fact involved releasing little atoms of private
power to a more remote authority. The authority in this case was
not the *res publica*, confused and uncontrollable but at least in principle influenceable and subject to constitutional rules, but the
mutual confidence of men in the city of London, some of the
gravest of whom might on occasion behave like children, and
who had no habit of responding to public criticism. The best way
of encouraging the habit of deposit banking, Bagehot says, no
doubt not unmindful of the affairs of the Somerset Bank and of
Uncle Vincent, was 'to allow the banker to issue bank-notes of a
small amount that can supersede the metal currency'. [*ibid.*, p. 60.]
This amounted to a subsidy to each banker – from whom he does
not say – to keep the banker going until people, impressed by this
mysterious power which makes money out of nothing, come
along bringing their deposits, real money to take the place of the
money the banker was in the first place allowed to imagine. One
can quite see the desirability of keeping this arcane privilege to a
few persons. Bagehot's account of this process is that of an acute
and interested observer. The reason for its success is that, in the
first instance, the initiative is entirely with the banker. All he
requires is a public docile enough to do nothing but take his
money and pass it from hand to hand. If people do not call his
bluff by presenting the notes for payment, all is well. In time
people begin to acquire piles of these notes. This makes them
think what a trustworthy character the banker is, so they take
along to him, and put on deposit, not merely his own notes but
good coin as well. By preserving a grave exterior the banker has
made money. One can understand the immense number of fail-
ures among early bankers, and the look of morality on the faces
of those that survived. It is this conjuror's smile that we see again
and again on the face of Walter Bagehot. He inherited it.

Bagehot recounts the history of the origin of the Bank of
England, which his favourite Macaulay has told in a manner so
suited to the exuberance of the age. Here was a Whig finance
company, set up on the principle that while a Whig government
was best for the city, even with such a government it was better
for city men to trust themselves than the government. The city

would give countenance to the government rather than the government to the city. It was a phenomenon of settled times. A large Whig debt having been established, it became impossible to recall the Stuarts because they might repudiate it. The money-lender's notion of his ultimate rights over government, which coloured so much of the city's relationship with government from that day onwards, derives from this situation. The essence of the Whig settlement was that the court should sue for the support of the city rather than the other way round. Bagehot is wholly of this tradition.

> Nothing can be truer in theory than the economical principle that banking is a trade and only a trade, and nothing can be more surely established by a larger experience than that a Government which interferes with any trade injures that trade. The best thing undeniably that a Government can do with the Money Market is to let it take care of itself. [*ibid.*, p. 70.]

One could not have a more categorical demand for 'hands off' the city. Such a demand is, in effect, a demand for the subordination of government to the men who trust one another with money. The idea of the government keeping its own money belonged to the infancy of the world. Happy if government had never meddled with banking at all. But in England it had done so, and a marvellous system, which could have regulated itself entirely on the self-interest of moneyed men, was now driven to rely in some measure on public opinion. The natural voice of this opinion was the Chancellor of the Exchequer, so we had better try and get one that knew his business. But Bagehot clearly conceives the Chancellor's main duty as being so to arrange his affairs that the money market is not upset, and that the game of confidence which begins with the local banker deciding whom to favour, and ends with the international market, can be played uninterruptedly in accordance with its own rules devised, of course, primarily for the benefit of the players.

It might be supposed that the Bank of England 'has some peculiar power of fixing the value of money'. [*ibid.*, p. 77.] Not so, however, according to Bagehot. Other people follow the Bank of England in what they charge for money, but there is no compulsion about this. They are quite free to do otherwise; it only happens that the Bank holds more money than other people and that has a certain influence on events. In effect it fixes a price, and what other people have to decide is whether they will enter into competition with this giantess, and offer money more cheaply, or whether they will charge a little more. It would seem that their freedom of action is somewhat limited. Unless anyone has an immense store of money, he will obviously get tired of offering it cheaply before the Bank offers to bring its own rate down. As for offering money at a price above the Bank's, that is unlikely to be very alluring to customers. The caprice of the Bank is important, therefore, though Bagehot explains how, through the operation of supply and demand, it all comes right in the end, so that the Bank's power is not permanent; it is only great and sudden. A small matter, he seems to imply, though it causes some inconveniences, for 'up to a certain point money is a necessity'. [*ibid.*, p. 80.] It is not the necessity of buying bread that Bagehot has in mind, but the anxiety of the merchant to find money in order to make more. 'If money were all held by the owners of it, or by banks which did not pay interest for it' – if it were designed solely for such low purposes as the exchange of directly usable goods, in other words – 'the value of money might not fail so fast. Money would in the market phrase, be "well held".' But in Lombard Street money is held mainly by people who are borrowers as well as lenders. They must keep up a constant juggling of borrowing and lending, trying to make sure that the balance of the transactions is in their favour. The final secret of the market is that it must be run to the bankers' own advantage. This vital interest depending on it, one naturally wants to see a certain steadiness in the Bank of England, so that the lesser usurers are able to keep up with it.

With these important issues at stake, it is hardly surprising that 'Lombard Street is often very dull, and sometimes very excited'. [*ibid.*, p. 82.] It is rather on the same principle that other professions seem always to be more excited about their own jokes and vendettas than about the earthquakes and famines of the world at large. As an immense credit rests on a relatively small cash reserve, events such as a threat of invasion or the failure of a harvest bring with them the more serious trouble of a panic among bankers. The sudden apprehension that they may be short of money casts a blight on the whole community. There are 'good' times and 'bad' times; those that are good for bankers are good for everybody, those that are bad for bankers are bad for everybody. Certainly these warlocks should be propitiated! The identity of interest between capital and labour is complete, for the latter cannot hope to eat if the former is unhappy. The manufacturer, that secondary capitalist who is the banker's direct client, does not, as you might think, produce goods so that they can be *used*; he produces them 'to be exchanged' [*ibid.*, p. 83] because this is the operation in which there is most scope for the money-lender. The brisker the rate of circulation, the more the scope for lending and borrowing. The harder the manufacturer can be pressed, by his debts, to get his goods moving, the better. A man who carves pieces of wood, and puts them on a shelf to grow dusty until someone happens to come along who thinks it worth while buying one, is no use at all to the banker. He wants a manufacturer whose primary concern is a return on his money, and who thinks he has completed his mission if he produces any trash which can be sold above its cost, and the more the better, so that he has always to borrow to expand and can spare a percentage for the banker in the process. A depression or a slowing down of the circulation of trade, can be caused by one of two great natural forces – a calamity to a particular industry, agriculture especially, which produces goods people want to eat even more than they want to exchange them – and a failure of credit, caused by head-aches and migraines suffered by men with money who, on account of some disappointment, no longer trust one another as much as they did. The two great natural forces are not uncon-nected. The picture is of the soul of the banker agonizing within the crude body of industry.

A flicker of historical recollection crosses Bagehot's mind at this point in the argument. 'In our common speculations', he says, 'we do not enough remember that interest on money is a refined idea, and not a universal one.' [*ibid.*, p. 86.] There are even now unenlightened countries – most of the world, indeed, Bagehot says, in his day – where people do not trust the process of letting out money at usury. The real progress of civilization came when people found they could have safe investments. There is an optimum stage of credit, attained in the year 1871 and character-ized in the *Economist* as follows: 'We are now trusting as many people as we ought to trust, and as yet there is no wild excess of misplaced confidence which would make us trust those whom we

ought not to trust.' [*ibid.*, p. 97.] These good times are times of
rising prices – produced by cheap corn, which the *Economist* was
founded to campaign for, and cheap money – and not very
welcome to 'quiet people' of 'slightly-varying and fixed incomes',
but then it is not such people that Bagehot wishes principally to
consider. They are, after all, unlikely to have their minds sufficiently on the kind of money games which mark our society with
its peculiar qualities. The people Bagehot admires are those who,
when a long-continued period of low interest has given way, by
processes he describes, to a high rate, feel a sudden excitement,
'work more than they should, and trade far above their means'.
[*ibid.*, p. 101.] These are 'the ablest and the cleverest' – the
money-makers, in short, those who have a peculiar gift for seeing
beyond the vulgar surface of physical objects to the magical
numbers which lie beyond.

Bagehot goes on to examine the role of the Bank of England
in the panic of 1866. The Bank conceived that it had a duty to
support the banking community, and so paid out its reserves till
it hurt. No legitimate request for help, backed by proper securi-
ties, was refused. The *Economist* was so exuberant in its praise of
these proceedings, and of what it took to be an admission by the
Bank that Mr Bagehot's analysis of its function was the correct
one, that Hankey, one of the directors, characterized the article
as containing 'the most mischievous doctrine ever broached in the
monetary or banking world in this country, viz. that it is the
proper function of the Bank of England to keep money available
at all times to supply the demands of bankers who have rendered
their own assets unavailable.' [*ibid.*, p. 108.] And indeed one can
see that, in the round of confidence tricks desiderated by Bagehot
for the proper maintenance of credit, there might well be some
harm in the flat assertion that the Bank of England would always
pay out to the lesser bankers. No doubt he had seen exactly where
the interest of the lesser bankers lay; he was moreover, a journalist,
and his striking and simple doctrine looked well in the *Economist*.
The passage between Hankey and the *Economist* characterizes
Bagehot's position as a writer on public affairs. On the one hand
he was never tired of pointing out, to the merely intellectual
world, the solid good sense of men of affairs, himself included. On
the other, he was delighted to exhibit to men of affairs, engrossed
in mere business, the superiority of intellectuals, once more

including himself. It is a position which gave him a sort of personal invulnerability, so long as he twisted and turned quickly enough, but one cannot be entirely without misgivings about so slippery an Achilles, with no heel. Bagehot's analysis of the ineptitude of men of affairs, in matters of theory, is admirable.

> The abstract thinking of the world is never to be expected from persons in high places; the administration of first-rate current transactions is a most engrossing business, and those charged with them are usually but little inclined to think on points of theory, even when such thinking most nearly concerns those transactions. No doubt when men's own fortunes are at stake, the instinct of the trader does somehow anticipate the conclusions of the closet. But a board has no instincts when it is not getting an income for its members, and when it is only discharging a duty of office. [*ibid.*, p. 113.]

Yet it is to these alarming characters, lurching as instinct directs them towards their private profit, that Bagehot assures us that the control of credit and the public fortunes can safely be left. And what of the commentator? If he intrudes remarks for their wit or general truth rather than for the appositeness to a particular practical situation, is he more than a public entertainer who bedevils further the problems of the men who, by virtue of their position, have to find solutions or at any rate next moves?

Still, Bagehot is, in spite of the temptations of journalism, something more than a mere commentator. He is a banker from the skin inwards, and the attraction of his work on financial matters is that it is that of a man who can actually talk, with some facility, about the operations which his ordinary colleagues, the ordinary sensible men of business, merely perform. *Lombard Street*, as Keynes says,

> is a piece of pamphleteering, levelled at the magnates of the City and designed to knock into their heads, for the guidance of future policy, two or three fundamental truths. ... Perhaps the most striking and fundamental doctrine ... is, in a sense, psychological rather than economic ... the doctrine of the Reserve, and that the right way to stop a crisis is to lend freely. [*loc. cit.*, pp. 371–2.]

Psychologically, it may be added, the appeal of the doctrine to

Bagehot was that he was recommending *other people* to lend freely, in time of panic, as a way of saving Bagehot. He describes the panic of the Money Market rather as one might have described the Fire of London, and indeed it must have been rather like that. The bad news would 'spread in an instant through all the Money Market at a moment of terror; no one can say exactly who carries it, but in half an hour it will be carried on all sides, and will intensify the terror everywhere.' [*Works*, VI, p. 125.] This was perhaps the central horror of his life, next to the madness of his mother.

Bagehot goes on to describe the government of the Bank of England, as it was in his day. The board was self-electing, and although in theory a certain number went out each year, it was always some of the younger ones who went, so that the real power lay in the hands of a collection of ripe old men. When they chose a new director they did so with scrupulous care – 'purity', is the word Bagehot uses, and it had a certain meaning for him – because if he stayed he would, twenty years later, infallibly become in turn Deputy Governor and Governor, for those offices were filled by seniority. They came to all in turn, and those who had held office – 'passed the Chair' – formed the Committee of Treasury which exercised the real power in the establishment. By custom, none of these directors was a banker, in the ordinary sense of the term; they were merchants coming from reputable city houses. No wonder they needed Stuckey's to lecture them on the principles of banking! Bagehot indeed had a revolutionary proposal. It was that, since the Bank did not have a permanent Governor, and moreover had no one but subordinates about the place who understood banking, they should employ a sort of Permanent Under Secretary, on the model of Whitehall, to run it. Such a man as Bagehot himself would have filled the bill entirely.

Lombard Street is, in many ways, the most personal of Bagehot's books. His heart lay not only in the money but in the game of confidence he had inherited from his father and uncle in Somerset. He saw that banking was changing, and, correctly, expected that private banking would come to an end. The paragraphs in which he celebrates the life of that milieu – his own – come nearer to poetry than anything he ever wrote:

> I can imagine nothing better in theory or more successful in practice than private banks as they were in the beginning. A

man of known wealth, known integrity, and known ability is largely entrusted with the money of his neighbours. The confidence is strictly personal. His neighbours know him, and trust him because they know him. They see daily his manner of life, and judge from it that their confidence is deserved. In rural districts, and in former times, it was difficult for a man to ruin himself except at the place in which he lived; for the most part he spent his money there, and speculated there if he speculated at all. Those who lived there also would soon see if he was acting in a manner to shake their confidence. Even in large cities, as cities then were, it was possible for most persons to ascertain with fair certainty the real position of conspicuous persons, and to learn all that was material in fixing their credit. Accordingly the bankers who for a long series of years passed successfully this strict and continual investigation, became very wealthy and very powerful.

The name 'London Banker' had especially a charm value. He was supposed to represent, and often did represent, a certain union of pecuniary sagacity and educated refinement which was scarcely to be found in any other part of society. In a time when the trading classes were much ruder than they now are, many private bankers possessed a variety of knowledge and a delicacy of attainment which would even now be very rare. Such a position is indeed singularly favourable. The calling is hereditary; the credit of the bank descends from father to son: this inherited wealth soon brings inherited refinement. Banking is a watchful, but not a laborious trade. A banker, even in large business, can feel pretty sure that all his transactions are sound, and yet have much spare mind. A certain part of his time, and a considerable part of his thoughts, he can readily devote to other pursuits. And a London banker can also have the most intellectual society in the world if he chooses it. There has probably very rarely ever been so happy a position as that of a London private banker; and never perhaps a happier. [*ibid.*, pp. 164–5.]

Lombard Street was finished in 1873. 1876 was the centenary of the publication of *The Wealth of Nations*. Bagehot wrote two essays on this occasion – or perhaps one should say an essay and an article, the latter for the *Economist*, the former, closely related and in points repetitive, for the *Fortnightly*. The contribution to the *Fortnightly*, 'Adam Smith as a Person', is perhaps Bagehot's best essay. He had a subject completely to his liking, and completely within his scope.

Adam Smith was a man Bagehot felt he could patronize. A man inferior to himself, and yet who had produced such notable results to the world: What might not then Bagehot himself produce? Smith was born in Kirkcaldy in 1723, in a world far enough off in time as in place from Bagehot's English province. 'He was never engaged in any sort of trade, and would probably never have made sixpence by any if he had been.' [*Works*, VII, p. 1.] This lack of practical experience, in a man who passed for the inventor of political economy, needed some explaining. He was an awkward, unplausible man in comparison with Bagehot. He had a scheme, typical of the more superficial side of the eighteenth century – the Whig-*encyclopédiste* side – for a vast work on the development of the human mind and of social laws, on everything, in short. He went at this with Scotch and professorial industry until the acquisition of a sinecure made all intellectual work impossible. He picked up and much elaborated the talk of Glasgow merchants, and spent three years in France as tutor to the Duke of Buccleuch and there, as Bagehot put it, observed the numerous 'errors, such as generally accompany a great Protective legislation'. [*ibid*., p. 18.] The administration of France, then as now, showed a certain weakness for logical complexity. Worse still was the tendency of this legislation. Bagehot says that 'her legislators for several generations had endeavoured to counteract the aim of nature' – which was to confine her to agriculture and so make room for the English trade – 'and had tried to make her a manufacturing country and an exporter of manufactures'. [*ibid*., p. 17.] Reasoning on all these matters was Quesnay, who had a place at Court and excited himself about '*acheter, c'est vendre*' while Madame de Pompadour ran the government downstairs. The frank admiration for competition, which would infallibly produce fair prices, made an impression on Adam Smith, whose academic mind was probably also not unsympathetic to the governmental fantasies of the *économistes* who had 'the natural wish of eager speculators, to have an irresistable despotism behind them and supporting them; and with the simplicity which marks so much of the political speculation of the eighteenth century, but which now seems so childlike', says Bagehot, 'never seemed to think how they were to get their despot, or how they were to ensure that he should be on their side.' [*ibid.*, p. 22.] The gruesome admiration of eighteenth-century intellectuals for such characters as Frederick the Great is no more comic than the delusions of those of the twentieth century who have imagined that a Communist government would do what they wanted. After his residence in France Adam Smith went back to Kircaldy and lived with his mother for six years. After this he spent three years in London, still thinking, and then *The Wealth of Nations* appeared.

There are some acute comments on Adam Smith's conception of political economy in Bagehot's *Economic Studies*. Bagehot points out that this aboriginal author

> never seems aware that he is dealing with what we should call an abstract science at all. *The Wealth of Nations* does not deal, as do our modern books, with a fictitious human being hypo-thetically simplified, but with the actual concrete men who live and move. It is concerned with Greeks and Romans, the nations of the middle ages, the Scotch and the English, and never diverges into the abstract world. [*ibid.*, pp. 176–7.]

On the other hand, because Adam Smith's mind was rather crabbed and limited, he thought people were far more rigorous in pursuit of gain than most of them in fact are. He mentions some of the other things that people get up to, but his description is one-sided. He does not abstract more than he can help, but his mind is really of a self-limiting and so abstracting kind. People think him very practical, as compared with modern economists, because he professes to deal with the whole of man, but they are impressed by him because he deals only with parts. By contrast, Bagehot says, the modern economists who make a deliberate abstraction of the economic man, while really, he implies, under-standing the whole range of human nature, strike people as mere theorists. This is an argument from which we can afford to stand aside, but it may be remarked that the simplicity of mind, which led Adam Smith to the Utopia of Free Trade, is not much compli-cated in his nineteenth-century successors who thought that nothing could go amiss if it were established without hindrance in their native land.

One can hardly do better, if one wants an impression of the
exuberance of solid men, in Bagehot's own circle, on the subject
of free trade, than look at the prospectus which formed the
preliminary number of the *Economist* (August, 1843). The immediate object of the new 'political, commercial, agricultural and
free-trade journal' was the abolition of the Corn Laws, on which
liberal opinion had fixed with the blinkered tenacity with which
it has seized, since that day, on a succession of high causes which,
viewed historically, are no more than successive expressions of the
growing appetite of industry. The argument of free trade was
from the first a financial argument. In James Wilson's eloquent
prospectus the actual trades and actions of men are made to disappear before our eyes – they are explicitly treated as non-existent
if they do not satisfy the financial conventions of the time. 'As
long as railways and canals are profitable', he says, 'they truly
represent in real wealth the capital invested; but diminish the
amount of traffic only so much as pays the profit – ... and they
are no longer wealth.' [prospectus, p. 5.] In these terms there was
over-production, even at this early stage of mechanized industry,
and

> There is no cure, there is no remedy, for all these evils but
> increased demand; and there can be no increased demand
> without increased markets; and we cannot secure larger
> markets without an unrestricted power of exchange, and by
> this means add to our territory of land, as far as productive
> utility is concerned, the corn fields of Poland, Prussia, and
> above all, the riches and endless acres of the United States.
> [*ibid.*, p. 7.]

There might well be some hesitation, less than a generation after
the Napoleonic wars, about a system based on the accessibility of
the fields of Prussia and Poland. Even if this were not so, one
might wonder how, on this basis of territorially expanding
markets, 'we might go on increasing our production without
limits'. The doctrine of free trade was, after all, no more than the
mood which went with markets which were in fact then
expanding. If it was, as for Wilson, 'this only natural state of
things', it was so for people who had rejected Hobbes's state of
nature in favour of a more optimistic tradition.

Bagehot had an eye for the entertaining detail of Adam Smith's work – how long it took waggons to go from Edinburgh to London, how many apprentices a master cutler could have in Sheffield, or a master weaver in Norwich. But the subject of his essay is Adam Smith himself, and there is a sort of personal curiosity about the way he treats the events of his fellow-economist's life. The parallel is never exact – indeed there is hardly a parallel at all – but Bagehot is thinking of his own involvement in practical affairs when he makes play with Adam Smith's appointment, after the publication of *The Wealth of Nations*, as a commissioner of customs. Well acquainted with the theory of taxation, 'he could have given a Minister in the capital better advice than anyone else as to what taxes he should impose'. [*Works*, VII, p. 27.] Just like me! Bagehot no doubt thought; was he not 'the spare Chancellor'? On the other hand, Adam Smith's not very weighty duties prevented him from writing any more. A point of contrast with the banker of Langport! 'And not unnaturally, for those who have ever been used to give all their days to literary work, rarely seem able to do that work when they are even in a slight degree struck and knocked against the world.' [*ibid.*, p. 28.] Bagehot puts on a brave face before the loss of his predecessor's works. He says, truly enough no doubt, that what was lost was probably not very valuable. So Adam Smith lived on for fifteen years after the publication of *The Wealth of Nations*, talking sense among the lawyers and professors of Edinburgh and saying, at the end, that he meant to have done more. His mind no doubt was still full of his great scheme, with which in the end he did not weary the world.

Bagehot himself was, towards the end of his life, occupied with a great work which Hutton appeared to think he might be finishing off in heaven. It was an economic treatise, to be in three parts, the first of general economic theory, the second a critique of some classic theorists, and the third containing portraits of great economists. The essay on Adam Smith is clearly the prototype of the work which would have made up the third part. What Bagehot had done of the first and second parts became the posthumous *Economic Studies* (1879). This work is therefore of a fragmentary nature, but perhaps we put up with the loss of the rest of it as well as Bagehot put up with the loss of the work Adam Smith did not do because he was distracted by the Customs. Bagehot is an

unsystematic writer and it is unlikely that his book would have
been a landmark in economic theory.

The *Economic Studies* open with an essay which appeared in the
Fortnightly in 1876 under the title of 'The Postulates of English
Political Economy'. The essay starts with a reference to Adam
Smith and goes on to inquire why English political economy was
not popular outside England. One reason he alleges is it was 'more
opposed to the action of Government in all ways than most such
theories. ... All Governments', he says, 'like to interfere; it
elevates their position to make out that they can cure the evils of
mankind' [*ibid.*, p. 94] – a role which, in Bagehot's view of things,
is rather that of bankers who, by the stimulation of trade through
moneylending, produce comfort, which is what we most desire.
Another reason was simply that political economy was 'the
science of business' which at that time was held to be fully developed only in this country, as nowadays it is held to be fully
developed only in the United States. Although he used this
phrase, Bagehot was hardly on the side of the 'scientists' in this
field. He was sceptical of the excessive hope in numeracy which
has now swept through the minds of experts in affairs like a
blinding lunacy. He was convinced of the treachery of figures; he
knew how 'the names remain, while the quality, the thing signi-
fied', changed. 'Statistical tables, even those which are most
elaborate and careful, are not substitutes for an actual cognizance
of the facts: they do not, as a rule convey a just idea of the movements of a trade to persons not *in* the trade.' [*ibid.*, p. 99.] Yet
Bagehot was not on the side of mere non-statistical common
sense either. He was superior to the academic student of business
because he was *in* trade, and to the ordinary man of business
because he was clever. He takes neither side of the argument very
far and characteristically rests in a position where he feels that no
one can get at him. As a conclusive illustration he alleges that,
'extraordinary as it may seem, the regular changes in the sun have
much to do with the regular recurrence of difficult times in the
money market'. [*ibid.*] It is a striking assertion, which perhaps goes
to the root of Bagehot's religious faith.

The essay goes on to comment on two unfruitful methods of
investigation, still in principle very popular. One is what he calls
the 'all-case' method, which pretends to the impossible task of
collecting all the facts before proceeding to a theory. This method

Bagehot traces to Bacon's early fumblings after an empirical method. The other unfruitful method is what he calls the 'single case' method, which consists in an exhaustive analysis of a particular group of facts. Bagehot quite rightly holds that no exercise in the manipulation of facts can be useful without a preliminary theory. Even so, with a sense of the fluctuation of things which almost overwhelms any belief in the existence of man as an, historically speaking, relatively unchanging species, he sees political economy – English Political Economy, as he calls it – as concerned only with a particular recent group of phenomena. 'It is the theory of commerce, as commerce tends more and more to be when capital increases and competition grows.' [*ibid.*, p. 108.] He proceeds to examine the conceptions of the transferability of labour and of capital in the light of these limitations. He has no difficulty in showing that there are many conditions of society in which these conceptions do not hold. The revelation will cause little astonishment to any reader who stands a little apart from the Great Commerce in which Bagehot revelled, but Bagehot himself certainly did not draw the full consequences from that glimpse of the subjectivity of economic notions. His common insistence on the superiority of common sense, and of the notions of practical men, in business or politics, over those of religious and political ideas which have a longer grip on the mind, is shown to be mere bravado, the valueless talk of a class of men who happen to be fashionable with themselves at a particular moment of history. Bagehot repeatedly claims that men of business, economists and bankers are concerned with 'hard' fact, as if it were a special kind of truth. It is simply the one he loves best. 'Now of course it is true that there are some things, though not many things, more important than money', he said in his centenary article on *The Wealth of Nations* in the *Economist*,

> and a nation may well be called on to abandon the maxims which would produce most money, for others which would promote some of these better ends. The case is much like that of health in the body. There are unquestionable circumstances in which a man may be called on to endanger and to sacrifice his health at some call of duty. But for all that bodily health is a most valuable thing, and the advice of the physician as to the best way of keeping it is very much to be heeded, and in the

same way, though the wealth is occasionally to be foregone, and the ordinary rules of industry abandoned, yet still national wealth is in itself and in its connections a great end, and economists who teach us to arrive at it are useful. [*Works*, IX, pp. 199–200.]

The key to this passage is the equation of wealth with money, an error which Adam Smith had sought to remove, and which Bagehot understood very well, only to forget it in his passion for the refinements of credit, of which he was a powerful and hereditary practitioner.

Songs in the Night:
The Work of Henry Vaughan the Silurist

I

'My brother and I', he wrote, 'were borne att Newton in the parish of St Brigets in the yeare 1621.' 'Newton by Uske near Sketh-Rock', he called it, in the parish of Llansantffraed in Breconshire. The senior twin was Thomas, the magician, hermetical philosopher, experimental chemist, Thomas Vaughan who died by getting mercury up his nose. The father of the two, also Thomas Vaughan, was of the old Welsh gentry, from Tretower, nearby, and the inventory of his estate included 'one table in the hall with 3 wainscot benches and 3 chaires', 'fower sheep & 1 ram and 2 lambs' and '8 acres or thereabouts of hard corn growing in the field called y Llaworth y Ty'. He also had a reputation for being less than precise in money matters. Henry Vaughan and his brother were fortunate in their schoolmaster, Matthew Herbert of Llangattock, a well-to-do clergyman who was a Latinist of some accomplishment. At the age of twenty they went to Oxford, where Henry stayed only two years before going to London to study law. That would be about 1640. He was therefore in the capital for the two years preceding the outbreak of the Rebellion, being called home by his father in 1642. Of course he observed the streets:

> Should we goe now a wandring, we should meet
> With Catchpoles, whores, and Carts in ev'ry street:
> Now when each narrow lane, each nooke and Cave,
> Signe-posts, & shop-doors, pimp for ev'ry street:
> When riotous sinfull plush, and tell-tale spurs
> Walk Fleet street, & the Strand, when the soft stirs
> Of bawdy, ruffled Silks, turne night to day;
> And the lowd whip, and Coach scolds all the way;
> When lust of all sorts, and each itchie bloud
> From the Tower-wharfe to Cymbelyne, and Lud,
> Hunts for a Mate, and the tyr'd footman reeles
> 'Twixt chaire-men, torches and the hackny wheels

– lines which owe something to the study of Juvenal as well as to observation. The two years in London included the impeachment of Laud and Strafford and a great deal of noise from Pym. No doubt the education begun by Matthew Herbert was furthered in a number of ways.

The rest of Vaughan's life was spent in Breconshire. He may have gone a little further afield in his early twenties and there is reason to think he saw service with the King's forces. But there he lived, till his death in 1695, having been, for a few years after his return, secretary to a Welsh judge and then settled into his native landscape as a physician, practising, he told Aubrey, 'with good successe (I thank god!) & a repute big enough for a person of greater parts than my selfe'. He married a Warwickshire girl of good family, whom he met in Brecon, and later his deceased wife's sister, having four children by each marriage. One of his daughters, soured perhaps because of a mutilated hand, burnt while she was still a baby, dunned him repeatedly for maintenance in his old age. He gave up his house to a son, also apparently restive, and spent his last years in a tiny cottage. He published books of poems in 1646, 1650, 1651, 1655, 1678 and 1679, the last being merely a re-issue of the volume of 1651 and the 1678 volume containing little which did not date from a much earlier period. Vaughan's main activity as a poet seems to have fallen between the ages of nineteen and thirty-four.

Vaughan considered that he lived in bad times: 'Sed ut mea Certus / Tempora Cognoscas, dura fuere, scias', he said when he addressed himself 'Ad Posteros'. In lines more bitter than any in his English verse and in the rural imagery which came so naturally to him he complains that the springs were befouled, the sweet fields and sacred rose trampled. This he wanted to set on record, as also – *scias* again – that he had no part in it: 'partem / Me nullam in tanti strage fuisse, scias'. Popular and theological fury were not for him. His answer – *more parentis* – after the fashion, no doubt, of his mother, the Church of England, as George Herbert had said – was to suffer with tears. The language may seem excessive, to a generation which keeps its expressions of passion for other concerns, but within a certain tradition it is restrained. He believed, as he said in his preface to his translation of the *Hermetical Physick* of Henry Nollius (1655), that 'as men are killed by fighting, so truth is lost by disputing'. The point is that, when he settled after whatever part he took in the troubles, it was to let the storm blow over him as far as it would. It would not leave him, for the revolution was long before the end carried into even obscure villages. The clergy were turned out, churches were closed and alienated, the services and sacraments prohibited. If the seventeenth century was the golden age of the Church of England, it is partly because, for so many years of it, she was then treated with every opprobrium. There were other matters contributing to Vaughan's sensitivity during his inventive years – the death of friends in the war and, not least, his own long illness during which he seems to have undergone something like a conversion at the hands of George Herbert's *Temple*.

Vaughan's gravestone in Llansantffraed churchyard bears, by his own instruction, the words:

SERVUS INUTILIS

PECCATOR MAXIMUS

HIC JACEO

†

GLORIA MISERERE

II

Thomas Vaughan stayed longer at Oxford than his brother, was certainly in arms on the King's side, was ordained, installed as rector of Llansantffraed, and ejected some years later by the Parliamentarians. After the Restoration he seems not to have returned to his cure; by this time he was deep in chemistry. Hostile witnesses describe him as 'a common drunkard, a common swearer, no preacher, a whoremaster' – but one has to allow for Puritan exaggeration. He died in 1665–6.

It is a delicate question how much attention should be given to Thomas Vaughan in the consideration of his brother. Given that they were twins, there may have been temperamental affinities as there were certainly affinities in their upbringing. Both were scholars. The prose of Henry reaches more easily than his brother's into the common-sense world of social and moral connections. About Thomas's – the curiosity of the subject-matter apart – there is a suggestion of something which might, in another time and place, have issued in something like the romanticism of Novalis. But the brothers were certainly complementary in profound ways, and if one is looking, not for overt influences, but for illustrations of related trains of thought, some acquaintance

with the works of Thomas Vaughan is necessary for the understanding of Henry.

The works of Thomas Vaughan are certainly bizarre, even by
the standards of the seventeenth century. Jonathan Swift may have
looked into them, or he may have relied on the unfriendly
account of it given by Henry More the Cambridge Platonist.
Anyhow he refers to *Anthroposophia Theomagica* as 'a Piece of the
most unintelligible Fustian, that, Perhaps, was ever published in
any language'. But as this is in a footnote to a passage in which
Swift reproached Homer with not having read the book, or
Böhme, and is part of the exuberance of *A Tale of a Tub*, it should
not be taken, without more, that Swift so judged the matter.
Thomas Vaughan was certainly not Swift's favourite reading, and
there is so much of the seventeenth century in the Dean of St
Patrick's — much more, indeed, than the ordinary reader of
Gulliver's Travels would be likely to imagine — that the magician
would certainly have been less use to him than he might be to us.
Thomas Vaughan called himself Eugenius Philalethes. He was
more than a little given to portentousness and mystification, a
weakness his brother was far from sharing. The titles of his
books are not intended to make light of their abstruseness: *Anthroposophia Theomagica* was supplemented by *Anima Magica
Abscondita*, *Magia Adamica*, *Coelum Terrae*, *Lumen de Lumine*, *Aula
Lucis*, *The Fraternity of the Rosy Cross* and *Euphrates*, and several of
these works bear even more portentous subtitles, as that of *Coelum
Terrae*, which is *The Magician's Heavenly Chaos, unfolding a Doctrine
concerning the Terrestrial Heaven*. That some rather pretentious
matter is to be found scattered throughout these works is not
surprising. Thomas Vaughan has, so to speak, the *hermetic touch*: 'I
was not trusted with more in relation to public and popular use'
(*Lumen de Lumine*); 'the eye of man never saw the earth, nor can
it be seen without Art' (*Magia Adamica*); and so on. At times his
overweening knowledge (never quite revealed) puts him in a
position which, to say the least, is odd for a priest: 'shew me but
one good Christian who is capable of and fit to receive such a
secret, and I will show him the right, infallible way to come to it'.
No doubt these airs reflect a certain lack of adaptation, on
Thomas's part, to the ordinary world.

But one should not be put off by these symptoms. Thomas
Vaughan was in fact attending to matters of importance. In the

first place, his eyes and all his senses were filled by the physical world. It is from *looking* that he starts such trains of thoughts as that on 'those herbs which open at the rising and shut towards the sunset, which motion is caused', he says, 'by the spirit being sensible of the approach and departure of the sun. For indeed flowers are – as it were – the spring of the spirit, where it breaks forth and streams, as it appears by the odours which are more celestial and comfortable there.' Indeed, when he asserted that 'the eye of man never saw the earth' it was because he had contemplated closely 'the feculent, gross body on which we walk' and messed about with it in test-tubes or the like. He thought that what ignorant nurses took for a mere desire to play was a manifestation of a desire for knowledge. The external world was where you got knowledge from. 'Indeed whiles we follow our own fancies and build on bottomless, unsettled imagination' – as he accused the Schoolmen of doing – 'we must needs wander and grope in the dark, like those that are blindfolded'. God had proposed the rules of enquiry in the creation. 'In vain hath He made Nature if we dwell on our own conceptions and make no use of her principles.' Thomas Vaughan is a man feeling his way into science through a world of vivid appearances – not, as so many now do, thinking he can break into nature with the help of one or two theoretical conceptions. 'It is true', he admits,

> that no man enters the Magical School but he wanders first in this region of chimaeras, for the inquiries we make before we attain to experimental truths are most of them erroneous. Howsoever, we should be so rational and patient in our disquisitions as not imperiously to obtrude and force them upon the world before we are able to verify them.

One could hardly better that.

At the root of Thomas Vaughan's apprehension of Nature was his apprehension of God. He denied that the two were contraries, as many had pretended and so 'weakened our confidence towards heaven'. The process of true knowledge consisted in undoing the effects of the Fall. God had 'made man – as it were – for His playfellow, that he might survey and examine his works'. The problem was to recover that condition. 'We should pray continually that God will open our eyes.' No doubt it is a kind of gnosticism, but Thomas Vaughan does not divide the world into

twin creations of Light and Darkness. On the contrary, he sees all
such dichotomies as resolved by the Incarnation. For 'no philosophy hath perfectly united God to His creature but the Christian,
wherefore also it is the only true philosophy and the only true religion'. Yet the doctrine of *Anthroposophia Theomagica* has more
than a touch of pantheism about it. 'For God breathes continually
and passeth through all things like an air that refresheth.' It is the
very wind blowing down the valley of the Usk.

III

Ben Jonson died in 1637 and in the 1640 folio the collection of
minor poems called *The Underwood* was published for the first
time. Henry Vaughan will have received the impact of this during
his formative two years in London. Jonson exercised on the poets
of the first half of the century an influence comparable only to that
of Pound in our own time – and for the same reason, that he was
a technical master of great solidity and learning and one whose
techniques poets of very different temperamental endowments
could put to good use. Vaughan was exceedingly unlike Jonson
in temperament, and unlike him ultimately in the use to which
his writing was put. But his first collection, *Poems with the tenth
Satyre of Juvenal Englished*, is very much a product of the Jonson
tradition. The prefatory address 'to all ingenious lovers of poesie',
is the rather precious stuff which might be expected of a young
dilettante of letters. There is an affectation of contempt for the
affairs of common men. Vaughan addresses himself to those
'alone, whose more refined Spirits out-wing these dull Times,
and soare above the drudgerie of durty Intelligence'. (It is a pity
that this last word has to be read as meaning *news*.) The volume
itself starts with a charming letter in verse, with enough marks of
grace and skill to be highly creditable to an aspirant to literary
performance:

> When we are dead, and now, no more
> Our harmless mirth, our wit, and score
> Distracts the Towne; when all is spent
> That the base niggard world hath lent
> Thy purse, or mine …

It is young man's stuff, with slightly more grandiose gestures than
the modest course of Henry Vaughan's life really called for, no
doubt. The 'Ingenuous friend' to whom it was addressed is Mr
R.W., and before the verses were published he had died fighting
at Rowton Heath, where Henry Vaughan may himself have been.
R.W. is commemorated in a moving elegy in Vaughan's second
volume, *Olor Iscanus* (1651). The bulk of the *Poems* of 1646 is made
up of somewhat slight verses to Amoret – some not without an
unmistakeable touch of personal feeling – and the Juvenal translation, a valuable literary exercise for which Matthew Herbert's
teaching had equipped the translator. Juvenal might seem a somewhat unsympathetic figure for Henry Vaughan to work on, but
the exercise will not have been the less valuable on that account.
The translation has its fortunate moments, but in a vein utterly
different from that of the original, as 'Smiles are an easy purchase,
but to weep / Is a hard act, for tears are fetch'd more deep.' No
doubt Vaughan was more at home with Virgil and the epigraph
of *Olor Iscanus* – an apt one – is from the *Georgics*: 'Flumina amo,
silvasque inglorius.' The first poem celebrates the Usk:

> But *Isca*, whenso'er those *shades* I see,
> And thy *lov'd Arbours* must no more *know* me,
> When I am layd to *rest* hard by thy *streams*,
> And my *Sun sets*, where first it *sprang* its beams,
> I'le leave behind me such a *large, kind light*,
> As shall *redeem* thee from *oblivious night*,
> And in these *vowes* which (living yet) I pay
> *Shed* such a *Previous* and *Enduring Ray*,
> As shall from age to age thy *fair name* lead
> 'Till *Rivers* leave to *run*, and *men* to *read*.

The volume contains, besides the elegy on R.W., another on 'Mr
R. Hall, slain at Pontefract, 1644'. The war engaged Vaughan
passionately, and in his closest connections. It is well to remember
this, when one thinks of him beside the Usk, in his long devotional retreat.

> Thou wert no *Wool-sack* souldier, nor of those
> Whose courage lies in *winking* at their foes,
> That live at *loop-holes*, and consume their breath
> On *Match* or *Pipes*, and sometimes *peepe* at death...

(Surely a reminiscence of some garrison where Vaughan had served.) There are further evidences of Latin studies in the verses from Ovid and Boethius, as well as in three of the short prose translations with which *Olor Iscanus* was, rather oddly, bound up. The prose pieces show in what direction Vaughan's mind was moving. The first was 'Of the Benefit wee may get by our enemies', a discourse of Plutarch which Vaughan took from a Latin version. The second, 'Of the Diseases of the Mind and the Body', from the same source. The third was a discourse on the same subject as the second, but from '*Maximus Tirius* a Platonick Philosopher'. The last of the four was 'The Praise and Happinesse of the Countrie-Life', from the Spanish of Antonio de Guevara. There is no doubt that Vaughan was a man of wide and curious reading – by modern standards probably a man of considerable learning. It was a mind of some instruction, as well as of some complexity and experience, which finally issued in the unassuming, and sometimes luminous, verse of *Silex Scintillans*.

Between *Olor Iscanus* and the first volume of *Silex Scintillans* came a volume of prose, *The Mount of Olives* (1652). This was intended as a practical manual of devotion, for a time when churches were 'vilified and shut up'. It is certainly composed in no spirit of mere political antagonism to the Puritans. Vaughan's revulsion is from their abstracted spirituality and their contempt of the physical world – precisely, their putting of their own conceptions before the evidence of the senses, by that trick of mind which Thomas Vaughan deplored in another context. 'Nor should they', Henry says in *The Mount of Olives*, 'who assume to themselves the glorious stile of Saints, be uncharitably moved, if we that are yet in the body, and carry our treasure in earthen vessels, have need of these helps.' The scope of the work is best given in the words of the address 'To the peaceful, humble and pious reader' prefixed to the volume.

> Here are Morning and Evening sacrifices, with holy and apposite Ejaculations for most times and occasions. And lastly, here are very faithful and necessary Precepts and Meditations before we come to the Lords Table. To which last part I have added a short and plaine Discourse of Death, with a Prayer in the houre thereof. And for thy comfort after thou hast past through that Golgotha, I have annexed a Dissertation of the

blessed state of the righteous after this life, written originally by holy Anselme sometime Arch-Bishop of Canterbury.

The whole production is written with simplicity and elegance, and absolute application to its purpose. It is eminently conciliatory, so far as it could be without any derogation from the experimental truth of the mystery 'where thy flesh is the meat, where thy blood is the drink, where the creature feeds upon the Creatour, and the Creatour is united unto the creature'. It is of course instinct with the language and spirit of the Prayer Book which had been replaced, by order of Parliament, by the Directory of Public Worship. Vaughan published a further series of reflective treatises, *Flores Solitudinis*, in 1654. These were all translations.

One hardly likes to draw attention to the preface of *Silex Scintillans*, so remote is it in spirit from anything now considered reasonable in a literary man. It is remote from what Vaughan himself had thought reasonable when he put together his first volume. 'Wits' are now treated with scant regard. 'Many of them', he says, 'having cast away all their fair portion of time, in no better imployments, then a deliberate search, or excogitation of idle words, and a most vain, insatiable desire to be reputed Poets'. Things do not change much. 'The first, that with any effectual success attempted a diversion of this foul and overflowing stream', he goes on, 'was the blessed man, Mr George Herbert'. But Herbert's imitators had 'more of fashion, than force'. Vaughan was not proposing a mere substitution of a sacred for a profane subject-matter. Indeed the clue to what he thought may be less in the preface than in the verse of Job he gives on the title-page: 'Where is God my Maker, who giveth Songs in the night?' He wrote the songs he was given. But the preface contains this critical severity on the subject of Herbert's imitators, that 'they aimed more at verse, then perfection'. The root of the matter for Vaughan was telling the truth, and having some truth to tell.

The best poems of *Silex Scintillans* are well known, but it is necessary to read the book as a whole to understand the temper from which they come. If the prejudice which most people now have against a devotional subject-matter is set aside, it will be seen that the reader is in the presence of a mind of unusual integrity

attempting to communicate experiences which are most often of
an untraceable privacy. He did this in the language of Anglican
Christianity because this was the natural language for him. It is
not merely the ebullition of 'I saw Eternity the other night' but
the more permanent moods which underlie it and make the
release possible: 'For sin (like water) hourly glides / By each man's
door.' Or this: 'My thoughts, like water which some stone doth
start'. The images of water are frequent – from the Usk, which
Thomas Vaughan also celebrated in a poem, or some deeper
stream. 'What sublime truths, and wholesome themes, / Lodge in
thy mystical, deep streams!' It is not merely that Vaughan moves
easily from natural observation to mysticism; but that the two are
inseparable for him.

> Dear stream! dear bank, where often I
> Have sate, and pleas'd my pensive eye,
> Why, since each drop of thy quick store
> Runs thither, whence it flowed before,
> Should poor souls fear a shade of night,
> Who came (sure) from a sea of light?

Light and darkness, storm and calm, are psychological as well as
outward realities, and the assimilation should make Vaughan intimately approachable even by those who are repelled by the
theological meanings which he sees simultaneously, as it were as
a third strand in the texture.

> There is in God (some say)
> A deep, but dazling darkness: As men here
> Say it is late and dusky, because they
>   See not all clear;
> O for that night! where I in him
> Might live invisible and dim.

It could be said that Vaughan's success or failure as a religious poet
– so far as one can distinguish such achievement from his
undoubted success as a poet of nature and psychology – is to be
judged by how far he succeeds in presenting the 'invisible and
dim' world of his inner life before the phenomena of nature as
necessarily one with theological humility: 'Sweet Jesu! will then;
Let no more / This Leper haunt, and soyl thy door.' Certain it is
that, when he spoke of being 'sick with desire' – for Vaughan used

the phrase as well as Yeats – it was, as he saw it, for the love of God, and that this was not because he had not known any other love, or the world, but because he had. Vaughan himself probably considered that he had achieved only a slight sketch of what he felt bound to try to convey, and that the second half of his life was as well spent in his labours as a country doctor, and his private devotions, as in further versifying – though no doubt his doctoring would not have stopped him writing verses, if he had been given more songs in the nights.

A final volume was published in 1678, though not, it would seem, on Vaughan's own initiative. It is a miscellaneous book, apparently made up of work written much earlier – worth saving, certainly. The 'Elegiac Eclogue' entitled *Daphnis* shows a very great skill in that classicizing tradition, from Ben Jonson to Dryden, with which Vaughan is not usually associated but in which he has a place:

> Here *Daphnis* sleeps! & while the great watch goes
> Of loud and restless Time, takes his repose.
> Fame is but noise, all Learning but a thought:
> Which one admires, another sets at nought.
> Nature Mocks both, and Wit still keeps adoe;
> But Death brings knowledge and assurance too.

IV

George Herbert, who came of an aristocratic and brilliant family, settled for the charge of the tiny church at Bemerton, lying between Salisbury Cathedral and the great house of Wilton which might well have been the poet's ordinary milieu. Henry Vaughan's grandfather was the Vaughan of Tretower – a great mediaeval house. In the courtyard three hundred archers who fought at Agincourt were mustered and behind lay the Norman keep. No doubt it had been a defended place time out of mind. The house as well as the castle were already reduced in compass in Sir Thomas Vaughan's time, and Sherriff's court was held next to the kitchen. The Usk, a wide and generally shallow, quick-moving stream, flows in a broad valley. There are swans on it; the Olor Iscanus was not imagined. Sketh-Rock is perhaps five miles upstream from Tretower. Between the two is Llansantffraed and in the churchyard, overlooking the Usk and faced by great sweeps of hillside which must always have been in Vaughan's eye, is the grave, under ancient yews. Green woodland, paler green hill-side, the water near.

Forewords from In the Trojan Ditch

Foreword to *Collected Poems*

The earliest poem here reprinted was written on a troopship going south through tropical waters. It is not altogether the work of an innocent beginner: I was nearly thirty. More poems were written in military camps in Bengal and the late North-West Frontier Province. There was a gap of several years, then the break to the surface which occurred with the poems entitled 'Fell-foot' and 'In a Dark Wood'.

That much of history explains how the bulk of the volume is the work of a man going onwards from thirty-five – poems of the return journey, therefore. My beginnings were altogether without facility, and when I was forced into verse it was through having something not altogether easy to say.

In a manner this defines the nature of the poet's problem. There is no question, as it has come to me, of filling note-books with what one knows already. Indeed as the inevitable facility comes, the conscious task becomes the rejection of whatever appears with the face of familiarity. The writing of poetry is, in a sense, the opposite of writing what one wants to write, and it is because of the embarrassing growth of the area of consciousness which writing, as indeed the other serious encounters of life, produces that one has recourse to the conscious manipulation of translation, as it were to distract one while the unwanted impulses free themselves under the provocation of another's thought. I have come in the end to have great sympathy with Dryden, who having pushed his way this way and that at the end of his days took pride in being able to do a translation better than any of them. He was glad, I imagine, to be able to release the energies of poetry without passing for having said anything of his own. I do not pretend that my path has led me so far. There are other enabling distractions – reasoning and analysis, mythology and other narrative, properly used. All these are really modes of the problem of form.

The claim of a collection like this is in the continuity of statement which underlies the historical recording, analysis or imitation and is recognizable in the development of rhythm rather than in overt logical connections. The proof of the poem – any poem – is in its rhythm and that is why critical determination has in the end to await that unarguable perception.

Foreword to *Selected Translations*

It is not an impertinence to try to translate great masters. It is a tribute that one pays. Dryden, who had a right to speak, claimed only that 'some of the beauties of the author ... appear sometimes in the dim mirror which I hold before you'.

The question is, What sort of mirror? There are several kinds of translation. None of those in this volume is for people who want help, in construing the sentences. But in a larger sense they are constructions, as any translation must be, a reading of the originals so that they make sense in our time. It will not do if one denatures the original, making out, for example, that Virgil was a smart-alec of the twentieth century. The aim must be to take what we can, and that can be no more than we can put into language that can be read. The argument is muddied by the critic's own reading of the original. A classical original is particularly susceptible of misconception, since people remember not only Virgil or Horace but the academy in which they were taught.

The method I adopted in translating Virgil is quite different from that used in my Catullus. There are two reasons for this. The first is the very different nature of the two texts. I am inclined to think that Landor was right in judging that a single poem of Catullus is worth the whole of the Eclogues. At any rate the language of Catullus is plainer and more direct, and that is what we now value, as Landor did, though in his day disapprobation of 'the Elizabethan style' was less common. It is proper to try to reproduce the plainness, as far as one can in the 'dim mirror' one holds. With Virgil the problem is different. There is a certain elaboration, very unfashionable in our time and perhaps of little use for contemporary literary purposes. There is also something which we ought to value. This is a deep movement of feeling, below the surface of our exacerbated daily life, and which has greater significance than any 'frankness' for those who want to understand the human brute. This is part of my excuse for translating Virgil on somewhat large lines. The other is that, for any poet, a translation serves a purpose and has a place in his own technical development. The exercise in plainness was what I wanted when I did the Catullus. The translation of Virgil was part of a movement away, as far as possible, from the merely personal concern, or from the presentation of our condition which has that appearance.

As to the versification, the publication of the Catullus has taught me that many critics will know what that should be. I have always found it a most difficult thing to know myself. Indeed I would say that there is no way of knowing except by doing it, and that all theory about the proper measures for a translation is out of place. There is no equivalent in English of Virgil's hexameter; it is not even the case that the regular couplets of Dryden represent it more exactly than a less regular measure. There should be a certain music, however faint. But it is an ineluctable law that a verse translation has to be done in the only verse that the translator, at the time of writing, can make; and that if he could not make verse before he will not suddenly become so gifted because he is faced with a classical text. Dryden wrote in the superb verse he was master of in his 'great climacteric'. For the Eclogues I wrote what I could manage at the age of fifty-three, after the last poem in *Metamorphoses* which in turn owed something to Charles d'Orléans. There is some development of the verse in the course of writing. The octosyllabic broke as I wrote, and although an *a priori* judge might object, a poet is not entitled to.

The translations here reproduced follow, more or less, a chronological order. The earliest are from Heine, an edition of whose *Meisterwerke in Vers und Prosa*, published in Holland in 1939 with an eye on the political relationships of the time, I carried in my pack when I went aboard the S.S. *Vollendam* at Liverpool early in 1943. The book stayed with me in the camps in Bengal and the North-West Frontier Province in which I whiled out my fruitless stay. The Heine who was the Sword and the Flame of the German revolutionary struggles of the first half of the nineteenth century became the companion of the British Other Rank in his oppressive situation in the last decade of the British Raj. The translations were done for distraction, but they were the work of someone intent on sharpening his literary weapons, in case there should ever be a time and a place in which he could use them.

The odd bit of a French medieval song which follows is the survivor of a very small number of similar exercises undertaken, for pleasure and as part of my late dilatory training as a writer, in the later forties but before I had resumed the writing of poetry. If I had been asked what I was after, I should have said *plainness*, not certain whether I meant in verse or in prose, and thinking more probably the latter. When I again took up, intermittently, the habit of writing verse of my own, my interest in translation became subdued. Yet the major outbreak represented by my *Catullus* began in a similar search for plainness, and with the conviction that one had not read the Latin properly until one could put it in language of one's own. By this time I had published *The London Zoo* and *Numbers*. The competition with Catullus – which even the best of writers must lose – certainly had its effect on the style of the succeeding volume, rather confusingly entitled *Metamorphoses* on account of some allusions to Ovid in the title poem. The Catullus translation began with a few specimens, the result of random browsings, and it was only at a later stage that it occurred to me – or rather to David Wright – that I might do the lot. I had had my eye on Catullus for years – as what poet would not who could make out even a little of the Latin? – but the actual translation was the work of a few months – months which were full enough already with business of a nonliterary kind. It was a piece of education for the translator which, if my life as a writer had had any logic in it, would have taken place at the outset.

The next major work was with Virgil, and of that enough has already been said, except this: that with 'Palinurus' and 'The Descent' the use made of the original is so indirect that there might be some hesitation as to whether they belonged to this or to the earlier part of the volume. It is the balance of dependence which brought them here, while 'Eurydice', with its slighter allusion to Ovid, finds a place among the Collected Poems. I have included in this part a frontal attack on Ovid, in the form of a version of the opening lines of Book I of the Metamorphoses. This is nearer than the Virgil to the spirit of the Catullus translations and was done between them and the Virgil.

The selection of my translations ends with some specimens of Horace, done with varying degrees of fidelity to the original. The version of the Carmen Saeculare comes near to being a new start from the old original, but it is closer to its text than the two extracts from the Aeneid, which are selected from a great number of lines, while this and still more the other Horatian translations attempt to find equivalents for at any rate most of the statements of the original. Horace is a hard nut to crack, and others before me have broken their teeth on him. But he does yield his nourishment and, in the measure that it is extracted, one becomes aware of a poet of great depth as well as polish – a poet invaluable in our time not least because of his lack of sympathy with our most current prejudices.

Looking Back on Maurras

I

The influence of Charles Maurras is something I should like to shake off. Its work on me was done long ago, so far as I can judge, and I am puzzled that he has not fallen into place, with Eliot, say, or Yeats, as a figure to whom I acknowledge a debt from a distance: an historical debt which, unpaid as such things always are, no longer concerns one very much. With Maurras it is different. The seduction remains, even though I cannot read through any of his books with approval. And if I am asked to summarize his achievements, I find myself usually talking about his limitations, even his vices. If I am asked what books of his one should read, to get some idea of his importance, I do not know what to point to. Did he in fact write a satisfactory book? Each of the books is nothing, in itself, and the compendia he himself produced – such as the *Essais politiques* in the volumes of *Oeuvres capitales* he prepared during his final imprisonment – seem jejune and inadequate when one turns to them after a long acquaintance with his performance. They must be a poor starting-point to the reader who comes fresh to his work, and give nothing at all to the inquirer who does not come with a measure of sympathy and understanding, from the rumours he has heard of them. And it has to be admitted that an intelligent inquirer, interested in the political questions which obsessed Maurras, is as likely to have gathered from rumours matter for a lack of sympathy, or for plain hostility.

Perhaps a parallel case, so far as the nature of influence is concerned, would be that of Voltaire. What did Voltaire write? Everything and nothing. If there are masterpieces, such as *Candide*, they are much as one might expect from a smaller man. All the life of Voltaire is in them, in a sense, yet none of them gives one anything which could possibly account for his influence. So it is with Maurras. If you turn to the *Enquête sur la monarchie*, which from its title one might suppose to be a magisterial demonstration of the case for the monarchy advanced by the most famous monarchist of the twentieth century, you find nothing but a number of beginnings. And so elsewhere. Everything is provisional, linked to the quarrels and events of the moment, or rather of a series of moments which have already passed, as moments do, leaving the need for a different approach to the apologia. The book most to be recommended to anyone seeking an initiation is the autobiographical *Au signe de Flore*, which deals with the foundation of the *Action française* between 1898 and 1900. But again, it is in the excitements of the moment – the Dreyfus affair in particular – that the author discovers his principles. The reader who finds other principles more vividly illustrated by those events, or who feels an understandable reluctance, at this time of day, to turn over that particular dunghill again, will not find this book a very good starting-point for an inquiry into the modern case for the monarchy, which might be supposed to be Maurras's central subject though, truth to tell, it is not, and the question of what does lie at the centre of his work is not easily answered.

The most sympathetic matter in the book, for the reader without passionate political bias, is likely to be the idyll the author there makes out of his early years in Provence. Avoiding the circumstantial except when it embellishes the romance he is building, Maurras sets out his early recollections of his childhood in Martigues, Bouches-du-Rhône. The whole aroma of old Provence rises from a few pages. Nothing of the more squalid predicaments of the family of a minor official, living in a little fishing town presumably already in steep decline. Not a word of the industrial menace of Marseilles, almost on the doorstep, and containing more Provençals than the whole of Provence, as the England of the villages and shires is outnumbered and over-whelmed by the inhabitants of Liverpool, Manchester, Birmingham and London. How narrow Maurras's basic sympathies were, how narrow, really, the world of his imagination is curiously indicated by his reference to Nîmes (in a letter of 9 June 1894, to Barrès) as 'un ramassis de protestants, de juifs, et d'anciens mercantis beaucairois'. Or to Marseilles itself (letter of January 1903) as 'une ville *ignoble*. J'y respire l'ignomonie', he goes on. 'Aix est pur. Martigues est chaste. Arles a le goût de tous les mystères de mort, Marseille est d'une vie obscène, et vous le pouvez constater.'

It is a Provence of the imagination, of which one cannot deny the seductions. And so, in Athens, where he went to report on the Olympic Games in 1896, at the age of twenty-eight, the splendours of the Acropolis leave him no eyes for anything else; as when he went to London two years later, it was to see the Elgin Marbles without being distracted for a moment by the living city which, after all, has and must have had a certain human interest. In Greece it was only the peak of the classical period which interested him; before and after that, there was only ugliness. It was the aesthetic of a man who had already found all he wanted to know, 'la science du sentiment', as he accurately defined it. 'Une ANTHINÉA, fleur du monde, printemps des pensées et des arts, s'élargit nécessairement.' It includes the country, 'douce et nerveuse' of Racine, Voltaire and La Fontaine. Maurras feels its intimate bonds with his own Provence. He has travelled, one may say, in order to find his roots. Yet it is not exactly that. For in *Anthinéa* itself he explains that beginnings are not beautiful. 'La beauté véritable est au terme des choses.' Dangerous to contemplate, one would think; and perhaps Maurras thought so. It is difficult to fix a point in the ultimate thoughts of this man who, for all his dogmatisms, was so full of reactions and qualifications. Looking at the instability of his own Martigues, built among the sand-dunes of the Étang de Berre, he reflects that it is a place of death, where 'le néant et la mort ont soulevé ... leur voile' and 'Celui qui ne meurt point de cette vue en tire une nourriture très forte.' The whole of Maurras's career is, in a sense, a revulsion from this vision of death, on which he none the less feeds all the time. The aesthetic of an unattainable finality broods over it all, yet Maurras knows better than to try to embody this finality in any work of his own.

All this may seem far from the Maurras known to those who see him only as a political figure, bitterly involved in the Dreyfus affair, in antagonism with Léon Blum and the *Front populaire*, standing behind Pétain during the occupation in 1940–4 or in the dock at Lyons in 1945. But it was never far away – not far enough, it might be said, for Maurras tried to impose his vision on that singularly inharmonious background, the technological Europe of the late nineteenth and the first half of the twentieth century.

II

Although I had some glimmerings of Maurras, while still an undergraduate in 1931–4, from the *Speculations* of T.E. Hulme and the pages of *The Criterion*, and indeed had read *L'Avenir de l'intelligence* without those glimmerings becoming a light, it was in the two following years, under the full impact of my first visits to the Continent and prolonged stays in Germany and in Paris at a time of tempestuous international politics, that I really had my apprenticeship. Everything in my approach to him was coloured by the dangers and controversies of those pre-war years. A residence of eight months in Hitler's Germany, with all the intimidations that offered to a very young Englishman whose heart did not readily beat in time, as invited, with the then thumping hearts of his German cousins, determined my direction. As an undergraduate, though at a provincial university, I had already undergone the full onslaught of left-wing politics. It was the time of unemployment and hunger marches, as well as of the early poems of W.H. Auden and Stephen Spender. The few fashionable intellectuals my university boasted were, as was proper, members of the Communist Party. My sympathies had been with the hunger marchers. I had gone to hear Saklatvala speak and had assumed that he was talking the language of the future. Through the good offices of T.E. Hulme, my scanty political reading had extended beyond *The Communist Manifesto* to take notice of Georges Sorel. The brilliant representatives of the Communist Party had not, however, talked me round. Auden and Spender were impressive in their language but their social attitudes were unconvincing to someone brought up in a working-class area and a complete stranger to the social facilities of the upper and even the middle classes. I belonged I supposed to one of the lower middle classes, those barely distinguishable people who – perhaps because I have belonged to them – I believe had their roots deeper than anyone, in what England used to be. At any rate I was, in the end, stubborn as a mule to the political dogmatisms of student politics, and when I set off for Germany, in October 1934, it was as a more or less complete political agnostic.

As I tried to arrive at an orientation of my own, living in the Hamburg and Berlin and Munich of the Storm Troopers and a Prague already threatened by the Sudeten Germans, it was not as an adherent of Right or Left – those great, vague, pan-European conceptions – but as an Englishman whose country was threatened by attack. The Nazi party at that time was putting itself out quite noticeably to be pleasant to the British. While a dogmatic anti-fascist passion raged among the British Liberals and Left, fanned by those who were particularly moved by the threat to the Jews, what one might call the ordinary stupid British tourist was not infrequently won over by the partly assumed, partly real, admiration of the Germans for the race which was supposed to be enjoying stable government, to be running a great empire, and anyhow to be given to manly sports in a manner which made them worthy companions of a movement in which young men were for ever flexing their muscles and admiring their physique. I was not a candidate for this ingenuous flattery and had no difficulty in seeing the Nazis for the menace they were. I was, moreover, of a reflective nature and thought of 1870 and 1914 as well as of 1933. My sympathy for France grew *pari passu* with my alarm for England. It never occurred to me to doubt that the French cause was also ours. When I finally got to the Rhine it was to hope that the poplars of Alsace concealed plenty of guns pointing east. It was at this time, while a student in Freiburg, that I sought out my first book by Léon Daudet and so came a step nearer to becoming an addict, as happened in Paris later in 1935, of the *Action française*.

The political events of those years were confusing enough, and did in fact confuse many better qualified observers than I. There was the Abyssinian war, to which the liberal reply was supposed to be in the operation of the League of Nations in Geneva, where H. M. Government, represented by Anthony Eden in his best-tailored period, still cut quite a figure. At home there was a Peace Ballot, a much-canvassed expression of the will to peace which was supposed to be an answer to rising militarism. Briefly, the politics of opinion, against the politics of action as represented by Hitler's Germany and Mussolini's Italy. All good courses were supported by the Soviet Union; all bad courses were supported by Hitler, Mussolini, and in due course, Franco. There was a high degree of plausibility in all this. The merit of the commentaries which, as I found when I got to Paris, appeared day by day over the signature of Charles Maurras, was not that they took a sympathetic view of Mussolini and, when he appeared, of Franco, or the

vain dream – not without connection with Maurras's Provençal
obsessions – of creating a Latin block against the Germans. It was
in the nature of the analysis which – this little Latin deviation apart
– ignored the clamour of sentiment, however popular, and operated wholly on a calculation of interests and forces. The rights and
wrongs of, say, the Abyssinian war, as they appeared to most of
the public in France as in England, the widespread sentiment
which supported the League of Nations for the good it was
supposed to be capable of, were brushed aside. England still had
a reputation for morality in those days, and all the manifestations
of that virtue were treated with a fine irony. Churchill, at this
stage still a relative outsider, was pointed to as a statesman with
the wit to support the League solely for the advantages of interest
which could be extracted from it. 'Cependant il n'est pas des
nôtres', I remember Maurras writing in one of his daily articles.
The interests Churchill sought to preserve were, of course, British
imperial interests. France must look to herself.

And so, day by day, I ingested these radical commentaries, in
cafés on the Boulevard St-Michel or in my little room in rue du
Cardinal Lemoine. I was living in a pension where the opinion
was, predominantly, liberal and leftish; and day by day I talked
over Maurras's analysis with people who did not agree with it.
What came out of all this, so far as I was concerned, was a
complete disenchantment with the popular categories of 'democratic' and 'fascist', at a time when it was usual to see all political
events, wherever in the world they took place, as a conflict
between these ill-defined antagonists.

I became so far a convert to the *Action française* as to try to see
these events from the point of view of the bleakest national
interest – but I retained wit enough to try to effect my calculations
from the point of view, not of France, but of my own native
country, which involved sometimes a certain effort of transposition. It was one of the enlightening features of the Maurrassien
analysis that the idea that Russia was on the side of European
socialist movements had no part in it. The Russian moves were
seen as manifestations of a government as conscious of its national
interests as was Hitler's or Mussolini's; from that point of view,
the European socialist movements were merely being *used*. While
the almost universal conviction in democratic circles, in France as
in England and elsewhere, was that the Soviets could be relied

upon in any struggle, Maurras was for ever pointing to areas in which the interests of the Germans and the Russians might be the same. So when 1939 came, and the Russo-German pact which brought an appalled astonishment to all liberal and socialistically-minded persons in the west, I felt not dissatisfied with the education I had in the pages of the *Action française*.

III

If this lesson in the operation of national interests, and in the secondary place of sentiments, was the most striking outcome of my apprenticeship with Maurras, as it affected my observation of practical politics, there were several other strands to his influence, and it is difficult to distinguish how far they went and where they led. It was the rich suggestiveness of many pages of Maurras, even of sentences, and their narcotic mellifluousness, which seduced me originally, and I certainly did not distinguish the elements of this charm, or give it a name. He was the proponent and carrier of a pre-digested Mediterranean culture, and I was the ignorant Anglo-Saxon lover, even in wintry Paris, of the land 'wo die Citronen blühen', or at any rate of the un–British lucidities of the superficies of Latin thought and expression. It was the sort of illusion which once affected young men before Walter Pater explaining the Renaissance, but this secret charm spread its tentacles right into the brutal day-to-day world of politics. It was years later that I came across Maurras's own explanation: 'Notre nationalisme commença par être esthétique.' Nor did I identify those more personal poisons of that love of death and emptiness which lurk under Maurras's devotions. However far back, psychologically, the attraction of Maurras's work began, the direction of my orientation was towards the open and public world. I saw Maurras, as he saw himself, as the defender of intelligence and of 'la cité', the western, ordered, Romanized world of which the traces round about me, in the thirties, were already faint enough. I might say that in Hitler's Germany I had smelt the wind from the steppes, the great formless wind of the barbarian invaders, the Attila of romanticism. This was not history but a vision. I had also read *La Défense de l'Occident* (Henry Massis) as well as dipped into Spengler. The Maurrasian analysis, which equated civilization with the boundaries of the Roman world, was for the time being acceptable to me, and I would not pretend that, in spite of all qualifications, it has not retained a certain hold, or at any rate a certain meaning for me. I certainly retain a profound conviction, in spite of all the frivolities we see in that field, that public life ought to be treated – and conducted – seriously. There is so much in the Maurrasian conception of these matters which is related specifically to French history and traditions that a continual work of interpretation is necessary if one is to understand its implications for us. It is in the direct irrelevance of much of Maurras's work that its fruitfulness for us lies. It does not so much command assent as work on the mind and provoke reflections.

The *Action Française* movement came to life on the dunghill of the Dreyfus affair. There are pitchforks still turning over that event and I feel no temptation to join them. The significant issues were the innocence or guilt of a particular army officer, in relation to a recurrently hostile foreign power, and the extent to which the considerations of justice to an individual should take precedence over the welfare and safety of the state. The liberal answer to that question is clear. It was not the answer Maurras gave. E.M. Forster put a softer – because imaginary – version of the same dilemma as follows: 'if I had to choose between betraying my country and betraying my friend, I hope I should have the guts to betray my country'. The historical background to all Maurras's political thinking was, of course, the French Revolution and the Reformation. There has been a continuous importing of French notions of abstract right, and social-democratic ideologies, into this country, but the *facts* behind us remain the constitutional struggles of the seventeenth century, with their very different outcome, and the Anglican church settlement which, whatever its defects, did not leave in the centre of the stage a bleak, individualistic Protestantism. And while Maurras brooded with anachronistic relish over Malherbe's admittedly magnificent verses inviting Louis XIII to 'take his thunder' against the Protestants of La Rochelle and destroy them, the most persistent political disruptors in England have been the Papists, who in Maurras's France can be cast in the role of defenders of order. No Englishman can swallow Maurras whole. That whole branch of Maurras's writing, which is concerned with a form of apologetics for the Roman church, is matter for digestion and reflection rather than assent. It consists in praise for her skill in bringing in a Latin discipline to destroy the pernicious judaizing element represented by the gospels themselves. Maurras knew how to give seductiveness to these paradoxes, with his references to Dante's 'sommo Giove / Che fosti in terra per noi crucifisso', and his assimilation of so much that is Christian to the pagan world.

IV

I find it difficult to imagine how far the work of Maurras can retain an interest for my juniors, among the different orientations of the present day. That it does retain some interest is a matter of fact, for here as well as in France there are people looking closely at his work who are young enough not to be blinded by the emotions of thirties' politics or of the quarrels surrounding Vichy and the occupation. For me it is a sympathetic and wrong-headed figure – as an actor on the scene rather than as a writer – that Maurras stays in my mind. It was a first visit to his native Provence, delayed till I was nearly sixty, and a visit to Martigues itself, which brought him vividly back to mind. He carried his complex and elaborately-related dogmatisms so consistently through his long life, to the court which condemned him for treason in 1945 and beyond that to his death, only a few months half-liberated, in 1952. His life was one of self-abnegation, if you call it abnegation to live toilsomely and simply, and without wife or family, in order to put your word in at each day's turn of public events. He founded his politics on his esthetics and that is a lunacy, and would be even if a man's esthetic were not, as it is, in the end something more personal and less admissible. I remember how, in one of his daily articles in 1935 or 1936, Maurras followed some even more than usually dashing excursion into the relationships existing between the then great powers with the apology: One would prefer to give this advice in the chamber of the king rather than in a public newspaper. The whole of his hallucination is there. For if there had been a king in France in the 1930s, it would not have been Maurras but Laval, or some similar master of sleight-of-hand, who would have been advising him. A publicist, even the most brilliant, and least of all the most honest, is not a politician. What really happens, in the political world, is a matter of the decisions of the men who, at a particular time, happen to be sitting in the seats of authority, subject to the pressures which, at that particular moment, bear upon them. It is not anyone's dream.

A Four Letter Word

It is an odd fact that, in a century in which it has, on the whole, paid writers to trade under a left-wing label, so few of the major figures have done so. For some of the most eminent figures – one need go no further than Yeats, Eliot, Pound, Lawrence, Wyndham Lewis – it has been necessary to enter special apologies, to explain how people so recalcitrant to the main stream of intellectual prejudice can be accepted as intellectually respectable in spite of it all. Something is wrong somewhere, and since the general managers of the trade cannot be at fault, something must be wrong with these eminent writers. It is fortunately not difficult to show that *something* is wrong, in each case, for anyone who dips a toe into the great sea of politics gets his feet dirty. None the less it is odd that none of these brilliant performers could quite swallow what might be called the great obligatory truths of the left, which all decent people take without choking: put compendiously, a belief in the harmony of democracy, large-scale organization, and individual self-expression. Of course the managers of the trade have become adept at various logomachies; one of the most useful has been the assimilation of literary innovation into the general notion of revolution, which has become a repository for all that is desirable. There are even people, not themselves anxious to promote the usual axioms of the left, who have been so far convinced by this as to be on the look-out for technical manifestations in literature which will reassure them that the world is not changing too fast.

But the world is changing fast, and not even formal rhyme-schemes will save us from this. The question remains, whether the hell-for-leather race for the incompatible goals of democracy, large-scale organization, and self-expression is the most intelligent form of political sport which can be engaged in at the present time. In raising this question here, there is no design of dragging *PN Review* into the combats which entertain politicians and their supporters, either in Parliament, the constituencies or the various perhaps more powerful fora which now exist outside. These have their proper places and actors. What has been lacking is the sort of pre-political discussion which the poetic intelligence can hardly avoid, when it becomes discursive, and which is of moment to everyone who has the interests of literature at heart, as distinct from the interests of the trade and its managers.

It is with this degree of disinterestedness, and no more, that this essay ventures upon an explanation so unfashionable that even my inured typewriter jibs at the enigmatic word. The word is – but before I utter it I must ask the reader to exercise an enormous forbearance and not to choke at it until he has digested several pages of my qualifications – the word is, *Tory*. It is as shop-soiled as any in the dictionary, and has long been the property of a political party which has no conception at all of its meaning, so that a voter who was a *Tory*, in the sense about to be elucidated, might as soon find himself voting Labour or Conservative – so-called Labour as soon as so-called Conservative; or he might, truth to tell, not think it worth his while to vote for either. Only I beg the reader, for a moment, to dissociate himself from these quarrels and to turn his mind to the quarrels of three centuries ago. They have their relevance to our affairs.

Dr Johnson, whose Erse was not very good, thought that the derivation of the word Tory was 'from an Irish word signifying a savage'. My own Erse is no better, but the compilers of the Oxford Dictionary, whom one must suppose to be careful about such matters, say the root of the word is *toraidhe, –aighe*, a pursuer, from *toir*, to pursue. As it was English settlers that these tories pursued, perhaps Johnson's rough translation was not so far out. It was by Cromwell's charmers that the word seems to have been given its first tinge of constitutional respectability, for they used it of any Irish Royalist in arms. In Charles II's reign it was used of those who thought that the hereditary principle, so recently reestablished by the Restoration, should not immediately be imperilled by the exclusion of James from the throne on the grounds that he was a Roman Catholic. The innuendo was that such persons, for the most part Anglican High Churchmen, were no better than a lot of murderous Teagues. Not for the first time in history, a name invented as a term of abuse was adopted as a label by the party so insulted. James did not repay this loyalty, but by the Declaration of Indulgence of 1687–8 attempted to remove the disabilities of all dissenters, Protestant and Papist alike. This unparalleled act of liberalism was not well received. Like most liberal acts of government it was open to other interpretations. James was suspected of indulging the Protestant dissenters only to make way for the Papists. Moreover, the Declaration purported to set aside Acts of Parliament, which did not promise a very liberal course once the Papists were in the saddle. The strongest opposition to James came from the very quarters which had insisted on his right to succeed Charles II. It was headed by the Archbishop of Canterbury, Sancroft, with the support of six other bishops including Ken of Bath and Wells, and Trelawny of Bristol. James was tactless enough to imprison these seven in the Tower, which did their cause a world of good. Too much good, it may be, for it was not the bishops' cause which triumphed. Soon James was out of the country and William and Mary were in his place. That was the Revolution miscalled Glorious.

The consequences of that affair are as complicated as the subsequent history of England. There were scrupulous persons who could not in conscience take the Oath of Allegiance to William and Mary because they could not break the oath they had sworn to James II and his heirs. These included eight bishops – Sancroft and Ken among them – and four hundred other clergy. Many would say they had more sanctity than sense. At least their action makes a pleasant change from the temporizing which usually wins the day in politics. They lost their day, and the non-juring group dwindled to nothing in the course of the eighteenth century. They had chosen a quixotic course, to an extent that disqualified them even from being Tories.

The bits that remained, for the Tories to pick up, were few and unsatisfactory. Yet nothing is more striking, in the eighteenth century which was given over increasingly to Whiggery – the forces of money taking over increasingly from the old landed rights while deism and rationalism ate away at the old foundations of theology and, it might be said, imagination – than the tenacity of the older constitutional thinking. Blackstone's *Commentaries on the Laws of England* so to speak demonstrated the value of what was being lost, while it was being lost. There is of course a sense in which any general exposition of the law gives the illusion of a stability which never existed, and of a coherence which owes more to the mind of the expositor than to the current facts of any one age. Blackstone did not exactly invent the constitution, but he drew attention to the great, half-forgotten residue of laws, written and unwritten, explicit and implied in the practice of Englishmen over the centuries of the country's formation. It is for this reason that the *Commentaries* retain their interest, to this day, for anyone who still thinks that it matters how the country is put together. There is much that throws light on our deepest political attitudes. That the work caused some shock among Blackstone's contemporaries may be gathered from his *Postscript* to the *Preface* of 1765; one may also gather in what quarters the shock was most felt.

Many of the positions in the work 'were vehemently attacked by zealots of all (even opposite) denominations, religious as well as civil; by some with a greater, by others with a less degree of acrimony.' Blackstone was the first Vinerian professor at Oxford. He was by way of being an intellectual innovator, attempting not only a new systematization of English law but a new method of education based on his more systematic elucidation of the subject. But in constitutional matters he was so far from being an inno-vator that his one passionate concern was to draw attention to what was *there*, as he conceived it, embedded in the laws and customs of the country; and in doing so he drew attention to much that the Whigs did not want to hear of, that they hoped to see eroded or merely wished away. Wishing away does in the end get rid of constitutional attitudes people can be taught not to like, and perhaps the great result of Blackstone's work was to set up a programme of what was to be abolished. The next stage was the Benthamite construction of a system of law based on the reformer's fantasy of what people wanted, or what a reasonable man ought to want, if he was reasonable in the way that Bentham was.

What Blackstone saw was that mixed constitution which became famous in the misinterpretations of foreign observers.

> If the supreme power were lodged in any one of the three branches separately, we must be exposed to the inconven-iences of either absolute monarchy, aristocracy, or democracy; and so want two of the three principal ingredients of good polity, either virtue, wisdom, or power... But the constitu-tional government of this island is so admirably tempered and compounded, that nothing can endanger or hurt it, but destroying the equilibrium of power between one branch of the legislature and the rest. For if ever it should happen that the independence of any one of the three should be lost, or

that it should become subservient to the views of either of the other two, there would soon be an end of our constitution.

It is hardly too much to say that to bring about this subservience, and so to subvert the constitution as understood by Blackstone, has been the standing objective, viewed with varying degrees of clarity, ever since, by those who are generally regarded as enlightened persons.

None of the subversions of the constitution has met with more general and more persistent approval than those which aimed at the position of the Church. So great is the success which has attended these subversions, that even among practising Anglicans there is scarcely even a shadowy apprehension of what has been given up. Since these subjects are now out of most people's way, it is perhaps necessary to say that the roots of the matter go back beyond the Reformation which for Romans – but not Anglicans – was the start of the Church of England. 'Christianity is part of the laws of England', says Blackstone, and backs this with the recital of a bit of an Act of Henry VI: 'Scripture est common ley, surquel touts manieres de leis sont fondues'. There would have been some confusion any time after the thirty-fourth year of Henry VI if that provision had been invoked in a literal sense. Still, the medieval, and the original Anglican assumption, was that members of the state were members of the Church, and it followed that there were certain disabilities for any who were not. In the medieval view, such outsiders were fit only for burning, and the law provided accordingly. The modern English view was less extreme, once Bloody Mary, in the last fling of papal power, had sickened people at large by her roastings at Smithfield and elsewhere. The laws against recusants under Elizabeth were laws against treason, for the Pope claimed to have absolved the Queen's subjects from their allegiance – a very practical point which was welcome to the King of Spain. As late as 1605 Guy Faux and his friends showed, also in the most practical way, that loyalty could not be counted on in Papists. This aroma of disaffection was not dissipated in a hurry. After the murder of Charles I by a tribunal without legal standing a certain aroma of disaffection hung about Protestant dissenters as well, though perhaps less pungent, for it was a *homely* smell, whereas the smell of Papists was not only suspect but *foreign*. It was in either case a doubt about loyalty, rather than a scruple on a point of doctrine, which lay at the root of the civil disabilities – of increasing mildness – suffered by dissenters up to the time of the Catholic Emancipation Act of the early nineteenth century. The two were never entirely disentangled; dissent whether Catholic or Protestant implied a degree of dissociation from the Christian polity which the realm was supposed, however implausibly, to be. All this seems nonsense now, for it is thought that everyone has a right to disaffection, and that religion is not a matter of truth but of opinion.

Looking now over the volumes of Blackstone, which I browsed over more than twenty-five years ago, I recognize that many of my notions of government must have been, if not formed, at any rate sharpened, on that work. It was the epoch of the 'Reflections on Marvell's Ode', if that is not too grand a way of referring to my preoccupations at the time. That meant that such writers as Filmer and Algernon Sidney, key figures of the political discussions of the seventeenth century, were in my mind. It is perhaps fair to make the point that such reading was the work of my odd moments, and that my days were spent, within earshot, so to speak, of the centre of government: so that, whatever the appearances to the contrary, the essays written at that time were not the product of someone ignorant of the mechanisms of government in the twentieth century, but on the contrary of someone who, in his brief leisures, was concerned to identify the elements which had somehow gone missing from the political discourse of the day, even though the realities of politics seemed to call for them.

There is no question now of resuscitating Samuel Johnson's definition of *Tory* and offering it to anyone as a political programme. It is not merely that no one prominently on the scene in politics would be likely to understand it; there is the more radical inconvenience that it is simply unusable. For Johnson a Tory was 'One who adheres to the ancient constitution of the state, and the apostolic hierarchy of the church of England'. The term was 'opposed to a *whig*', and *Whig* was 'The name of a faction'. If these notions, and the history which lies behind them, are not directly usable in a party programme, they at least provide the elements of a possible criticism of contemporary political manners.

A *Toryism* of this kind not ambitious of political success but only of contributing a little, in time, to the reorientation of minds which – whatever else may be said about them – certainly require some treatment of that kind. One would have to start by washing away all that rubbish of imaginary rights which are conceived of as a sort of metaphysical property of each individual, as if there could be rights which did not impose a duty on somebody else. 'The Rights of Man' is a cant phrase, covering a series of quite concrete problems involved in some proposed redistribution of social duties. The 'rights of women', as we have the phrase now, does not have quite the same degree of abstract futility, for no one is in any doubt that whatever is claimed is at the expense of somebody.

Once the abstract 'individual', with his imaginary 'rights' is out of the way, one can, starting from the limited physical person, who moves around on the earth, identify the particular obligations which arise from the presence, round about, of other physical persons in like case. The web is of great complexity, in the twentieth century, and one of the few certain things about it is that it is *local*, not quite the same in one place as in another, in spite of the kaleidoscopic effect produced by rapid transport. Another certainty, well understood in the past but now also subject to kaleidoscopic effects which produce a faint dizziness, is that the web is *temporal*, has its place in time and cannot be the instantaneous creation of someone who happens to be thinking something at the moment. In fact our thoughts, our language, our institutions, our *rights* – if the word cannot be escaped – are historical. The present moment was preceded by the previous moment which was preceded by ... and there never was a moment when any of these things changed in a flash. So we are caught in space and time, whether we like it or not. If you go forward without looking back you are still impelled by the past. It is a highly inadequate realism, whether in literature or in politics, which pretends to take account only of contemporary influences.

One cannot argue from these considerations to the maintenance of ancient institutions. Everything temporal will also crumble in time. But one can argue from them to the need for understanding old institutions, especially those still surviving in some form, which may therefore still serve us, indeed other things being equal are more likely to serve us lastingly than is last week's so-called invention, about which the most certain thing is that it is not so new as is at the moment made out.

So much – and it is not much, except an invitation to reflection – for Johnson's 'ancient constitution of the state'. For the 'apostolical hierarchy of the church of England', its public character as a vehicle of truth was impugned by the temporizing of politicians. The two key dates are 1689 and 1850. At the former date, under the same Crown, the religion of Scotland became different from the religion of England. At the latter date, a collateral apostolic line was brought to this country, with territorial claims which drove a wedge into the fabric of the church of England. On both these occasions the state was announcing that it dissociated itself from the truth and was concerned only with political expediency. This should be understood by all who expect a government to espouse a cause, uphold a right or right a wrong.

So the surviving Tory lives on, in an obscure ill-understood opposition, profoundly sceptical in all those fields in which popular belief is most widespread and passion rises highest; credulous himself, most would say, in an ill-defined faith going back for two thousand years or established from all eternity, as he would by definition say. At least the profound scepticism with regard to contemporary politics will not seem out of place, to anyone who sets a value on any truth at all.

Poetry and Myth

The assertion about the myth-kitty with which Philip Larkin astonished the world some years ago is perhaps better understood as a piece of autobiography than as a statement about poetry at large. The young man bemused by Yeats had the impression of being relieved of his load of dreams by Thomas Hardy, whose dreams were certainly of a different kind. One might leave it at that, had not the author of this dramatic announcement added glosses which suggested that he was putting forward a critical principle. You 'have to be terribly educated, you have to have read everything, to know these things', and that would not do for a man from St John's College, who has spent most of his life in libraries.

> As a guiding principle I believe that every poem must be its own sole freshly-created universe, and therefore have no belief in 'tradition' or a common myth-kitty or casual allusions in poems to other poems or poets, which last I find unpleasantly like the talk of literary understrappers letting you see they know the right people.

This last, rather spiteful little point, must be one to which Larkin attaches some importance, for he makes it again elsewhere: 'you've got somehow to work them' – your bits of reading – 'in to show that you are working them in'. These asides are probably meant to be read as the apologia of a poet who had evaded the impact of Eliot and Pound, and wished to make this a matter for congratulation. It is, however, hardly possible to ignore major innovations, made by one's seniors, without paying a penalty – which some think Larkin has paid.

Larkin's contention seems to be that he has exemplified a higher form of originality than that of the mere literary innovator. 'Its own sole freshly-created universe' – there must be some exaggeration in that, surely! It suggests a dynamic which puts to shame the hero of the first chapter of *Genesis*. In any age other than ours the phrase would have been regarded as mere wind; but that, perhaps, shows how truly original and – at the same time – of the age, it is. It is one step beyond that originality of the 'individual' expressing 'himself' ('herself') of which we hear so much. But of course it is only rhetoric, or nonsense. A poem can have meaning only in terms of words other people use, and which we have from our ancestors. It is a part and not a whole or, if one allows it to be a whole, it can be so only in the sense in which individual people may be 'wholes', as members of a company.

When, therefore, Larkin says, 'But to me the whole of the ancient world, the whole of classical and biblical mythology means very little', it must be taken either as confessing, how properly it is not for me to say, to intellectual and imaginative limitations of asphyxiating narrowness, or as a boast of staggering proportions. For he goes on, 'and I think using them today not only fills poems full of dead spots but dodges the writer's duty to be original.' Why 'today'? How does it differ from other days? Because the reader cannot be expected to know anything of the things of which he must know something if he is to read any of the European masters from Homer to – up to but not including – Philip Larkin.

The truth is, one must know something, in order to read anything. Knowing less does not increase one's chances of being original, though it may increase one's chances of imagining that one is. Certainly, if one can attach no meaning to 'the whole of the ancient world, the whole of classical and biblical mythology', better keep clear of those subjects in one's poetry. None the less, it is proper to concede that these are matters about which every literate person – including Larkin – has some knowledge. Nobody could pursue his reading of English poetry very far without picking up a smattering, and a more intensive reading is likely to take one deeper in. Better understand something about the Christian religion if you want to read Herbert or Dr Johnson, let alone such a damned foreigner as Dante, who by the way seems to have been incapable of distinguishing between pagan and Christian mythology, for he speaks of 'il sommo Giove, / Che fosti in terra per noi crucifisso'. There is however the other question, of 'the writer's duty'. Clearly a man may *write* poems without much consciousness of Christianity or of pagan mythology, though of course he will, in the west, not have escaped their influence entirely, for our languages are full of it. If he does use this material overtly, he will make 'dead spots' – lucky if they are only *spots* – unless his understanding, however fragmentary, reaches to a grasp of some contemporary significance it might have, which can only appear in the language in which he speaks of it. So, unless one is to say *a priori* that references to this material are banned, which would be a political, not a critical principle, then we are back at the most solid of all critical dogmas, That the proof of the pudding is in the eating. Yet the problem of mythology is deeper than this. It has to do, precisely, with the standing of that 'experience' of which the twentieth century makes so much. Of course we all have experience; it would be difficult to avoid, as one knocks around the world, or even if one stayed in one place, behind drawn curtains. It is the conscious – though, maybe, not the most important – part of this beastly business of living that we all engage in. The question is, are our feelings about things some sort of absolute? Or can they be checked against some wider reference? And if so, how? It is certainly essential to the possibility of any sort of civilization that the answers to these latter questions should not be entirely negative. It is essential to any communication, to human life itself which, whatever it may be, is certainly not that of any individual floating in space. Mythology is one of the vehicles by which the human being can escape from his solipsism. Through it, one stands for all, as in the Christian religion, or for some of all, or for part of all, as in the pagan mythologies. The old gods were put to flight, but not altogether chased off the scene, by Christ, and if he could be erased from men's apprehension it would not be in favour of a vacuum.

The subject, like any of the fundamental questions which can be asked about art, takes one beyond the frontiers of literary criticism, and deep into it. Is a girl called Sue less a figure of mythology than one called Diana? The question in each case is the reach of her typicality, which is a measure of her significance for other people. Perhaps Larkin should read Hardy again, and consider this question.

II

Sir Philip Sidney, who says he 'slipped into the title of a poet', and that it was for him an 'unelected vocation', was driven to *An Apologie for Poetry* by the silly things that were said about it. His explanations creak a little, because of the Platonic machinery, which we do not handle very well in our century, but they contain a remarkable amount of sense and observation. With a wholesome emphasis on what is *made*, for all to see, as against the modern emphasis on what is alleged to have been felt, he says that the poet, 'lifted up with the vigour of his own invention, doth grow in effect another nature, in making things either better than nature bringeth forth, or, quite anew'. It is the Aristotelian *mimesis*, an imitation of the processes of nature, rather than a copying from her. So, in place of Larkin's 'prime responsibility ... to the experience itself', which he is 'trying to keep from oblivion for its own sake', we have the invention of 'forms such as never were in Nature, as the Heroes, Demigods, Cyclops, Chimeras, Furies, and such like'. That might bring a laugh of triumph to the lips of all who can make nothing of 'the whole of the ancient world'. A large claque can be organized, at any moment, for doing without the heraldic beasts. But Sidney can restate his argument in a manner which makes it less easy to set aside. For 'right poets', he says, 'be they which most properly do imitate to teach and delight, and to imitate borrow nothing of what is, hath been, or shall be; but range, only reined with learned discretion, into the divine consideration of what may be, and should be.' That is to say, the party of the hippogriff is the party of invention, which takes its stand on bringing something new into the world, as against the party of preservatism, which thinks, with Larkin, that 'the impulse to preserve lies at the bottom of all art'.

Sidney's conception of poetry has to be considered in relation to a vatic function, of those 'that did imitate the inconceivable excellencies of God'. That language may not suit, but it is important to realize that the imitation in order to set examples, of which Sidney and other older writers make so much, is a doctrine of *creation*. It is easy to read as a mere bit of school moralism, Sidney's summary: 'whatsoever the philosopher saith shall be done, he' – the peerless poet – 'giveth a perfect picture of it in some one by whom he presupposeth it was done'. In fact, Sidney emphasizes 'a perfect picture', and says that the poet 'yieldeth to the powers of the mind an image of that whereof the philosopher bestoweth but a wordish description'. It is a process which involves a 'purifying of wit', an 'enriching of memory, enabling of judgement, and enlarging of conceit' – precisely, the rewards of a humane education, as they ought to be. And so it is that such a figure as

Sue Bridehead enabled readers of *Jude the Obscure* to understand better what was happening to themselves and others. The image did undoubtedly 'strike, pierce' and 'possess the sight of the soul' more than any mere theory, defined the type and, for good or ill, gave it followers. It is not for the poet to follow, but to invent.

That leaves us with the problem – a whole range of problems – about the relationships of what is invented to the world supposed real. Bacon, who had, no doubt, read the *Apologie*, took this matter up in *The Advancement of Learning*, with less sureness of touch, it may be, because he was not himself of the 'unelected vocation' of poet. For him poetry was 'nothing else but FEIGNED HISTORY'; the use of it was

> to give some shadow of satisfaction to the mind of man in those points wherein the nature of things doth deny it ... because true History representeth actions and events more ordinary and less interchanged, therefore Poesy feigns them with more rareness and more unexpected and alternative variations.

We are approaching the realm of half-truth which confuses art with sentimentality, art with ingenuity, and art with mere vicarious sexual satisfaction, and cuts it off from reality. That was not Sidney's notion. For him it was a form of reality, which was invented. But Bacon goes on, with a sentence which seems to sweep away both the poetical and the divine: 'And therefore [Poesy] was ever thought to have some participation of divineness, because it doth raise and erect the mind, by submitting the shows of things to the desires of the mind, whereas reason doth buckle and bow the mind unto the nature of things.' The coming thing was not poetry but the inductive method.

III

With Shelley the unkillable spirit of Platonism is with us again, to bedevil our understanding of his formulations. But, in one respect at least, we are better off than with the author of *The Advancement of Learning*. For Shelley was undoubtedly a poet, though he is an unfashionable one. So he occupies the essential common ground with Sidney, and states his claim in a more unmistakeable manner than the modest soldier, who merely 'slipped into' being a poet. 'Poetry ... differs in this respect from logic, that it is not subject to the control of the active powers of the mind, and that its birth and recurrence have no necessary connexion with the consciousness or will.' So much for recording that moment when Philip Larkin got up for a piss. The claim that it is with the recording of some such precious moment of consciousness that poetry is primarily concerned is implicit in acres of journalistic verse produced in our time, but it is a fiction of the critics, not unrelated to the attempt made by I.A. Richards, in *Principles of Literary Criticism*, to establish a positive basis for the valuation of literature. In practice the poet finds himself with a poem, which cannot be checked, by the poet or anyone else, against the golden moment which is to be kept from oblivion 'for its own sake'.

Despite Shelley's manic tone, and his much greater facility in handling abstractions, the poetic function as he defines it is recognizably the same as that of which Sidney speaks. In neither is a mere copying of the everyday world what is in question; for Shelley poetry 'strips the veil of familiarity from the world, and lays bare the naked and sleeping beauty, which is the spirit of its forms'. Again, it 'transmutes all that it touches, and every form moving within the radiance of its presence is changed by wondrous sympathy to an incarnation of the spirit which it breathes'. He is, decidedly, of the party of the hippogriff. Yet all the poet's inventions have their origin in a human faculty, which is 'a going out of our own nature, and an identification of ourselves with the beautiful which exists in thought, action, or person, not our own'. To 'imagine intensively and comprehensively', a man 'must put himself in the place of another and of many others; the pains and pleasures of the species must become his own.' Sidney makes more of the example, Shelley more of abstract laws, but for both what gives the poet's images their significance is the generality perceived in and through the sensible presentation.

Mere Platonism! But not at all. Both Sidney and Shelley are observers of a process in which they have participated. The involuntary element in composition, of which both speak, is that which 'defeats the curse which binds us to be subjected to the accident of surrounding impressions', in Shelley's words. 'It makes us the inhabitants of a world to which the familiar world

is a chaos. ... It creates anew the universe, after it has been anni-
hilated in our minds by the recurrence of impressions blunted by
iteration.' Precisely; what we have seen and felt, over the years,
establish their own relationships, among themselves, and the
poem which emerges is a piece of stuff torn from that pattern.

But what is that pattern? No one can say exactly. But the
figures which appear in it – which move in it, for nothing is stable
– are the giants and heroes of the world, as far as we have made
them our own, as far, that is, as our nature has been capable of
'going out', and so far as 'the pains and pleasures of the species'
have become our 'own'. Such figures, half-figures, ghosts, fragments, are, of their nature, mythological, whether or not they
bear, for us, a name you could find in Lemprière.

Poetry and Sincerity

Modernity has been going on for a long time. Not within living memory has there ever been a day when young writers were not coming up, with shining faces and a threat of iconoclasm, to destroy the illusions of their elders and the forms and rules into which they had hardened. Indeed such conduct has, for several generations at least, been so perfectly the tradition that most of the old now belong to it. It is *the* tradition, so far as the literature of the twentieth century is concerned, just as revolution, in some degree or other, has become the political tradition – the amount of novelty, in both cases, being much exaggerated by the patter that goes with it.

The theory of modernity propounded by Donald Wesling in *The Chances of Rhyme: Device and Modernity* (1980) is that there are a lot of rules of rhyme and prosody – all pretty well bashed by now, one would think – and that to be modern is to bash still harder, yet to find, miracle of miracles, that the structure never entirely disintegrates. What is the hammer which is used in this vain effort at destruction? It is 'sincerity' – that venerable *pons asinorum* – so that the whole thing boils down to what was neatly put by Herbert Read, more than fifty years ago, as follows:

> The modern poet does not deny the right of regular verse to exist, or to be poetic. He merely affirms that poetry is sincerity, and has no essential alliance with regular schemes of any sort. He reserves the right to adapt his rhythm to his mood, to modulate his metre as he progresses.

For 'poetry is sincerity' Professor Wesling reads 'everything in the poem, even the prosody, bears the mark of the poet's personality'. These are not easy conceptions. Nor does one get out of the difficulties by asserting, with Philip Larkin – in unfamiliar guise as a metaphysician – that 'every poem must be its own freshly created universe'.

W.P. Ker said soberly, some seventy years ago:

> When you talk about the form of a poem, what do you mean? We talk of the form of a poem, we talk of its matter: it may be assumed that in this case as in others the two terms are correlative.

But as soon as one begins to examine into the meaning of the terms, they not only elude you, but they even exchange their meanings.

For the poet actually writing a poem these categories simply do not exist at all. The first necessity is to have something to say, but even this will be present only as an impending cloud, and to assert its necessity is to make an *ex post facto* analysis. The moment announces itself by words conveying a rhythm or, it may be, by a rhythm conveying a few words. There must be poets – Roy Fuller or the Poet Laureate – who take a solemn decision at some stage that there shall be *x* syllables to a line and a rhyme-scheme *abab* or whatever it is. I suspect that, in the heyday of, say, the sonnet, it was rather that the rhythms and rhymes so presented themselves, the language being at a stage in which that form was the natural vehicle for minds heavy with a certain class of utter-ance. For Sidney to 'look in his heart and write' was to write a sonnet; this form, then so little exploited in England, offering a way so clear that it was *the* way to say what he had to say. For the Elizabethan and Jacobean dramatists, some variant of the iambic pentameter was the indisputable language of the stage, so that the discourse came in that form till Shakespeare tore the medium to pieces and there seemed to be no more to be said that way. The makers of the ballads must be supposed not to have hesitated over the form they should use. For the contemporary writer, no such resolute direction presents itself. Yet the problem remains the same: How is the poet to disburden himself of his thoughts with conviction?

The history of versification is really nothing else than the history of how such utterance has been possible, and there is more of necessity than of freedom in it, unless one can talk of a freedom to avoid the unnecessary. The conception Wesling appears to have, of 'art sentences' supported by all manner of rhetorical devices, so that the writer 'separates his language from ordinary language by a conscious patterning' is surely utterly wrong-headed, the product of a critical decadence which is suffering from too many books, too much leisure, too much discourse accompanying a shrivelled performance. Only the rhetorician, not of a silver age but of an age of tin or plastic, could ask 'what devices a work employs to achieve a relative transparence, or

seeming spontaneity of rhetoric'. Such a question is surely
designed to mislead both reader and writer as to the nature of its
alleged subject-matter. It is calculated to increase the already
overwhelming number of transgressions in verse by people nature
never intended for poets. No less sinister is the spurious contrast
between 'literary dialect' and 'the vernacular' and between
'literary poetry and inferior or non-literary poetry'.

Such an emphasis on the wilful elements in verse reflects a critical milieu in which too much is made of the separateness of
'poetry' from ordinary speech on the one hand and from good
workmanlike prose on the other. The root of language is that
vulgar *eloquentia* of which Dante wrote, and which he distinguished from the secondary speech 'which the Romans called
grammar' in which we can be 'guided and instructed' only by 'the
expenditure of much time, and by assiduous study'. 'Of these two
kinds of speech', as Dante says, 'the vernacular is the nobler ...
necessary for all ... even women and children.' (It is universality
Dante is seeking to indicate by this last, now offensive, phrase.)
The nursery rhyme is so far from being something to be dismissed
with 'failed poetry' and other 'sub-literary genres' that it is the
original and most important element in poetic education. Lose
that – as it is being lost – and an essential tie with the language we
learned 'by imitating our nurses', as Dante says, is gone:

> Gay go up and gay go down
> To ring the bells of London Town

or

> Hink, spink, the puddings stink,
> The fat begins to fry,
> Nobody at home but jumping Joan,
> Father, mother and I.

Without such things it is not conceivable that Shakespeare would
have written – if he did not rather heave out of memory, with
more or less variation:

> Jog on, jog on, the footpath way,
> And merrily hent the stile-a;
> A merry heart goes all the day,
> Your sad tires in a mile-a.

'Poetry takes on a life beyond techniques', says Wesling, meaning that this happens after 1795 – his date for the beginning of Romanticism and so of modernism – and that thereafter rhymes and all his array of other devices are suspect. This timing is historically myopic. Poetry as the thing to be said, the thought to be disburdened, has *always* taken priority over the abstractions of 'technique'. Nursery rhymes actually *say* things; even the counting-out of a game rhyme is a meaning to be conveyed and one of great seriousness.

To maintain the relationship of verse with workmanlike prose is a need not less frequently ignored. Because the writing of 'poetry' is encouraged on a doctrine of self-expression – a luxury-derivative from that religion of democracy which has so largely replaced Christianity – there is a sort of vulgarization of creation, of the kind adumbrated by Philip Larkin. Thousands who could not write a straight sentence of prose to convey some ordinary matter of fact, are encouraged to believe that they are engaged in a superior activity because their lines do not quite reach the margin and are therefore called verse.

It might be too much to say that no one who cannot write prose should be allowed to write verse, but certainly no one should be admitted to any of those myriad courses which purport to teach the writing of verse, until he has read at least one book each of Swift and Defoe and can write a page which is not too utterly disgraceful by their standards.

Poetry – verse in any serious usage of the term – is a receptacle for sense which cannot be put into prose, and which burdens the speaker until it is said. 'Lully, lulla, thou little tiny child' is a paradigm of the art; the assonance and half rhyme, and the rhythm, are rigorously essential to the meaning to be unloaded. The line says what cannot be said otherwise. Poetry is precisely that; all other speech hangs more or less loosely. Only the greatest poets maintain this degree of rigour at any length.

We live amidst such a plethora of bad verse, in an age of such disastrous facility of speech and writing of all kinds, that the very notion of the rarity of humanly indispensable utterance is on the way to being lost. Real speech has to be surrounded by silence. We get this impression – in part, admittedly, because of what has been lost – in the fragments which remain to us of early literatures – from our own Anglo-Saxon, for example. What is certainly not illusory is the growing facility, over the centuries, in the use of specific forms. We see the author of *Gawain* introducing variants to avoid the facility into which Langland is already falling. I regret not having made more use of the opportunities I once had for learning Anglo-Saxon and Middle English, and speak very tentatively on these matters, but I suppose that the relative slackness of Langland's verse represents the growing unsuitability, for the language of the fourteenth century, of a form of parallelism which was the product of a stronger, inflected, language.

Chaucer's triumphant solution to the problem was the adaptation of French versification and rhyme-schemes, so far as but not farther than the language allowed. This adaptation must have been felt as a release, not as the entry into new trammels. It brought a new clarity into English verse; the language itself grew clearer:

> Hyd, Absolon, thy gilte tresses clere;
> Ester, ley thou thye mekness al a-doun;
> Hyd, Ionathas, al thy friendly manere;
> Penalopee, and Marcia Catoun,
> Mak of your wyfhod no comparisoun;
> Hyde ye your beautes...

– and so on. It is a measure of the genius of Chaucer that he could perceive and realize these new possibilities of the language throughout the eight thousand lines or so of *Troilus and Criseyde*. His contemporary, John Gower, is fumbling by comparison, or at any rate mechanical. Gower's French poems are better than his English poems and that was no doubt because there was more in his aural memory to help him in French.

The balance between the degree of memory which indicates a direction of movement, and a degree of emancipation from it which enables the words to come freshly, is what determines the rise and fall of particular verse forms. The work of Chaucer determined without appeal the direction of the future development of English verse, but it is rarely that one feels that his immediate successors are as at home as he was with the new demands, while the old way had fallen into a measure of old-fashionedness which made it unusable. There are those in whom a residual alliteration remains; there are those in whom rhyme falls into a simple trot; there are – even up to Sackville, magnificent though he some-

times is – those who appear to find the structures they use somewhat unwieldy. Some of the best verse of the fifteenth and early
sixteenth centuries is by men who were applying Chaucer's
discoveries to a different variant of the language – Scots – without
much in the way of technical novelty. The real infusion of easiness
into a variety of rhymed forms in English must have come from
popular poetry:

> I have a newe gardyn,
> & newe is be-gunne;
> swych an-other gardyn
> know I not under sunne,

or

> I must go walke the wood so wyld,
> & wander here & there.

Conflating the history, one may say that perfection in a new kind
– a lesser achievement than Chaucer's but still an immense
triumph of lucidity – came with Wyatt, who of course drew on
the technical achievements of French and Italian. He may be said
to have made these achievements truly at home by assimilating to
his versions of them the singableness of popular verse. One knows
how, a little later, Sidney still had an ear for the border ballads,
and no doubt he was not alone in this. Perhaps it is not fair to take
Charles d'Orléans, in spite of his long years in England, as an
example of the difficulty of making a transfer of techniques from
one language to another, but it is worth noting how his competent enough English verses fail altogether to show the life of his
rondeaux and ballades in French.

Marks of a new confidence at once in the aural qualities of
English verse and in its ability to convey whatever needs to be
said, are everywhere in Elizabethan poetry. Something new
appears with Gascoigne – whose merits are still hardly enough
recognized – in the realistic ease with which he lays before us,
when a prisoner in the Low Countries, his insistent worries about
the fate of his gun. Not for nothing did this accomplished
performer urge poets not to worry too much about technique but
first to be sure that they really had something to say. In the move
towards suppleness and lucidity, verse, at this epoch, leads prose
by rather more than a short head, and it is this, no doubt, which

gave confidence – sometimes excessive confidence – in the writing of long poems. The pressure to speak in ways prose cannot manage must always be the motive for verse, and there was still much that prose could not manage. It is in Spenser that the ability to speak at length without losing the thread either of aural or semantic satisfactions, first achieved a new suppleness. He demonstrated this suppleness through complicated stanzas and thousands of lines, and his occasional superficial archaisms will not distract anyone who reads him at length from the general urbanity of his language – an indispensable contribution to later developments.

The Elizabethan and Jacobean eras left English a mature language – that is to say one always threatened by the nibblings of decline. It seems odd if not ungrateful to talk of the varied achievements of the seventeenth century in this way, but they became varied by limiting themselves in one direction or another – as who could do otherwise, after Shakespeare? There are the refinements of the song-writers, often exquisite, but unable to go beyond Campion and Shakespeare; there are the specialist achievements of the Metaphysicals and related poets. There is Milton's personal form of elaboration. Above all – as regards significance for later times – there is the movement which took the heroic couplet from Ben Jonson to Dryden, with a variety of interesting manifestations on the way. With the possible exception of the song-writers – who however have a new tone to offer, identifiable only in their day – these were all ways of pushing the subject-matter of poetry in new directions. The couplet was perhaps the nearest thing to a deliberate aim at a new rhetoric, an attempt to look smarter than prose which was in fact overtaking verse as an expository medium. This is one of the few examples in the history of English verse of a development which put a lid on what the poet had to say rather than took it off and here, a driving force was the sharper opportunities which the closed couplet gave to satire.

Until perfected. For when Pope had done all that could be done in the way of closing the couplet and regulating the caesura it was not long before the familiarity of the preferred pattern became too great to be borne. Whatever may be said for this or that later exponent of the form, it needed the full mind of Wordsworth to replace it decisively; he felt the need to do away

with baubles and to speak as 'a man speaking to men'. At this
point, Wesling would say, a new world began, although others
would say that there was the same motive for change that there
had always been.

That is already nearly two hundred years ago. Wesling sees a
new Romantic rocket shot from the first about 1910, and
although he speaks boldly of 'many major poets' since that date,
in any serious historical perspective it would be difficult to
substantiate that description. It is hard to find much radical
novelty in English verse (in which I include that written in
America) after 1920, which is not to say that there are not to be
found a few people who have been impelled by a hitherto
unspoken content to invent new tones and occasional new
rhythms. To liberate the language, even ever so little, from the
shadow of what has become familiar, and walk a few paces on firm
ground, is still the business of the poet, as it always was. A
language so worn by use as ours is may give the illusion that
anything can be said in it, but the difficulties are certainly not less
than they were, and may well be greater. Professor Wesling tells
us that Miss Wesling, a poet aged seven, speaks 'as an individual'.
She should place a steadying hand on her father's arm and suggest
that he looks up her sources.

The Poet and the Translator

The man whose memory we are honouring this evening was one for whom Latin was assuredly not a dead language. He was moreover one who knew what poetry is — a qualification by no means to be taken for granted. 'The words which Vergil uses and the verse in which he sets them', as he put it at the beginning of *Vergil's Troy*, mattered to him not for any technical points that could be made about them but for their relationship to what used to be called — and what Jackson Knight calls — the poet's 'vision'. 'It is worth while,' he says, 'to watch how they dominate perception.' I should prefer to say: how the poet's perceptions dominate and determine the words and rhythms, but perhaps the difference of meaning is not so great as it seems. A similar sensitivity to the essentials of poetry is indicated by an incident recorded in Wilson Knight's biography of his brother. He tells how Jackson once heard an actor who had 'a striking voice, perfect modulation, and continual variation, speaking Shakespeare.' Jackson was not taken in. With these charms ringing in his ears, he objected that the actor was 'always delivering the same pattern.' Wilson Knight comments — and who should know better than he? — 'The vocal patterns were themselves complicated, but they recurred; they were not freshly made in correspondence to every new twist in the poetry.' That is fine criticism. It comes very near to the elusive difficulties I want to explore — or rather make an excursion into — tonight.

I am not a scholar. I am not even — as I fear will be too evident — a lecturer: a less grave deficiency perhaps, still it is one, on an occasion such as this. These memorial lectures are, charitably, allowed to be given not only by classical scholars but by 'other persons with classical interests'. I must be one of those. There are people who will put up even with poetry for the sake of classical studies but that is not precisely my line. Some old schoolbooks give the impression that if Virgil — or whoever the author might be — had been to a good school he would not have been allowed to put things in quite the way he did. 'But there,' one imagines such editors saying, 'we must bear with the poetry somehow.' It does not sound very affectionate. 'Inaccurate and inconsistent if it is pressed' — and here I am actually quoting — A. Sidgwick, no less — 'but' — and he seems to be choking back his disapproval — 'there

is no difficulty about such a phrase in poetry.' Why not? one may
ask. Are inaccuracy and inconsistency the marks of poetry? If so,
we really should be better without it. These remarks of Sidgwick's
are in aid of a phrase about the Tiber flowing backwards and stopping at the same time. The phrase is a terse and vivid presentation
of the extraordinary portent which met Aeneas's eyes; for an
instant in passing, it can astonish the reader too. It is above all
accurate, and fits what is seen: a supernatural event but also a
contradiction one might understand in a flash, looking at a stream
which seems at once moving and stationary.

These physical realities, which correspond closely to nature or
to our perceptions of her, are an important part of the solid
ground of poetry. There they take precedence over the mere
explanation which is the normal business of prose. Between the
time when I first read at bits of the Latin poets at school and my
return to them later I had travelled considerably among other
poets. Mostly they were English poets but I had also read, with
various degrees of understanding, some who wrote in French,
German or Italian. I had also written poems of my own, though
it was a number of years before I had admitted to being a poet.
Prudently or imprudently, I have since accepted this designation.
It is all I have now to bolster up my claims to be an 'other person
with classical interests.' That is the sort of 'other person' I am.

This does not amount to a claim to represent Virgil or Dante
on earth. I have observed that, when one publishes a translation
– a thing I have done rather more often than most people – there
is sure to be some reviewer who will assert that it is not as good
as the original. As a way of taking the translator down a peg, the
assertion seems to me rather ineffective. Where are these translations of the great masters which *are* the equal of the original? The
reviewer perhaps has one of his own in a drawer, and is only
holding his fire before he astonishes us all? But Dryden did not
suppose that he had done as well as Virgil. Ezra Pound asserted
that Gavin Douglas's version was '*better* than the original', but it
is not on record that Gavin Douglas thought the same. It is not
my contention that there exist in English satisfactory equivalents
for *any* poem in a foreign language, much less for masterpieces.

I might put it the other way round. It is my positive
contention that no line of poetry in one language corresponds in
any exact way with a line in another. This is a commonplace; like

most commonplaces it is frequently overlooked. Think of the claims some people make to familiarity with foreign poetry, in languages they do not understand. Relatively few people know Russian, but the place is swarming with people who are willing to give their opinion on Russian poets. The same – well, almost the same – goes for Polish, Hungarian, Bulgarian, what you will. It is a comedy. For of course if one does not know something of a language one knows nothing of much importance about its poetry. One might add that with the availability of instant translation the market is open to the intrusion of mere reputations without our having much clue as to whether they are deserved or not. Generally, of course, the reputations of contemporary poets are not deserved.

If any of us knows anything about poetry, if we really care for it – and the taste is perhaps rarer than the diffusion of verse would lead one to suppose – it can only be because we have first of all recognized its existence in our own language. I am not talking now about the opinions of literary critics, even of the most serious ones. I am talking about the moment when the child, or more often the adolescent, is so possessed by a poem or by some lines that he cannot escape from the experience. It is like love; the possession does not necessarily go on in that way; it certainly does not go on like that all the time but it reveals something new, the ramifications of which are never completely grasped. Behind the adolescent illumination which seems in some form to come to most people who are really to care about poetry, there is that first blind association of words and rhythms which the child makes before he has as much as heard of literary critics or even of experts in linguistics. The apprehension of poetry, whenever it comes, is of an indissoluble connection of words and rhythms with a perception. At a certain moment a line of poetry may fill the mind; thereafter it may re-appear from time to time on the edge of consciousness, bringing more or less of itself with it. The part such things play in the operations of the mind as a whole must differ enormously from one person to another, but the ghostly presence of poetry in the mind is not easily eradicated. Nor is it very easily simulated when it is not there, though the attempt is often made and even attended with worldly success.

These general reflections on poetry, unsatisfactory and elusive as such reflections almost always are, will I hope serve to indicate

the direction in which the problems of the translator lie. What
one is asked to translate is something which is essentially indivis-
ible, the boundaries of which are indecipherable. It is because
translation cannot be done that the habit of doing it can become
so intractable. We may puzzle over the instructions on a packet,
in a language we do not know. That is the simplest form of the
disease. What we are concerned with this evening is at the other
end of the scale, the ultimate impossibility. Perhaps the best way
of getting a glimpse of what is involved is to look at an historical
line of translations, the successive attempts which have been
made, over the centuries, on some well-known classical text. In
century after century people have read the text, taken a pen and
produced things so different from one another that one rubs one's
eyes. Can these successive versions, so different in language, in
rhythm, in tone, really be drawn from the same original? Of
course the connections are there; the elements of what is rather
lightly called the simple prose meanings, turn up. There is the
pious Aeneas, maltreating his lady friend in Africa; there is
Catullus, deploring the death of what is said to be his girlfriend's
sparrow. But such correspondences do not take us very far. The
tone, the rhythm, the language, are predominantly those of the
age in which the translation was written. How could it be otherwise? Yet the next translator who comes along is quite likely to
announce that, unlike his predecessors, he has at last made the
essential connections and somehow syphoned off the essential
Virgil or the essential Catullus. I have seen American prospectuses
which allege that a certain eminent, but rather wooden, translator
has faithfully reproduced all the poetry and rhythms of Virgil.
Well, trade is trade, but poetry is quite another thing.

Is the Scottish-Chaucerian couplet of Gavin Douglas, the
blank verse of Surrey, the almost-Augustan couplet of Dryden,
the right medium for translating Virgil? Are the near-hexameters
of one of my predecessors in this lectureship right? At a little
distance in time it is evident that none of these forms is *right*; it is
merely the best that a particular translator could do at the time of
his attempt. Here I may remark that it has been one of the delusions of the twentieth century that the translator ought to imitate
the verse-form of the original. The temptation is greatest in relation to modern languages because the verse-forms are,
superficially at least, akin to our own. I have elsewhere arraigned

the commercially very successful pretensions of the late Dorothy Sayers to copy the verse form and rhyme scheme of Dante, in her deplorable version of the *Divine Comedy*. Such a copy of course cannot be made. The relative availability and non-availability of rhymes in English and Italian, the relative lack of feminine endings in the former, should themselves have been enough to deter a sensible woman. No one with an ear for Dante, or indeed for the historical performance and present possibilities of English verse, could have written as she has done. What she has done is less to translate Dante than to take up one or two crude notions of what Dante is like and to produce a plausible mock-up on that basis. A similar plan has been followed, with varying degrees of subtlety and skill, by contemporary translators from a variety of languages.

I am not asserting that the translator has no business to use a line or a rhyme-scheme which pretends to correspond to that of his original. What I am saying is that the starting-point cannot be any analytical notion of what ought to be preserved but must be the translator's apprehension of the original as a whole, the physical presence of the poem, of the line, which includes its rhythms, the choice and placing of the words, their meanings and resonances − in short the perceptions of the poet with the language which is inseparable from them. This is the poetry, the poem − that elusive thing which is, none the less, the one really important thing. I might here observe that the likelihood of a translator, intent upon the whole presence of the poem rather than upon certain analytically ascertained characteristics, getting near to the metres and rhymes of an original, is different in relation to different languages. Anyone who attempts a version of Heine or, say, Andreas Gryphius, is likely to feel himself impelled to allow those features to show up rather prominently in his English version, even if he is not meticulous about the scheme. This is because German has certain inescapable affinities with the radical parts of English. English has been moving away for many centuries, and with Chaucer it has assimilated something of the forms of French. It is arguable that the current disposition to think that the verse forms of an original ought so far as possible to be followed in a translation is a result of the German influences which spread into English literature with the Romantics and above all with the Victorians. Those bouncing Victorian ballad metres are as much German as authentically English.

It would be wrong to make light of the analytical skills which seem in theory at least to offer the chance of rebuilding a poem in another language – sticking to the dimensions, matching up the bricks, and so on. I am not against analysis, only against an analysis taking the place of the poem. The first impact must be of the poem as a whole, 'understood' or not, the final judgement – if there is such a thing – must take one back to the whole poem. How one tries to sharpen one's reading in the interval is another matter. There are various devices; not least, making such use as one can of the labour of scholars. I like to think that, although I am not a scholar, I know enough to make some use of them. I am told that Ellis's commentary on Catullus is not quite the latest thing, but I can bear witness to the fact that to read through the poems with the help of it is far more rewarding, poetically, than floundering on without such help. The only point I am trying to make is that when one comes to the actual moment of translation, one has to let the text operate as it will on the mind. Then one has to say as best one can what the poet says – in practice, some of what the poet says. At that moment it is the poet's perception, rather than his words, that one has to find one's own words for; yet his words are part of his perception and are part of the matter one is apprehending.

To understand the process it is well to start not from the notion of a literal version, but from the large and ill-defined field of English poetry which without aspiring – or it may be sinking – to the condition of translation, is impregnated with a foreign original. Examples will most often be found in the works of poets who have had Latin originals in mind. It is a commonplace that the whole tradition of our poetry – indeed that of the whole western world – would not have been what it is without the Latin influence. To take a relatively narrow illustration, can one imagine the existence of Ben Jonson and his school without Horace and Martial? Campion is thinking of Propertius 11.28 in the twentieth poem of Rosseter's *Book of Ayres*. The English of the lines of Propertius reads in Butler's version as follows: 'There are so many thousand beauties among the dead; let one fair one, if so may be, abide on earth. With you is Iope, with you snowy Tyro, with you Europe and impious Pasiphaë, and all the beauties that Troy and Achaea bore of old…'. It is touching matter, even in that bald version. But when the memory of the passage floats up into the mind of Campion we get:

> When thou must home to shades of underground,
> And there arrived, a new admired guest,
> The beauteous spirits do engirt thee round,
> White Iope, blithe Helen, and the rest
> To hear the stories of thy finished love
> From that smooth tongue whose music hell can move…

It is something different from Propertius, but it is something which could not have been there without Propertius. So with the first poem in Rosseter's *Book*. There the ghost who rises to Campion's lips is that of Catullus, in one of his most famous poems, remembered by poets again and again throughout the centuries. In Cornish's version it begins: 'Let us live, my Lesbia, and love, and value at one farthing all the talk of crabbed old men. Suns may set and rise again. For us, when the short night has once set, remains to be slept the sleep of one unbroken night…'. It is not very elegant. Campion begins close to his text:

> My sweetest Lesbia, let us live and love;
> And though the sager sort our deeds reprove,
> Let us not weigh them: heaven's great lamps do dive
> Into their west, and straight again revive:
> But soon as once set is our little light,
> Then must we sleep one ever-during night.

Then we get:

> If all would lead their lives in love like me,
> Then bloody swords and armour should not be;
> No drum nor trumpet peaceful sleeps should move,
> Unless alarm came from the camp of love:
> But fools do live, and waste their little light,
> And seek with pain their ever-during night.

Campion starts close to his original, but he soars away from it. The new poem is his own poem, and it is a superb one. It is also part of the gift which Latin literature has made to English literature.

This is something different from translation proper, but the borders of indiscipline are far from clear. Since there can be no point-by-point correspondence between a line of verse in one

language and a line of verse in another, how far off can the translator be allowed to go? The question may look precise but the
answer is not. When we say a translation is free we should
consider the ways in which it could be bound. What is usually
meant is being tied up with what one might call the fiction of
literal meanings, according to which there are words corresponding with other words. The real situation is much more complex.
A crib is a useful instrument, but it is no more than that. It may
help us to get inside a poem, if we are in certain sorts of difficulty,
but it is not the poem. There is a sense in which almost any line
of poetry is nearer to Catullus than the complete prose version of
Cornish is. I do not want to enter into the ancient controversy
about what used to be called 'poetical prose' or 'When is prose as
poetical as verse?' The crib cannot tell you what the poet says
because what the poet says is not a bare meaning tricked out with
lovely words and rhythms but something which is conveyed, in
varying degrees to various people, in a unique complex of words
and rhythms which are inseparable from his perceptions. Even a
translator of genius – say Dryden – cannot give you his author's
line. The most he can do is to offer you a *related* line, a related
poem. That is something. It omits matter you could find in such
as Cornish, and it is complicated by the words and rhythms of a
different language, a different age and a different tradition. That
takes us far from the original, it may be said. But we *are* far from
our classic originals. We are less far, evidently, from some poets
nearer our own time. When I was translating *Les Regrets* of Du
Bellay it occurred to me that one of the reasons why he attracted
me was that he was a man of affairs, messing about with the business of Popes and cardinals at the court of Rome – a situation I
could have some sympathy with, as one who had earned his living
messing about in Whitehall. That was of course a very minor
reason for the attraction, which had in fact begun before I had
even started on that searing experience; but when I came to translate it helped me to see what Du Bellay was complaining about.
You might call that an accidental qualification. There are of
course differences as well as resemblances between the court of
Rome in the sixteenth century and Whitehall in the twentieth,
and obviously the translator would be wrong if he presumed too
much on his small bit of luck. The real difficulty, as always, is that
when one sits down to translate a poet of a different epoch one is

stretching out one's sympathy through the veils of two languages and two – I am afraid I have to use that objectionable word – cultures, one's own and the author's.

This is perhaps the place to comment on a curious practice current among certain contemporaries. What I have in mind is the business of doing a job on a foreign poet without wrestling with the original text. The method is – incredibly, as it seems to me – to start from someone else's 'literal translation', or to persuade some willing scholar to explain what the original says without bothering to try to learn the language in which the author wrote. I confess that I am at a loss to know what satisfaction a poet can take in such a procedure or, quite simply, what is the point of it. When I do a translation it is primarily because I want to get closer to the author. When one has translated one's Lucretius, or Dante, or whatever it may be, one has at least got as close as one is ever likely to get. One has done some real reading – maybe also some real writing but that, in a sense, is incidental. Of course one hopes someone will find some use for the translation but if not, it's too bad. The struggle to apprehend what came into the mind of another person in another place and time is itself productive. One is struggling with another culture – that word again! – as well as another poet. For my part, I have felt so strongly the need of a certain gap across which understanding can sometimes spark that the prospect of translating contemporary work does not attract me.

A lot is talked in our time about 'the individual', but of course individual variants are as nothing compared with the great weight of thoughts and words which bear down on us from the past. Virgil was no doubt Virgil, but he would not have been what he was without the agonies of Roman history behind him, to go no further afield. We all live in a language which brings with it more of the past than we can hope to discern; we have to read the poets of the past from where we are and as who we are. When we speak, we speak as we are made. Dryden translated Virgil into heroic couplets because of what Ben Jonson, Waller and Denham had done. He wrote distinctively none the less, but he could do no more than swim in a current that was already flowing. So it is with any poet and with any translator. That is why some of the best translations we have are partial and as it were incidental to the English poet's own work. Of these the poems I have quoted from Campion may stand as the type. Reference to Latin poets in English verse ranges from the merest allusion – perhaps only a name or a phrase – through such cases as Campion, through that interesting form of reference known as the imitation, to the complete translation such as Dryden's. It would be interesting to construct a chain of examples to show the full range. Milton is full of allusions: 'Thick as Autumnal Leaves that strow the Brooks / In Vallombrosa...' One could go on for ever in *Paradise Lost*. Milton is an exceptionally literary poet but all poets – even Shakespeare – are affected by what they read as well as by what they see, and a gift for combining the two in a living way is almost a defining characteristic of the poet. The involuntary attraction which results in the practice of allusion is certainly largely responsible for the sort of imitation which flourished in the late seventeenth and in the eighteenth centuries, when the fantasy of living in an age which resembled the world of Augustus rose to its greatest heights. It was not entirely a fantasy, because the human race has not changed much since Adam and the successive great centres of civilization have characteristics in common. The relevance of what the old poets had said about Rome to what the new ones saw in London was striking enough. The classic example is Samuel Johnson's 'London', 'A Poem,' says the subtitle, 'in imitation of the Third Satire of Juvenal'. Old editions – I suppose all good editions – set opposite the texts the extracts from the Third Satire which have most direct relevance to Johnson's verses. We start with the first three lines of the Latin. Then there is a break, of little more than a line but set after a sizeable space while Johnson disports himself in English. Then follow five lines more, and another gap to allow the English poet to catch up, although there is no gap in the Latin text. Then ten lines of the Latin are missing; there is a gap while Johnson goes his own way. Then the two texts meet up again – more or less. Johnson is picking and choosing, maybe as bits floated into his memory, which was capacious.

Such a combination of literary recollection and contemporary observation as there is in Johnson's 'London' gives the version a raciness which, even with so accomplished a performer as Johnson, might have been inhibited by any strict rules of translation. What I suppose in the Latin is something on four wheels becomes – with a vivid evocation of the London watermen – a 'wherry'. And these splendid verses, one of the passages which has something to show on the opposite page in the way of a Latin original, depart from that original when Johnson's own impulses call him more strongly.

> For who wou'd leave, unbrib'd, Hibernia's land,
> Or change the rocks of Scotland for the Strand?
> There none are swept by sudden fate away,
> But all whom hunger spares, with age decay:
> Here malice, rapine, accident, conspire,
> And now a rabble rages, now a fire;
> Their ambush here relentless ruffians lay,
> And here the fell attorney prowls for prey;
> Here falling houses thunder on your head,
> And here a female atheist talks you dead.

In this last couplet there must have been a momentary conflict in Johnson's mind. For where Juvenal's target was poets reciting their poems – a target which might reasonably have appealed to Johnson – I am afraid that a touch of male chauvinism, in that unenlightened man, carried the day.

There are obvious risks about this form of imitation. So much weight may be given to the contemporary, as against the matter of the original, its manner and its tone, that we may not feel that we are in contact with the original at all. That is not the case with Johnson, who surely – with Dryden – gives us something as near as we can get to the spirit of Juvenal in English. I would give a similar, if slightly less powerful, commendation to John Oldham's imitation of the *Ars Poetica* of Horace, to which I have drawn attention in the introduction to my own version. 'I was resolved', says Oldham, 'to alter the scene from Rome to London, and to make use of English Names of Men, Places, and Customs, where the Parallel would decently permit, which I conceived would give a kind of new Air to the Poem, and render it more agreeable to the Relish of the present Age.' Obviously in such matters something depends on what the relish of the present age is. We may not be so well off as Oldham in this respect.

It will be a rare poet who manages to continue, through any prolonged work whether of imitation or of translation proper, the degree of assimilation which he might be capable of in the occasional involuntary allusion but, after the first, perhaps more or less involuntary start, assimilation is what he will strive for. The decision that has to be taken, as he approaches his work, is not so much how it *should* be done as how it *can* be done. The distinction is important. If we are merely to construe a text, there is nothing to stop us taking a dictionary and whatever other aids we need and getting on with it. For such labours a plain 'should' may be appropriate. For the poet the matter is more deeply troubling. He *should* do only what he can, and for him this 'can' means being able to give us his author's matter without violence to his – the translator's – own natural language. This does not mean that his own style will not be extended as he goes along, by the text before him: indeed one of the benefits of the practice of translation is that it demands just such extensions. There is a tension between the original author and his translator which involves language and thought and the whole world each of them moves in. It is the establishment of this relationship which so to speak constitutes the moment of discovery in which the poet-translator finds that he *can* venture on his subject. A great poet – any real poet – is present in every line of his work; the essence of his work can be received in a flash from a single poem or from a few lines, and what follows is a deepening of that insight. The poet-translator cannot begin until he has gone a stage further. He has to find the tone in which he can speak. This is not a deliberate search; it is a revelation which can only come to him involuntarily, as a line of his own may come to him, out of the blue. It must come to him concretely, a few words or a rhythm suddenly emerging, a few lines and – suddenly, he knows how the thing can be done. After that he can go on, through all the intervening hours of labour, to the end. No doubt the quality of the intuition varies, and the work that follows can be more or less true to that initial hunch, but some hunch there must be if a poem in a foreign language is to find a voice in this one.

Here I must return to the delicate subject of what English verse is appropriate in a translation. This is part of the hunch and is absolutely not a thing to be determined *a priori*. The writing of verse can in no wise be separated from the words that are used in it. It has always struck me as odd that there have been people who have written no poems of their own but have none the less thought that, faced with a classical text, they suddenly knew how to write verse. It is frankly ridiculous. One thing – if no more –

is lacking: the subjective experience of how verse comes to be written, which is of necessity rather than of choice. A poet will not be tempted to say in verse what he could say in prose, but there will be moments when words come to him in a rhythmic form which will admit of no other way of saying them. It is his sense of the sequence of rhythms which will determine what words he takes and what he lays aside during the process of composition. The sense of language which demands that the choice shall be made in this way cannot suddenly be summoned up by any act of will or by a publisher's contract. The suitability of a specific kind of verse is an expression of the relationship established between the translator and his author, between one age and one language, and another age and another language. What we call a translation is no more than a reading, in one time and place, of a text from another place and time. It syphons off something from the original, but as much only as we in our different world are able to take. A successful translation – the concrete embodiment of a reading – does not preclude other attempts, it invites them. All are partial, all give the original a particular twist. That is why, beside the word 'translation', which implies the removal of something from one place to another, we should set the word 'version', which emphasizes the twist.

Twisters are rightly suspect, but a recognition by the operator of what he is up to should be beneficial rather than otherwise. The danger comes when the operator is so pleased with his own cleverness that he reckons himself above his text. The perfect translation would give way entirely before the text, but that is impossible. The translator remains stubbornly himself, like it or not – like him or not. Of course critics, from heights towering above those of Parnassus itself, will continue to demand the impossible. But for the poet it is a consolation to have made a readable book in the English language.

Notes

Poems

The selection follows the order in *Collected Poems* (1998). A few of the departures from this in the original volumes are noted below. A note to *In the Trojan Ditch* (1974) reads: 'Hitherto unpublished earlier poems have been put more or less in their chronological places'.

From *The London Zoo* (1961) and other early poems

The London Zoo (London, New York, Toronto: Abelard-Schuman, 1961) was Sisson's first book of verse proper. It was narrowly preceded by two pamphlets: *Poems* (London: Peter Russell, 1959), which did not appear until 1961, and the privately printed *Twenty-one Poems* (Sevenoaks, 1960). There is no overlap between the two pamphlets; *The London Zoo* takes thirteen of the *Twenty-one* and sixteen from *Poems*, and adds seven new poems. Here, the poems 'On a Troopship' to 'Silence' appeared in *Poems*, 'Ightham Woods' to 'Knole' in *Twenty-one Poems*. All are to be found in *The London Zoo* apart from the first three and 'In London'.

On a Troopship
Written 'on a troopship off Freetown' (*Collected Poems* (1998), p. 499) in 1943. Since *In the Trojan Ditch* the 'official' first (or last) poem, though the 1998 *Collected Poems* includes an appendix of earlier poems written 1931–35, and 'On a Civil Servant' is also earlier. For two further early poems (written in India), see *PN Review* 217 (May–June 2014).

The Body in Asia
First published in *New English Weekly* (31 August 1944).

In a Dark Wood
Also used, without the title, as a kind of introit to the novel *Christopher Homm* (1965).

Maurras Young and Old
See the three essays on Maurras: 'Charles Maurras and the Idea of the

Patriot King' (1937), 'Charles Maurras' (1950), and 'Looking Back on Maurras' (1976); and the later poem, 'Martigues' (1974).

Family Fortunes
In *Twenty-one Poems* this poem has an extra section at the end.

Cranmer
Called 'The Village' in *Twenty-one Poems*.

Knole
Called 'Knole Park' in *Twenty-one Poems*.

On a Civil Servant
First published in *New English Weekly* (23 February 1939), under the title 'Epitaph'.

The London Zoo
In *The London Zoo*, the opening poem.

From *Numbers* (1965)

Numbers was published by Methuen and carries the epigraph 'If it were not, my masters, for the beasts, we should live like clerks. *Rabelais*, I, xvi.' Methuen also brought out Sisson's second novel, *Christopher Homm*, at the same time and, later that year, *Art and Action*, his first collection of essays.

A Letter to John Donne
Not part of *Numbers*. First published in *In the Trojan Ditch* (1974), and included under *Numbers* in both *Collected Poems* (1984 and 1998). The same goes for 'Words', below, and two other poems not included here: 'Act Munday' and 'At First'.

From *Metamorphoses* (1968)

The fourth and last of Sisson's books to be published by Methuen. It has as epigraphs: 'Though fleshe cannot believe, yet God is true' (Fulke Greville) and 'Et ici, sans nous perdre dans des subtilités, constatons que le monde n'est devenu une telle cochonnerie que parce qu'il a été si bien, si totalement, empli de Dieu' (René Crevel) [And here, without losing ourselves in subtleties, let us note that the world has become the mess it is only because it was so well and truly, so totally, filled with

God]. A long Ovidian poem, 'Metamorphoses', has not been included. An unfinished translation 'From Book I of the *Metamorphoses*' also dates from this period and first appeared in *In the Trojan Ditch*. See *Collected Translations*, pp. 285–91.

Catullus
Not in *Metamorphoses* but added in *In the Trojan Ditch* and subsequently put with the *Metamorphoses* poems, along with two others not included here: 'In Preparation for an Epitaph' and 'The Queen of Lydia'. Originally published as a Preface to *Catullus* (1966), with the Valediction at the end.

In Allusion to Propertius, I, iii
Included among the translations in *In the Trojan Ditch* but also to be found in both *Collected Poems*, as well as in *Collected Translations*.

From the new poems in *In the Trojan Ditch* (1974)
In the Trojan Ditch, Sisson's first book from Carcanet, was not so much a collection, though it is often referred to as such, but, as the subtitle says, 'collected poems and selected translations'. It came with two forewords, which are included among the essays below. It gathers, in the words of its 'Note', 'most of the poems from *The London Zoo*, *Numbers* and *Metamorphoses* and more than enough new matter to have made another volume of the same kind', plus 'translations selected from *Versions and Perversions of Heine*' (Gaberbocchus, 1955) and *Catullus* (MacGibbon & Kee, 1966), together with unpublished work including the whole of a version of Vergil's Eclogues'. As in the novel *Christopher Homm*, the chronology is reversed, with 'Martigues', the most recent poem, coming first and 'On a Troopship' last. This habit is not observed for the translations. 'New poems' here, following both *Collected Poems*, mostly means poems written after those in *Metamorphoses*, since some unpublished earlier poems were later slotted in chronologically as noted above.

The Discarnation
First printed privately in 1967.

The Usk
Can be read alongside the essay 'Songs in the Night: Henry Vaughan the Silurist', written at about the same time.

A Ghost
Uncollected. Appeared in *New Poems 1973–1974: A P.E.N. Anthology of Contemporary Poetry*, edited by Stewart Conn (London: Hutchinson, 1974).

From *Anchises* (1976)

Anchises has the epigraph: 'La vie est un sommeil: les vieillards sont ceux dont le sommeil a été plus long; ils ne commencent à se réveiller que quand il faut mourir' (La Bruyère) [Life is a sleep: old men are those whose sleep has been longer; they start to wake up only when it's time to die]. The translation of Lucretius appeared in the same year.

From *Exactions* (1980)

Exactions has another epigraph in French: 'Le bout de la rue qui fait le coin / Amour tu n'entends point / Le bout de la rue qui fait le coin'. The Dante translation appeared in the same year.

From the new poems in *Collected Poems* (1984)

Collected Poems undoes the reverse chronology of *In the Trojan Ditch* and has a closing epigraph from John Gower: 'O gentile Engleterre, a toi j'escrits'. It includes the poems *Night Thoughts and Other Chronicles* (Inky Parrot Press, 1983), none of which has been selected here. Also published this year: *The Regrets* of Du Bellay.

From *God Bless Karl Marx!* (1987)

The Racine plays came out the same year, and Virgil's *Aeneid* the year before.

From *Antidotes* (1991)

This volume bears a dedication: 'for DAVID WRIGHT *no surfett in word ne in langage*'.

Fifteen Sonnets
Originally published as *16 Sonnets* (1990) – one was cut.

Muchelney Abbey (from *On the Departure*)
The third poem of a six-poem sequence.

Translations

'Translations' is one way of putting it, and the word nearly always used by Sisson himself, in *In the Trojan Ditch, Collected Translations*, and elsewhere. But more evocatively he spoke of 'fishing in other men's waters', or 'versions and perversions'. Sisson's work as a translator is considerable – few poets have translated anything like as much. To focus just on the books, there is: *Versions and Perversions of Heine* (1955), *Catullus* (1966), Horace's *Poetic Art* (1975), Lucretius's *Poem on Nature* (1976), *Some Tales of La Fontaine* (1979), Dante's *Divine Comedy* (1980), the *Song of Roland* (1983), Du Bellay's *Regrets* (1984), Virgil's *Aeneid* (1986), and three plays by Racine (1987). A great deal else is gathered in *Collected Translations* (1996). All this is severely underrepresented here. The *Roman Poems* (see below) exemplify the sharply divergent and inventive form of translation where the 'use made of the original' is 'indirect' (Foreword to the translations in *In the Trojan Ditch*). There is also a much more literal mode, for example in the Dante.

Roman Poems

The five versions grouped together here were first published privately, in the same order, as *Roman Poems*, a pamphlet printed in Sevenoaks in 1968. All were then included in *In the Trojan Ditch*.

Carmen Saeculare (Horace)
In *Roman Poems* this poem has the title 'Public Ode' and comes with a short preface: '*The carmen saeculare of Horace, to which this bears some resemblance, was composed for the secular games held by Augustus in 17 BC on the occasion of the renewal of his mandate. It was sung by a chorus of boys and girls.*'

Hactenus arvorum cultus (Virgil, *Georgics* II)
The last of the *Roman Poems*. It takes the opening line of *Georgics* II as its starting-point but then distances itself rapidly. In *In the Trojan Ditch* it was included among the poems rather than the translations, and unlike the other *Roman Poems* is in both *Collected Poems* and *Collected Translations*.

Eheu fugaces, Postume, Postume (Horace, *Odes* II, xiv)
In *In the Trojan Ditch*, the final poem.

Essays

The bulk of Sisson's most important essays are to be found in *The Avoidance of Literature: Collected Essays*, edited by Michael Schmidt (Carcanet, 1978), referred to as *Avoidance* below. Substantial book as this is (over 550 closely printed pages), still it doesn't print everything essay-like that Sisson had written up to 1978, though it does contain a complete bibliography. The first prose book, apart from the novel *An Asiatic Romance* (Gabberbocchus, 1953), was *The Spirit of British Administration and some European Comparisons* (Faber, 1959; 2nd edition 1966), written while Sisson held a Senior Research Fellowship from the University of Manchester. *Art and Action* (Methuen, 1965) was the first gathering of essays published in the *New English Weekly*, X, and elsewhere, with a handful of unpublished essays. It is dedicated 'to Philip Mairet, *veridicum oraclum*' – Mairet had been the editor of the *New English Weekly*. The privately printed *Essays* (1967) were entirely new. *English Poetry 1900– 1950: An Assessment* (Rupert Hart-Davis, 1971) incorporated some essays published separately (notably essays on Yeats and Pound) but mostly contains new material, only a little of which has been reprinted elsewhere. Next came *The Case of Walter Bagehot* (Faber, 1972), a major piece of polemic reproduced entire in *Avoidance*, and a short study of *David Hume* (The Ramsay Head Press, 1976), which has not been reprinted anywhere. After *The Avoidance of Literature*, Carcanet published a volume of *Anglican Essays* in 1983 which contained essays (mostly reviews) written 1979–83. Then in the early 90s the critical prose was re-collected into three volumes of essays roughly literary (*In Two Minds: Guesses at other Writers*, 1990), political (*English Perspectives: Essays on Liberty and Government*, 1992) and ecclesiastical (*Is there a Church of England?*, 1993), though of course these categories are rarely distinct in the writing itself. *In Two Minds* and *Is there a Church of England?* focus on essays post-*Avoidance*, though reaching back where necessary, so despite quite a lot of overlap, especially with *English Perspectives*, these three volumes certainly don't supersede the 1978 collection.

From the *New English Weekly* (1937–1949)

Charles Maurras and the Idea of a Patriot King
NEW: 22 July 1937. Collected in *Avoidance* and *English Perspectives*.

Prejudice as an Aid to Government
NEW: 7 April 1938. Collected in *Avoidance* and *English Perspectives*.

English Liberalism
NEW: 9 March 1939. Collected in *Avoidance* and *English Perspectives*.

The Civil Service
NEW: 19 June 1941. Collected in *Avoidance*.

Charles Péguy
NEW: 14 November 1946. Collected in *Art and Action*, *Avoidance* and *English Perspectives*.

Epitaph on Nuremberg
NEW: 15 May 1947. Collected in *Avoidance* and *English Perspectives*.

T.S. Eliot on Culture
NEW: 2 December 1948. Collected in *Art and Action* (with the title 'T.S. Eliot' and slightly edited), *Avoidance* and *English Perspectives*. In *NEW* and *Avoidance* the title is 'What is Culture?'

Ego Scriptor: The Pisan Cantos of Ezra Pound
NEW: 28 July 1949. Collected in *Art and Action* and *Avoidance*.

Order and Anarchy: An Essay on Intellectual Liberty
A shortened version, 'Order and Anarchy: Extracts from an Essay on Intellectual Liberty', appeared in *Purpose: A Quarterly Magazine*, XI (Oct.–Dec. 1939). First published uncut in *Avoidance*, and then in *English Perspectives*, with the subtitle.

Charles Maurras
First published in *The Catacomb*, New Series, Vol. I, No. 3 (Winter 1950–51). Then in *Art and Action*, *Avoidance*, and *English Perspectives*.

Reflections on Marvell's Ode
First published in *The Catacomb*, New Series, Vol. II, No. 1 (Spring 1951). Then in *Art and Action*, *Avoidance*, and *In Two Minds*.

The Nature of Public Administration
First published in *The Cambridge Journal*, Vol. VI, No. 7 (April 1953), under the pseudonym 'Philonous'. Then in *Avoidance* and *English Perspectives*. Much of this article went into Chapter 1 ('What Administration Is') of *The Spirit of British Administration* which, with 'A Note on the Monarchy', it thus represents here.

A Note on the Monarchy

First published in the *Church Quarterly Review*, Vol. CLIV, No. 313 (Oct.–Dec. 1953). Then in *Avoidance* and *English Perspectives*. Parts of this essay went into the final chapter ('The Civil Service and the Crown') of *The Spirit of British Administration*.

Autobiographical Reflections on Politics

Written in January 1954 but not published until 1978 in *Avoidance*.

Natural History

First published in *X: A Quarterly Review*, Vol. II, No. 1 (1961). Then in *Art and Action*, *Avoidance*, and *In Two Minds*. The 'long essay' referred to on p. 281 is 'Order and Anarchy', also mentioned in 'Autobiographical Reflections on Politics'. The 'twenty lines' are the poem 'In a Dark Wood'.

The Study of Affairs

First published in *Art and Action*, then in *Avoidance*.

William Barnes

Written 1961. First published in *Art and Action*, then in *Avoidance* and *In Two Minds*.

Sevenoaks Essays/Native Ruminations

First printed privately as *Essays* (Sevenoaks, 1967). Then as 'Sevenoaks Essays' in *Avoidance*; and as 'Native Ruminations' in *English Perspectives* and *Is there a Church of England?*

The Politics of Wyndham Lewis

First published in *Agenda*, Vol. VII, No. 3/Vol. VIII, No. 1 (1969–70). Reprinted in *Avoidance*.

From *English Poetry 1900–1950: An Assessment* (1971)

W.B. Yeats

First published in *Ishmael*, Vol. I, No.1 (November 1970). In slightly expanded form this was Chapter 8 of *English Poetry*. Included in *Avoidance*.

T.S. Eliot

Chapter 7 of *English Poetry*. Included in *Avoidance*.

Edward Thomas
Part of Chapter 5 of *English Poetry*. Included in *Avoidance*.

From *The Case of Walter Bagehot* (1972)

Chapter Four: The Art of Money
Chapter Four from the book on, or against, Walter Bagehot, which bears the epigraphs 'Any old lie to cheat England out of the best so that the tenth best may have a chance' (E. Gordon Craig) and 'O, das grässliche Lachen des Golds' [O the hideous laughter of gold] (Georg Trakl). Bagehot's works included *The English Constitution* (1867), which is tackled in Chapter III, and *Lombard Street* (1873), on banking, the main subject of this chapter. The book as a whole is an attack on liberalism in the sense of 'possessive individualism' (Raymond Williams).

Songs in the Night: The Work of Henry Vaughan the Silurist
First published in *Ishmael*, Vol. I, No. 3 (Winter/Spring 1972–73). Then in *Avoidance*, and *In Two Minds* (simply as 'Henry Vaughan the Silurist'). Vaughan called himself a 'Silurist' after the British tribe of the Silures who anciently inhabited the Brecon district he came from. Compare the poem 'The Usk', written in 1973.

Forewords from *In the Trojan Ditch*
First published in *In the Trojan Ditch*, then in *Avoidance* and *In Two Minds*.

Looking Back on Maurras
First published in *PN Review* 1 (1977). Then in *Avoidance* and *English Perspectives*.

A Four-Letter Word
First published in *PN Review* 1 (1977). Then in *Avoidance* and *Is there a Church of England?*

Poetry and Myth
First published in *Agenda*, Vol. XV, Nos. 2–3 (Summer/Autumn 1977). Then in *Avoidance* and *In Two Minds*.

Poetry and Sincerity
First published in the *Times Literary Supplement* (12 September 1980). Then in *Anglican Essays* and *In Two Minds*.

The Poet and the Translator
Given as the sixteenth Jackson Knight Memorial Lecture at the University of Exeter on 8 November 1984, and published by them in 1985. Collected in *In Two Minds*. Jackson Knight (1895–1964) was a classical scholar who published several books on Virgil, including a translation of the *Aeneid*.

Bibliography

Books and pamphlets by C.H. Sisson

The Curious Democrat (Peter Russell, 1950) [under the pseudonym Richard Ampers]

An Asiatic Romance (Gaberbocchus, 1953; Carcanet, 1995)

(tr.) *Versions and Perversions of Heine* (Gaberbocchus, 1955)

The Spirit of British Administration and some European Comparisons (Faber, 1959; second edition, 1966)

Poems (Peter Russell, 1959; appeared 1961)

Twenty-one Poems (privately printed, The Westerham Press, 1960)

The London Zoo (Abelard-Schuman, 1961)

Numbers (Methuen, 1965)

Christopher Homm (Methuen, 1965; Carcanet, 1975, 1984, 1997)

Art and Action (Methuen, 1965)

(tr.) *Catullus* (MacGibbon & Kee, 1966) / *The Poetry of Catullus: A Modern Translation with the Complete Latin Text* (Orion, 1967; Viking, 1969)

The Discarnation (privately printed, The Westerham Press, 1967)

Essays (privately printed, Knole Park Press, 1967)

Roman Poems (privately printed, The Westerham Press, 1968)

Metamorphoses (Methuen, 1968)

English Poetry 1900–1950: An Assessment (Rupert Hart-Davis, 1971; Carcanet, 1981; Methuen [University Paperbacks], 1981)

The Case of Walter Bagehot (Faber, 1972)

In the Trojan Ditch: Collected Poems & Selected Translations (Carcanet, 1974)

The Corridor (Mandeville Press, 1975)

(tr.) *The Poetic Art: A Translation of Horace's* Ars Poetica (Carcanet, 1975)

Anchises (Carcanet, 1976)

(tr.) *Lucretius: The Poem on Nature* (Carcanet, 1976)

(ed.) *The English Sermon 1650–1750: An Anthology* (Carcanet, 1976)

David Hume (The Ramsay Head Press, 1976)

(ed.) *David Wright: A South African Album* (Mantis Editions, 1976)

(ed.) *Jonathan Swift: Selected Poems* (Carcanet, 1977)

The Avoidance of Literature: Collected Essays, ed. Michael Schmidt (Carcanet, 1978)

(ed.) *Thomas Hardy: Jude the Obscure* (Penguin, 1978)

(tr.) *Some Tales of La Fontaine* (Carcanet, 1979)
Moon-Rise and Other Poems (Snake River Press, 1979)
Exactions (Carcanet, 1980)
(tr.) *Dante: The Divine Comedy* (Carcanet, 1980; Pan, 1981; OUP, 1993)
Selected Poems (Carcanet, 1981; 1990)
(ed.) *Philip Mairet: Autobiographical and Other Papers* (Carcanet, 1981)
Anglican Essays (Carcanet, 1983)
(tr.) *The Song of Roland* (Carcanet, 1983)
Night Thoughts and Other Poems (Inky Parrot Press, 1983)
(ed.) Ford Madox Ford, *The English Novel* (Carcanet, 1983)
(tr.) *Joachim du Bellay: The Regrets* (Carcanet, 1984)
Collected Poems (Carcanet, 1984)
(ed.) *Christina Rossetti: Selected Poems* (Carcanet, 1984)
The Poet and the Translator (The Sixteenth Jackson Knight Memorial
    Lecture) (University of Exeter, 1985)
(tr.) *Virgil: The Aeneid* (Carcanet, 1986; Everyman, 1998)
God Bless Karl Marx! (Carcanet, 1987)
(tr.) *Jean Racine: Britannicus, Phaedra, Athaliah* (OUP, 1987)
(ed.) Ford Madox Ford, *A Call* (Carcanet, 1988)
On the Look-Out: A Partial Autobiography (Carcanet, 1989)
16 Sonnets (privately printed, H & C Laserprint, 1990)
(ed.) *Jeremy Taylor: Selected Writings* (Carcanet, 1990)
In Two Minds: Guesses at Other Writers (Carcanet, 1990)
Antidotes (Carcanet, 1991)
Nine Sonnets (Greville Press, 1991)
English Perspectives: Essays on Liberty and Government (Carcanet, 1992)
The Pattern (Enitharmon, 1993)
Is there a Church of England? Reflections on Permanence and Progression
    (Carcanet, 1993)
(ed.) Ford Madox Ford, *Ladies Whose Bright Eyes* (Carcanet, 1993)
What and Who (Carcanet, 1994)
Poems: Selected (Carcanet, 1995; New Directions, 1996)
(ed.) *Edgar Allan Poe: Poems and Essays on Poetry* (Carcanet, 1995)
Collected Translations (Carcanet, 1996)
(ed.) Ford Madox Ford, *The Rash Act* (Carcanet, 1996)
Collected Poems (Carcanet, 1998)

See also

Angels and Beasts: New Short Stories from France, edited by Denis Saurat
    (Westhouse, 1947) [contains four stories by Jules Supervielle trans-
    lated by CHS]

Contemporary Authors Autobiography Series, Vol. 3, edited by Adele Sarkissian (Gale, 1986), pp. 293–309 [autobiographical essay by CHS]

Letters to an Editor, edited by Mark Fisher (Carcanet, 1989) [contains many letters from CHS to Michael Schmidt]

The Poet's Voice and Craft, edited by C.B. McCully (Carcanet, 1994) [includes a response by CHS: 'The best words in the best order']

Interview with John Burney, in *New Yorkshire Writing* 2 (Autumn 1977)

Interview in *Yorick* 2: 'An Ironic Contribution to a Hopeless Situation'

Interview with Clive Wilmer, in *Poets Talking: Poet of the Month interviews from BBC Radio 3* (Carcanet, 1994)

Interview with Nicholas Tredell, in *Conversations with Critics* (Carcanet, 1994)

Ghosts in the Corridor: Andrew Crozier, Donald Davie, C.H. Sisson, Paladin Re/Active Anthology No. 2 (Paladin, 1992)

Selected criticism on Sisson

PN Review 39 (1984), *C.H. Sisson at Seventy: A Special Issue* [includes an interview with Michael Schmidt]

Richard Poole, 'The Poetry of C.H. Sisson', *Agenda* 22/2 (Summer 1984)

Donald Davie, 'C.H. Sisson's Politics' and 'C.H. Sisson's Poetry', in *Under Briggflatts: A History of Poetry in Great Britain 1960–1988* (Carcanet, 1989)

Robert Wells, 'Sisson, Charles Hubert (1914–2003)', *The Oxford Dictionary of National Biography*, online edition (2009)

Agenda 45/2 (Spring 2010), *C.H. Sisson Special Issue*

Natalie Pollard, *Speaking to You: Contemporary Poetry and Public Address* (OUP, 2012) [includes three chapters on CHS, who is considered alongside W.S. Graham, Geoffrey Hill and Don Paterson]

Henry King, 'Out from under the Body Politic: Poetry and Government in the Work of C.H. Sisson, 1937–80' (PhD thesis, University of Glasgow, 2013)

PN Review 217 (2014), supplement: *C.H. Sisson at 100*

Index of Poem Titles

Index of First Lines